CW00762047

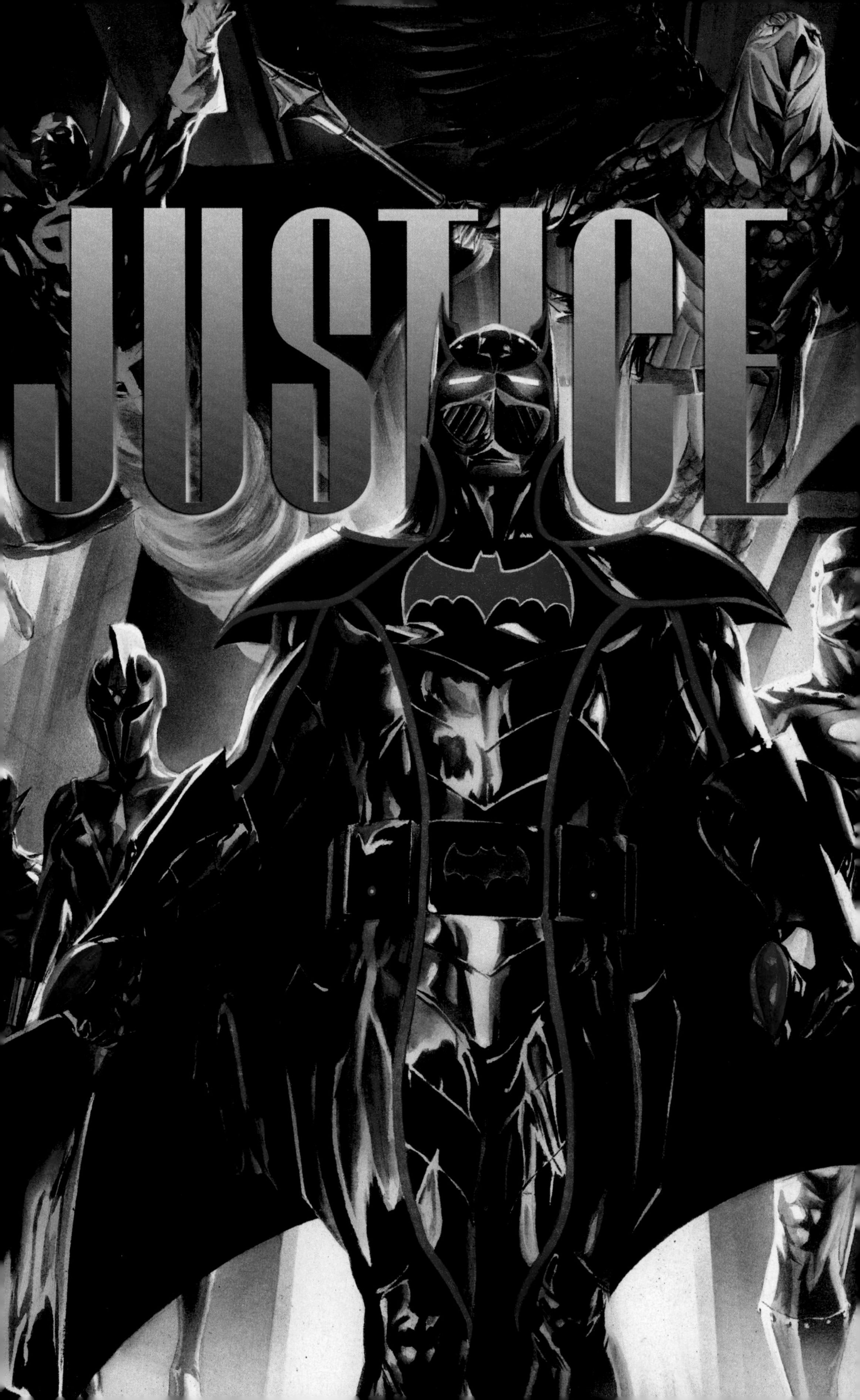
JUSTICE

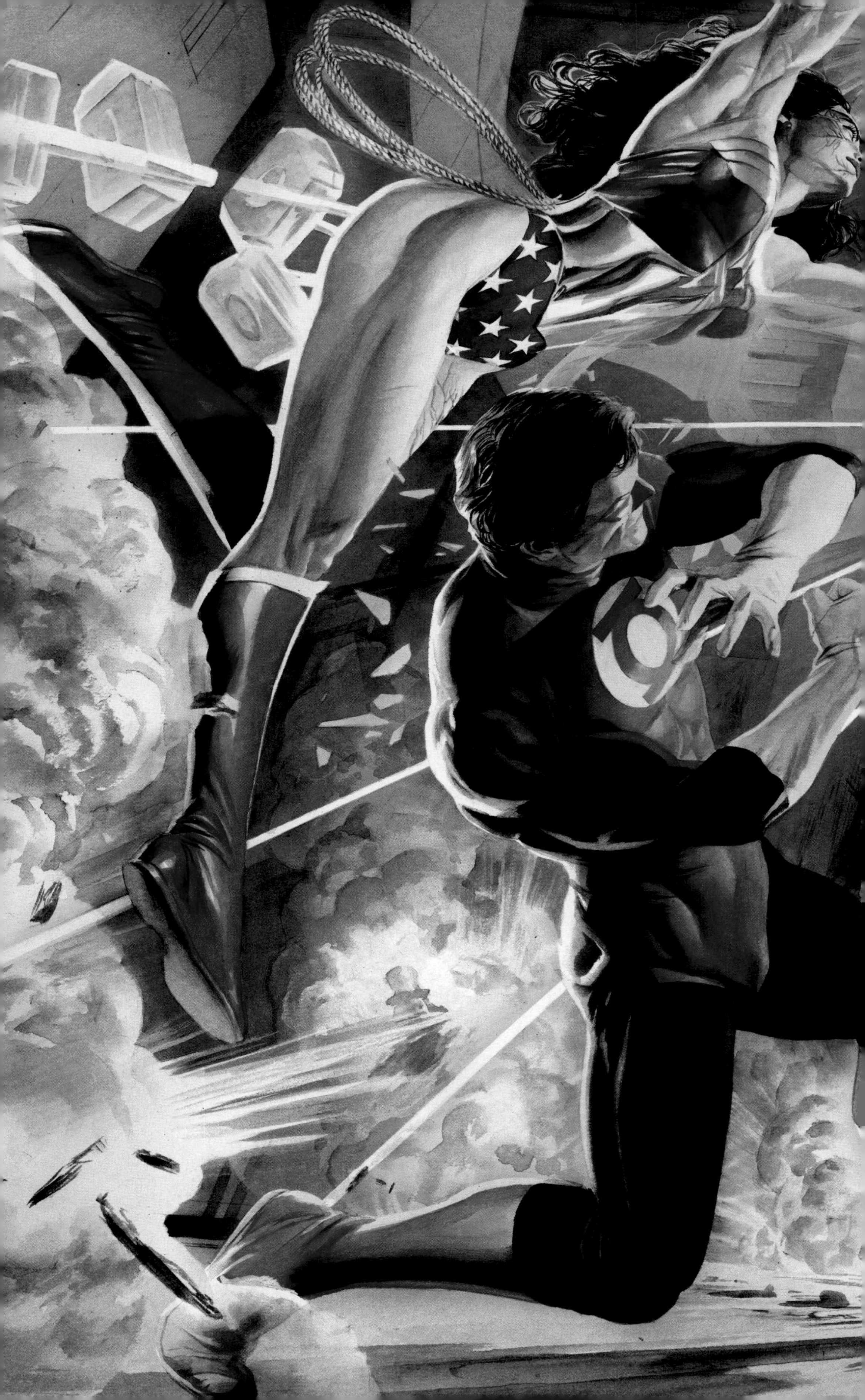

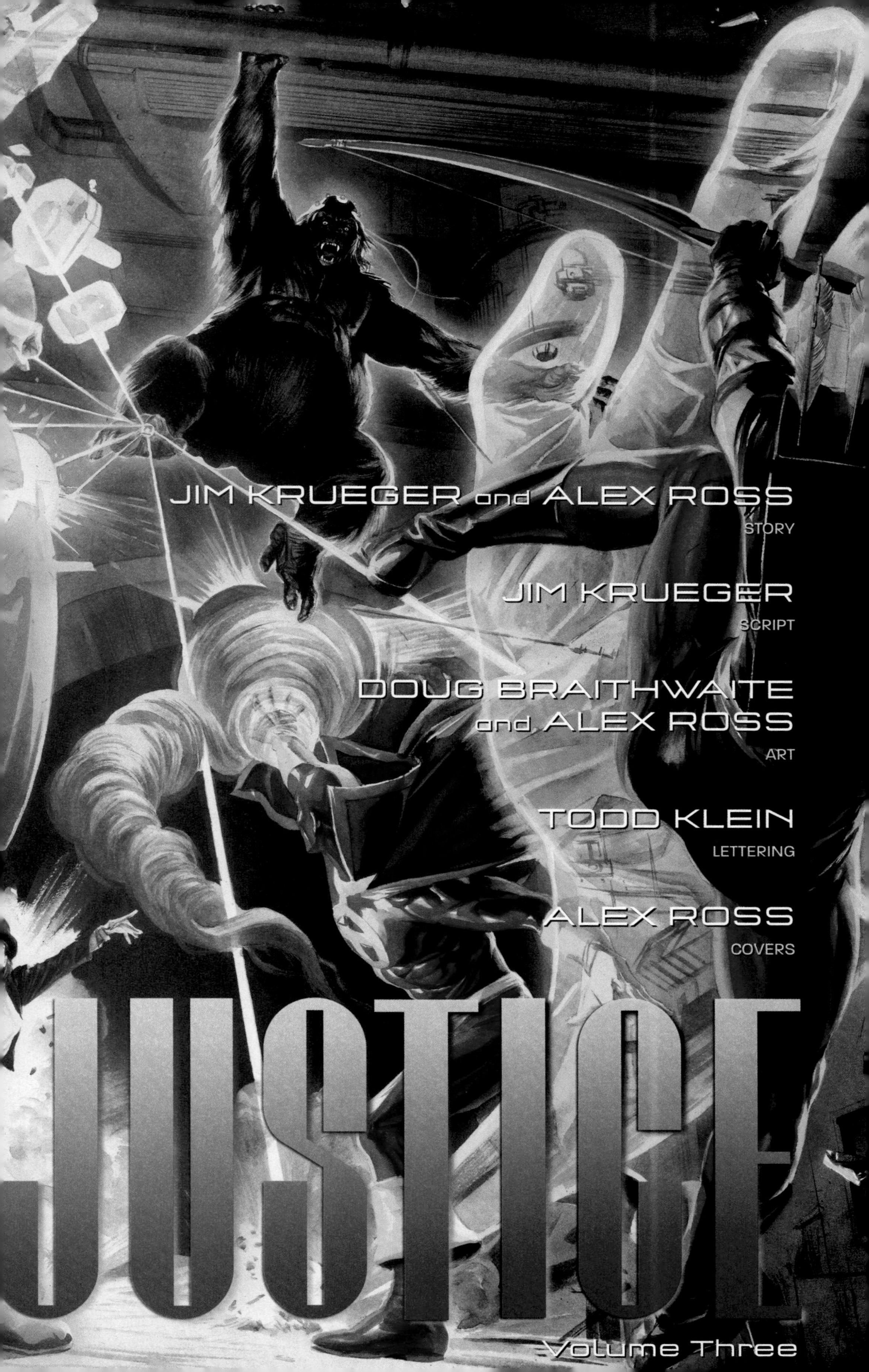

JIM KRUEGER and ALEX ROSS
STORY

JIM KRUEGER
SCRIPT

DOUG BRAITHWAITE
and ALEX ROSS
ART

TODD KLEIN
LETTERING

ALEX ROSS
COVERS

JUSTICE

Volume Three

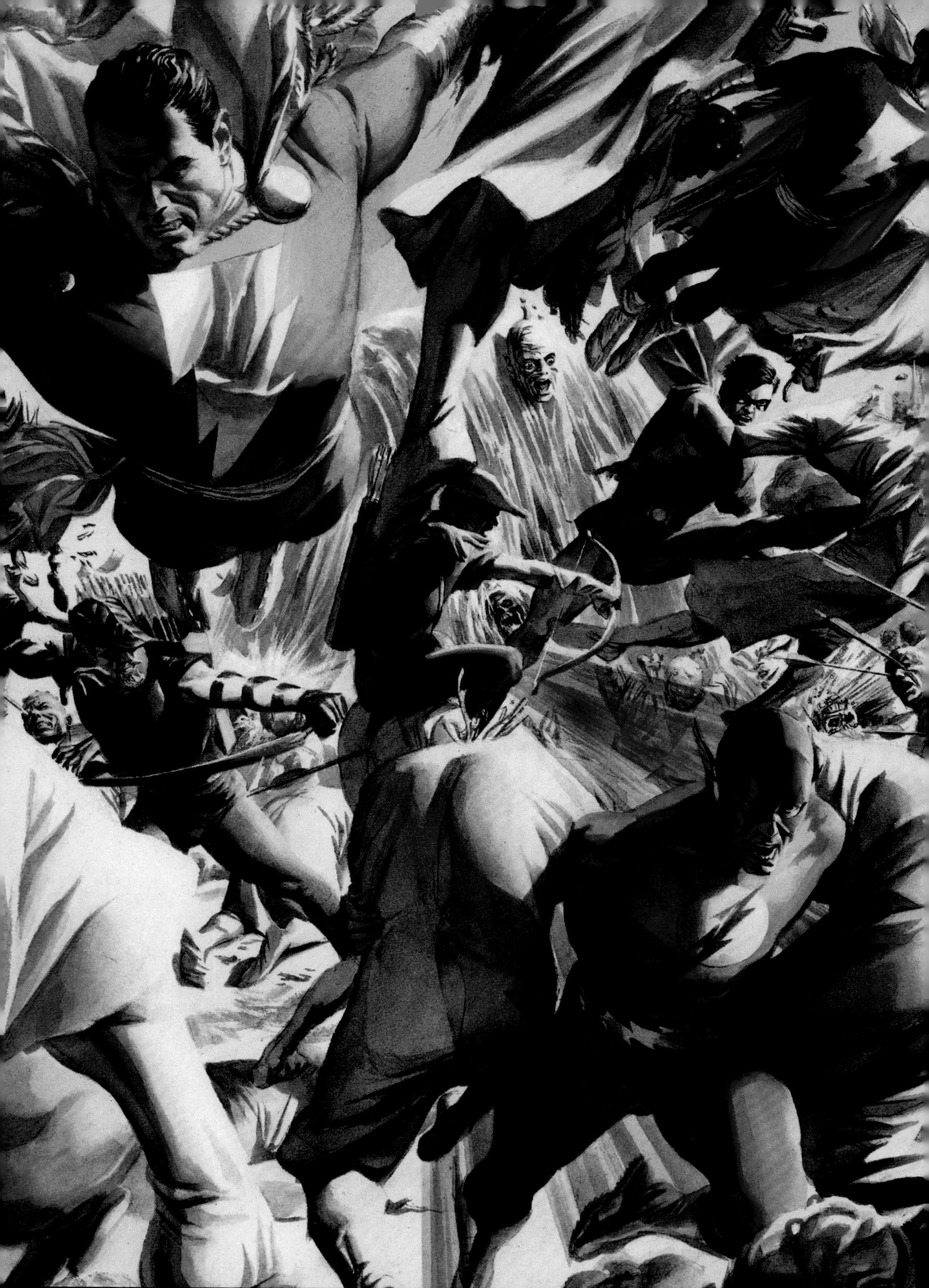

JUSTICE VOLUME THREE
Published by DC Comics.

DC Comics, 1700 Broadway, New York, NY 10019.

Dan DiDio *Senior VP-Executive Editor* • Joey Cavalieri *Editor-original series* • Michael Wright *Associate Editor-origina*
Stephanie Buscema *Assistant Editor-original series* • Anton Kawasaki *Editor-collected edition* • Robbin Brosterman *Senior Art*
Paul Levitz *President & Publisher* • Georg Brewer *VP-Design & DC Direct Creative* • Richard Bruning *Senior VP-Creative*
Patrick Caldon *Executive VP-Finance & Operations* • Chris Caramalis *VP-Finance* • John Cunningham *VP-Ma*
Terri Cunningham *VP-Managing Editor* • Alison Gill *VP-Manufacturing* • Hank Kanalz *VP-General Manager, Wi*
Jim Lee *Editorial Director-WildStorm* • Paula Lowitt *Senior VP-Business & Legal Affairs* • MaryEllen McLaughlin *VP-Adv*
& Custom Publishing • John Nee *VP-Business Development* • Gregory Noveck *Senior VP-Creative Affairs* • Sue Pohja *V*
Trade Sales • Cheryl Rubin *Senior VP-Brand Management* • Jeff Trojan *VP-Business Development, DC Direct* • Bob Wayne *V*

Cover by Alex Ross. Publication design by Brainchild Studios/NYC.

by Alex Ross

...the project's true inspiration
was from an old Saturday morning
cartoon show we watched as kids,
The Challenge of the Super Friends.

ersus. VS.

hat was the original working title for this toryline that pitted the greatest DC heroes gainst their greatest, most classic villains. S. embodied the concept that we wanted his to be seen as that ultimate good guy/ ad guy struggle given operatic form. truth, no matter what name we gave it, he project's true inspiration was from an d Saturday morning cartoon show we watched as kids, *The Challenge of the uper Friends.* Starring the Justice League f America, pitted against their greatest es in the form of the Legion of Doom, his series was the first of its kind, both n television and in comics.

uper-heroes' battles rarely put them up gainst a genuine roll call of villain favorites. es, there were many super-villain groups e the Secret Society of Super-Villains, ut mostly their rosters were made up f secondary bad guys and not lead rchnemeses working together en masse.

illains like Lex Luthor, Brainiac, Sinestro, iddler, Cheetah, and others being the

framework of an assembly equally impressive to the Justice League was a fan's dream come true. Previous work I've done in comics paid small tribute to certain details of this show, such as using the designs for the "Hall of Doom" and "Hall of Justice" as the basis for building structures in the series KINGDOM COME. I wasn't quite sure, when I did that work a decade ago, just how much untapped inspiration still remained in me from that original source. For myself, in my own evolution as a storyteller and DC Comics fan, I had to find that right point in my career to realize that I had never done a project like JUSTICE. In almost all of my previous jobs, I was telling stories about how super-heroes dealt with the world and each other, but never truly dealing with their common burden, super-villains. For a time, I almost didn't think that it was important for me to contribute my time to that never-ending battle that occupies most comic books. What I had to realize was that I needed to get off my high horse and dig in to try to produce the kind of drama and

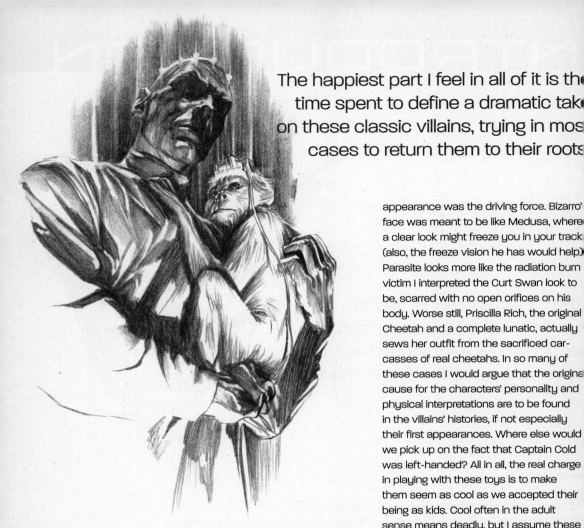

The happiest part I feel in all of it is the
time spent to define a dramatic take
on these classic villains, trying in most
cases to return them to their roots

appearance was the driving force. Bizarro'
face was meant to be like Medusa, where
a clear look might freeze you in your track
(also, the freeze vision he has would help).
Parasite looks more like the radiation burn
victim I interpreted the Curt Swan look to
be, scarred with no open orifices on his
body. Worse still, Priscilla Rich, the original
Cheetah and a complete lunatic, actually
sews her outfit from the sacrificed car-
casses of real cheetahs. In so many of
these cases I would argue that the original
cause for the characters' personality and
physical interpretations are to be found
in the villains' histories, if not especially
their first appearances. Where else would
we pick up on the fact that Captain Cold
was left-handed? All in all, the real charge
in playing with these toys is to make
them seem as cool as we accepted their
being as kids. Cool often in the adult
sense means deadly, but I assume these
characters were intended by their original
creators to be a striking and respectable
threat level.

entertainment that comics history is built
upon. Once I knew that, this book was all I
thought of and lived for almost three years.
After its inception and our run of twelve
issues, I find myself exhausted from trying
to live up to what normal comics do all
the time. Even with two artists working in
tandem and an excruciatingly planned-out
storyline, this series was a strained
endeavor.

The happiest part I feel in all of it is the
time spent to define a dramatic take on
these classic villains, trying in most cases
to return them to their roots. With Metallo,
one of the more recognizable Superman
villains by name but not by a single physical appearance, we played him mysterious
by showing the mustached Superman
look-alike that he first showed up as. Only
when he opens a metal door in his chest
are we to know by his kryptonite heart that
he is the cyborg Metallo. With others, the
intent to horrify the reader by the villains'

Speaking of toys, as many readers already
know, one of the joys of this series has
been the run of action figure merchandise
released in cooperation with the series. Not
since DC's "Super Powers" toy line from
twenty years ago have a comic and action
figure line worked together so successfully.
Working with DC Direct, I was allowed
to collaborate with the art directors, Jim
Fletcher and Georg Brewer, and many
talented sculptors to match the look and
style presented in the series. Most days I
was concentrating on painting the pages
to JUSTICE, but on others I was doing the
turnaround art for so many figures I had
always wanted DC to create, and now I
had a hand in getting them made. It was a
gratifying and nerve-racking experience.
It's an awesome feeling to see that bridge
built between the story you're imagining

nd illustrating and a three-dimensional
eality. I'm still hoping to get them to make
he oversized Giganta figure.

till, the comic book's reason for being
erves a multitude of ambitions. JUSTICE
lso exists to embrace a timeless
ontinuity, where the mostly Silver Age
oncepts of DC live and breathe and
opefully harness the creative core of
ho those characters are to the world at
rge. Within JUSTICE, Barry Allen still lives,
ick Grayson is still Robin, and most of
he heroes, villains, and supergroups that
efine DC appear as they first did. This
pocket universe" of DC is a privilege I've
njoyed for some time — to get to pay
omage to the comics era of my youth,
st to the side of the evolving modern
ontinuity. JUSTICE may be the final
ulmination of that joyful look at these
haracters, but I always hope that the
onic nature of super-heroes will always
ring the characters back to their simplest
orm and origins.

ve said it before of other books I've
vorked on, but it has never been more true
han with this series: It is a love letter to a
ctional universe, attempting to do justice
its inspiration.

LEX ROSS
ugust, 2007

WHAT HAS COME BEFORE

It begins with a dream...or rather a nightmare.

DC
Jim Krueger • Alex Ross • Doug Braithwaite
JUSTICE

DC
Jim Krueger • Alex Ross • Doug Braithwaite
JUSTICE

The world's vilest villains all wake up from the same feverish glimpse of a possible near-future: one in which the combined might of the fabled Justice League of America is not enough to save the world from total disaster. Humanity has relied too much on its heroes and has become too weak to defend itself. So now the greatest criminal minds on Earth have decided that the only way to save the world is by taking down the members of the Justice League... one by one.

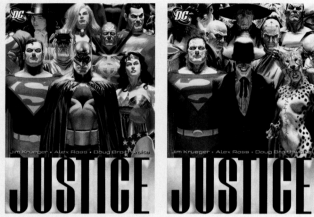

The villains begin to change the world around them in dramatic ways that the JLA couldn't or wouldn't — as desert wastelands bloom with life, people with disabilities walk again, and the end of world hunger is in sight. But the criminals' deeds are not entirely altruistic, as they discover the secret identities of the heroes, and several members of the JLA fall by their hand.

The villains present to the Earth's population their plan of changing the world. Accusing the heroes of being absent and unable to make the real changes needed for a better society, the villains build "perfect" cities without disease or poverty, and invite the people whom they've cured to live in them.

But with the help of other heroes, the JLA begins to regain their footing — and a final war with the villains is just on the horizon. When family members and loved ones of several of the heroes are kidnapped, the battle lines are drawn...

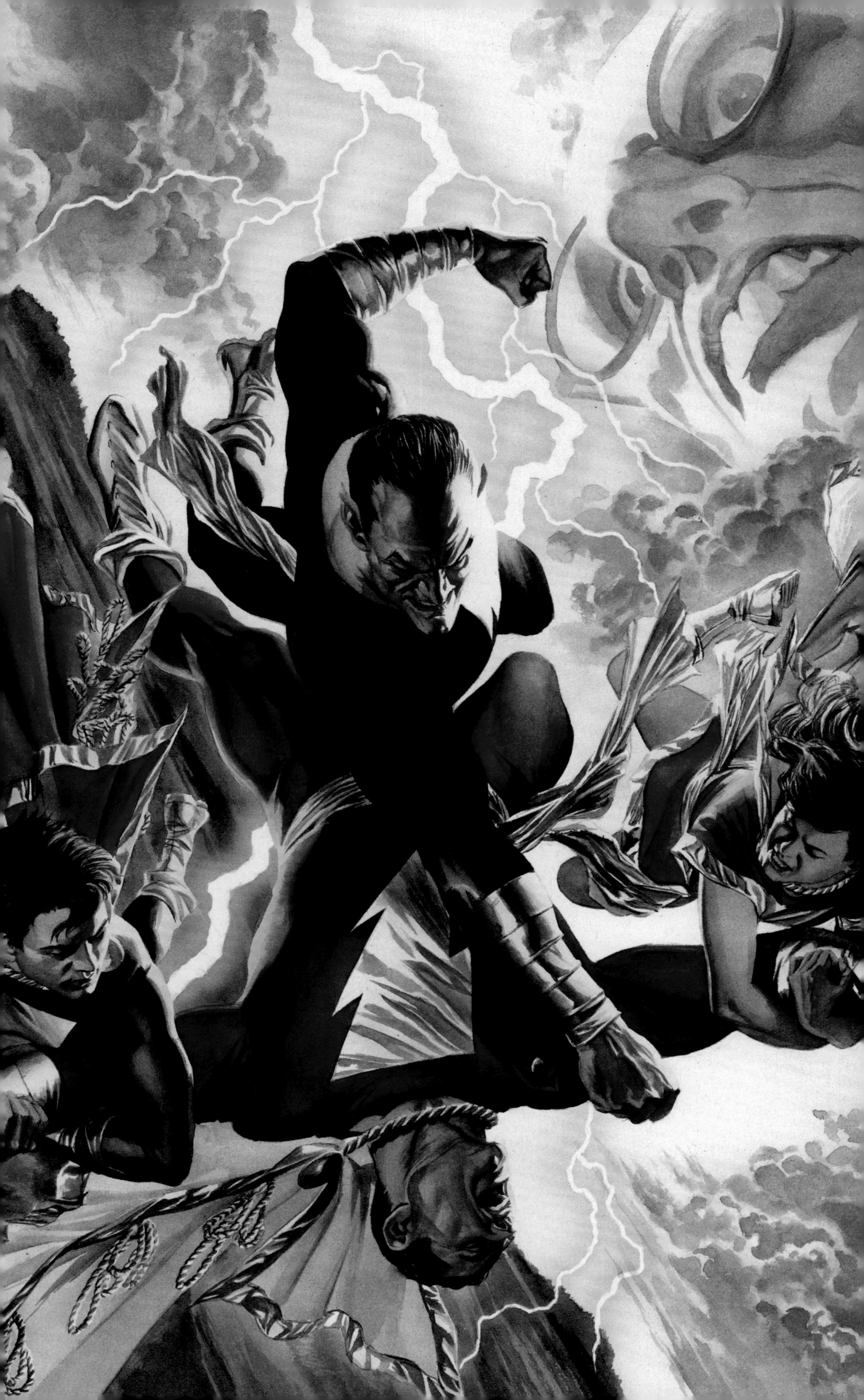

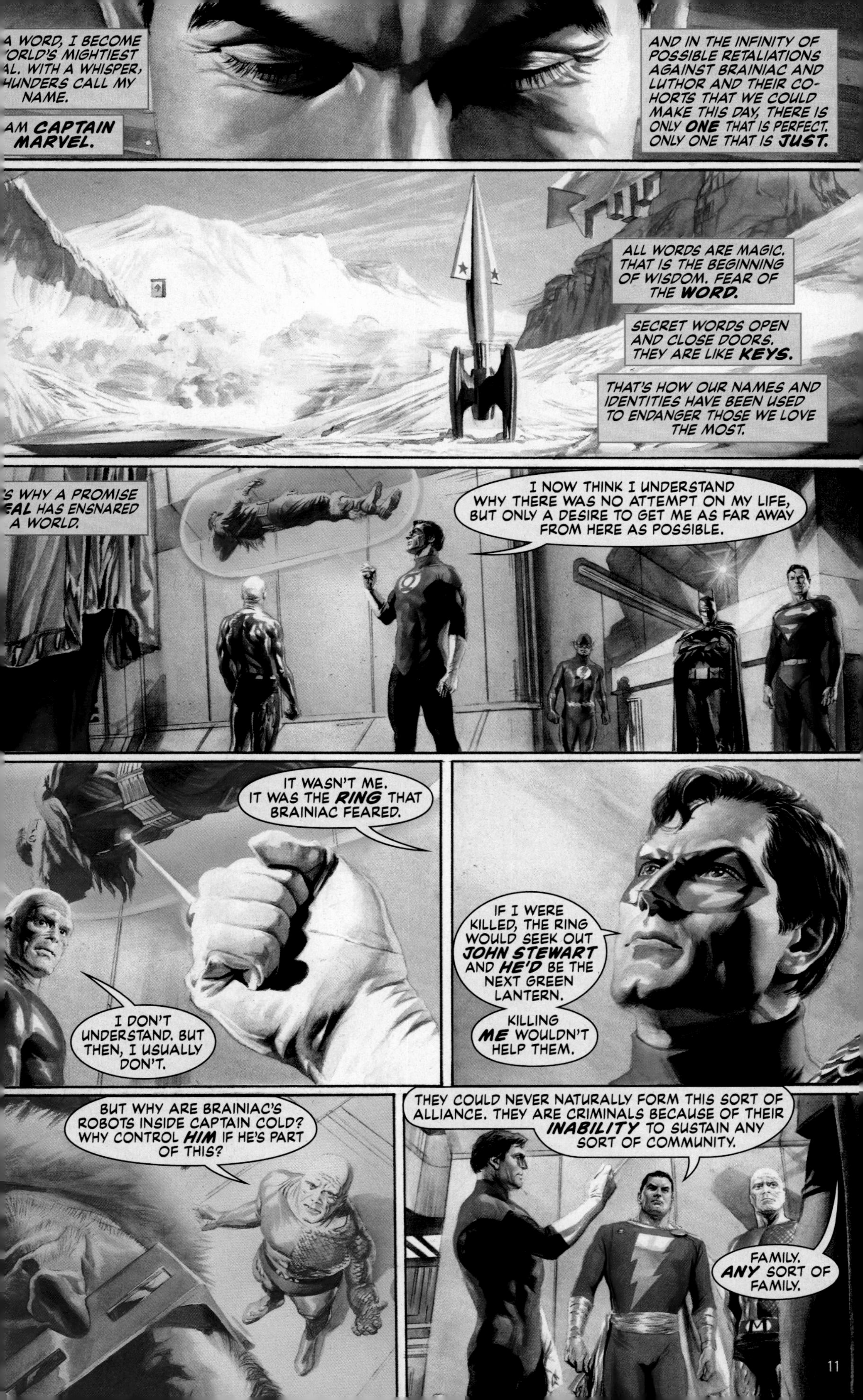
A WORD, I BECOME
ORLD'S MIGHTIEST
AL. WITH A WHISPER,
HUNDERS CALL MY
NAME.
AM CAPTAIN MARVEL.
AND IN THE INFINITY OF POSSIBLE RETALIATIONS AGAINST BRAINIAC AND LUTHOR AND THEIR CO-HORTS THAT WE COULD MAKE THIS DAY, THERE IS ONLY ONE THAT IS PERFECT. ONLY ONE THAT IS JUST.
ALL WORDS ARE MAGIC. THAT IS THE BEGINNING OF WISDOM. FEAR OF THE WORD.
SECRET WORDS OPEN AND CLOSE DOORS. THEY ARE LIKE KEYS.
THAT'S HOW OUR NAMES AND IDENTITIES HAVE BEEN USED TO ENDANGER THOSE WE LOVE THE MOST.
'S WHY A PROMISE
EAL HAS ENSNARED
A WORLD.
I NOW THINK I UNDERSTAND WHY THERE WAS NO ATTEMPT ON MY LIFE, BUT ONLY A DESIRE TO GET ME AS FAR AWAY FROM HERE AS POSSIBLE.
IT WASN'T ME. IT WAS THE RING THAT BRAINIAC FEARED.
I DON'T UNDERSTAND. BUT THEN, I USUALLY DON'T.
IF I WERE KILLED, THE RING WOULD SEEK OUT JOHN STEWART AND HE'D BE THE NEXT GREEN LANTERN.
KILLING ME WOULDN'T HELP THEM.
BUT WHY ARE BRAINIAC'S ROBOTS INSIDE CAPTAIN COLD? WHY CONTROL HIM IF HE'S PART OF THIS?
THEY COULD NEVER NATURALLY FORM THIS SORT OF ALLIANCE. THEY ARE CRIMINALS BECAUSE OF THEIR INABILITY TO SUSTAIN ANY SORT OF COMMUNITY.
FAMILY. ANY SORT OF FAMILY.

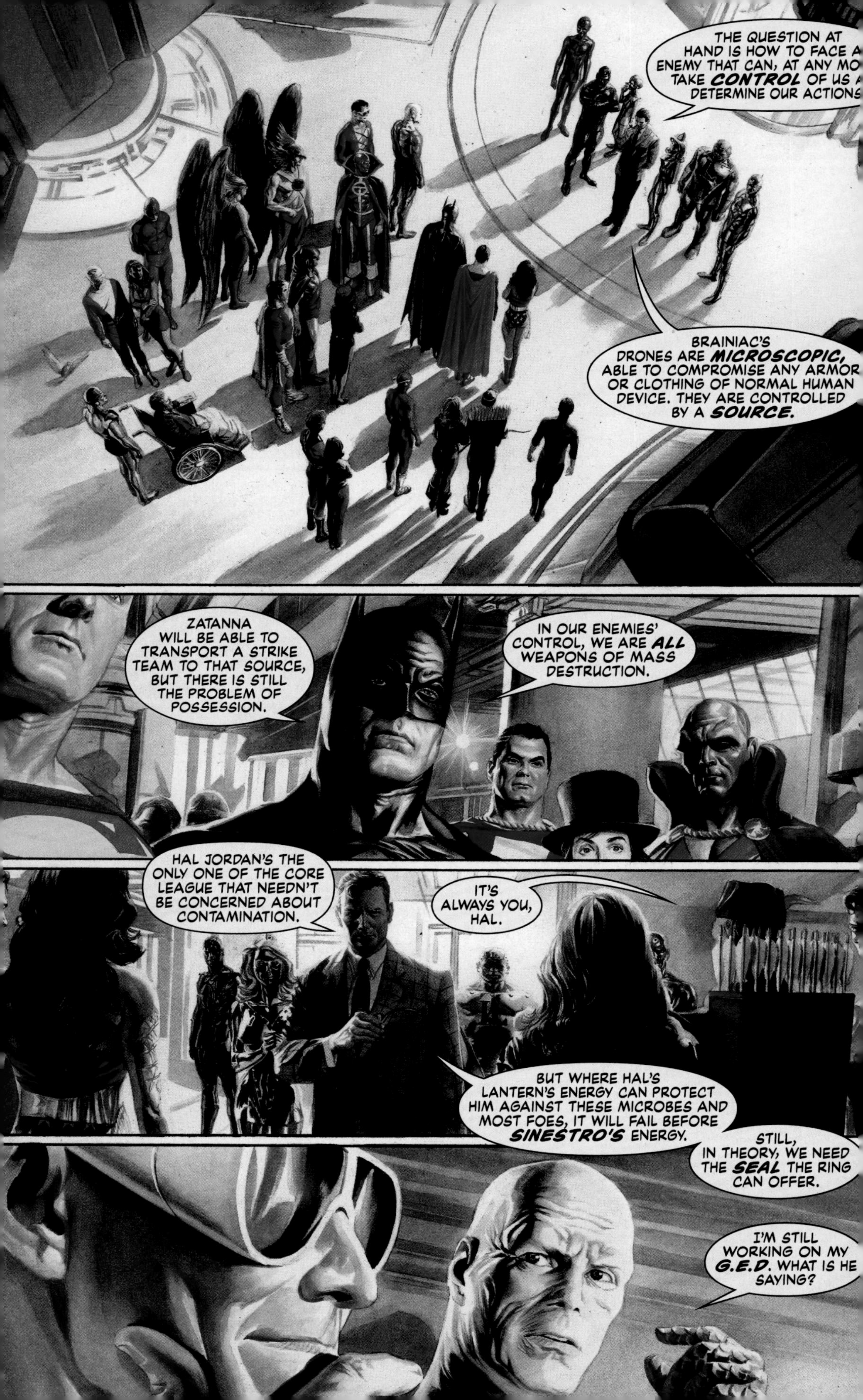
THE QUESTION AT HAND IS HOW TO FACE A ENEMY THAT CAN, AT ANY MO TAKE CONTROL OF US A DETERMINE OUR ACTIONS
BRAINIAC'S DRONES ARE MICROSCOPIC, ABLE TO COMPROMISE ANY ARMOR OR CLOTHING OF NORMAL HUMAN DEVICE. THEY ARE CONTROLLED BY A SOURCE.
ZATANNA WILL BE ABLE TO TRANSPORT A STRIKE TEAM TO THAT SOURCE, BUT THERE IS STILL THE PROBLEM OF POSSESSION.
IN OUR ENEMIES' CONTROL, WE ARE ALL WEAPONS OF MASS DESTRUCTION.
HAL JORDAN'S THE ONLY ONE OF THE CORE LEAGUE THAT NEEDN'T BE CONCERNED ABOUT CONTAMINATION.
IT'S ALWAYS YOU, HAL.
BUT WHERE HAL'S LANTERN'S ENERGY CAN PROTECT HIM AGAINST THESE MICROBES AND MOST FOES, IT WILL FAIL BEFORE SINESTRO'S ENERGY.
STILL, IN THEORY, WE NEED THE SEAL THE RING CAN OFFER.
I'M STILL WORKING ON MY G.E.D. WHAT IS HE SAYING?

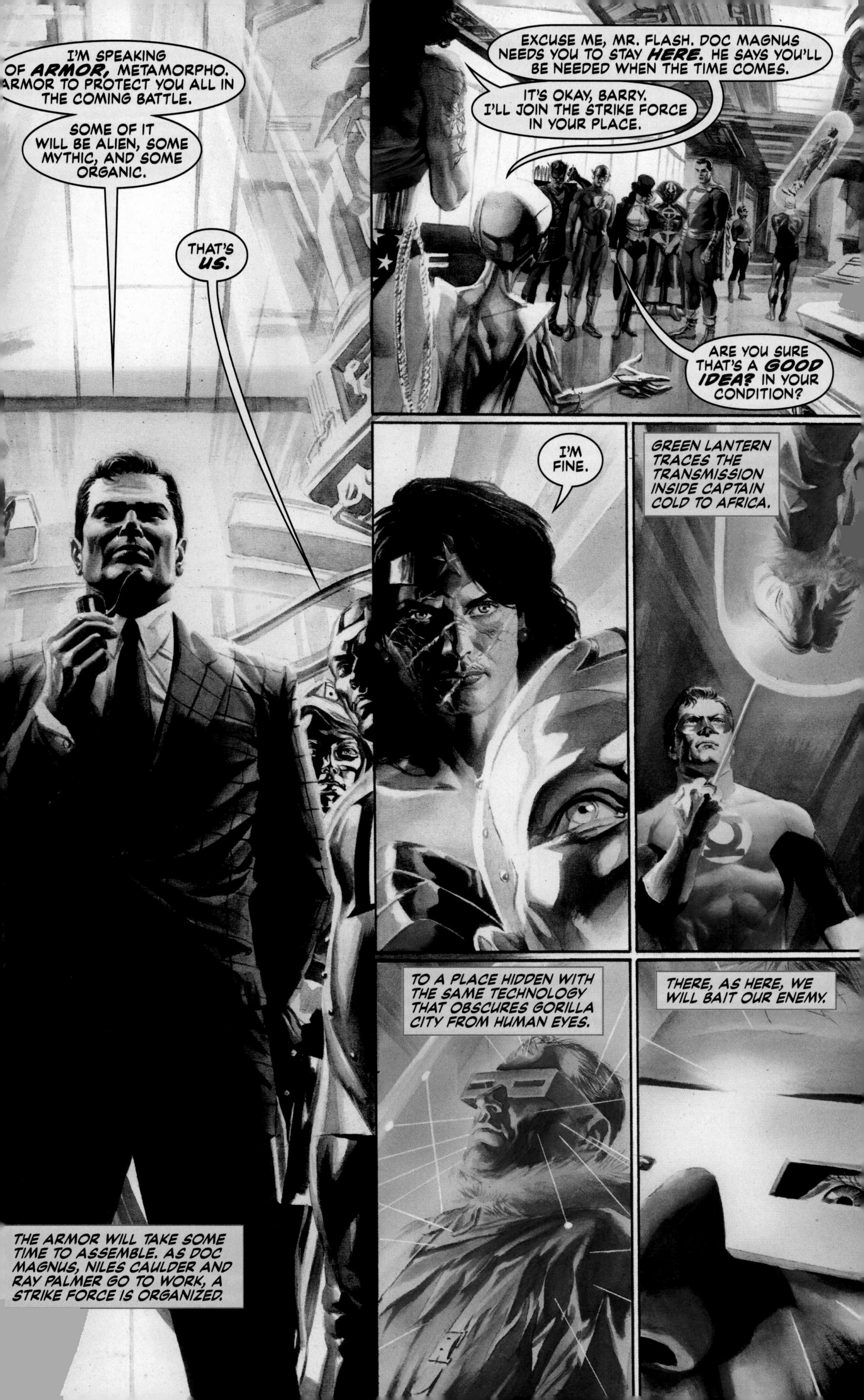

I'M SPEAKING OF ARMOR, METAMORPHO. ARMOR TO PROTECT YOU ALL IN THE COMING BATTLE.
SOME OF IT WILL BE ALIEN, SOME MYTHIC, AND SOME ORGANIC.
THAT'S US.
THE ARMOR WILL TAKE SOME TIME TO ASSEMBLE. AS DOC MAGNUS, NILES CAULDER AND RAY PALMER GO TO WORK, A STRIKE FORCE IS ORGANIZED.
EXCUSE ME, MR. FLASH. DOC MAGNUS NEEDS YOU TO STAY HERE. HE SAYS YOU'LL BE NEEDED WHEN THE TIME COMES.
IT'S OKAY, BARRY. I'LL JOIN THE STRIKE FORCE IN YOUR PLACE.
ARE YOU SURE THAT'S A GOOD IDEA? IN YOUR CONDITION?
I'M FINE.
GREEN LANTERN TRACES THE TRANSMISSION INSIDE CAPTAIN COLD TO AFRICA.
TO A PLACE HIDDEN WITH THE SAME TECHNOLOGY THAT OBSCURES GORILLA CITY FROM HUMAN EYES.
THERE, AS HERE, WE WILL BAIT OUR ENEMY.

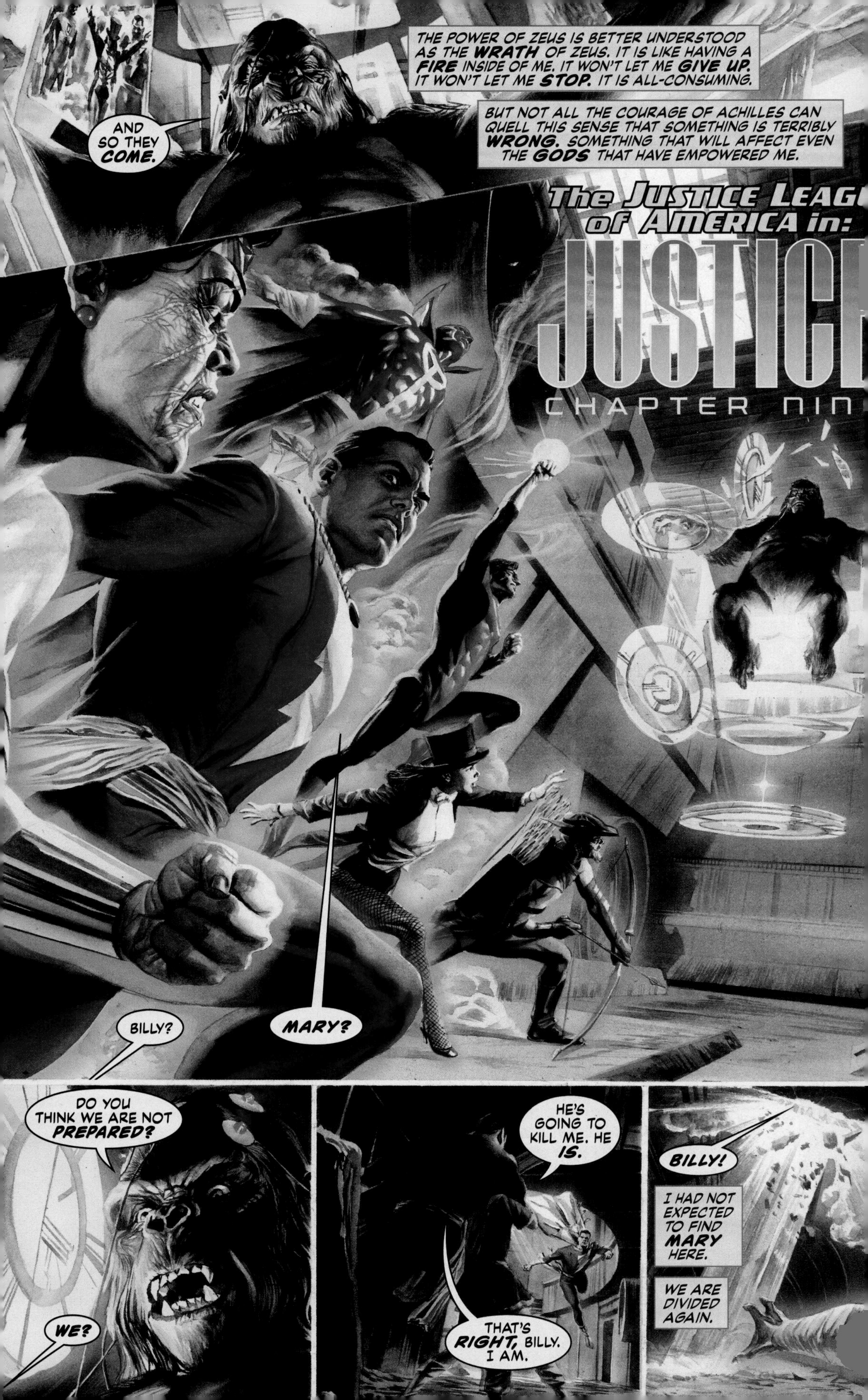
THE POWER OF ZEUS IS BETTER UNDERSTOOD AS THE WRATH OF ZEUS. IT IS LIKE HAVING A FIRE INSIDE OF ME. IT WON'T LET ME GIVE UP. IT WON'T LET ME STOP. IT IS ALL-CONSUMING.
AND SO THEY COME.
BUT NOT ALL THE COURAGE OF ACHILLES CAN QUELL THIS SENSE THAT SOMETHING IS TERRIBLY WRONG. SOMETHING THAT WILL AFFECT EVEN THE GODS THAT HAVE EMPOWERED ME.
The JUSTICE LEAG
of AMERICA in:
JUSTICE
CHAPTER NIN
BILLY?
MARY?
DO YOU THINK WE ARE NOT PREPARED?
WE?
HE'S GOING TO KILL ME. HE IS.
THAT'S RIGHT, BILLY. I AM.
BILLY!
I HAD NOT EXPECTED TO FIND MARY HERE.
WE ARE DIVIDED AGAIN.

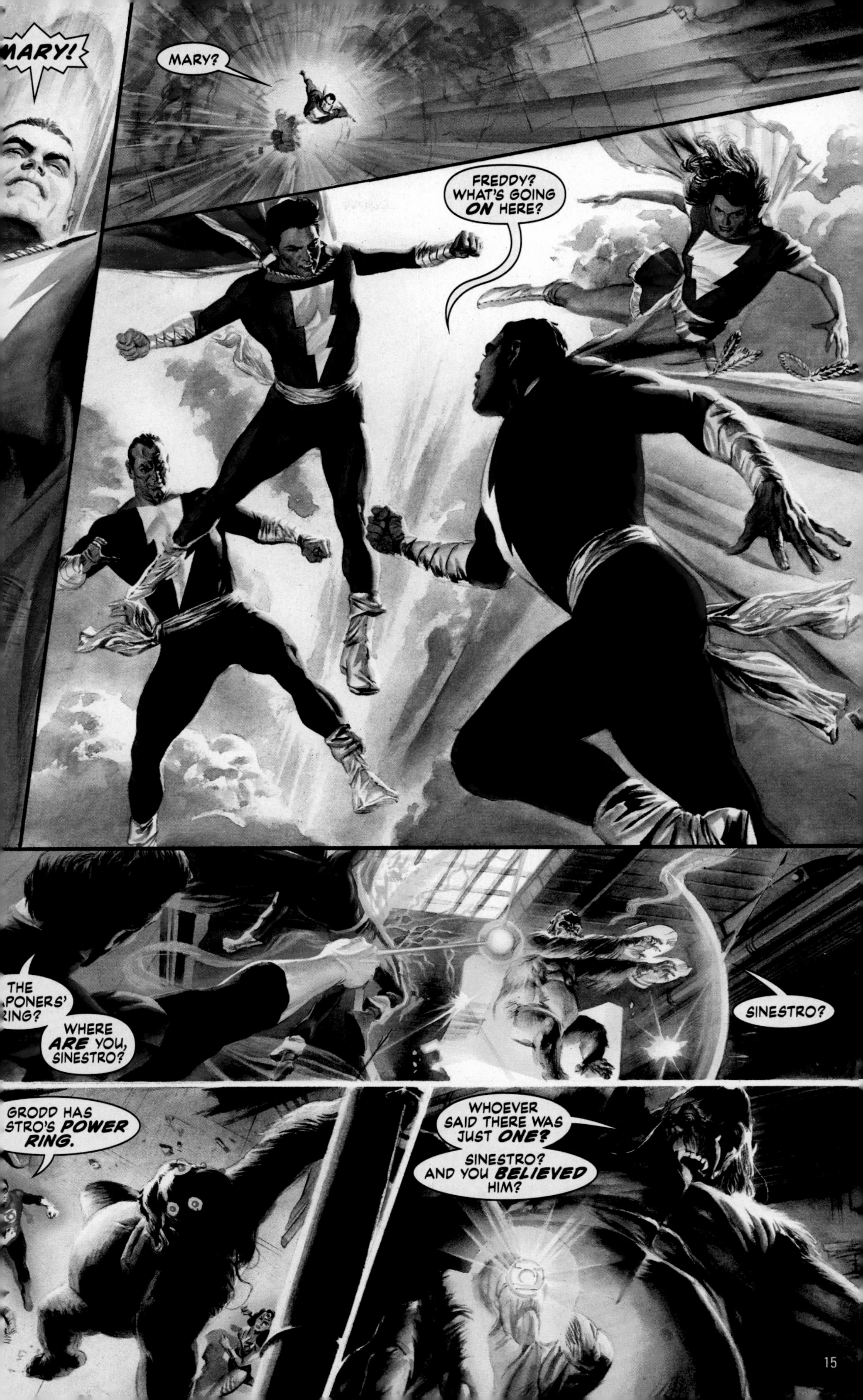
MARY!
MARY?
FREDDY? WHAT'S GOING ON HERE?
THE PONERS' RING?
WHERE ARE YOU, SINESTRO?
SINESTRO?
GRODD HAS STRO'S POWER RING.
WHOEVER SAID THERE WAS JUST ONE?
SINESTRO? AND YOU BELIEVED HIM?

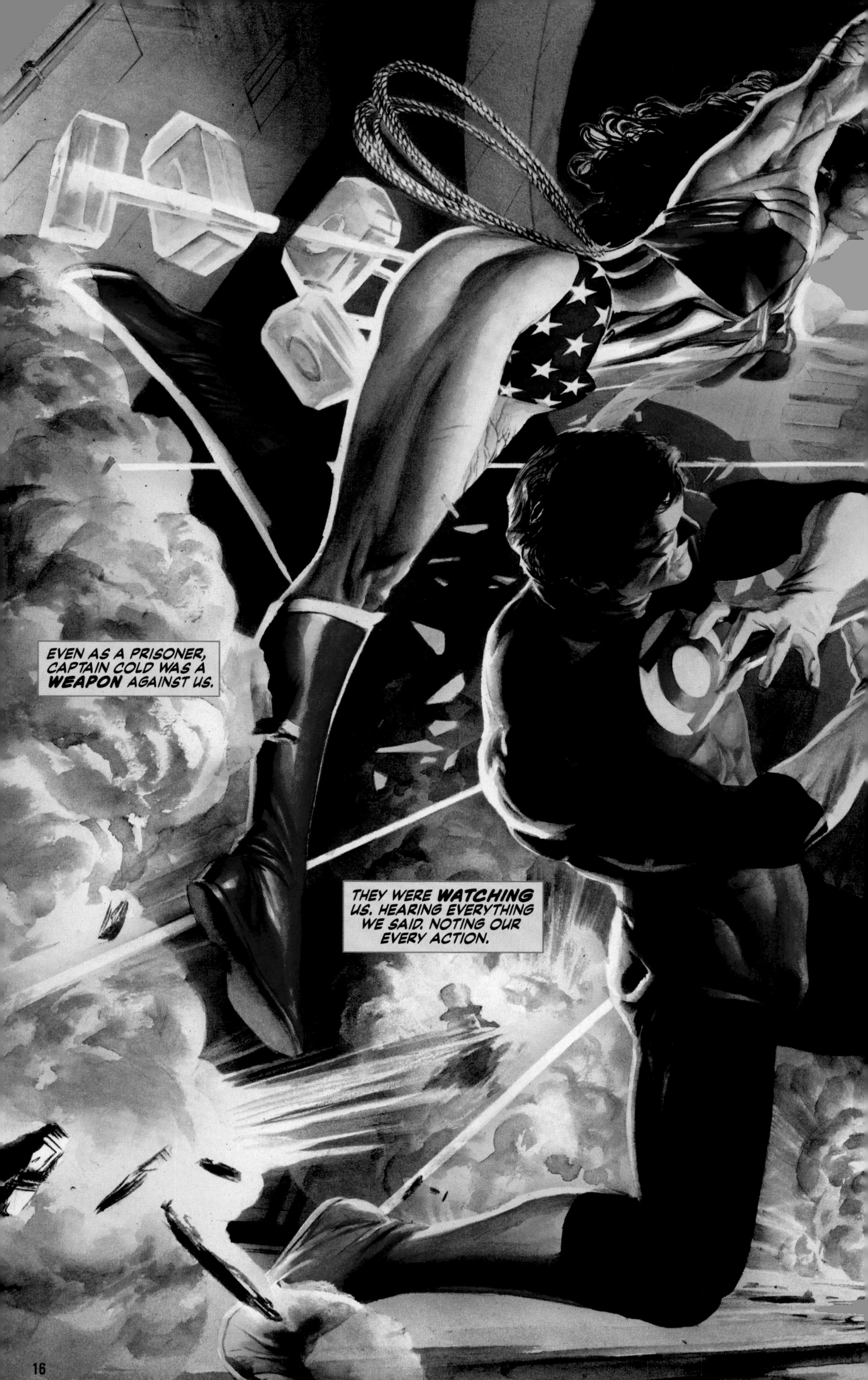
EVEN AS A PRISONER, CAPTAIN COLD WAS A WEAPON AGAINST US.
THEY WERE WATCHING US. HEARING EVERYTHING WE SAID. NOTING OUR EVERY ACTION.

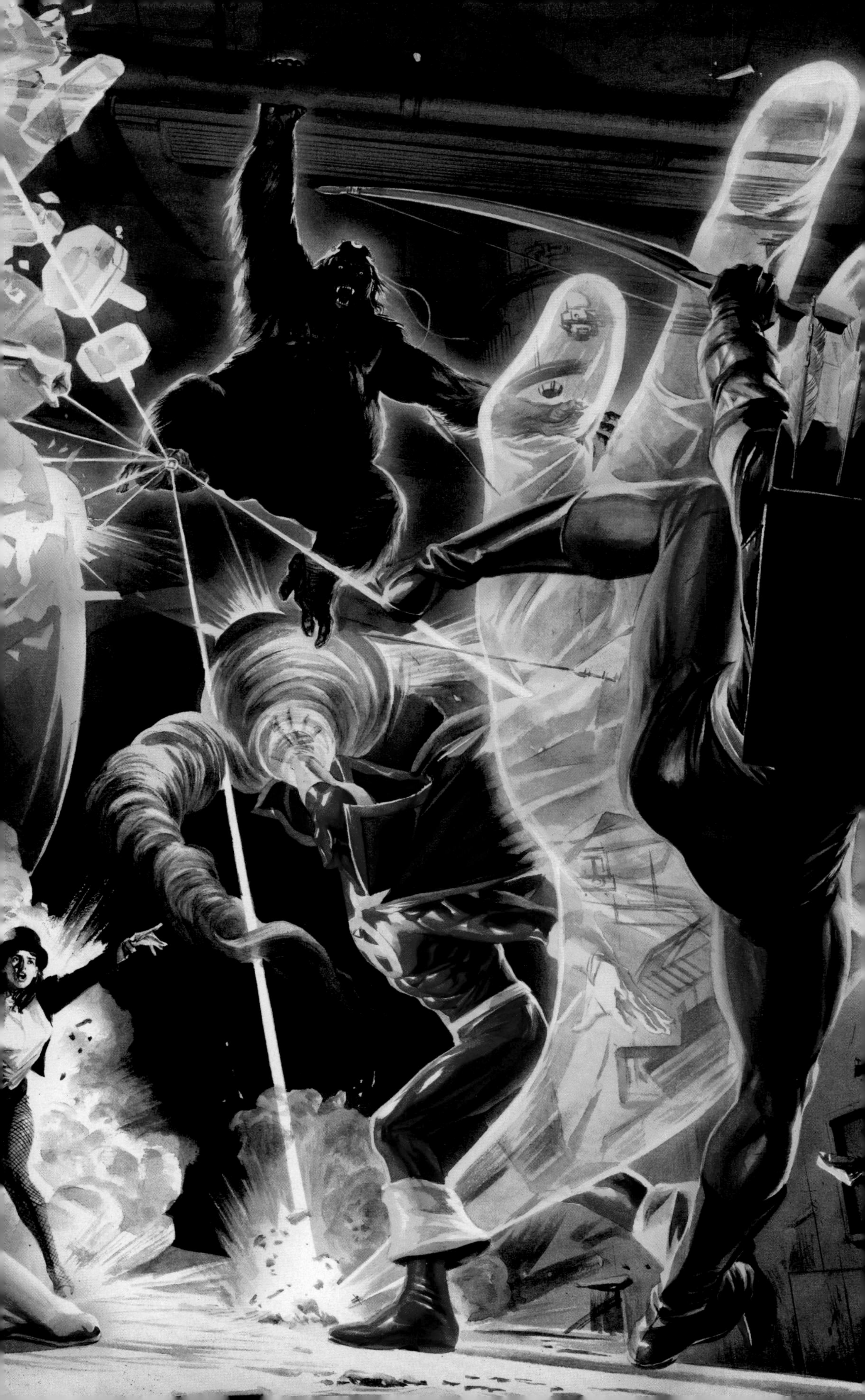

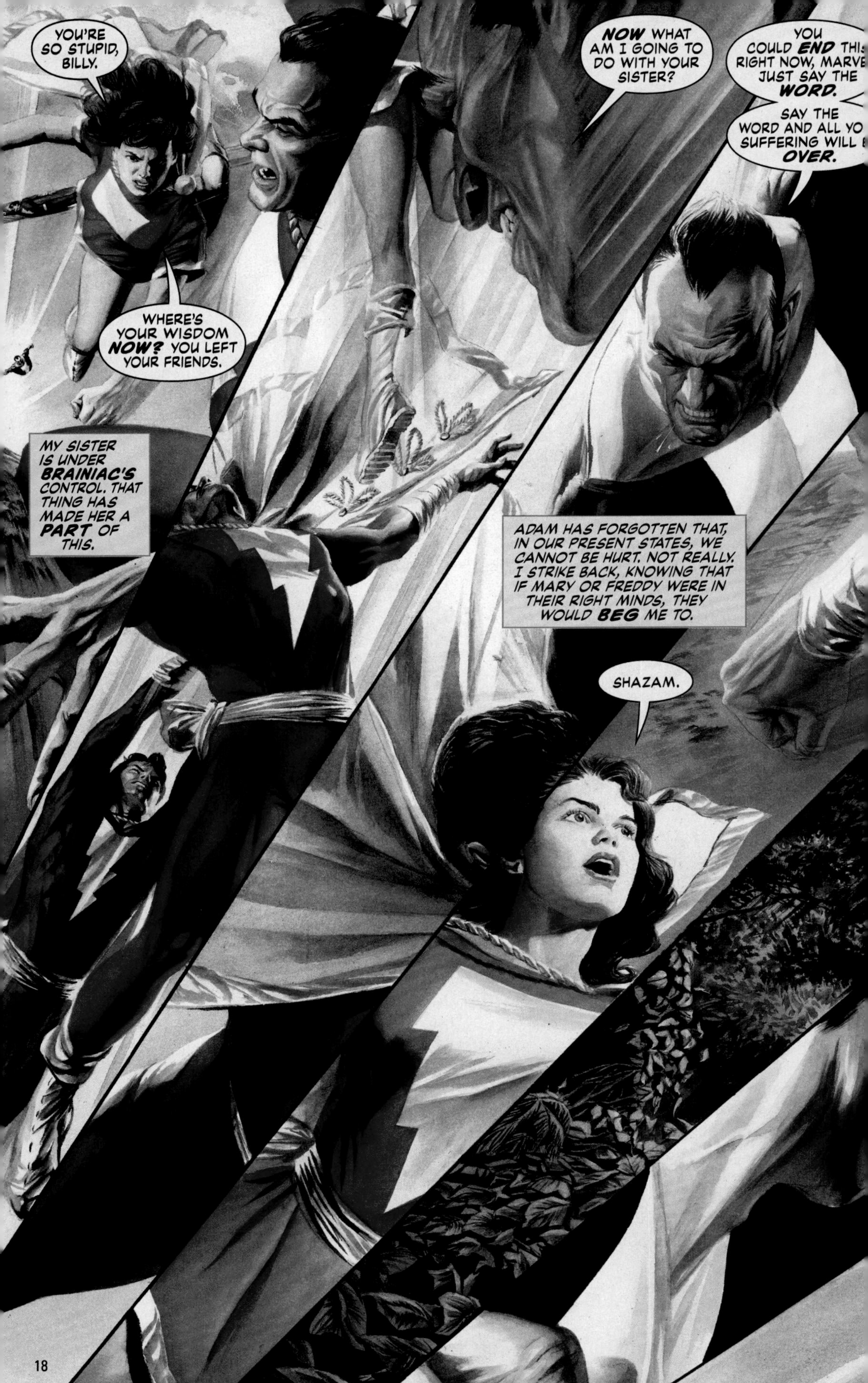
YOU'RE SO STUPID, BILLY.
WHERE'S YOUR WISDOM NOW? YOU LEFT YOUR FRIENDS.
MY SISTER IS UNDER BRAINIAC'S CONTROL. THAT THING HAS MADE HER A PART OF THIS.
NOW WHAT AM I GOING TO DO WITH YOUR SISTER?
YOU COULD END THIS RIGHT NOW, MARVE JUST SAY THE WORD.
SAY THE WORD AND ALL YO SUFFERING WILL OVER.
ADAM HAS FORGOTTEN THAT, IN OUR PRESENT STATES, WE CANNOT BE HURT. NOT REALLY. I STRIKE BACK, KNOWING THAT IF MARY OR FREDDY WERE IN THEIR RIGHT MINDS, THEY WOULD BEG ME TO.
SHAZAM.

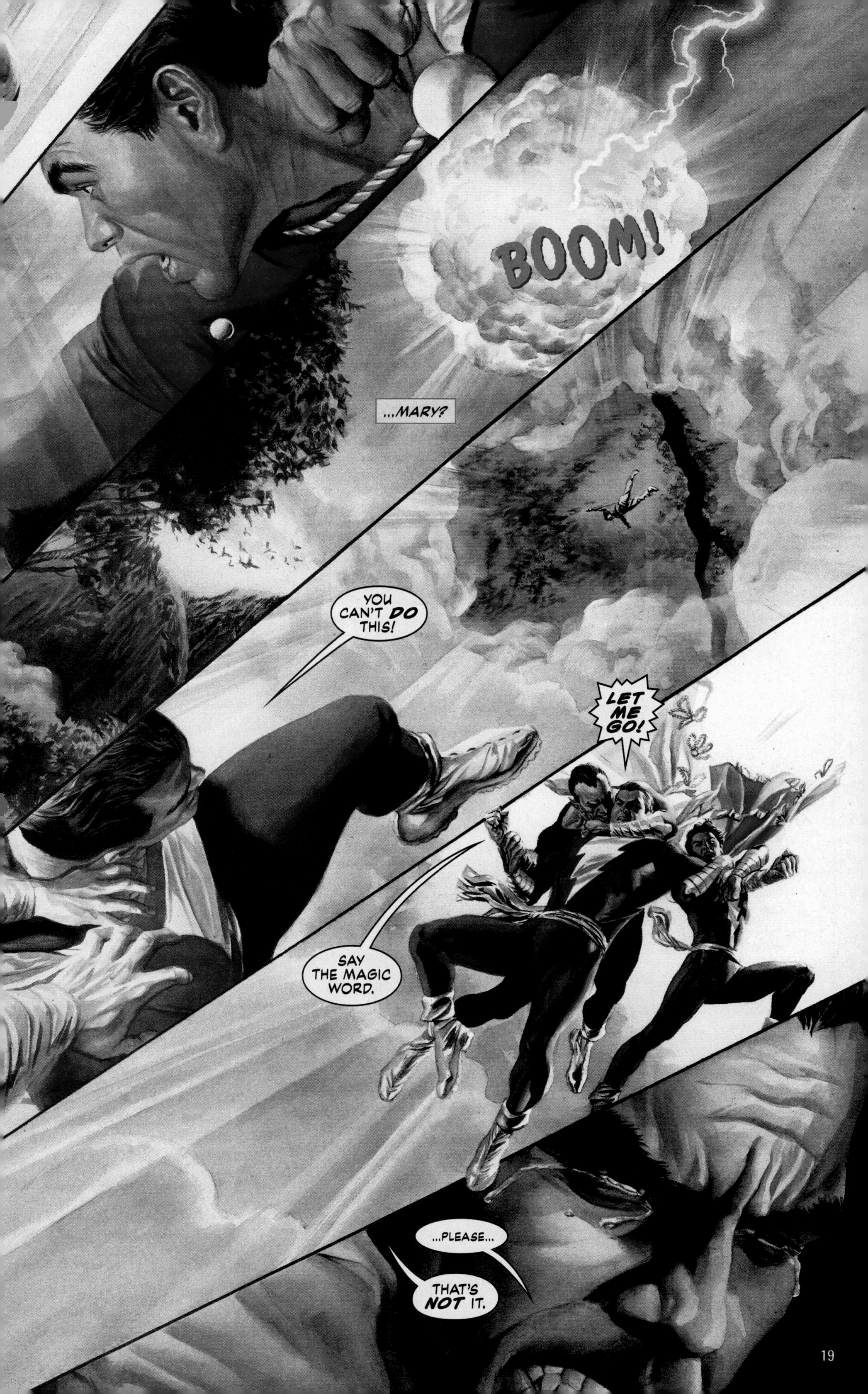
BOOM!
...MARY?
YOU CAN'T DO THIS!
LET ME GO!
SAY THE MAGIC WORD.
...PLEASE...
THAT'S NOT IT.

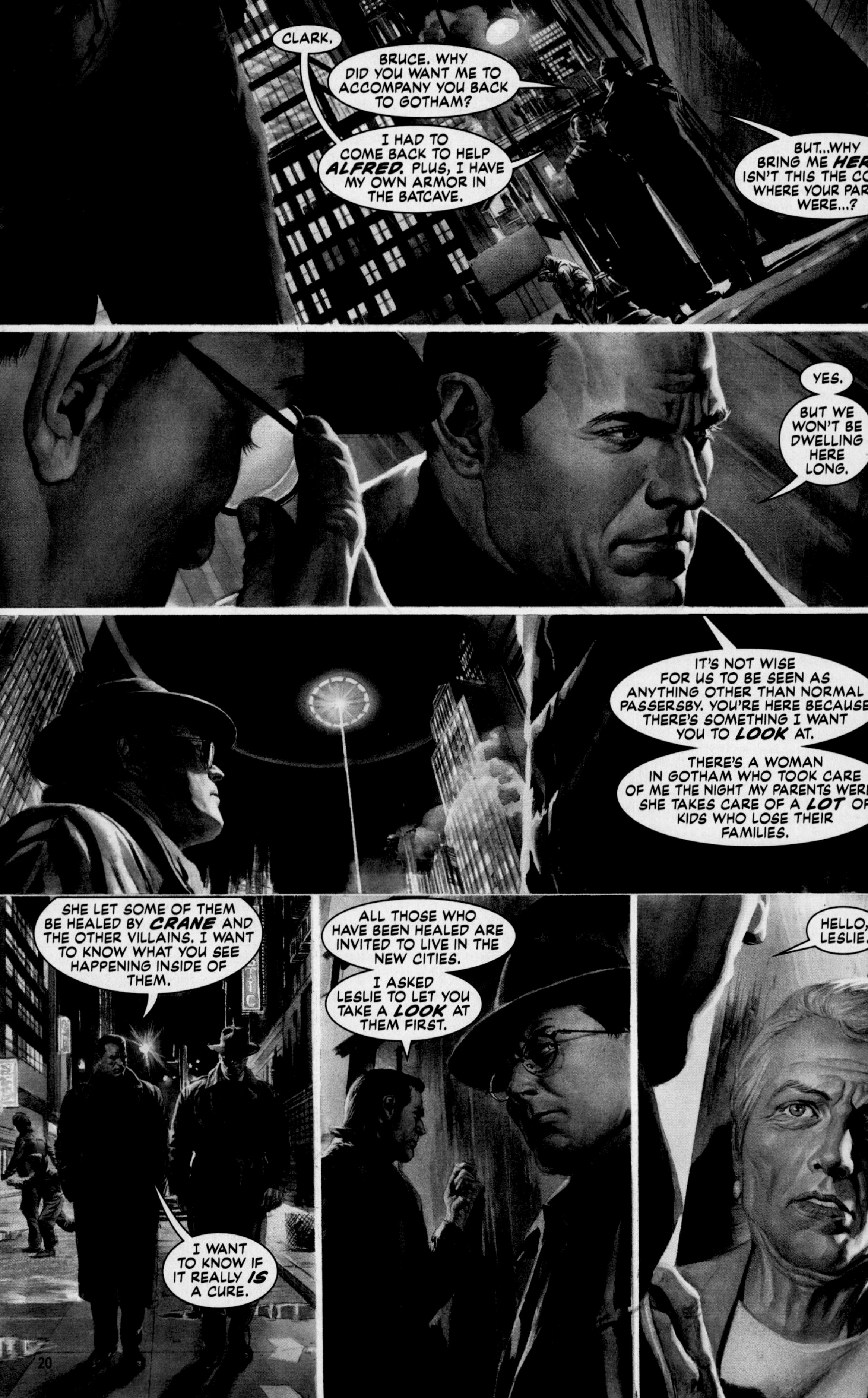
CLARK.
BRUCE. WHY DID YOU WANT ME TO ACCOMPANY YOU BACK TO GOTHAM?
I HAD TO COME BACK TO HELP ALFRED. PLUS, I HAVE MY OWN ARMOR IN THE BATCAVE.
BUT...WHY BRING ME HER ISN'T THIS THE CO WHERE YOUR PAR WERE...?
YES.
BUT WE WON'T BE DWELLING HERE LONG.
IT'S NOT WISE FOR US TO BE SEEN AS ANYTHING OTHER THAN NORMAL PASSERSBY. YOU'RE HERE BECAUSE THERE'S SOMETHING I WANT YOU TO LOOK AT.
THERE'S A WOMAN IN GOTHAM WHO TOOK CARE OF ME THE NIGHT MY PARENTS WER SHE TAKES CARE OF A LOT OF KIDS WHO LOSE THEIR FAMILIES.
SHE LET SOME OF THEM BE HEALED BY CRANE AND THE OTHER VILLAINS. I WANT TO KNOW WHAT YOU SEE HAPPENING INSIDE OF THEM.
I WANT TO KNOW IF IT REALLY IS A CURE.
ALL THOSE WHO HAVE BEEN HEALED ARE INVITED TO LIVE IN THE NEW CITIES.
I ASKED LESLIE TO LET YOU TAKE A LOOK AT THEM FIRST.
HELLO, LESLIE.

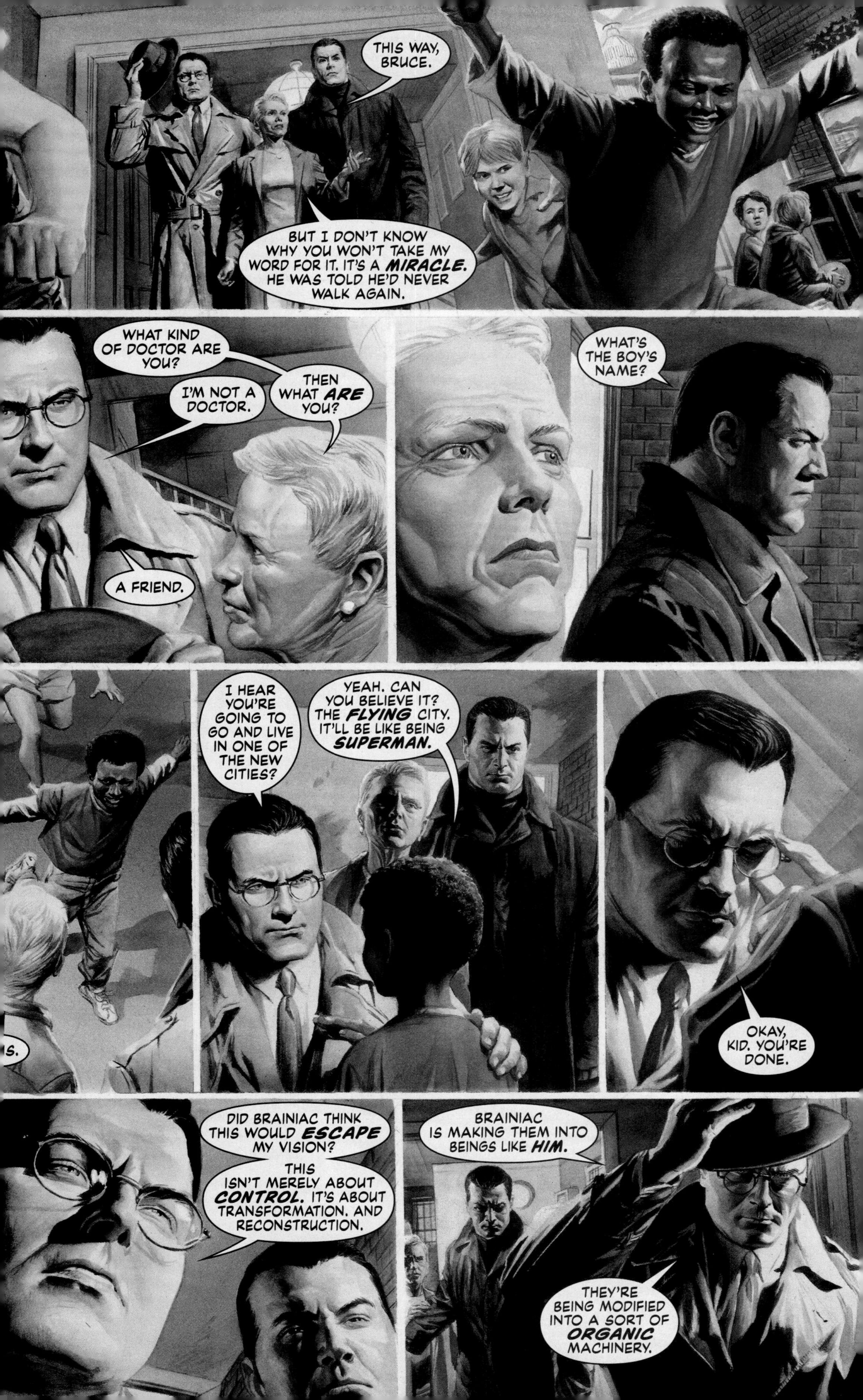
THIS WAY, BRUCE.
BUT I DON'T KNOW WHY YOU WON'T TAKE MY WORD FOR IT. IT'S A *MIRACLE.* HE WAS TOLD HE'D NEVER WALK AGAIN.
WHAT KIND OF DOCTOR ARE YOU?
I'M NOT A DOCTOR.
THEN WHAT *ARE* YOU?
A FRIEND.
WHAT'S THE BOY'S NAME?
I HEAR YOU'RE GOING TO GO AND LIVE IN ONE OF THE NEW CITIES?
YEAH. CAN YOU BELIEVE IT? THE *FLYING* CITY. IT'LL BE LIKE BEING *SUPERMAN.*
OKAY, KID. YOU'RE DONE.
DID BRAINIAC THINK THIS WOULD *ESCAPE* MY VISION?
THIS ISN'T MERELY ABOUT *CONTROL.* IT'S ABOUT TRANSFORMATION. AND RECONSTRUCTION.
BRAINIAC IS MAKING THEM INTO BEINGS LIKE *HIM.*
THEY'RE BEING MODIFIED INTO A SORT OF *ORGANIC* MACHINERY.

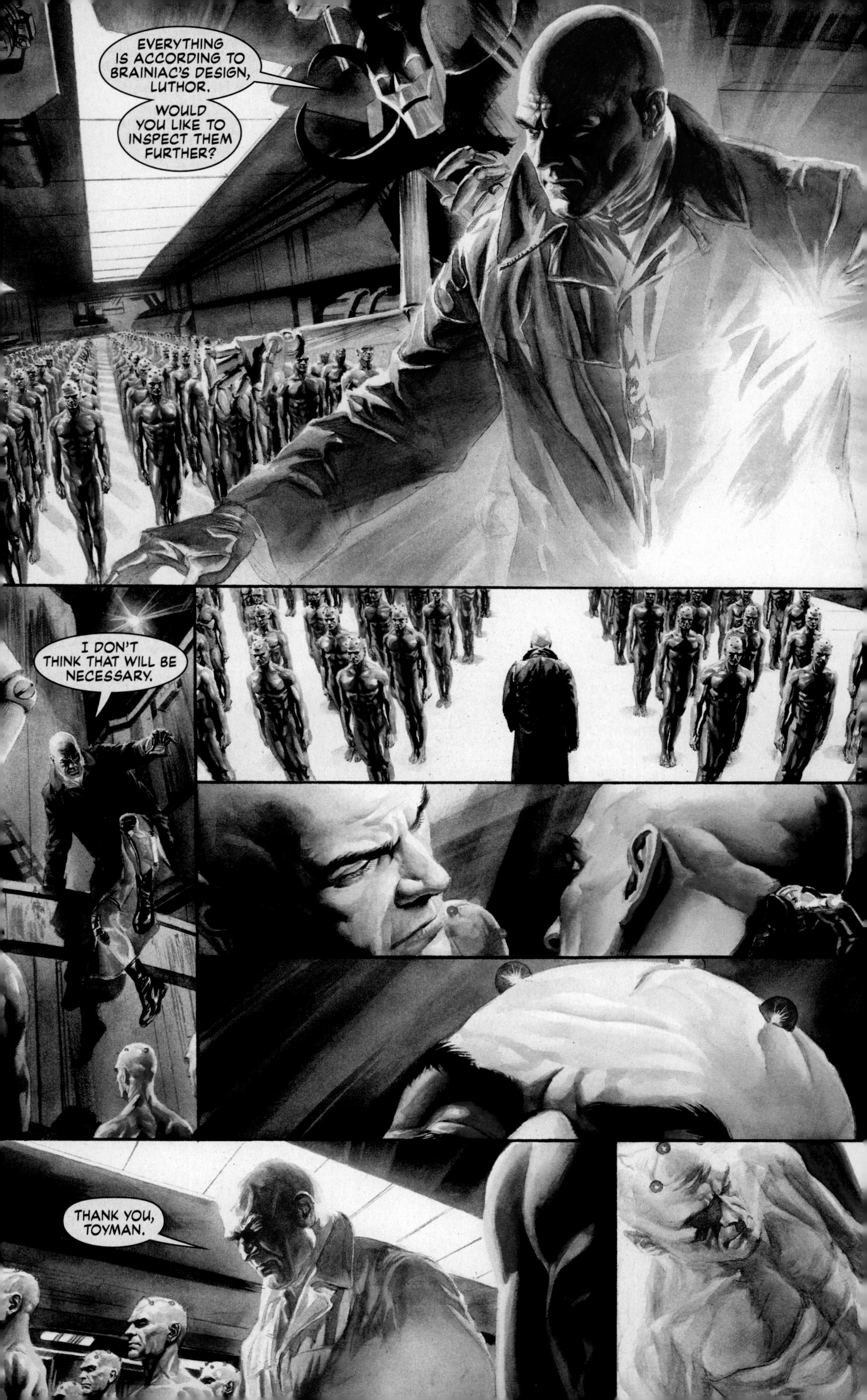
EVERYTHING IS ACCORDING TO BRAINIAC'S DESIGN, LUTHOR.
WOULD YOU LIKE TO INSPECT THEM FURTHER?
I DON'T THINK THAT WILL BE NECESSARY.
THANK YOU, TOYMAN.

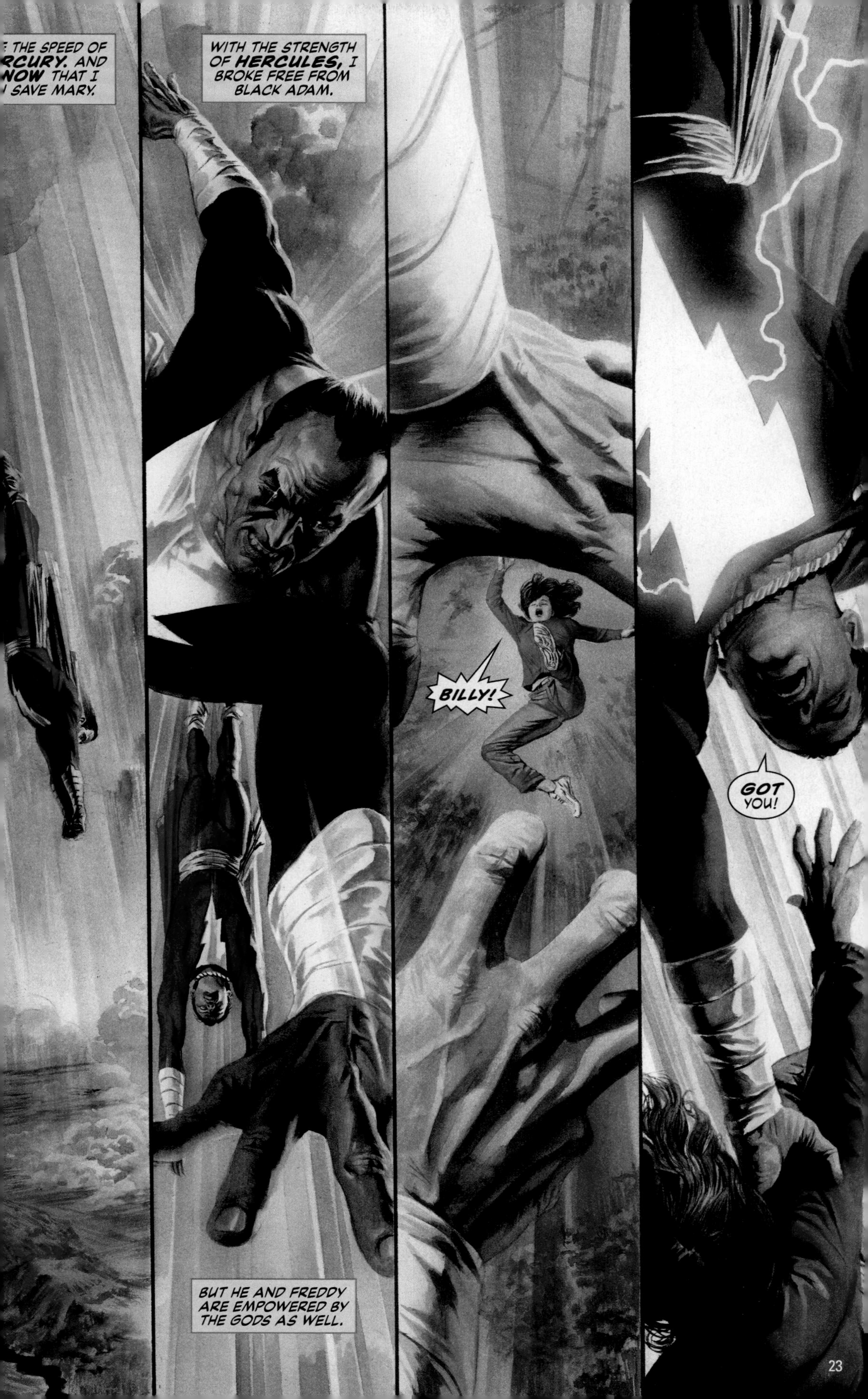

E THE SPEED OF RCURY. AND NOW THAT I I SAVE MARY.
WITH THE STRENGTH OF HERCULES, I BROKE FREE FROM BLACK ADAM.
BUT HE AND FREDDY ARE EMPOWERED BY THE GODS AS WELL.
BILLY!
GOT YOU!

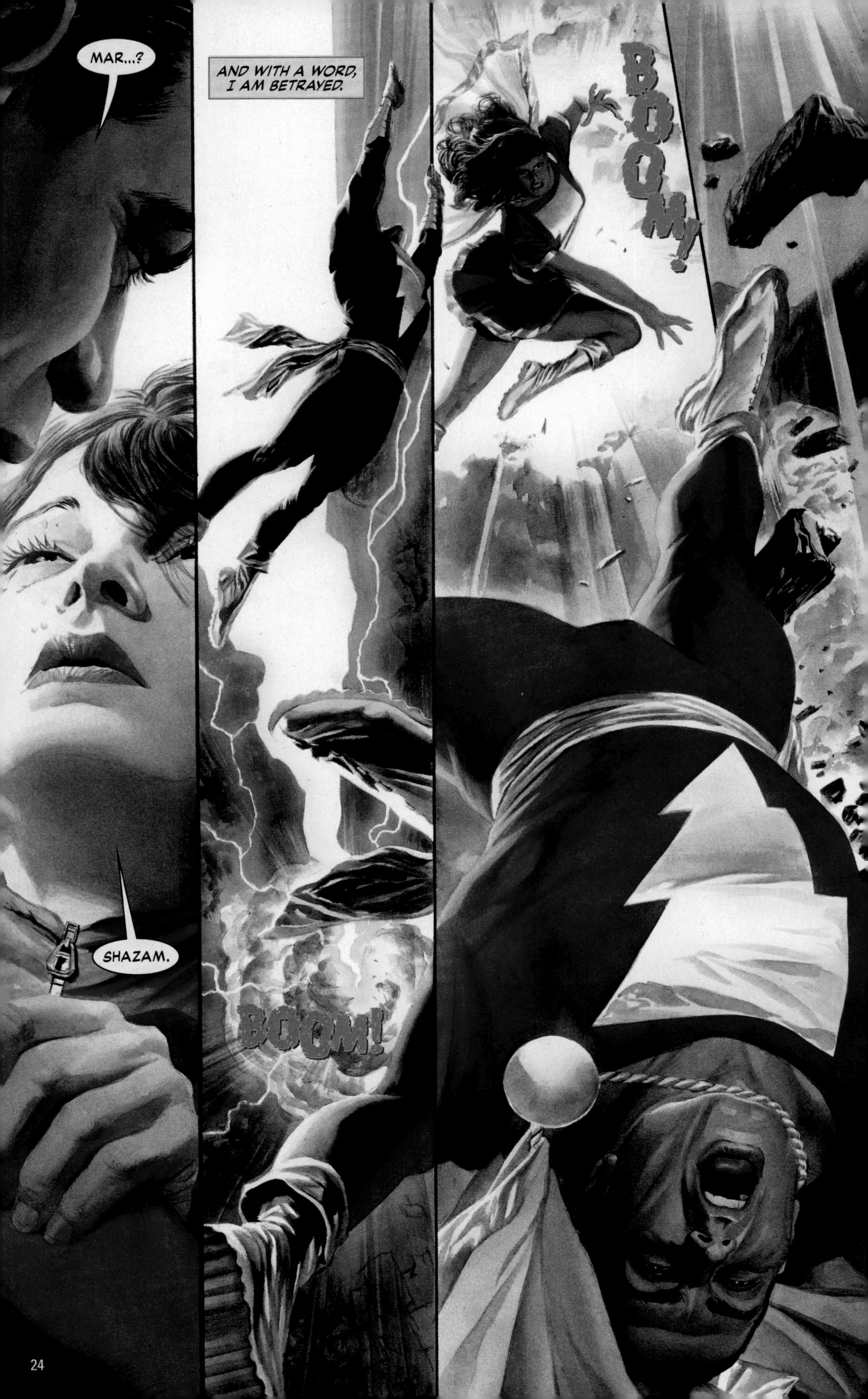
MAR...?
SHAZAM.
AND WITH A WORD, I AM BETRAYED.
BOOM!
BOOM!

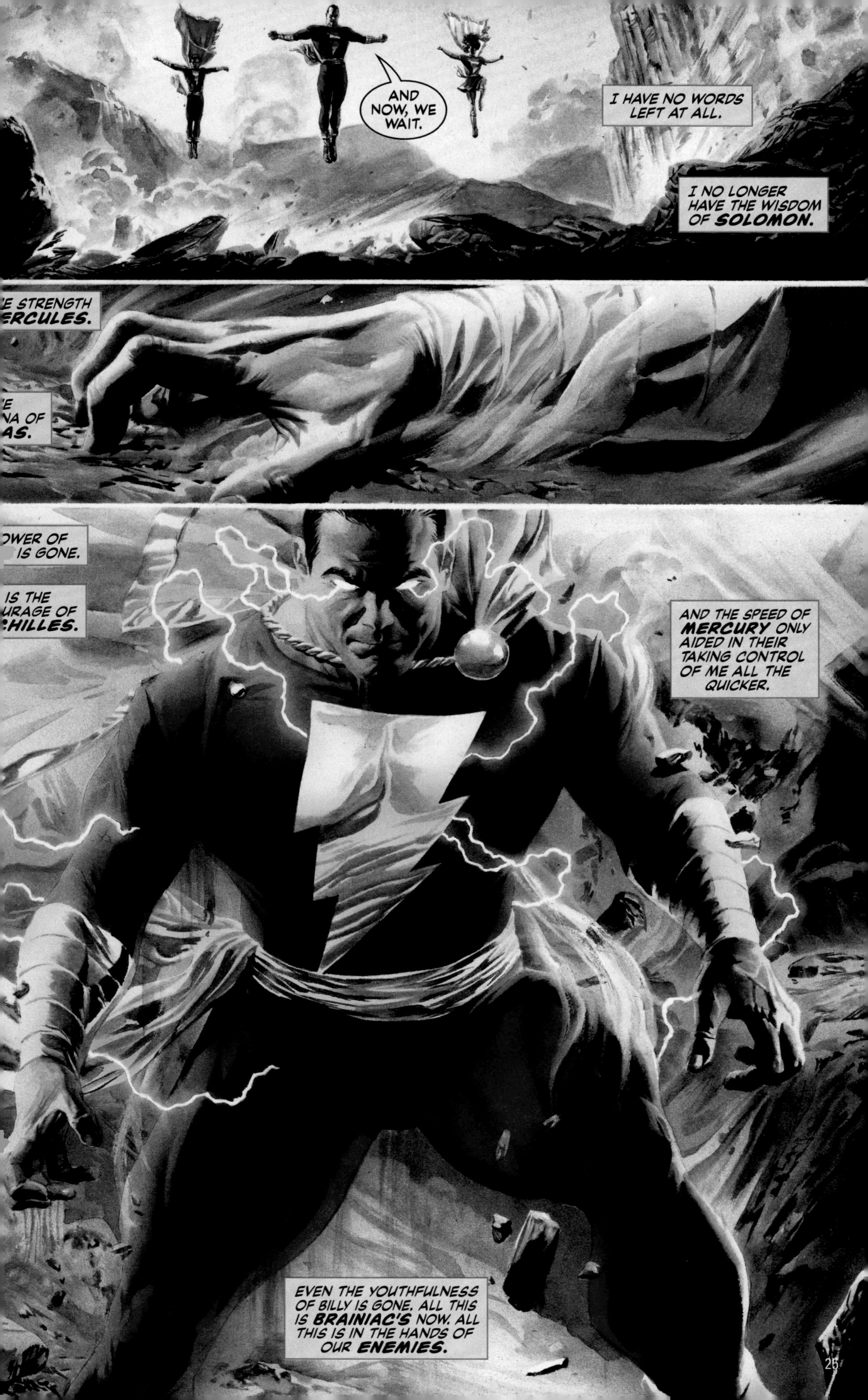
AND NOW, WE WAIT.
I HAVE NO WORDS LEFT AT ALL.
I NO LONGER HAVE THE WISDOM OF SOLOMON.
E STRENGTH ERCULES.
E NA OF AS.
OWER OF IS GONE.
IS THE URAGE OF CHILLES.
AND THE SPEED OF MERCURY ONLY AIDED IN THEIR TAKING CONTROL OF ME ALL THE QUICKER.
EVEN THE YOUTHFULNESS OF BILLY IS GONE. ALL THIS IS BRAINIAC'S NOW. ALL THIS IS IN THE HANDS OF OUR ENEMIES.

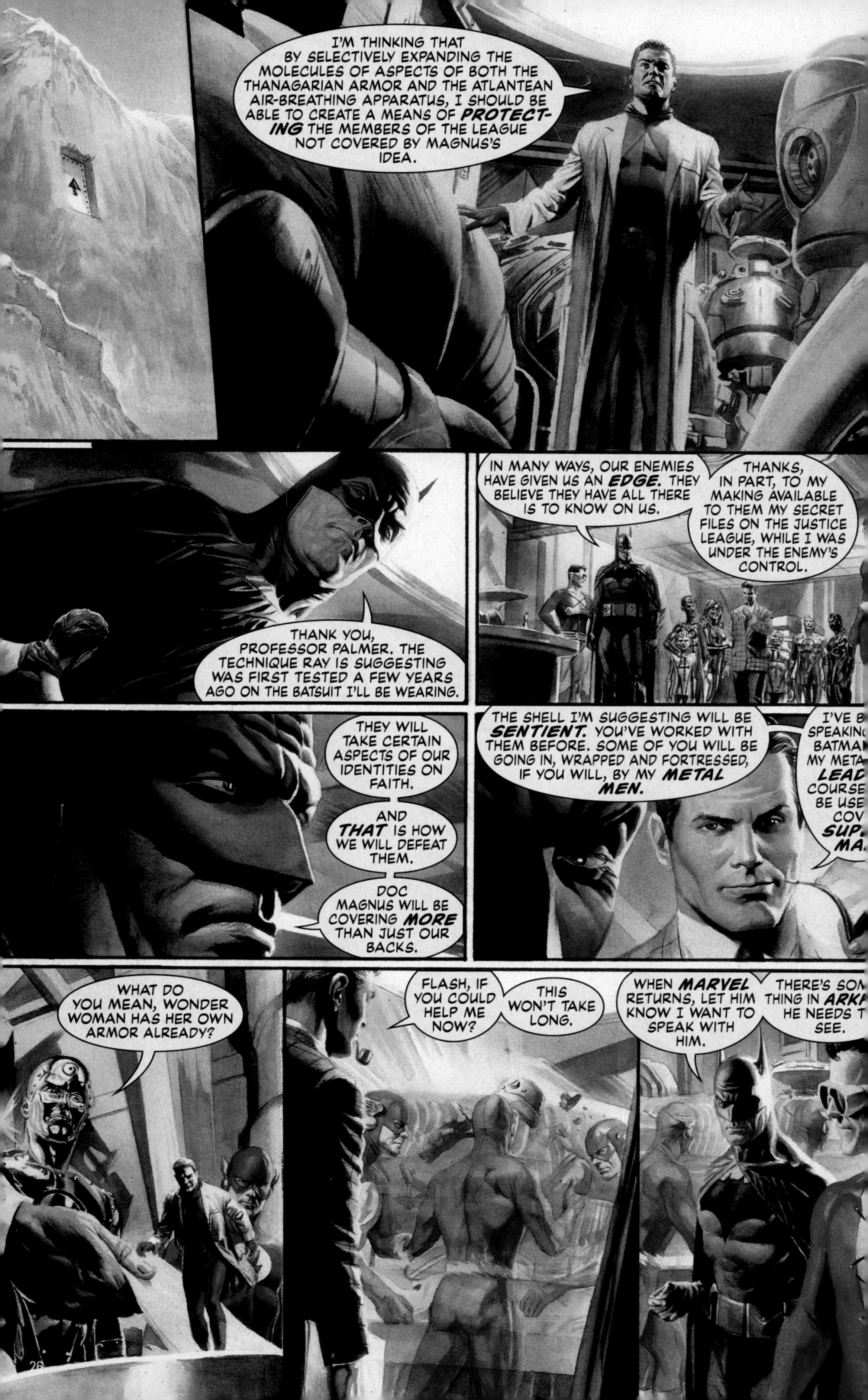
I'M THINKING THAT BY SELECTIVELY EXPANDING THE MOLECULES OF ASPECTS OF BOTH THE THANAGARIAN ARMOR AND THE ATLANTEAN AIR-BREATHING APPARATUS, I SHOULD BE ABLE TO CREATE A MEANS OF ***PROTECTING*** THE MEMBERS OF THE LEAGUE NOT COVERED BY MAGNUS'S IDEA.
THANK YOU, PROFESSOR PALMER. THE TECHNIQUE RAY IS SUGGESTING WAS FIRST TESTED A FEW YEARS AGO ON THE BATSUIT I'LL BE WEARING.
IN MANY WAYS, OUR ENEMIES HAVE GIVEN US AN ***EDGE.*** THEY BELIEVE THEY HAVE ALL THERE IS TO KNOW ON US.
THANKS, IN PART, TO MY MAKING AVAILABLE TO THEM MY SECRET FILES ON THE JUSTICE LEAGUE, WHILE I WAS UNDER THE ENEMY'S CONTROL.
THEY WILL TAKE CERTAIN ASPECTS OF OUR IDENTITIES ON FAITH.
AND ***THAT*** IS HOW WE WILL DEFEAT THEM.
DOC MAGNUS WILL BE COVERING ***MORE*** THAN JUST OUR BACKS.
THE SHELL I'M SUGGESTING WILL BE ***SENTIENT.*** YOU'VE WORKED WITH THEM BEFORE. SOME OF YOU WILL BE GOING IN, WRAPPED AND FORTRESSED, IF YOU WILL, BY MY ***METAL MEN.***
I'VE B SPEAKIN BATMA MY META ***LEAD*** COURSE BE USE COV ***SUP. MA.***
WHAT DO YOU MEAN, WONDER WOMAN HAS HER OWN ARMOR ALREADY?
FLASH, IF YOU COULD HELP ME NOW?
THIS WON'T TAKE LONG.
WHEN ***MARVEL*** RETURNS, LET HIM KNOW I WANT TO SPEAK WITH HIM.
THERE'S SOM THING IN ***ARK*** HE NEEDS T SEE.

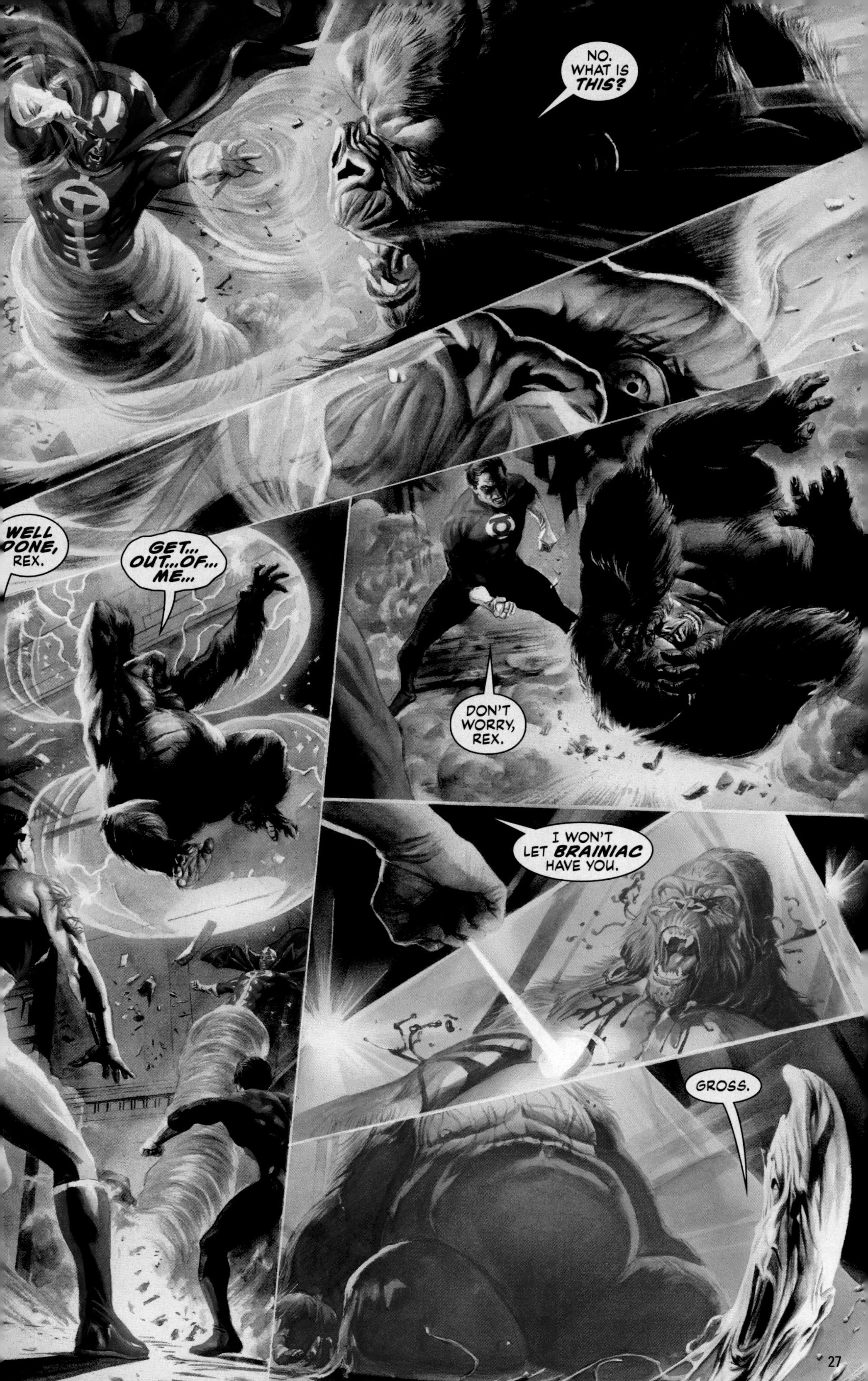
NO. WHAT IS THIS?
WELL DONE, REX.
GET... OUT...OF... ME...
DON'T WORRY, REX.
I WON'T LET BRAINIAC HAVE YOU.
GROSS.

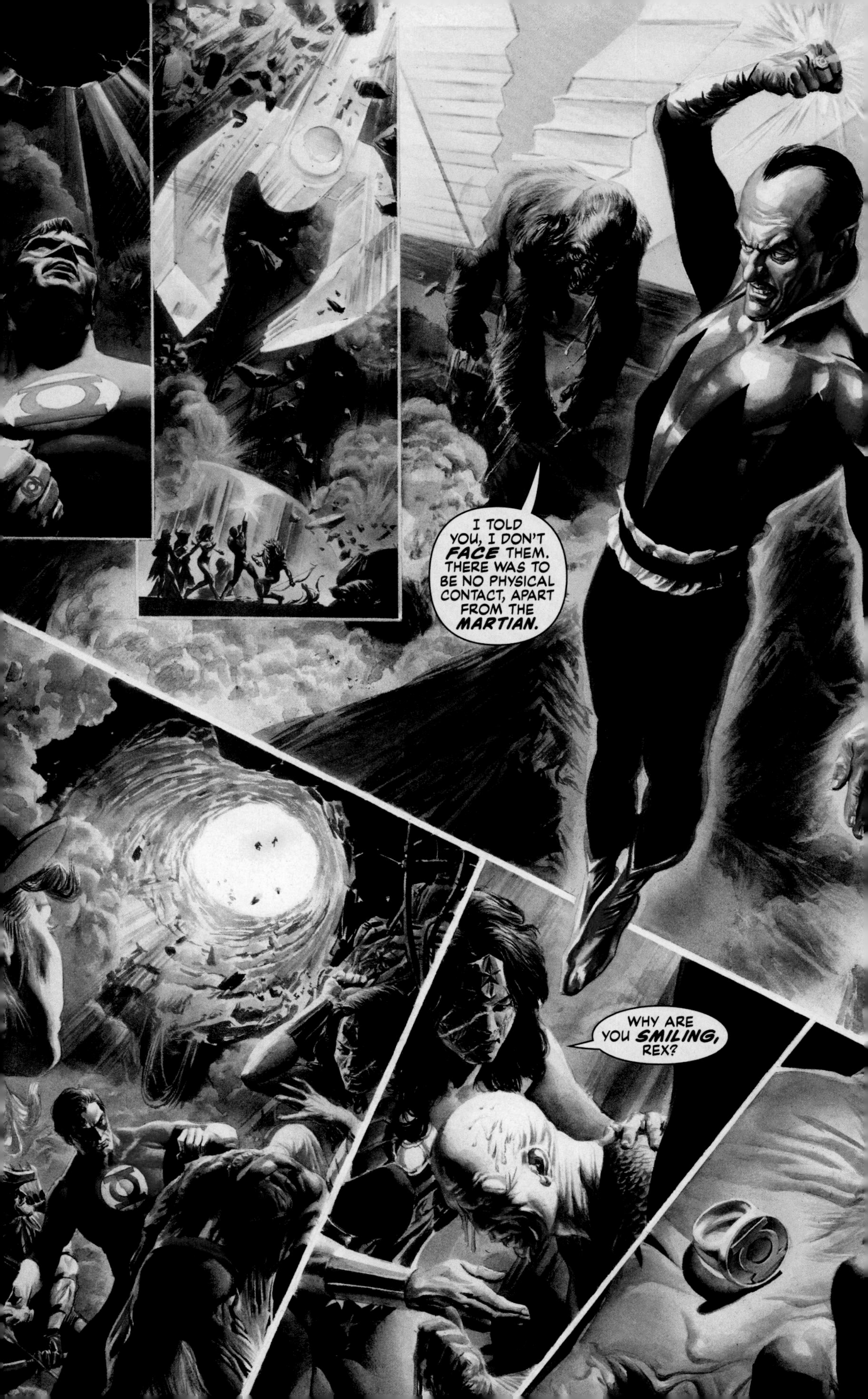
I TOLD YOU, I DON'T FACE THEM. THERE WAS TO BE NO PHYSICAL CONTACT, APART FROM THE MARTIAN.
WHY ARE YOU SMILING, REX?

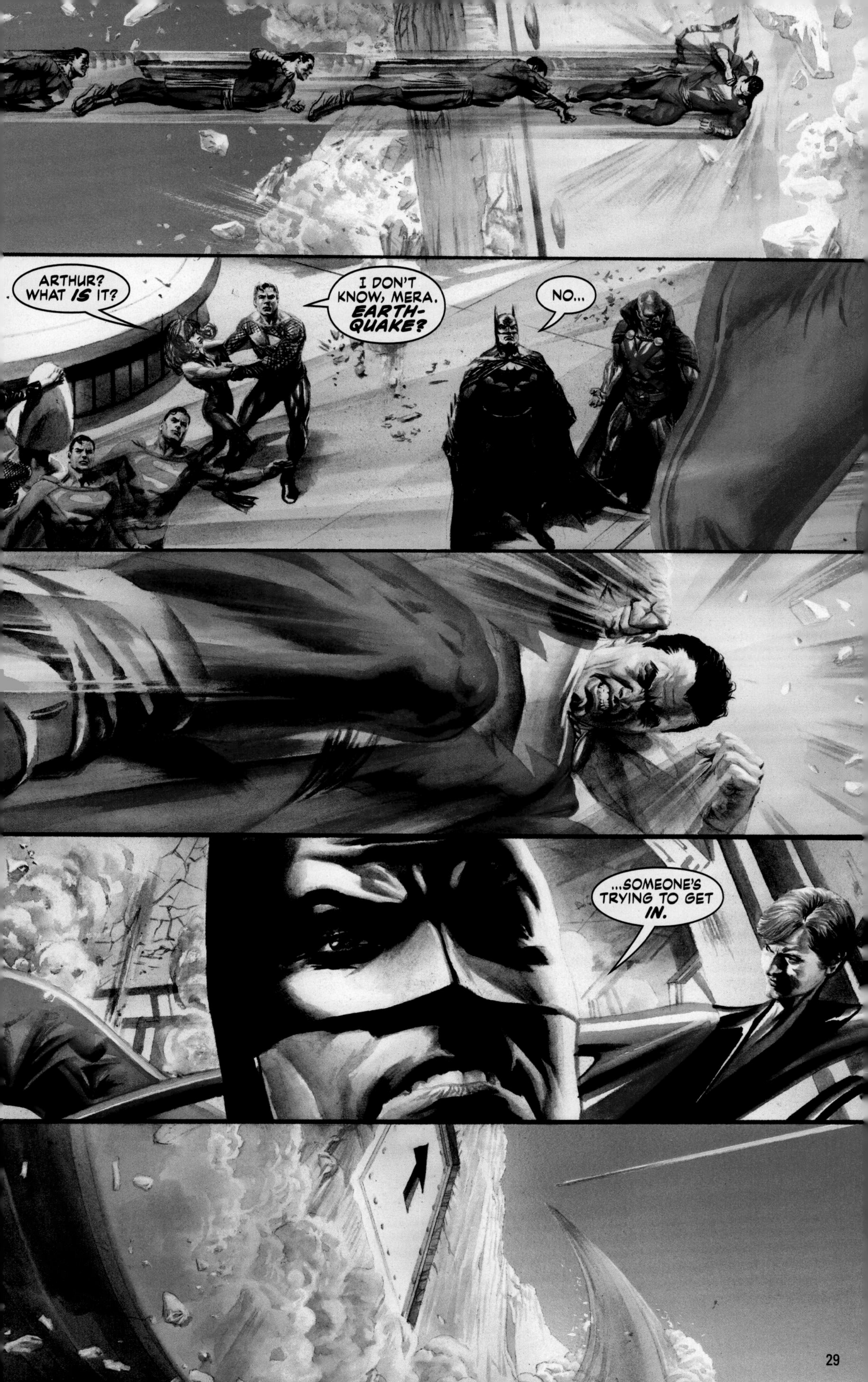
ARTHUR? WHAT *IS* IT?
I DON'T KNOW, MERA. ***EARTH-QUAKE?***
NO...
...SOMEONE'S TRYING TO GET ***IN.***

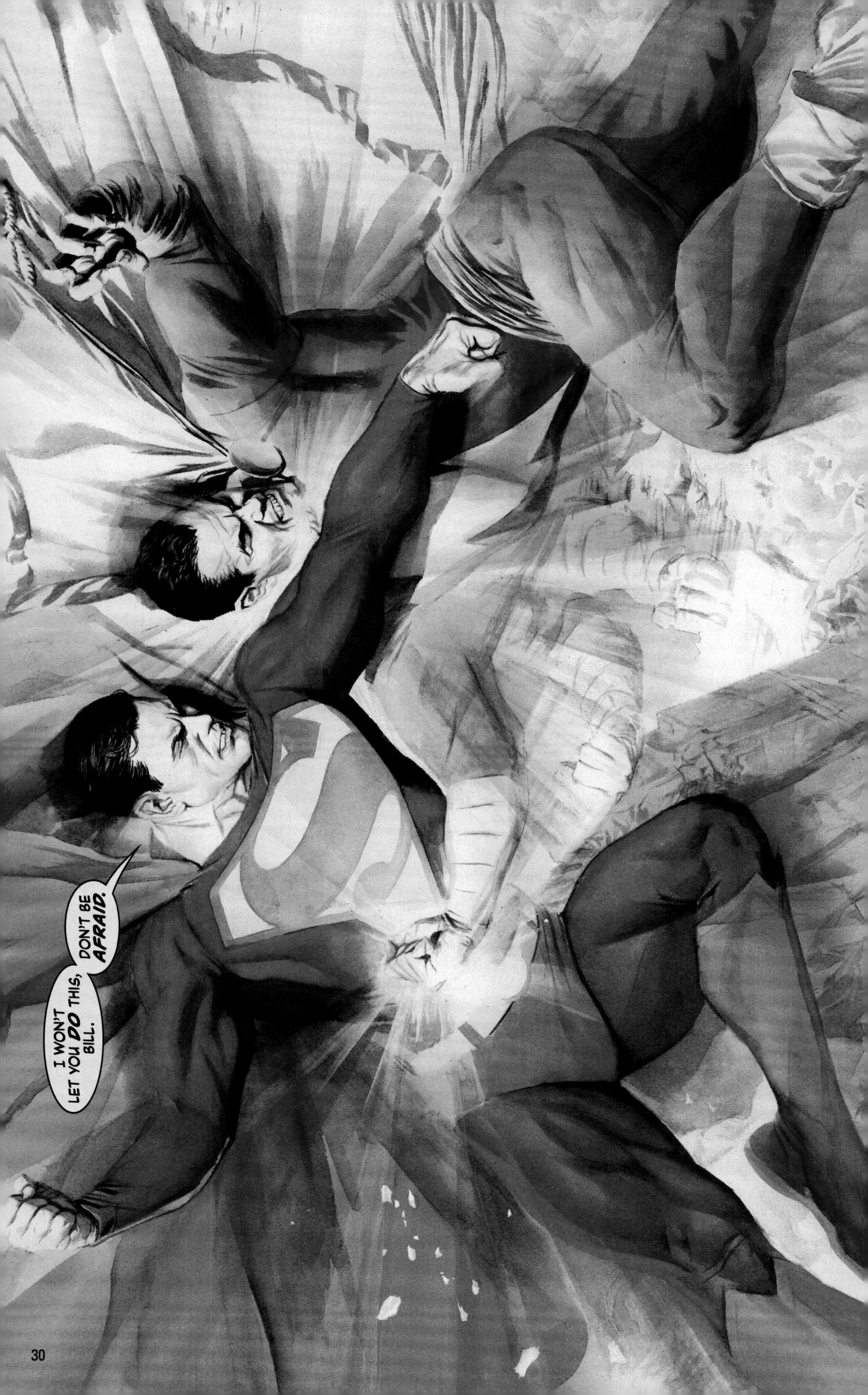
I WON'T LET YOU DO THIS, BILL.
DON'T BE AFRAID.

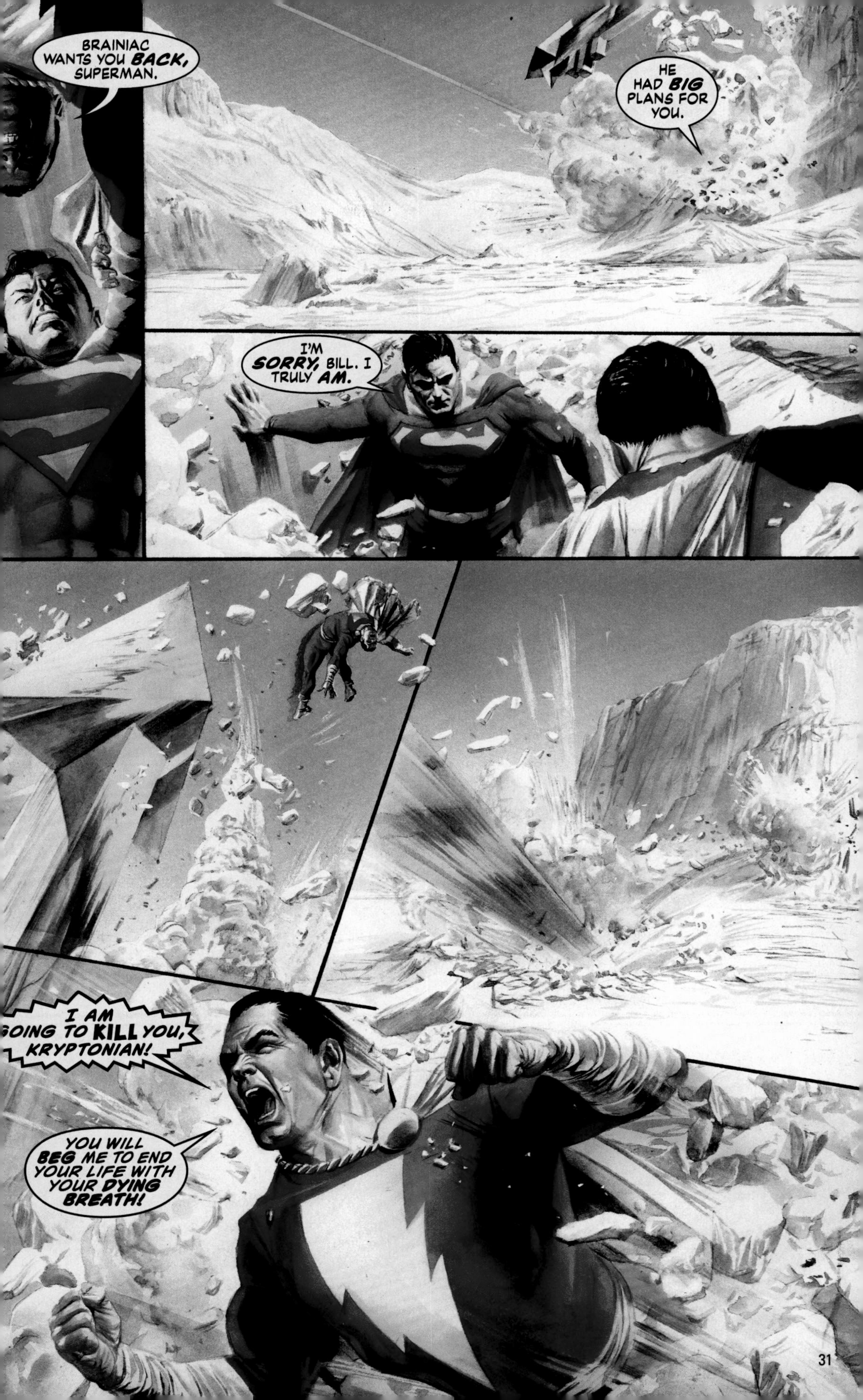
BRAINIAC WANTS YOU BACK, SUPERMAN.
HE HAD BIG PLANS FOR YOU.
I'M SORRY, BILL. I TRULY AM.
I AM GOING TO KILL YOU, KRYPTONIAN!
YOU WILL BEG ME TO END YOUR LIFE WITH YOUR DYING BREATH!

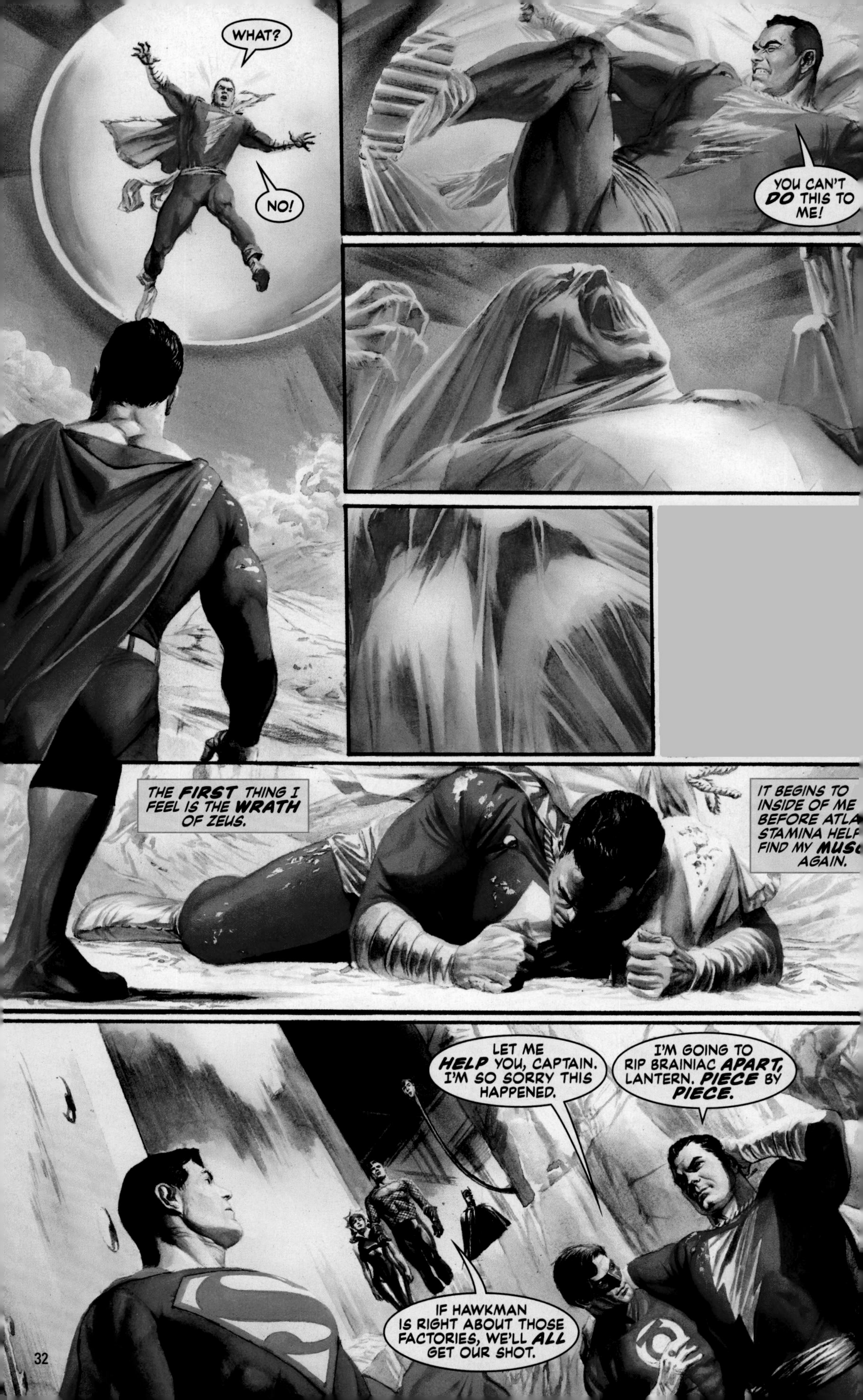
WHAT?
NO!
YOU CAN'T DO THIS TO ME!
THE FIRST THING I FEEL IS THE WRATH OF ZEUS.
IT BEGINS TO INSIDE OF ME BEFORE ATLA STAMINA HELF FIND MY MUS AGAIN.
LET ME HELP YOU, CAPTAIN. I'M SO SORRY THIS HAPPENED.
I'M GOING TO RIP BRAINIAC APART, LANTERN. PIECE BY PIECE.
IF HAWKMAN IS RIGHT ABOUT THOSE FACTORIES, WE'LL ALL GET OUR SHOT.

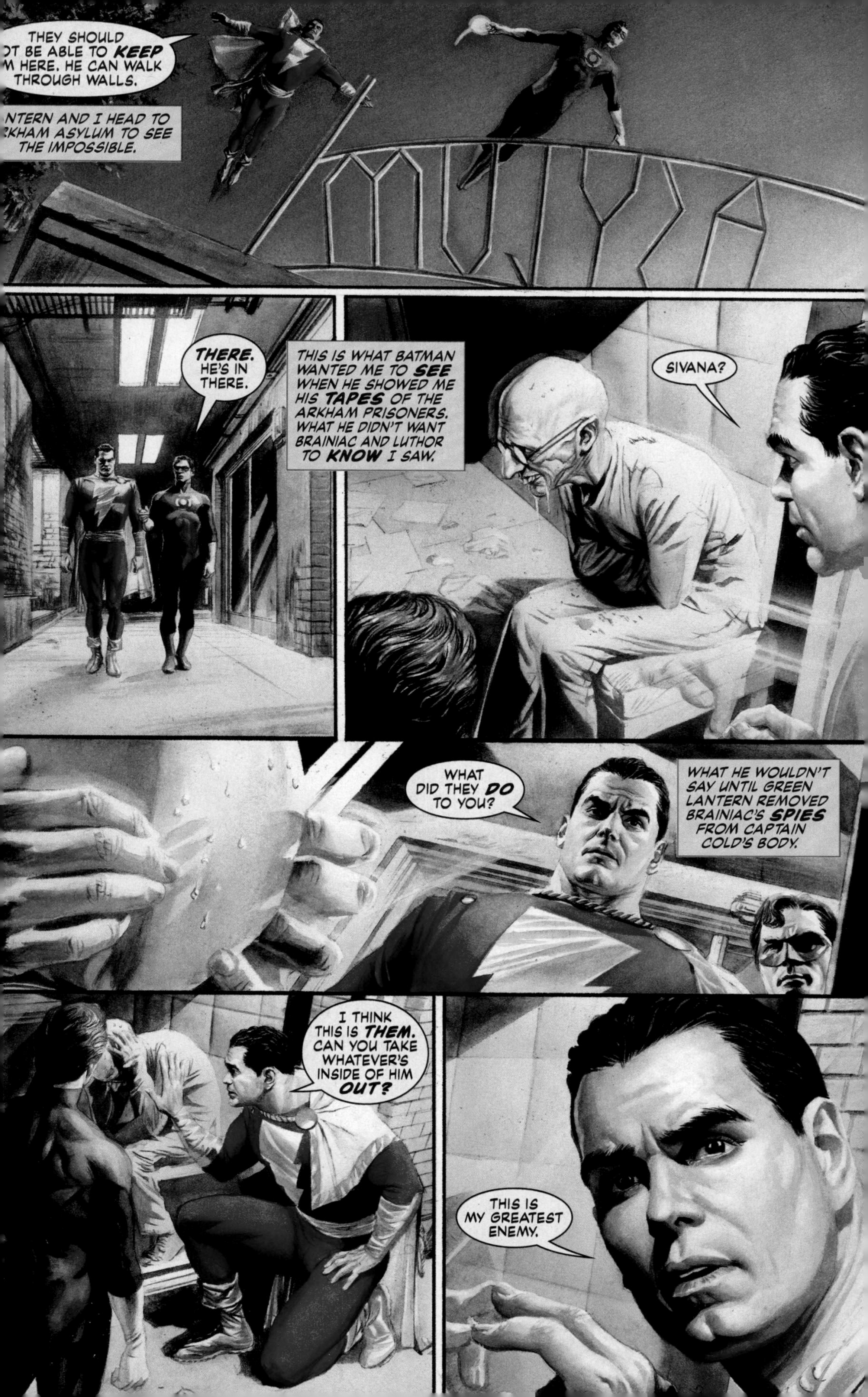

THEY SHOULD
OT BE ABLE TO KEEP
M HERE. HE CAN WALK
THROUGH WALLS.
NTERN AND I HEAD TO
KHAM ASYLUM TO SEE
THE IMPOSSIBLE.
THERE. HE'S IN THERE.
THIS IS WHAT BATMAN WANTED ME TO SEE WHEN HE SHOWED ME HIS TAPES OF THE ARKHAM PRISONERS. WHAT HE DIDN'T WANT BRAINIAC AND LUTHOR TO KNOW I SAW.
SIVANA?
WHAT DID THEY DO TO YOU?
WHAT HE WOULDN'T SAY UNTIL GREEN LANTERN REMOVED BRAINIAC'S SPIES FROM CAPTAIN COLD'S BODY.
I THINK THIS IS THEM. CAN YOU TAKE WHATEVER'S INSIDE OF HIM OUT?
THIS IS MY GREATEST ENEMY.

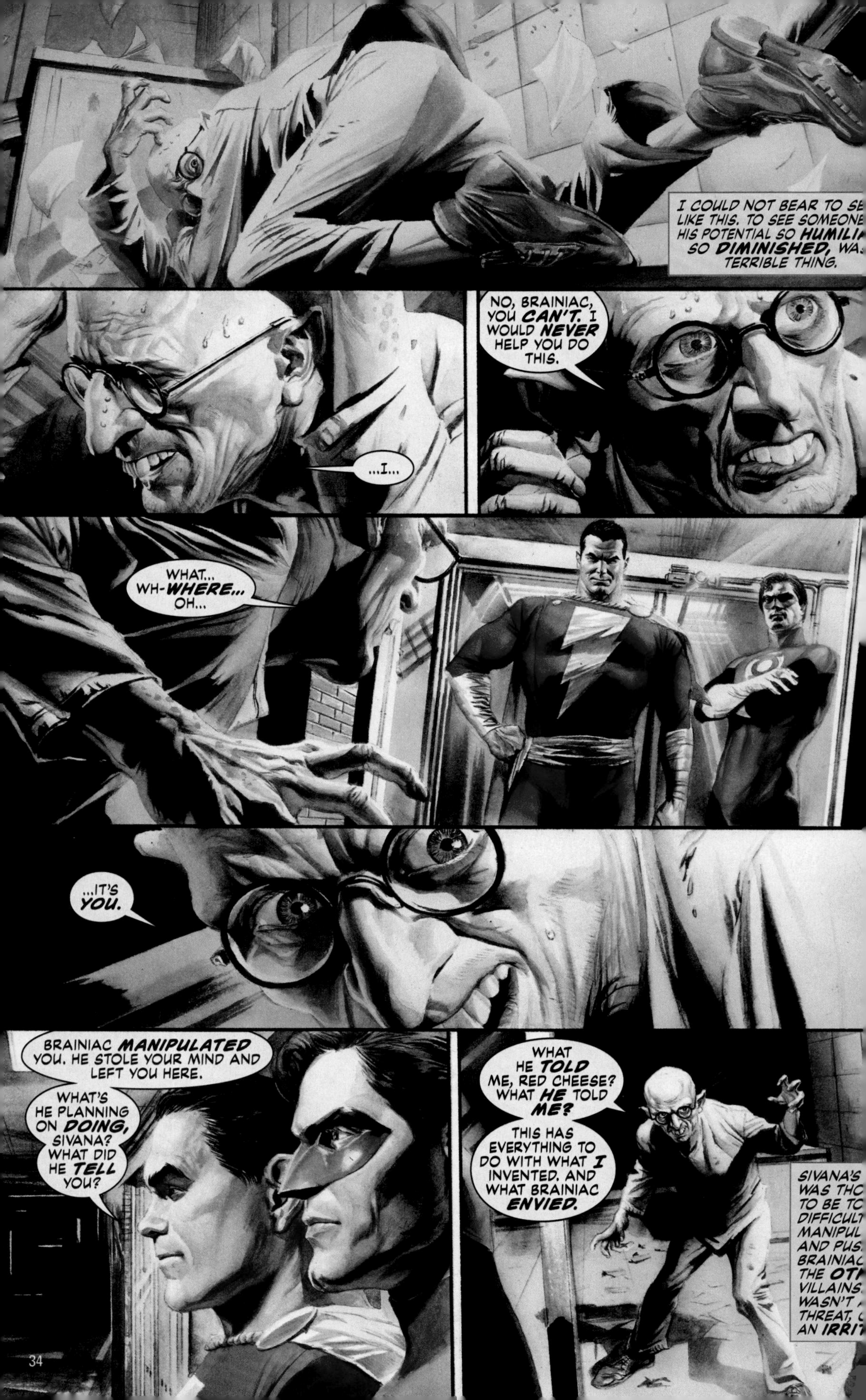
I COULD NOT BEAR TO SE LIKE THIS. TO SEE SOMEONE HIS POTENTIAL SO HUMILI SO DIMINISHED, WA TERRIBLE THING.
...I...
NO, BRAINIAC, YOU CAN'T. I WOULD NEVER HELP YOU DO THIS.
WHAT... WH-WHERE... OH...
...IT'S YOU.
BRAINIAC MANIPULATED YOU. HE STOLE YOUR MIND AND LEFT YOU HERE.
WHAT'S HE PLANNING ON DOING, SIVANA? WHAT DID HE TELL YOU?
WHAT HE TOLD ME, RED CHEESE? WHAT HE TOLD ME?
THIS HAS EVERYTHING TO DO WITH WHAT I INVENTED. AND WHAT BRAINIAC ENVIED.
SIVANA'S WAS THO TO BE TO DIFFICULT MANIPUL AND PUS BRAINIAC THE OT VILLAINS WASN'T THREAT, AN IRRI

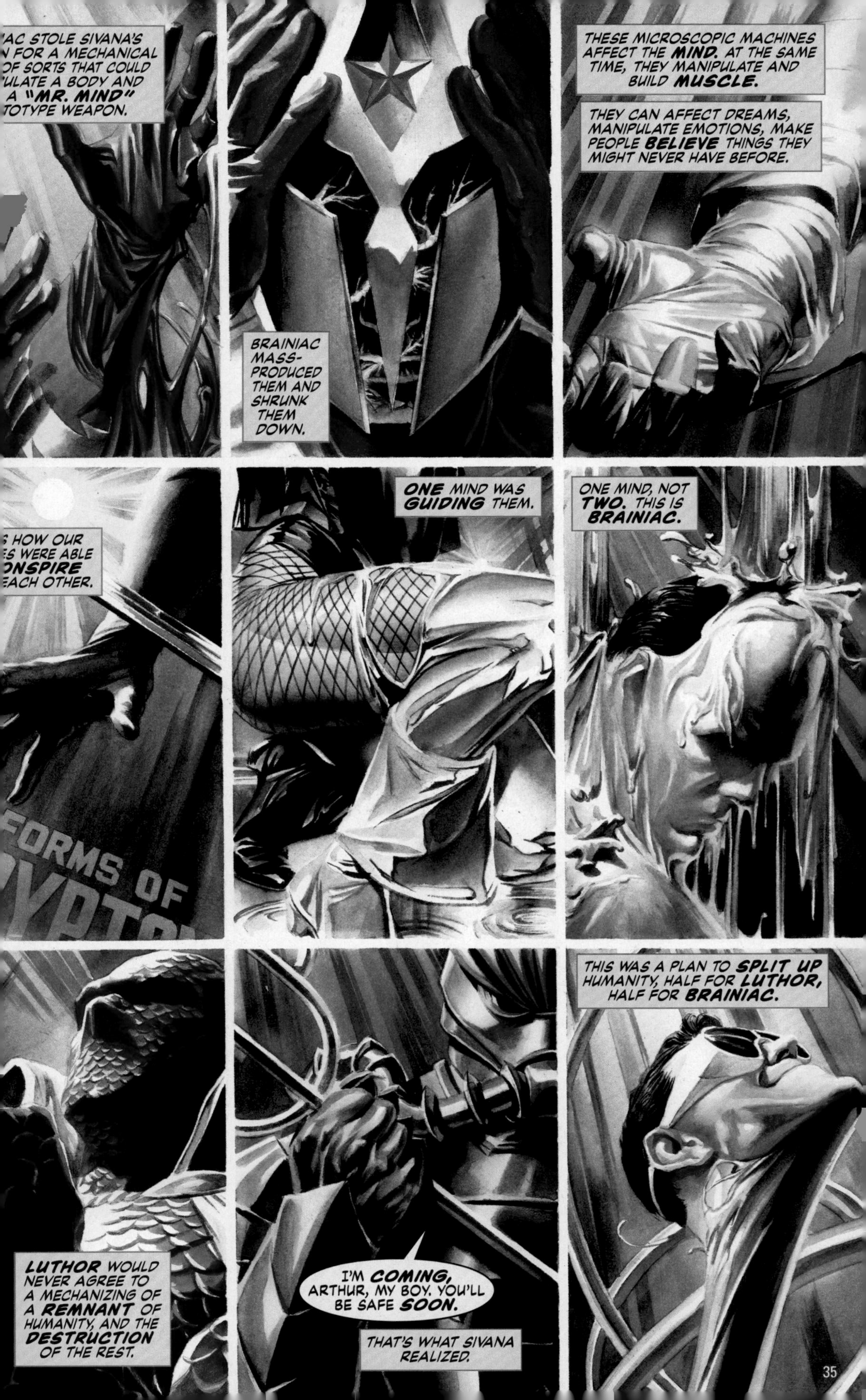

IAC STOLE SIVANA'S
N FOR A MECHANICAL
OF SORTS THAT COULD
PULATE A BODY AND
A "MR. MIND"
TOTYPE WEAPON.
BRAINIAC MASS-PRODUCED THEM AND SHRUNK THEM DOWN.
THESE MICROSCOPIC MACHINES AFFECT THE MIND. AT THE SAME TIME, THEY MANIPULATE AND BUILD MUSCLE.
THEY CAN AFFECT DREAMS, MANIPULATE EMOTIONS, MAKE PEOPLE BELIEVE THINGS THEY MIGHT NEVER HAVE BEFORE.
S HOW OUR
ES WERE ABLE
ONSPIRE
EACH OTHER.
FORMS OF
YPTO
ONE MIND WAS GUIDING THEM.
ONE MIND, NOT TWO. THIS IS BRAINIAC.
LUTHOR WOULD NEVER AGREE TO A MECHANIZING OF A REMNANT OF HUMANITY, AND THE DESTRUCTION OF THE REST.
I'M COMING, ARTHUR, MY BOY. YOU'LL BE SAFE SOON.
THAT'S WHAT SIVANA REALIZED.
THIS WAS A PLAN TO SPLIT UP HUMANITY, HALF FOR LUTHOR, HALF FOR BRAINIAC.

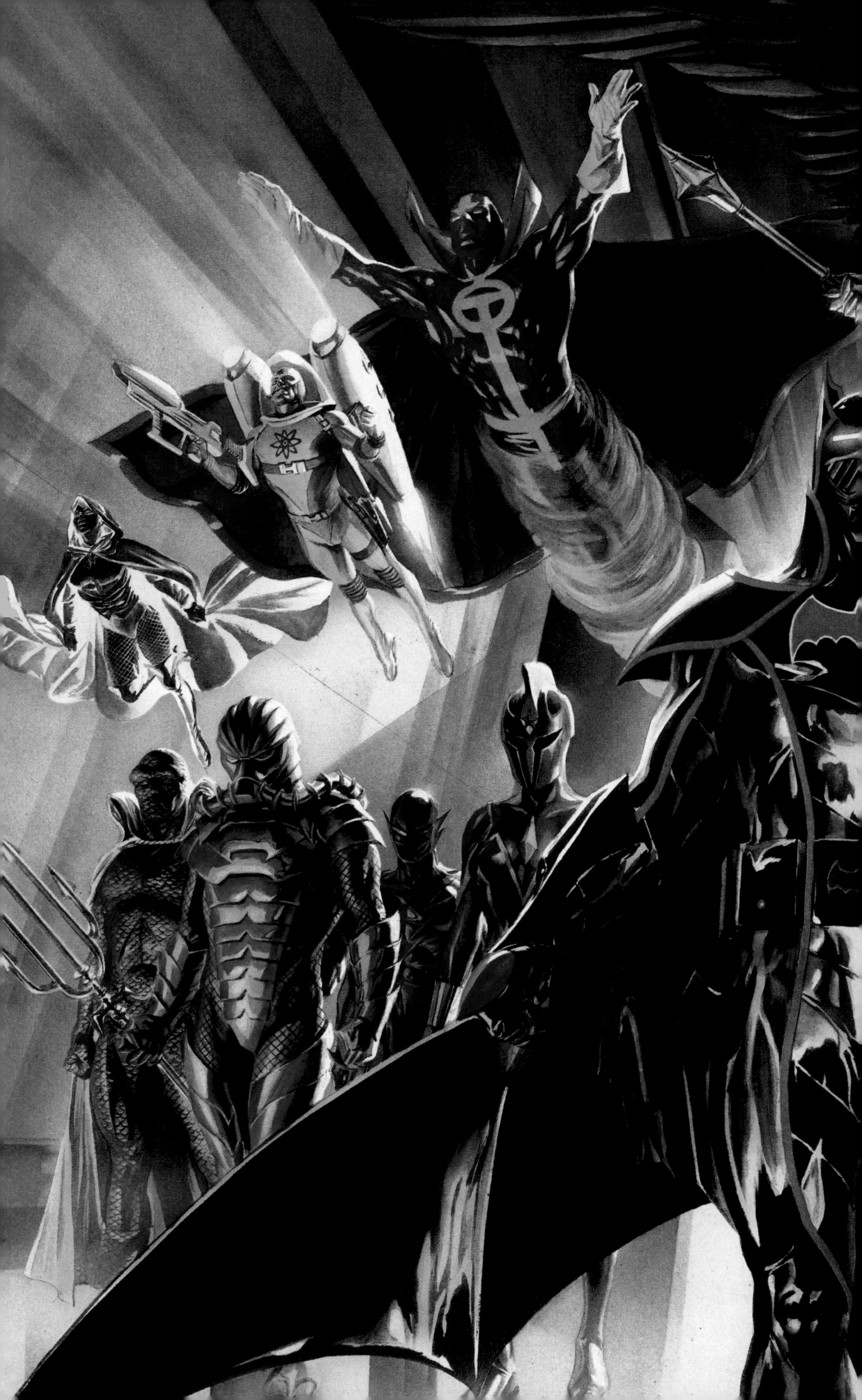

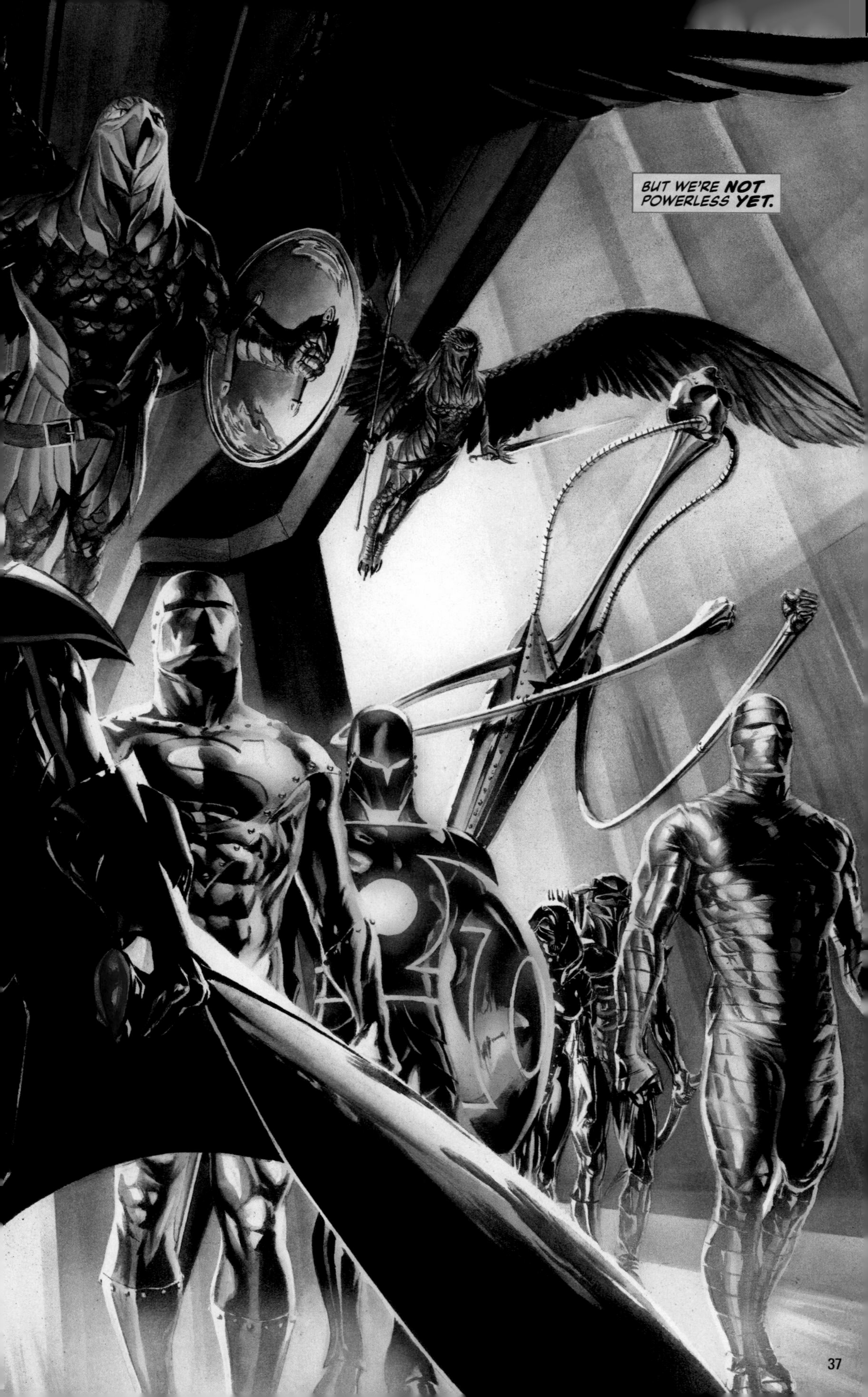
BUT WE'RE **NOT** POWERLESS **YET**.

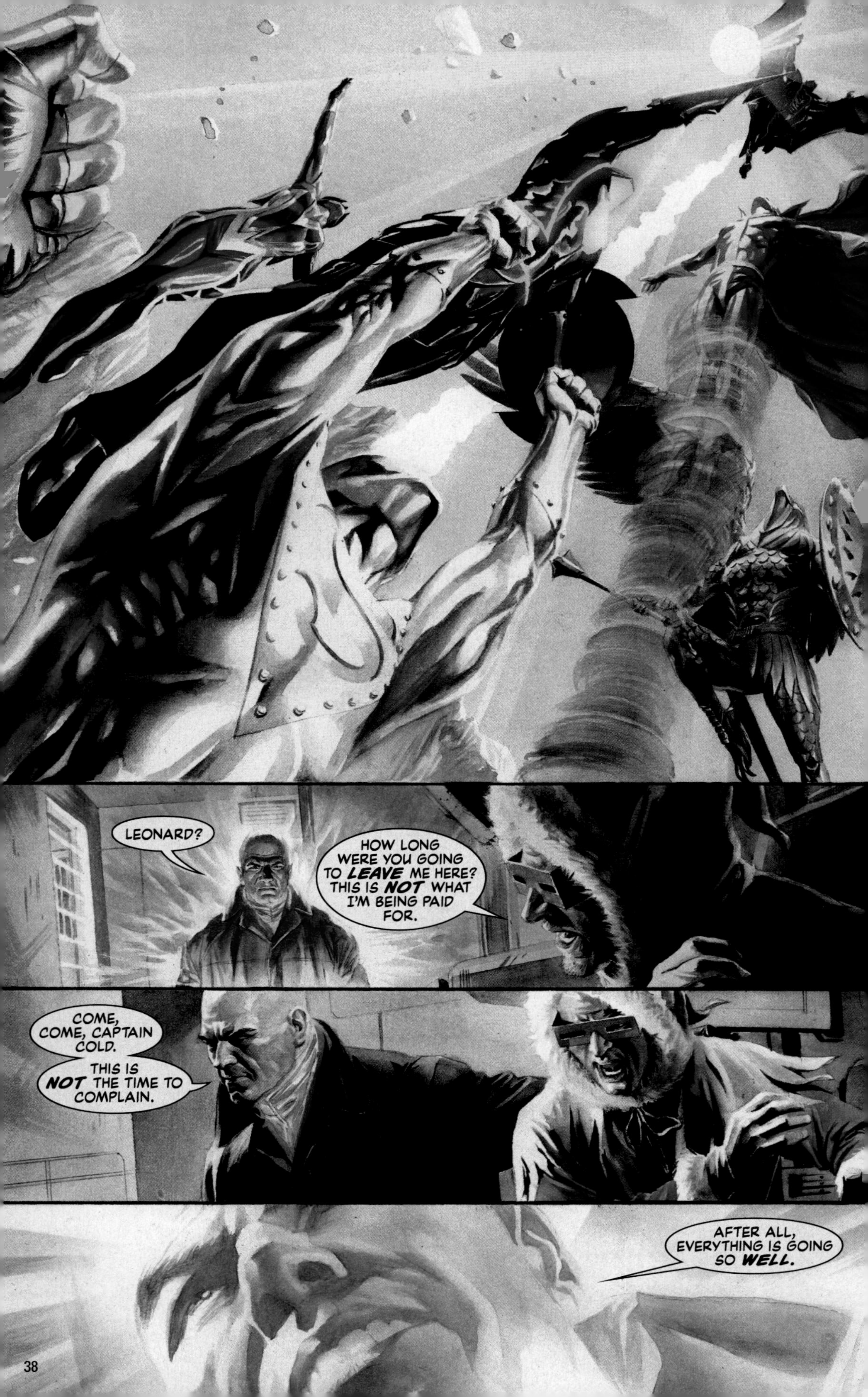
LEONARD?
HOW LONG WERE YOU GOING TO LEAVE ME HERE? THIS IS NOT WHAT I'M BEING PAID FOR.
COME, COME, CAPTAIN COLD.
THIS IS NOT THE TIME TO COMPLAIN.
AFTER ALL, EVERYTHING IS GOING SO WELL.

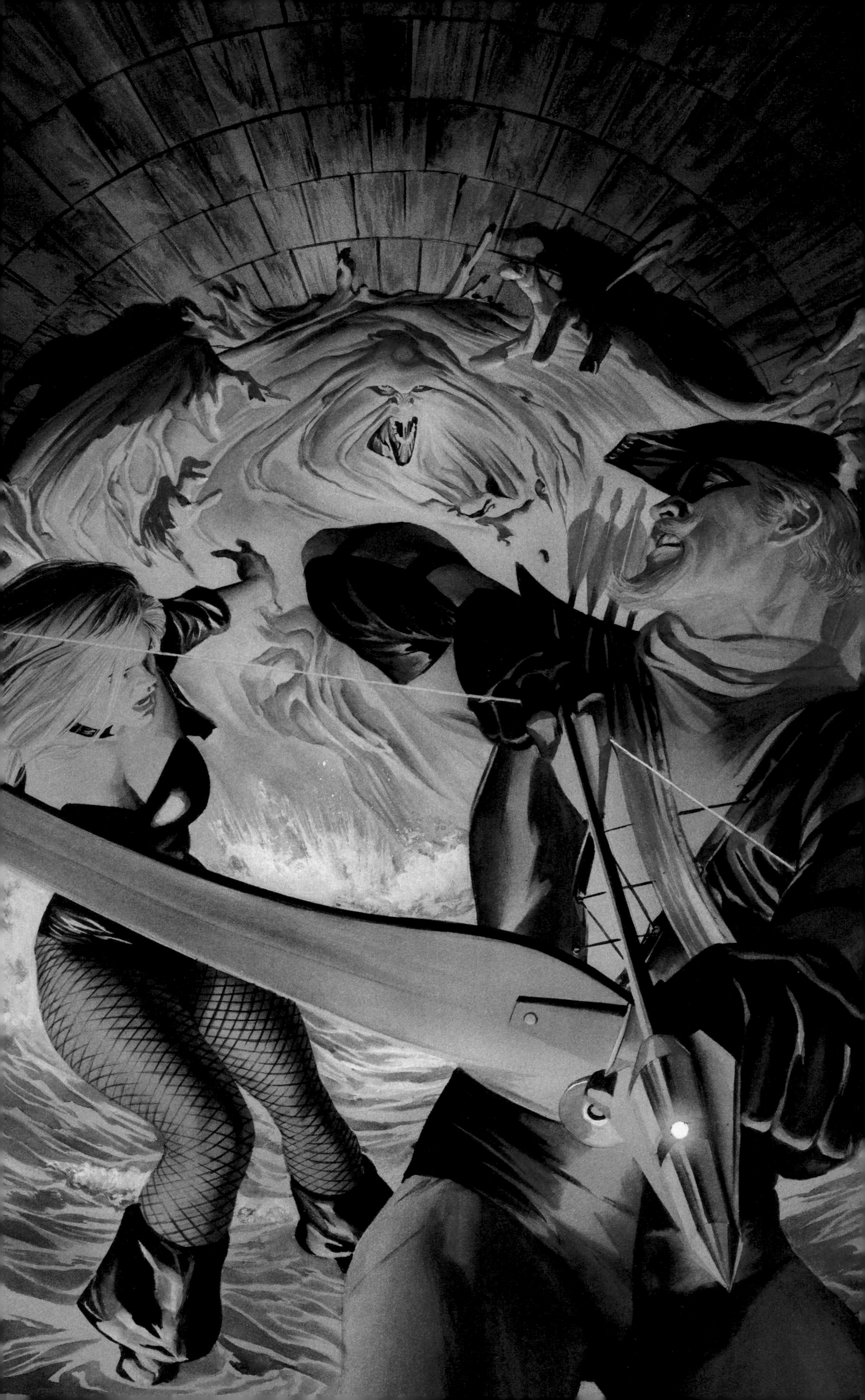

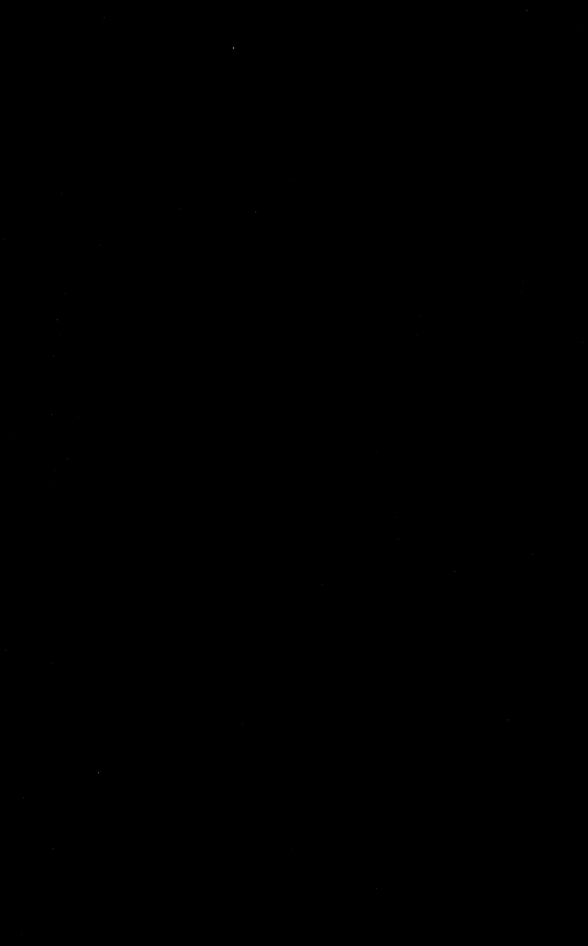

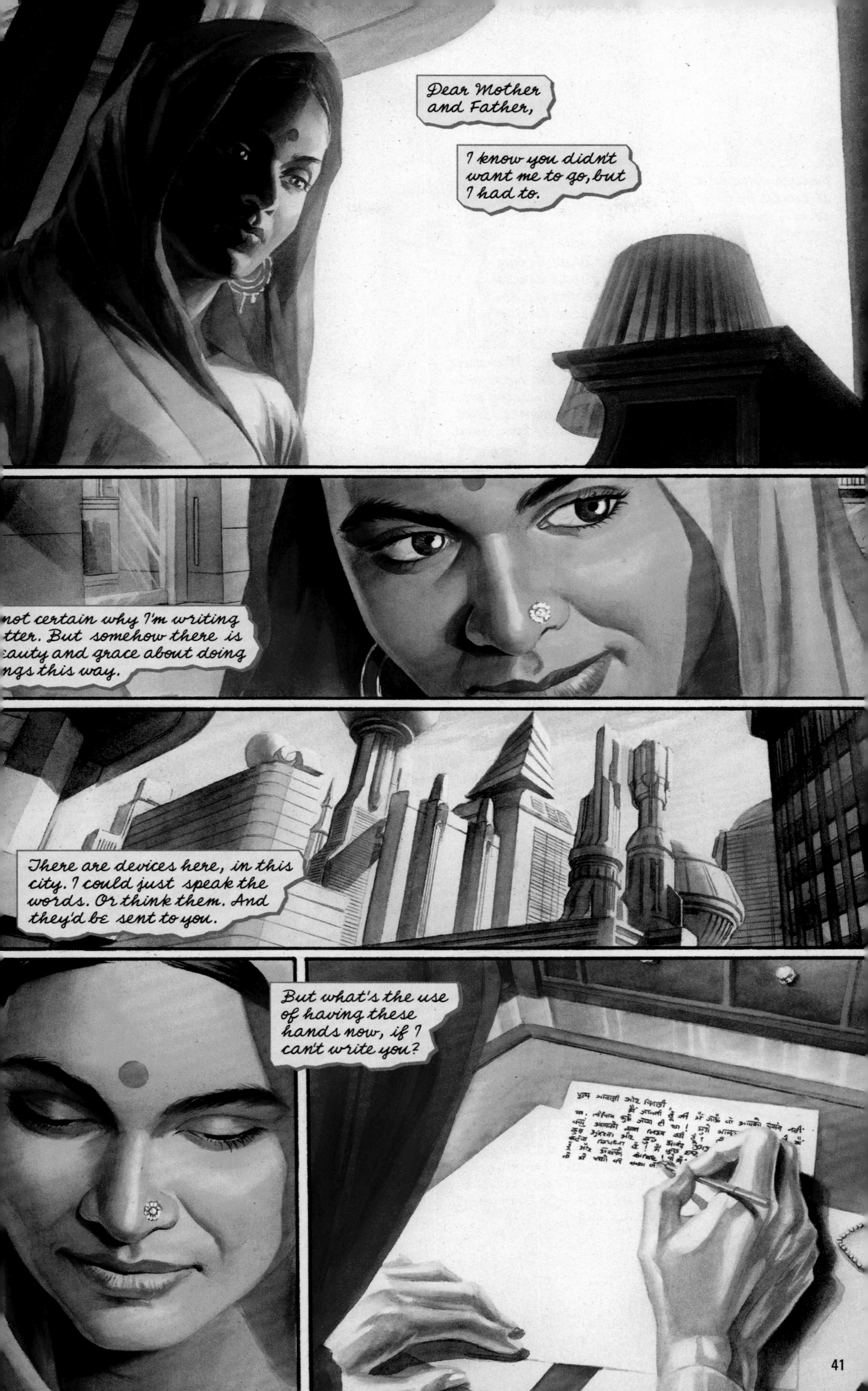

Dear Mother and Father,
I know you didn't want me to go, but I had to.
not certain why I'm writing
tter. But somehow there is
eauty and grace about doing
ngs this way.
There are devices here, in this city. I could just speak the words. Or think them. And they'd be sent to you.
But what's the use of having these hands now, if I can't write you?

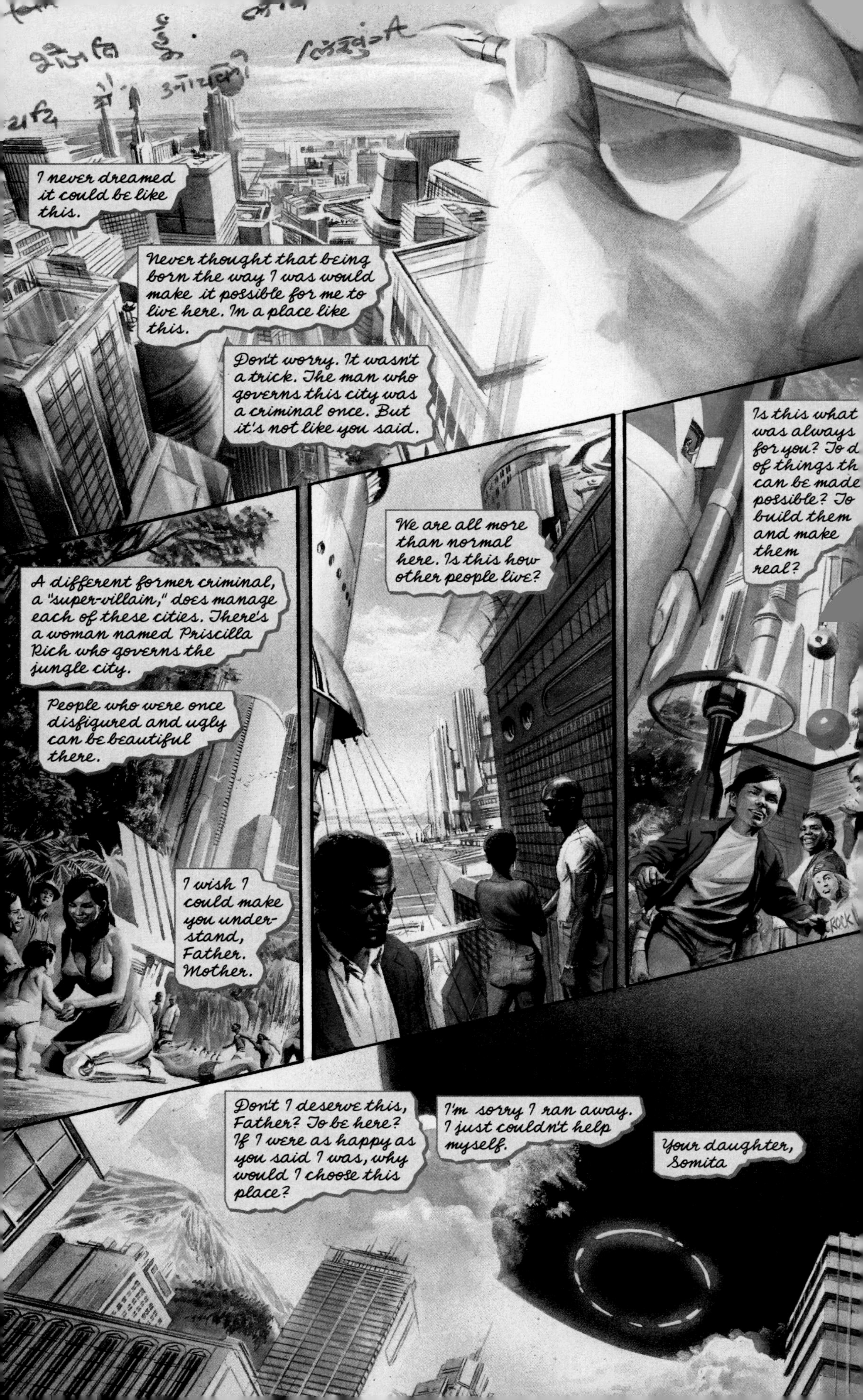
I never dreamed it could be like this.
Never thought that being born the way I was would make it possible for me to live here. In a place like this.
Don't worry. It wasn't a trick. The man who governs this city was a criminal once. But it's not like you said.
A different former criminal, a "super-villain," does manage each of these cities. There's a woman named Priscilla Rich who governs the jungle city.
People who were once disfigured and ugly can be beautiful there.
I wish I could make you understand, Father. Mother.
We are all more than normal here. Is this how other people live?
Is this what was always for you? To d of things th can be made possible? To build them and make them real?
Don't I deserve this, Father? To be here? If I were as happy as you said I was, why would I choose this place?
I'm sorry I ran away. I just couldn't help myself.
Your daughter, Somita

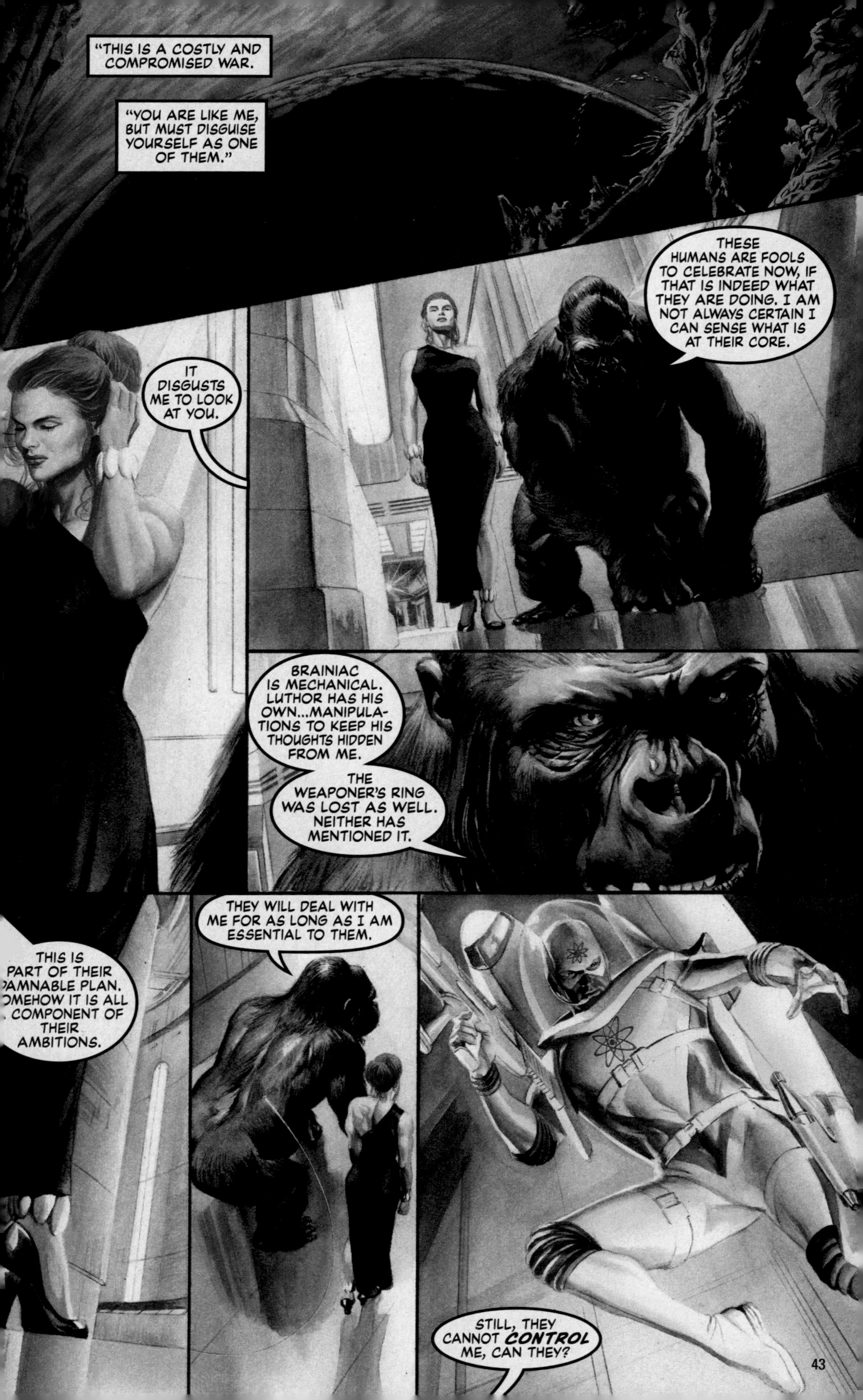

"THIS IS A COSTLY AND COMPROMISED WAR.
"YOU ARE LIKE ME, BUT MUST DISGUISE YOURSELF AS ONE OF THEM."
THESE HUMANS ARE FOOLS TO CELEBRATE NOW, IF THAT IS INDEED WHAT THEY ARE DOING. I AM NOT ALWAYS CERTAIN I CAN SENSE WHAT IS AT THEIR CORE.
IT DISGUSTS ME TO LOOK AT YOU.
BRAINIAC IS MECHANICAL. LUTHOR HAS HIS OWN...MANIPULATIONS TO KEEP HIS THOUGHTS HIDDEN FROM ME.
THE WEAPONER'S RING WAS LOST AS WELL. NEITHER HAS MENTIONED IT.
THIS IS PART OF THEIR DAMNABLE PLAN. SOMEHOW IT IS ALL A COMPONENT OF THEIR AMBITIONS.
THEY WILL DEAL WITH ME FOR AS LONG AS I AM ESSENTIAL TO THEM.
STILL, THEY CANNOT CONTROL ME, CAN THEY?

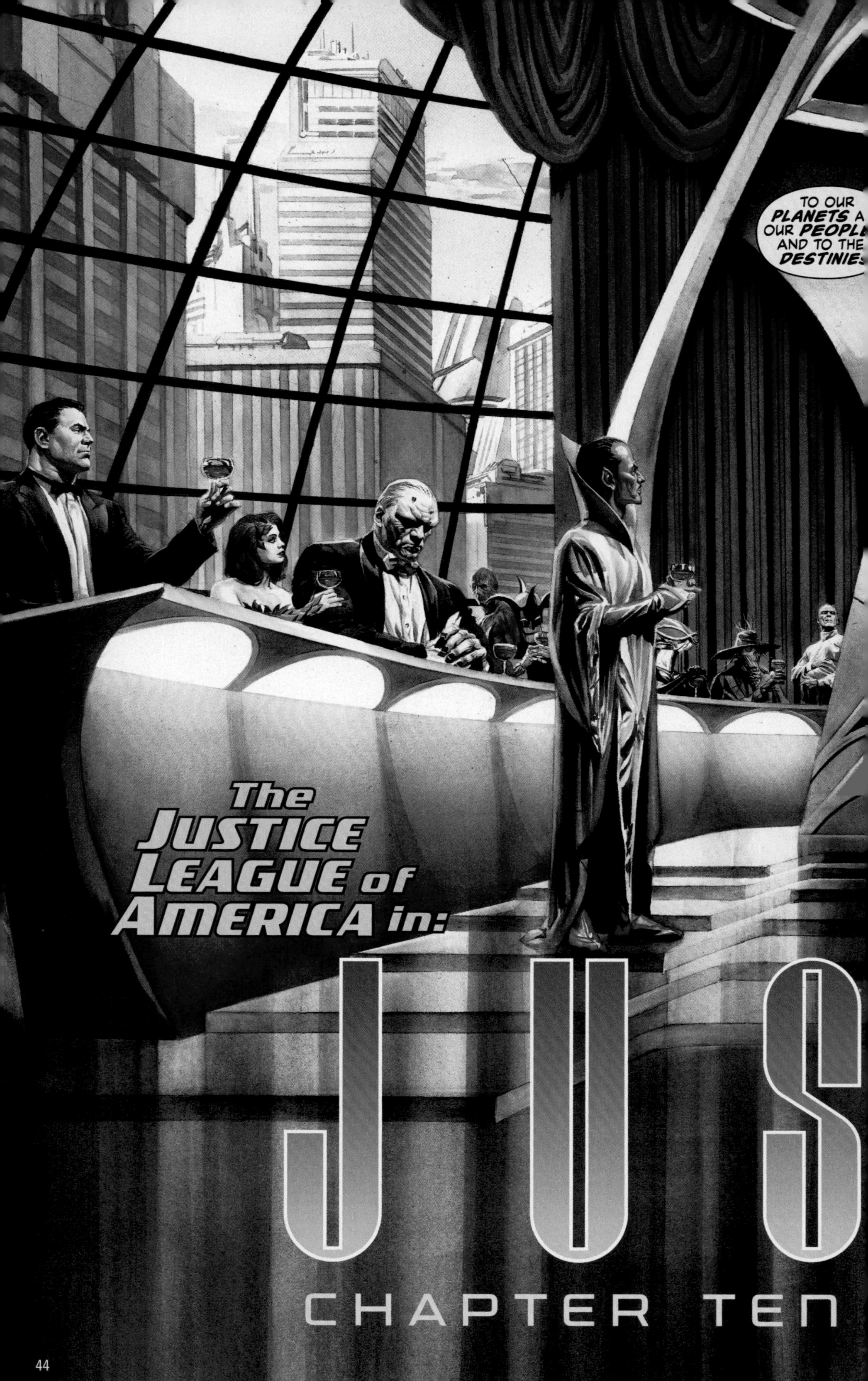
TO OUR PLANETS A OUR PEOPL AND TO THE DESTINIES
The JUSTICE LEAGUE of AMERICA in:
JUS
CHAPTER TEN

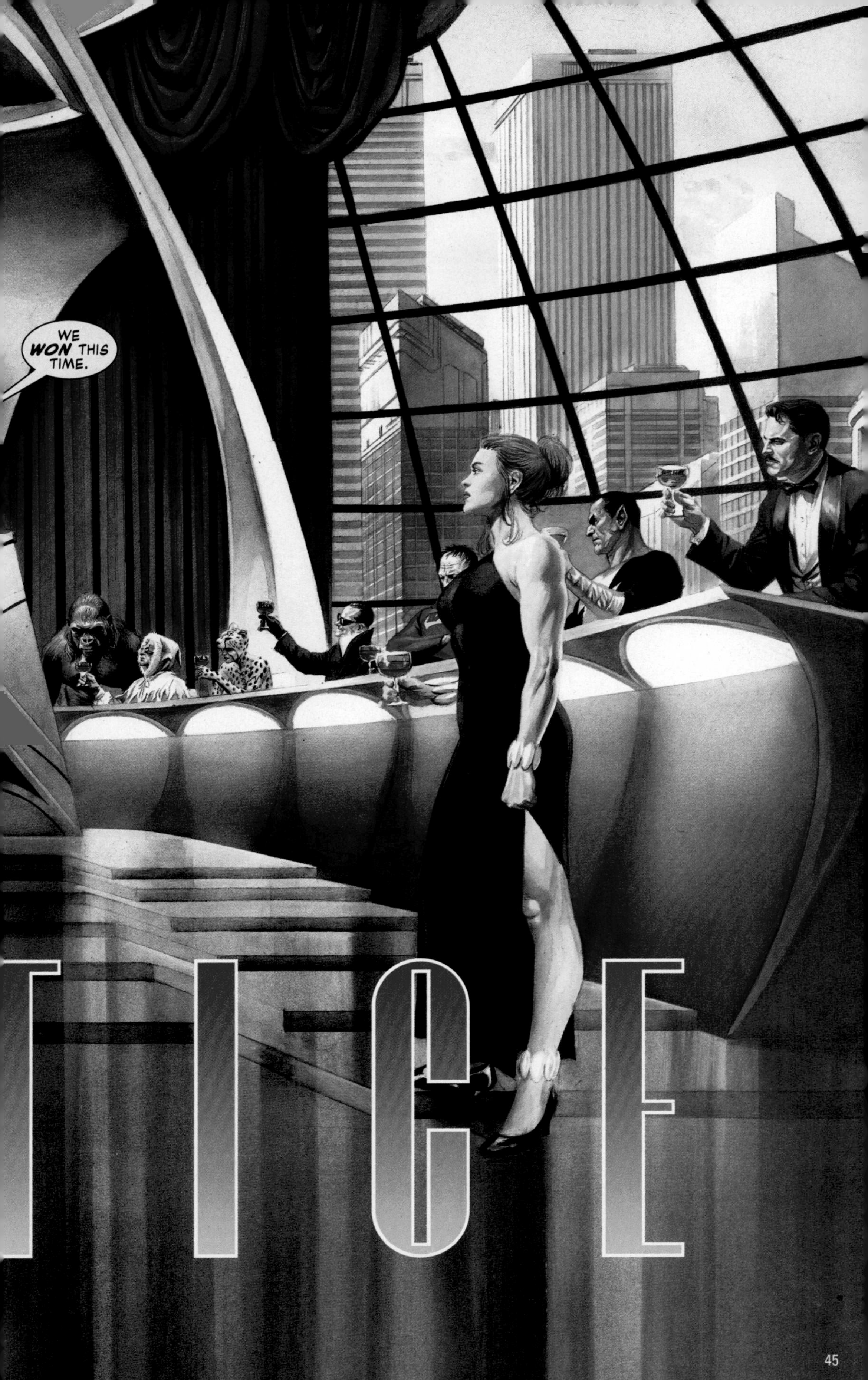
WE WON THIS TIME.
TICE

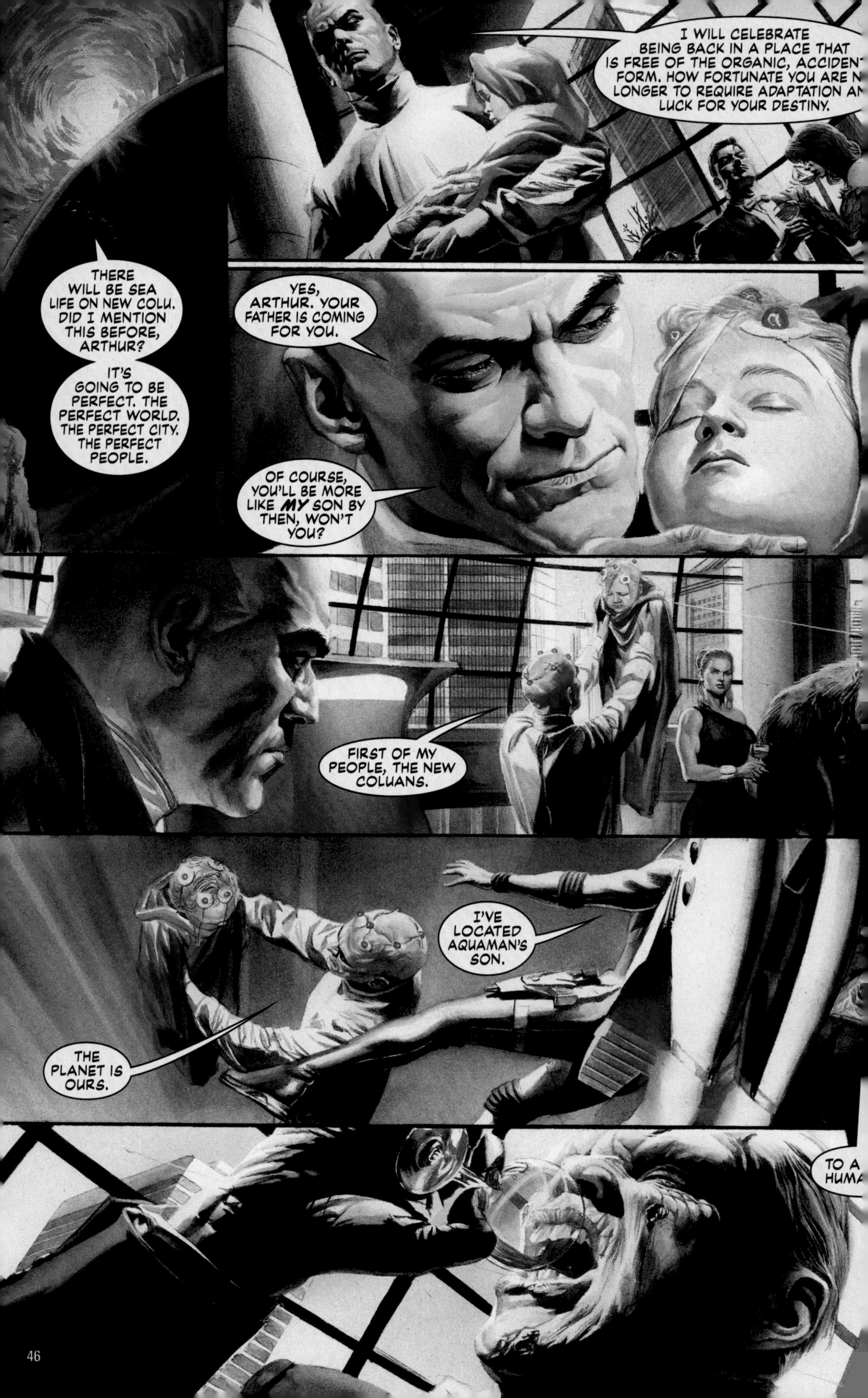
I WILL CELEBRATE BEING BACK IN A PLACE THAT IS FREE OF THE ORGANIC, ACCIDENT FORM. HOW FORTUNATE YOU ARE N LONGER TO REQUIRE ADAPTATION AN LUCK FOR YOUR DESTINY.
THERE WILL BE SEA LIFE ON NEW COLU. DID I MENTION THIS BEFORE, ARTHUR?
IT'S GOING TO BE PERFECT. THE PERFECT WORLD. THE PERFECT CITY. THE PERFECT PEOPLE.
YES, ARTHUR. YOUR FATHER IS COMING FOR YOU.
OF COURSE, YOU'LL BE MORE LIKE MY SON BY THEN, WON'T YOU?
FIRST OF MY PEOPLE, THE NEW COLUANS.
I'VE LOCATED AQUAMAN'S SON.
THE PLANET IS OURS.
TO A HUMA

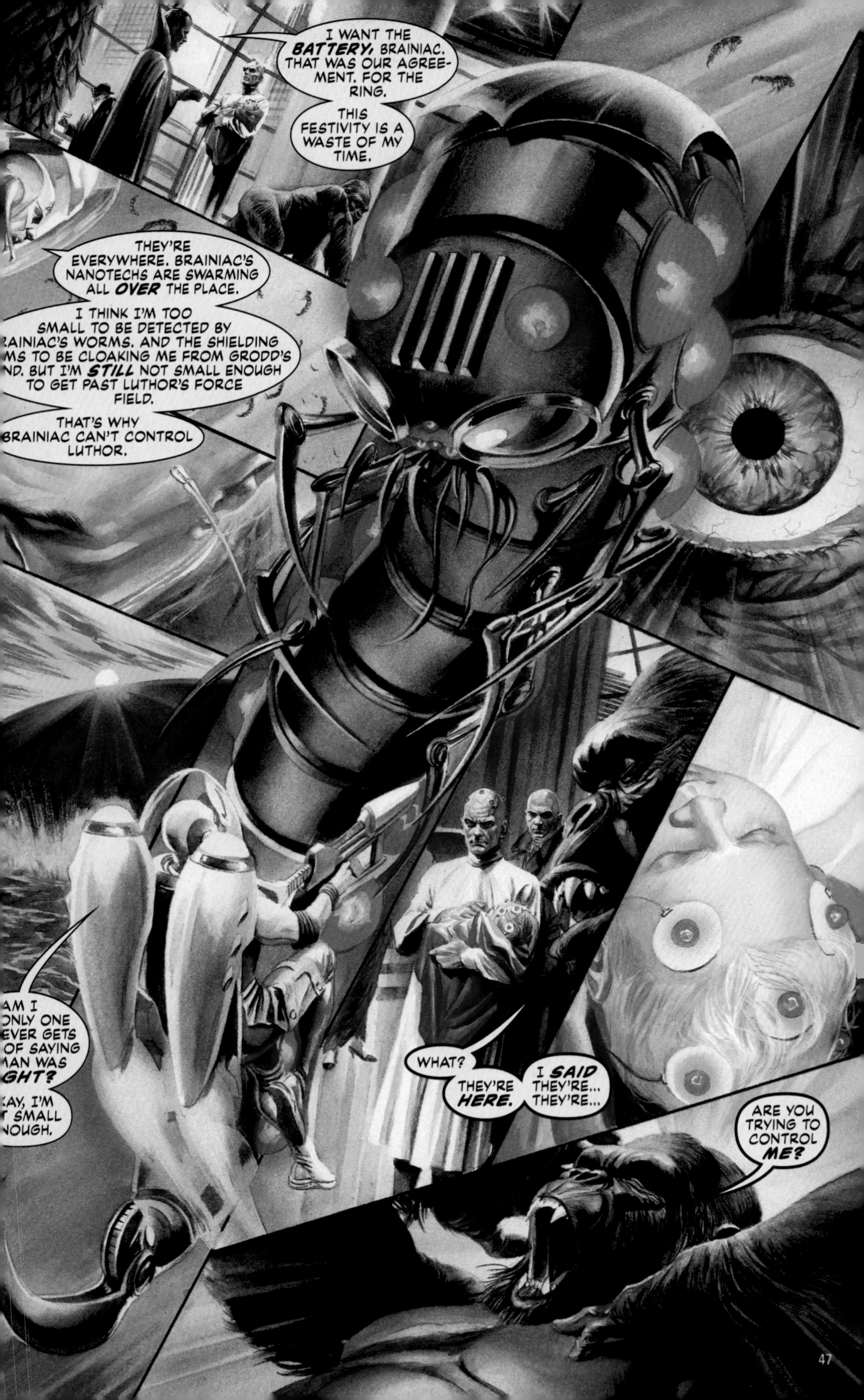

I WANT THE BATTERY, BRAINIAC. THAT WAS OUR AGREE-MENT. FOR THE RING.
THIS FESTIVITY IS A WASTE OF MY TIME.
THEY'RE EVERYWHERE. BRAINIAC'S NANOTECHS ARE SWARMING ALL OVER THE PLACE.
I THINK I'M TOO SMALL TO BE DETECTED BY RAINIAC'S WORMS. AND THE SHIELDING MS TO BE CLOAKING ME FROM GRODD'S ND. BUT I'M STILL NOT SMALL ENOUGH TO GET PAST LUTHOR'S FORCE FIELD.
THAT'S WHY BRAINIAC CAN'T CONTROL LUTHOR.
AM I ONLY ONE EVER GETS OF SAYING MAN WAS GHT?
KAY, I'M T SMALL NOUGH.
WHAT?
THEY'RE HERE.
I SAID THEY'RE... THEY'RE...
ARE YOU TRYING TO CONTROL ME?

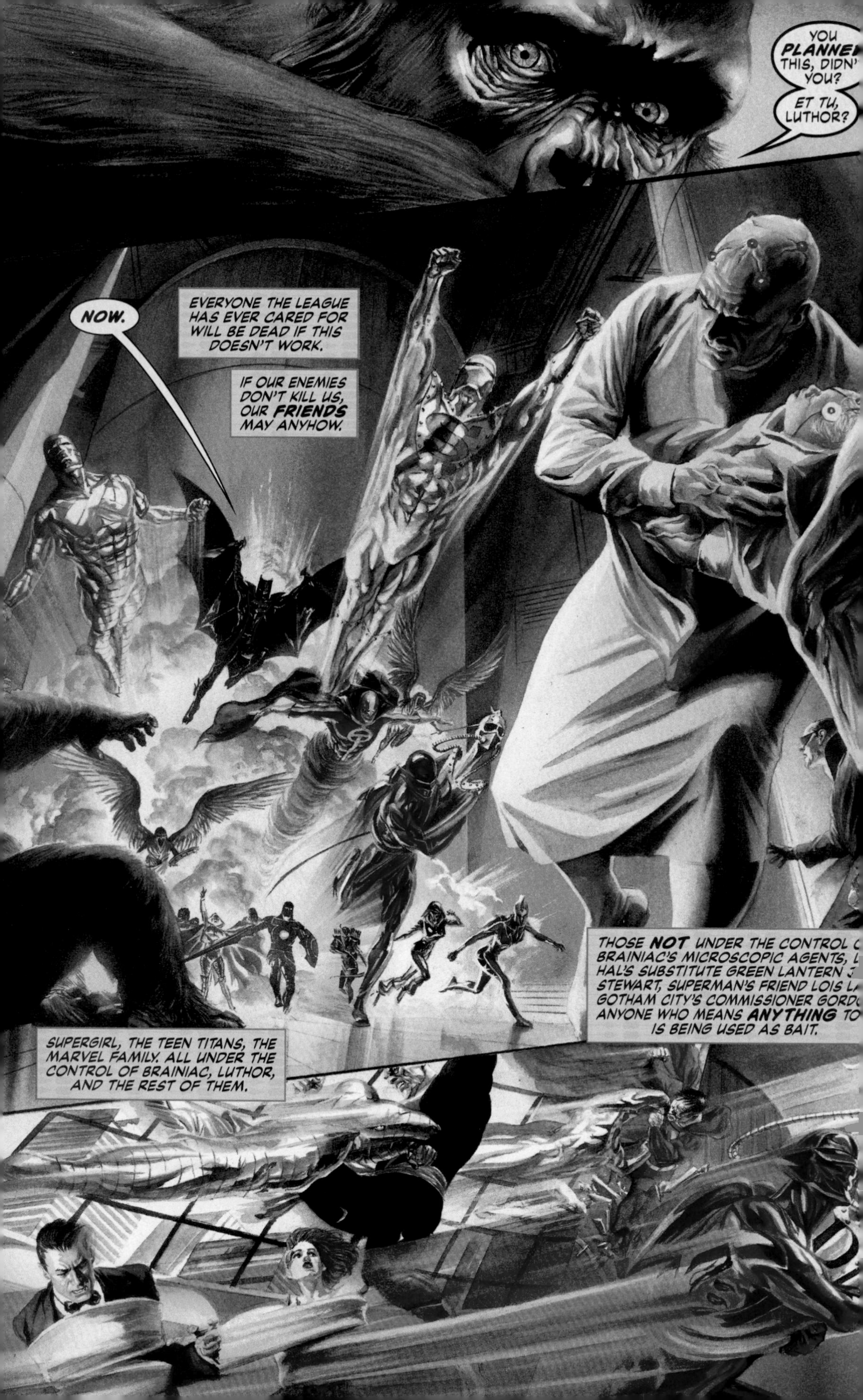

YOU PLANNE THIS, DIDN' YOU?
ET TU, LUTHOR?
NOW.
EVERYONE THE LEAGUE HAS EVER CARED FOR WILL BE DEAD IF THIS DOESN'T WORK.
IF OUR ENEMIES DON'T KILL US, OUR FRIENDS MAY ANYHOW.
THOSE NOT UNDER THE CONTROL BRAINIAC'S MICROSCOPIC AGENTS, HAL'S SUBSTITUTE GREEN LANTERN STEWART, SUPERMAN'S FRIEND LOIS GOTHAM CITY'S COMMISSIONER GORD ANYONE WHO MEANS ANYTHING TO IS BEING USED AS BAIT.
SUPERGIRL, THE TEEN TITANS, THE MARVEL FAMILY. ALL UNDER THE CONTROL OF BRAINIAC, LUTHOR, AND THE REST OF THEM.

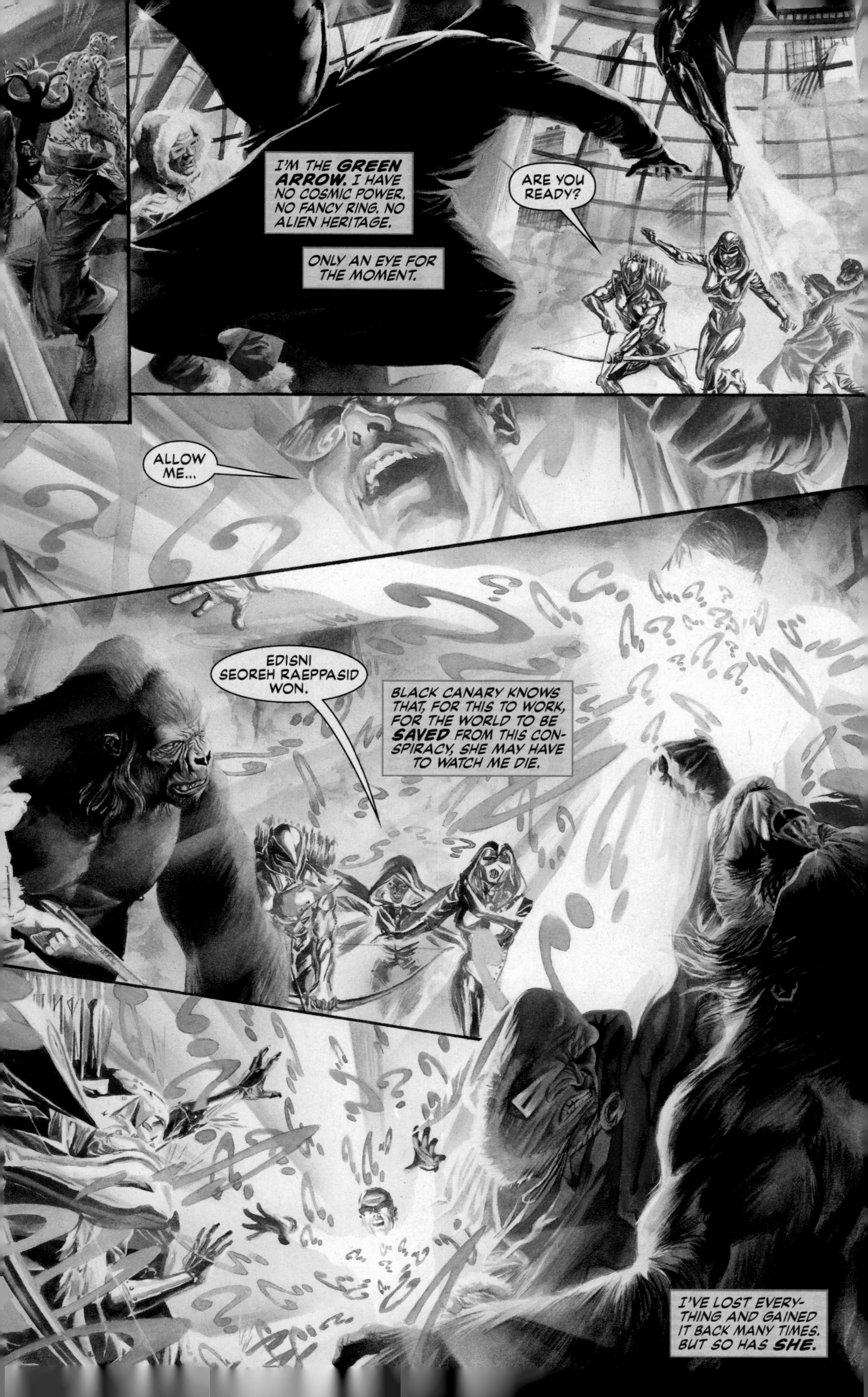
I'M THE **GREEN ARROW.** I HAVE NO COSMIC POWER. NO FANCY RING. NO ALIEN HERITAGE.
ONLY AN EYE FOR THE MOMENT.
ARE YOU READY?
ALLOW ME...
EDISNI SEOREH RAEPPASID WON.
BLACK CANARY KNOWS THAT, FOR THIS TO WORK, FOR THE WORLD TO BE **SAVED** FROM THIS CONSPIRACY, SHE MAY HAVE TO WATCH ME DIE.
I'VE LOST EVERYTHING AND GAINED IT BACK MANY TIMES. BUT SO HAS **SHE.**

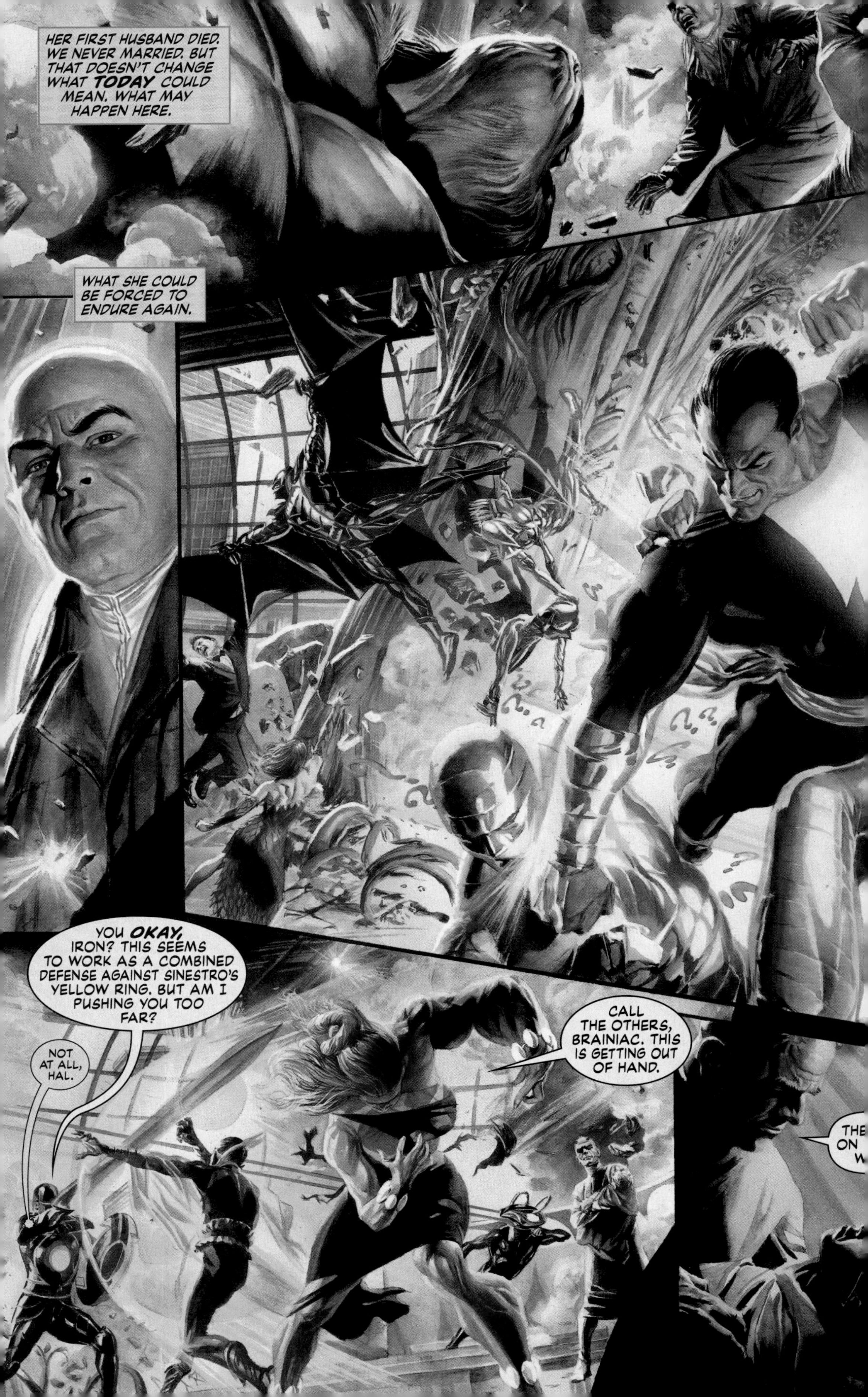
HER FIRST HUSBAND DIED. WE NEVER MARRIED. BUT THAT DOESN'T CHANGE WHAT TODAY COULD MEAN. WHAT MAY HAPPEN HERE.
WHAT SHE COULD BE FORCED TO ENDURE AGAIN.
YOU OKAY, IRON? THIS SEEMS TO WORK AS A COMBINED DEFENSE AGAINST SINESTRO'S YELLOW RING. BUT AM I PUSHING YOU TOO FAR?
NOT AT ALL, HAL.
CALL THE OTHERS, BRAINIAC. THIS IS GETTING OUT OF HAND.

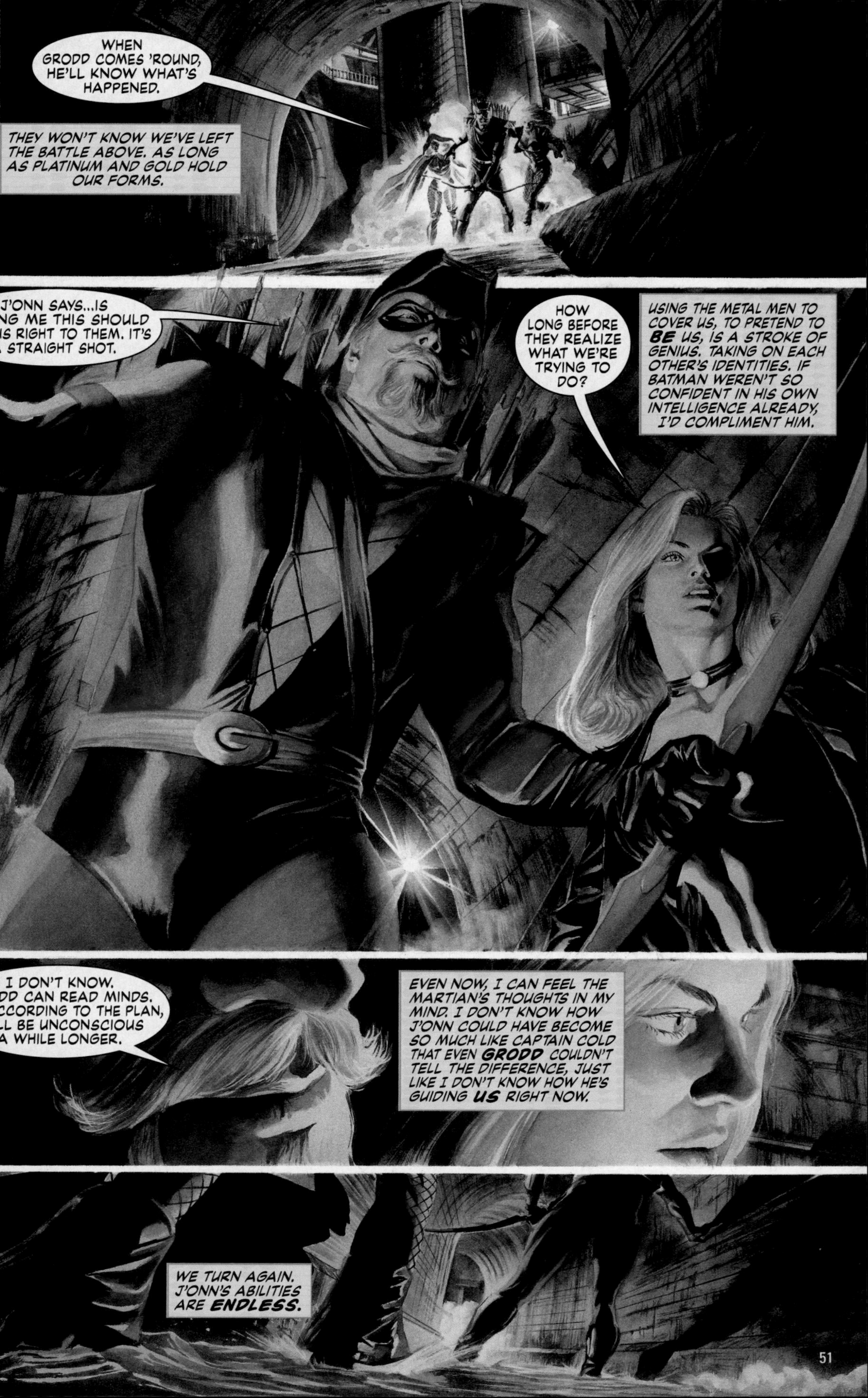
WHEN GRODD COMES 'ROUND, HE'LL KNOW WHAT'S HAPPENED.
THEY WON'T KNOW WE'VE LEFT THE BATTLE ABOVE. AS LONG AS PLATINUM AND GOLD HOLD OUR FORMS.
J'ONN SAYS...IS
NG ME THIS SHOULD
S RIGHT TO THEM. IT'S
STRAIGHT SHOT.
HOW LONG BEFORE THEY REALIZE WHAT WE'RE TRYING TO DO?
USING THE METAL MEN TO COVER US, TO PRETEND TO BE US, IS A STROKE OF GENIUS. TAKING ON EACH OTHER'S IDENTITIES. IF BATMAN WEREN'T SO CONFIDENT IN HIS OWN INTELLIGENCE ALREADY, I'D COMPLIMENT HIM.
I DON'T KNOW.
DD CAN READ MINDS.
CCORDING TO THE PLAN,
LL BE UNCONSCIOUS
A WHILE LONGER.
EVEN NOW, I CAN FEEL THE MARTIAN'S THOUGHTS IN MY MIND. I DON'T KNOW HOW J'ONN COULD HAVE BECOME SO MUCH LIKE CAPTAIN COLD THAT EVEN GRODD COULDN'T TELL THE DIFFERENCE, JUST LIKE I DON'T KNOW HOW HE'S GUIDING US RIGHT NOW.
WE TURN AGAIN. J'ONN'S ABILITIES ARE ENDLESS.

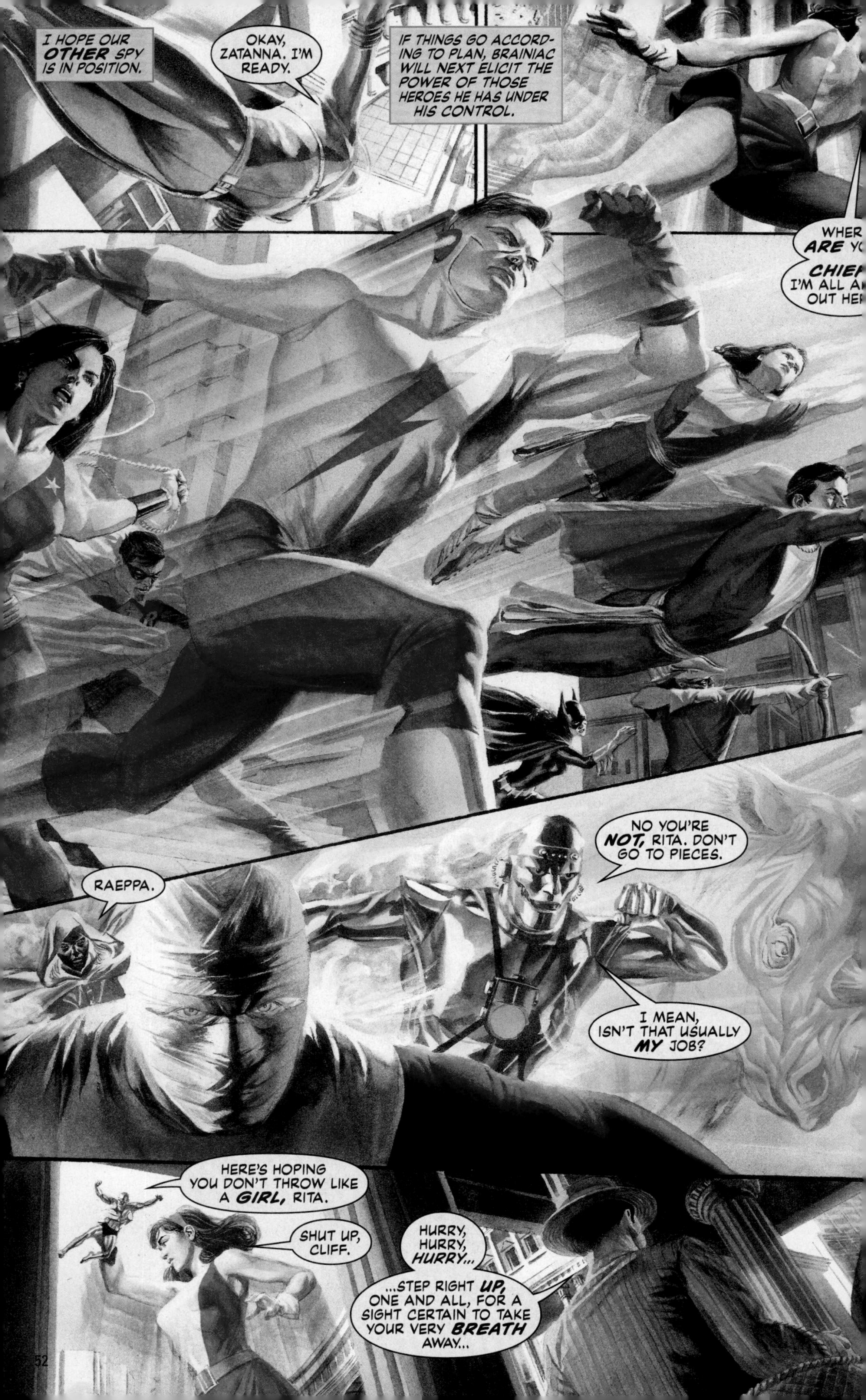

I HOPE OUR OTHER SPY IS IN POSITION.
OKAY, ZATANNA. I'M READY.
IF THINGS GO ACCORDING TO PLAN, BRAINIAC WILL NEXT ELICIT THE POWER OF THOSE HEROES HE HAS UNDER HIS CONTROL.
RAEPPA.
NO YOU'RE NOT, RITA. DON'T GO TO PIECES.
I MEAN, ISN'T THAT USUALLY MY JOB?
HERE'S HOPING YOU DON'T THROW LIKE A GIRL, RITA.
SHUT UP, CLIFF.
HURRY, HURRY, HURRY...
...STEP RIGHT UP, ONE AND ALL, FOR A SIGHT CERTAIN TO TAKE YOUR VERY BREATH AWAY...

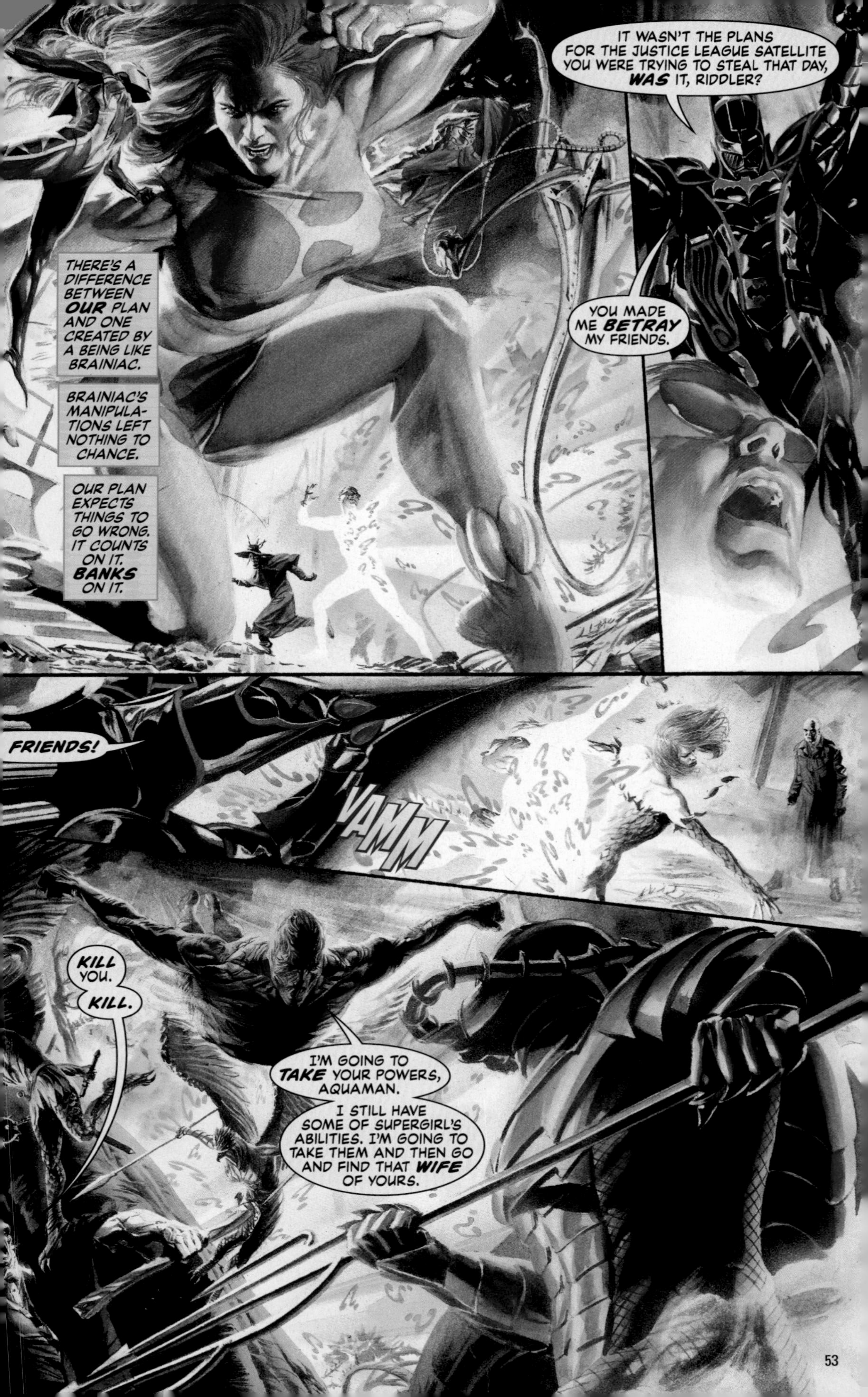
THERE'S A DIFFERENCE BETWEEN **OUR** PLAN AND ONE CREATED BY A BEING LIKE BRAINIAC.
BRAINIAC'S MANIPULATIONS LEFT NOTHING TO CHANCE.
OUR PLAN EXPECTS THINGS TO GO WRONG. IT COUNTS ON IT. **BANKS** ON IT.
IT WASN'T THE PLANS FOR THE JUSTICE LEAGUE SATELLITE YOU WERE TRYING TO STEAL THAT DAY, **WAS** IT, RIDDLER?
YOU MADE ME **BETRAY** MY FRIENDS.
FRIENDS!
VAMM
KILL YOU. **KILL.**
I'M GOING TO **TAKE** YOUR POWERS, AQUAMAN.
I STILL HAVE SOME OF SUPERGIRL'S ABILITIES. I'M GOING TO TAKE THEM AND THEN GO AND FIND THAT **WIFE** OF YOURS.

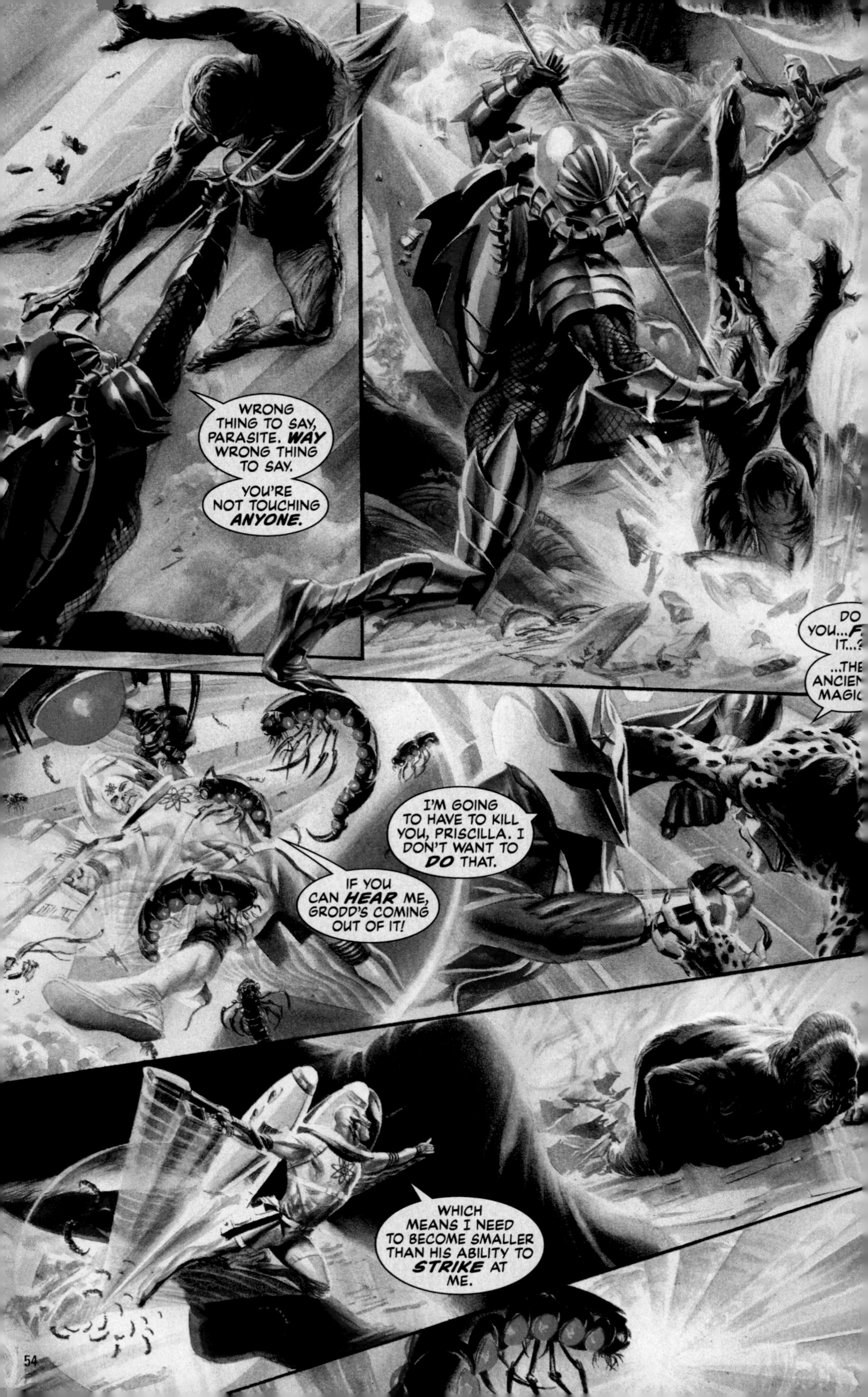
WRONG THING TO SAY, PARASITE. WAY WRONG THING TO SAY.
YOU'RE NOT TOUCHING ANYONE.
DO YOU...F IT...?
...THE ANCIEN MAGIC
I'M GOING TO HAVE TO KILL YOU, PRISCILLA. I DON'T WANT TO DO THAT.
IF YOU CAN HEAR ME, GRODD'S COMING OUT OF IT!
WHICH MEANS I NEED TO BECOME SMALLER THAN HIS ABILITY TO STRIKE AT ME.

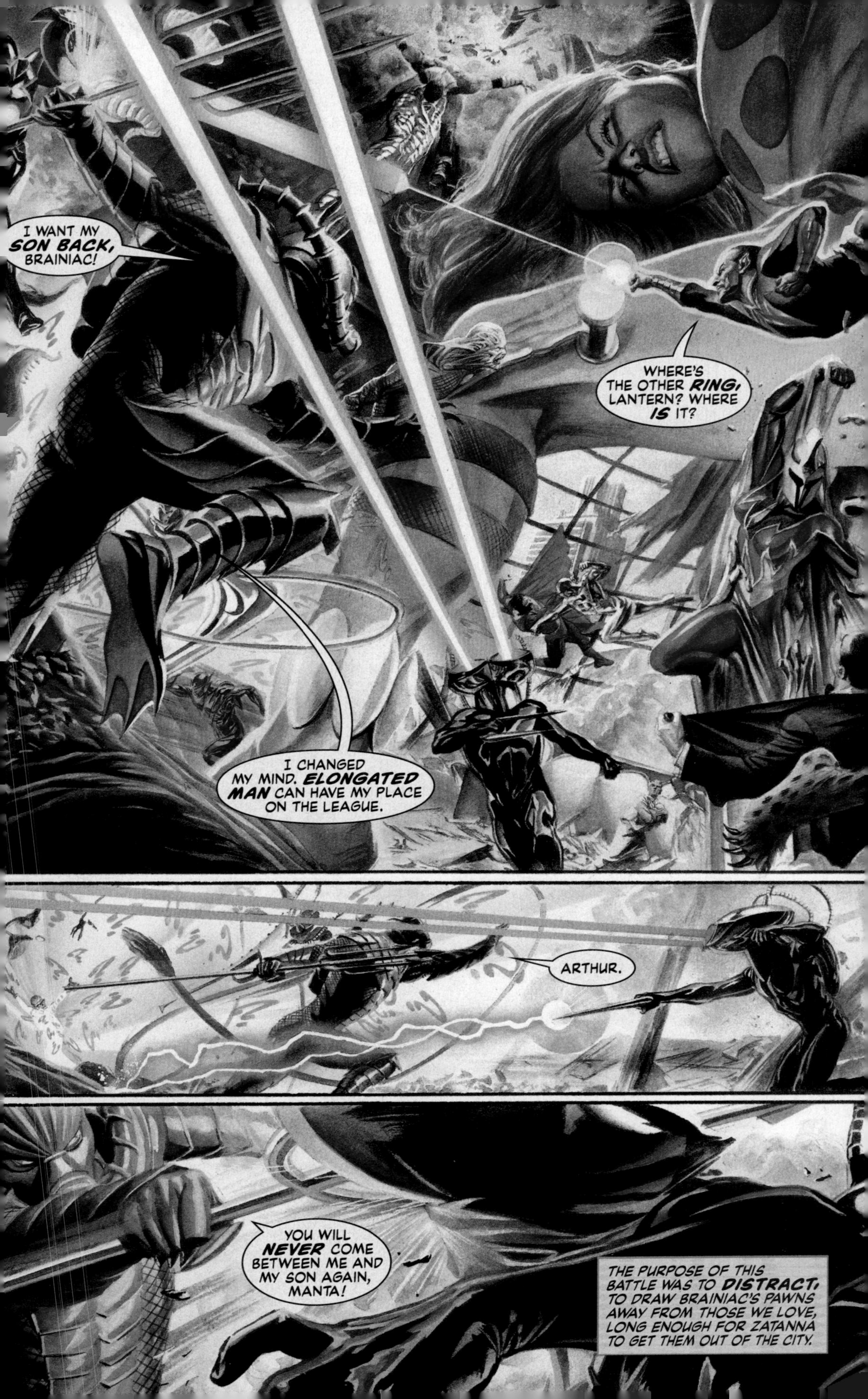
I WANT MY **SON BACK,** BRAINIAC!
WHERE'S THE OTHER **RING,** LANTERN? WHERE **IS** IT?
I CHANGED MY MIND. **ELONGATED MAN** CAN HAVE MY PLACE ON THE LEAGUE.
ARTHUR.
YOU WILL **NEVER** COME BETWEEN ME AND MY SON AGAIN, MANTA!
*THE PURPOSE OF THIS BATTLE WAS TO **DISTRACT,** TO DRAW BRAINIAC'S PAWNS AWAY FROM THOSE WE LOVE, LONG ENOUGH FOR ZATANNA TO GET THEM OUT OF THE CITY.*

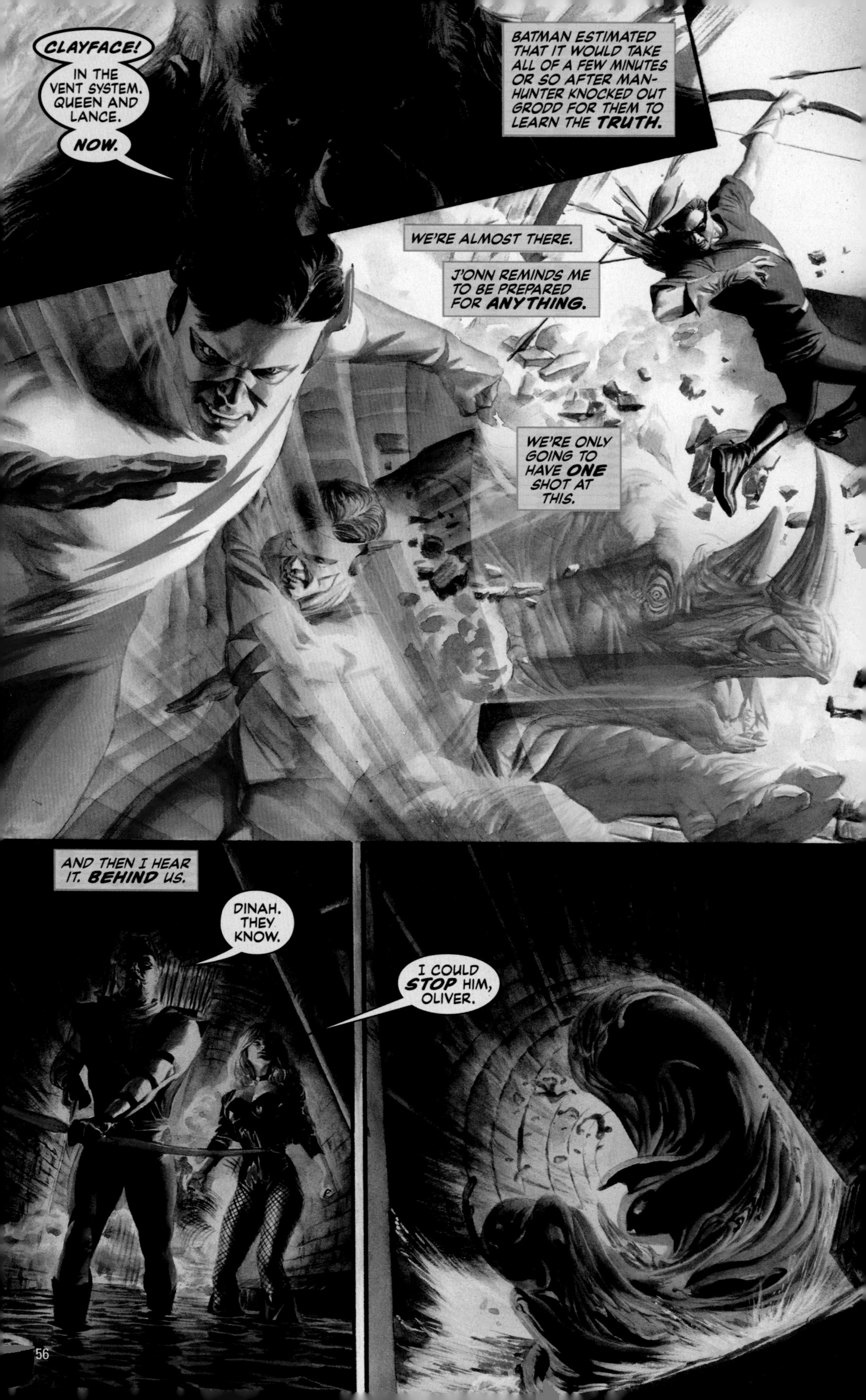
CLAYFACE!
IN THE VENT SYSTEM. QUEEN AND LANCE.
NOW.
BATMAN ESTIMATED THAT IT WOULD TAKE ALL OF A FEW MINUTES OR SO AFTER MAN-HUNTER KNOCKED OUT GRODD FOR THEM TO LEARN THE TRUTH.
WE'RE ALMOST THERE.
J'ONN REMINDS ME TO BE PREPARED FOR ANYTHING.
WE'RE ONLY GOING TO HAVE ONE SHOT AT THIS.
AND THEN I HEAR IT. BEHIND US.
DINAH. THEY KNOW.
I COULD STOP HIM, OLIVER.

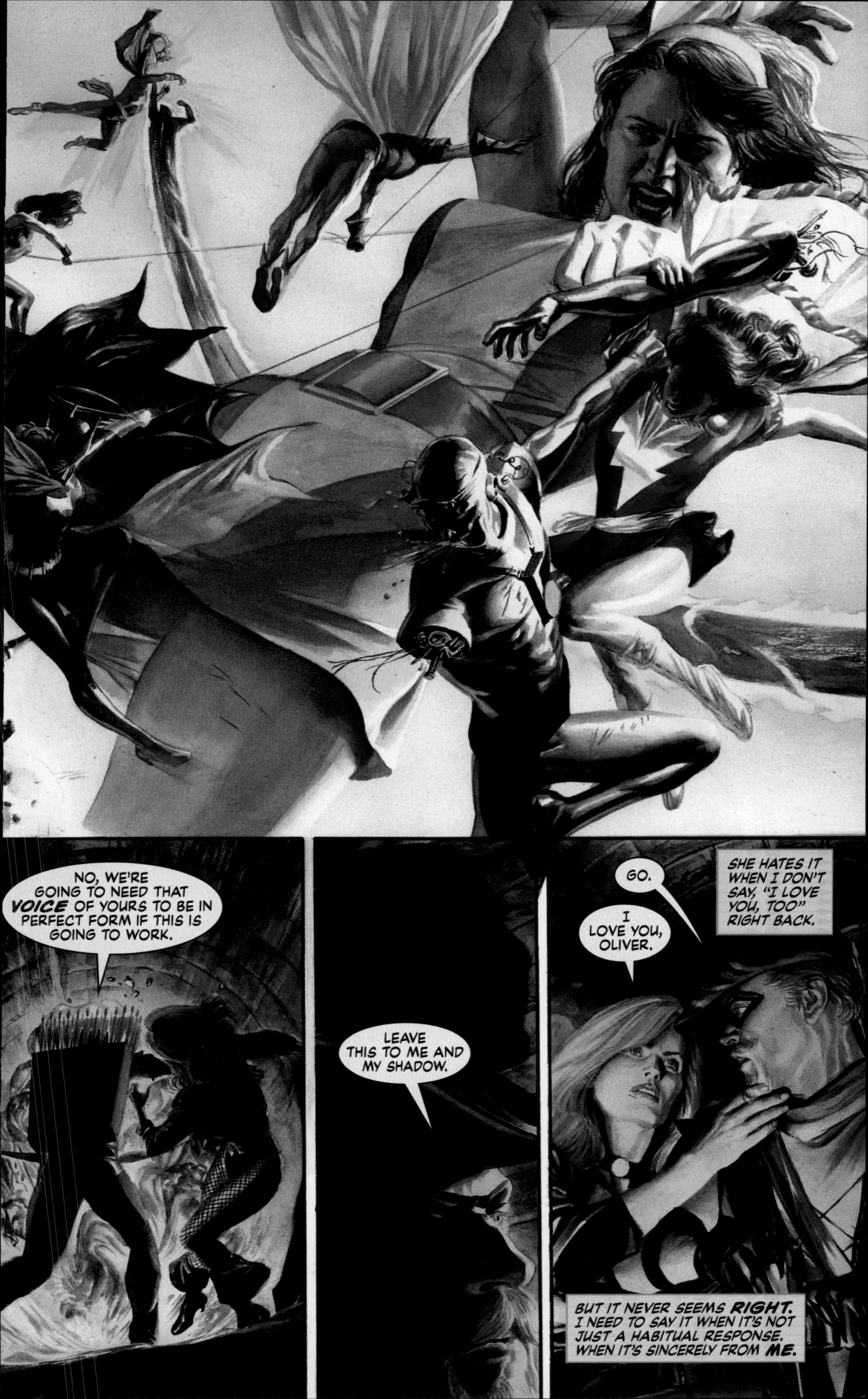
NO, WE'RE GOING TO NEED THAT VOICE OF YOURS TO BE IN PERFECT FORM IF THIS IS GOING TO WORK.
LEAVE THIS TO ME AND MY SHADOW.
GO.
I LOVE YOU, OLIVER.
SHE HATES IT WHEN I DON'T SAY, "I LOVE YOU, TOO" RIGHT BACK.
BUT IT NEVER SEEMS RIGHT. I NEED TO SAY IT WHEN IT'S NOT JUST A HABITUAL RESPONSE. WHEN IT'S SINCERELY FROM ME.

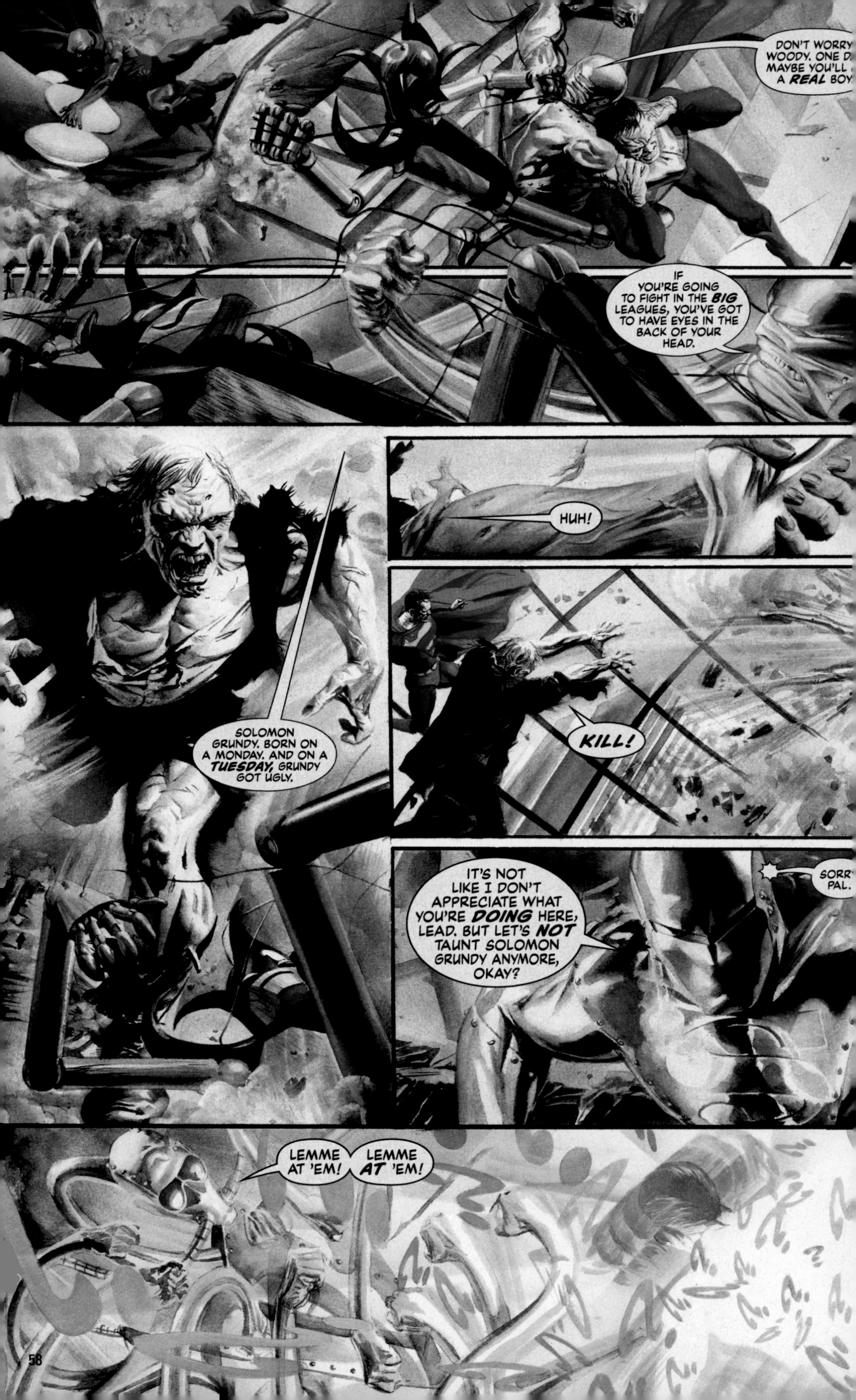
DON'T WORRY, WOODY. ONE DA MAYBE YOU'LL A REAL BOY
IF YOU'RE GOING TO FIGHT IN THE BIG LEAGUES, YOU'VE GOT TO HAVE EYES IN THE BACK OF YOUR HEAD.
SOLOMON GRUNDY. BORN ON A MONDAY. AND ON A TUESDAY, GRUNDY GOT UGLY.
HUH!
KILL!
IT'S NOT LIKE I DON'T APPRECIATE WHAT YOU'RE DOING HERE, LEAD. BUT LET'S NOT TAUNT SOLOMON GRUNDY ANYMORE, OKAY?
SORR PAL.
LEMME AT 'EM!
LEMME AT 'EM!

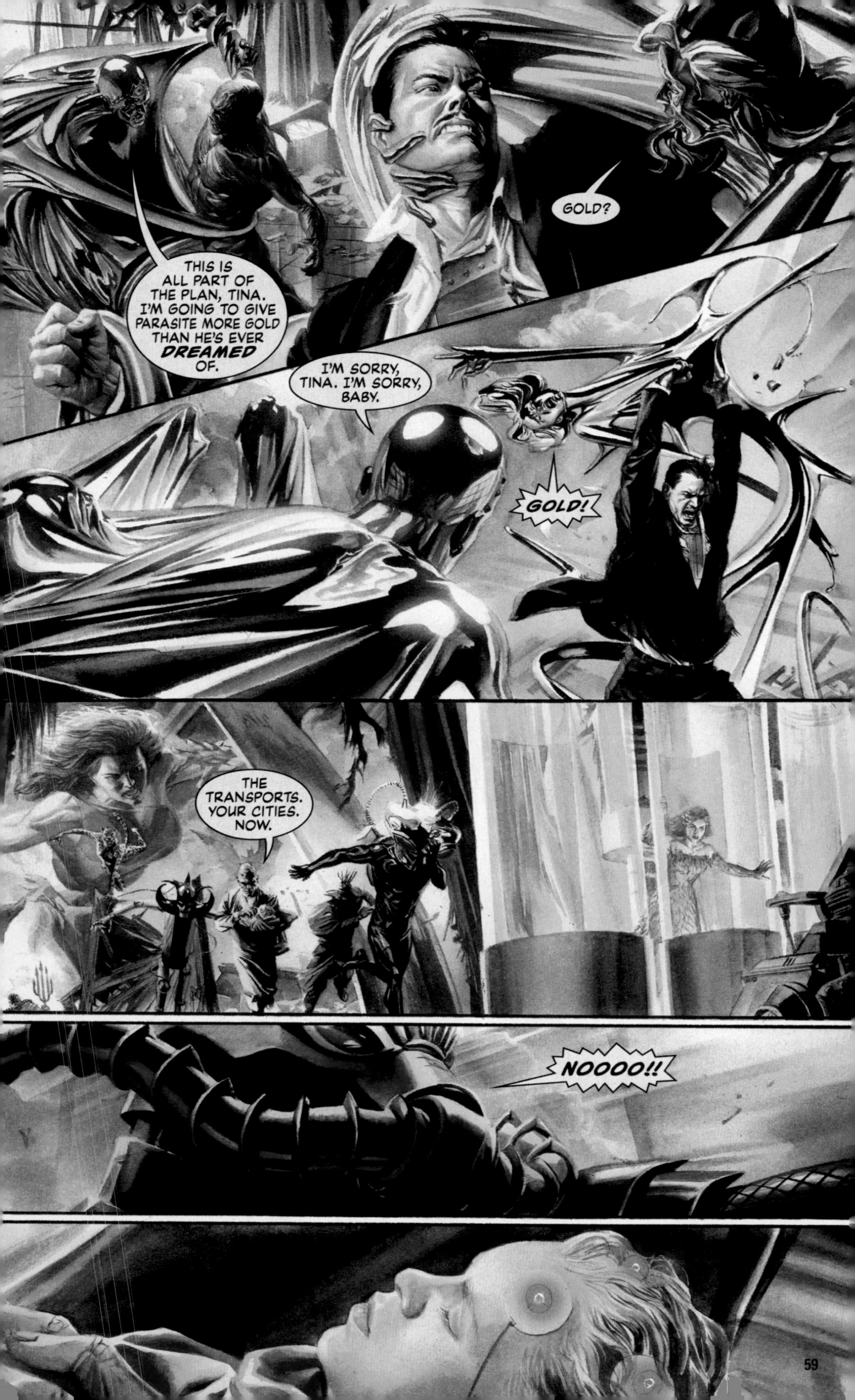
GOLD?
THIS IS ALL PART OF THE PLAN, TINA. I'M GOING TO GIVE PARASITE MORE GOLD THAN HE'S EVER DREAMED OF.
I'M SORRY, TINA. I'M SORRY, BABY.
GOLD!
THE TRANSPORTS. YOUR CITIES. NOW.
NOOOO!!

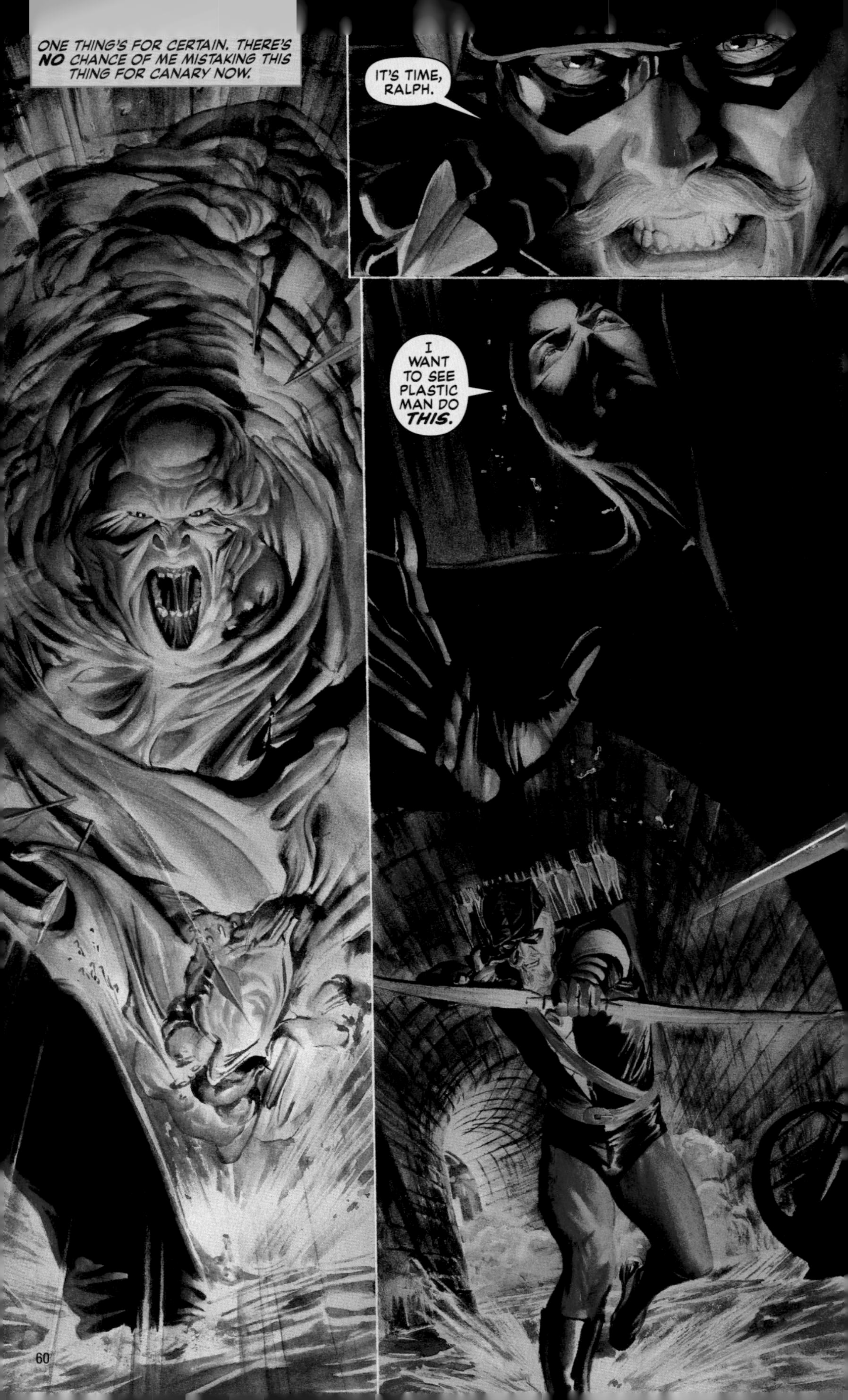
ONE THING'S FOR CERTAIN. THERE'S **NO** CHANCE OF ME MISTAKING THIS THING FOR CANARY NOW.
IT'S TIME, RALPH.
I WANT TO SEE PLASTIC MAN DO ***THIS.***

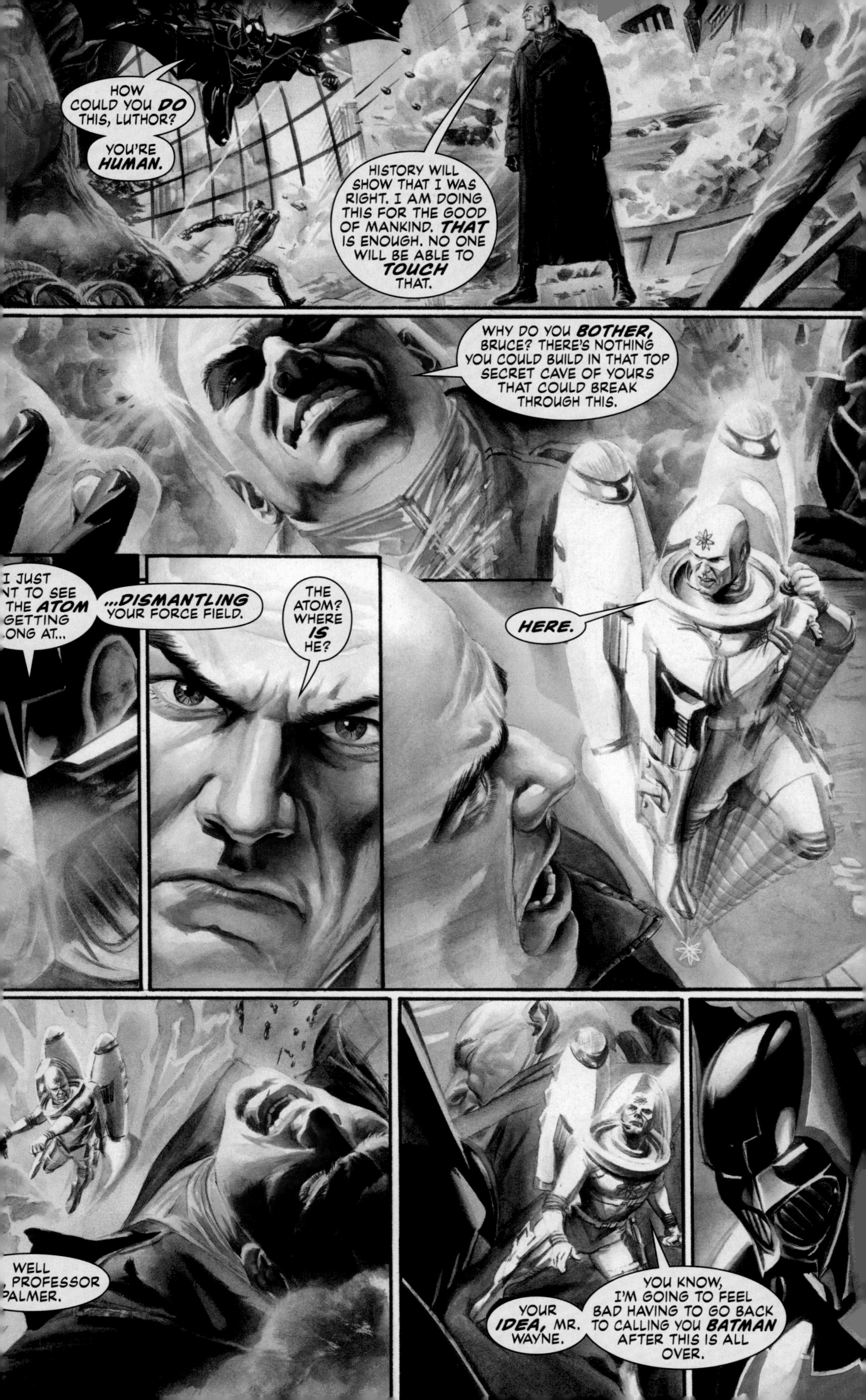

HOW COULD YOU DO THIS, LUTHOR?
YOU'RE HUMAN.
HISTORY WILL SHOW THAT I WAS RIGHT. I AM DOING THIS FOR THE GOOD OF MANKIND. THAT IS ENOUGH. NO ONE WILL BE ABLE TO TOUCH THAT.
WHY DO YOU BOTHER, BRUCE? THERE'S NOTHING YOU COULD BUILD IN THAT TOP SECRET CAVE OF YOURS THAT COULD BREAK THROUGH THIS.
I JUST NT TO SEE THE ATOM GETTING ONG AT...
...DISMANTLING YOUR FORCE FIELD.
THE ATOM? WHERE IS HE?
HERE.
WELL , PROFESSOR PALMER.
YOUR IDEA, MR. WAYNE.
YOU KNOW, I'M GOING TO FEEL BAD HAVING TO GO BACK TO CALLING YOU BATMAN AFTER THIS IS ALL OVER.

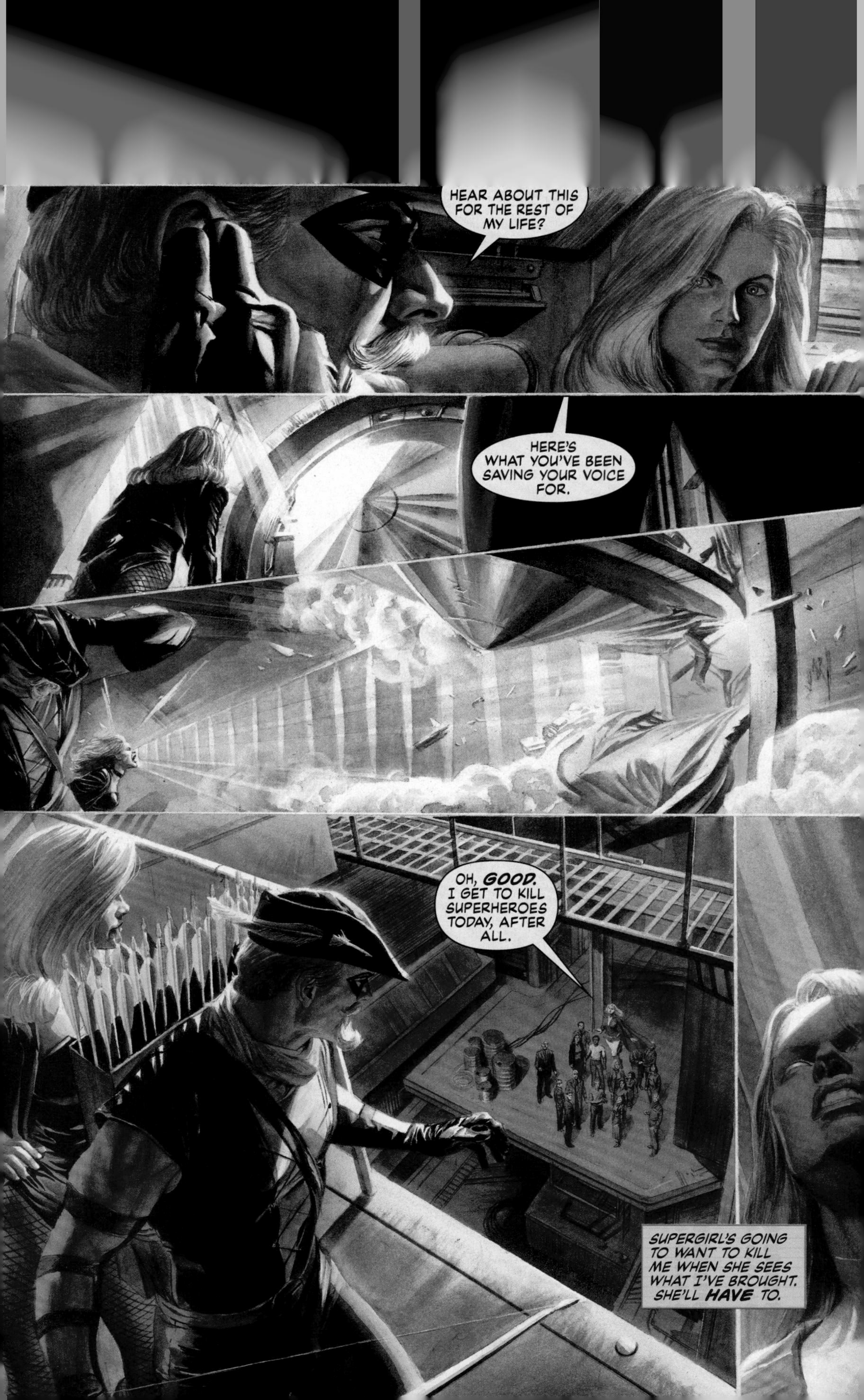
HEAR ABOUT THIS FOR THE REST OF MY LIFE?
HERE'S WHAT YOU'VE BEEN SAVING YOUR VOICE FOR.
OH, GOOD. I GET TO KILL SUPERHEROES TODAY, AFTER ALL.
SUPERGIRL'S GOING TO WANT TO KILL ME WHEN SHE SEES WHAT I'VE BROUGHT. SHE'LL HAVE TO.

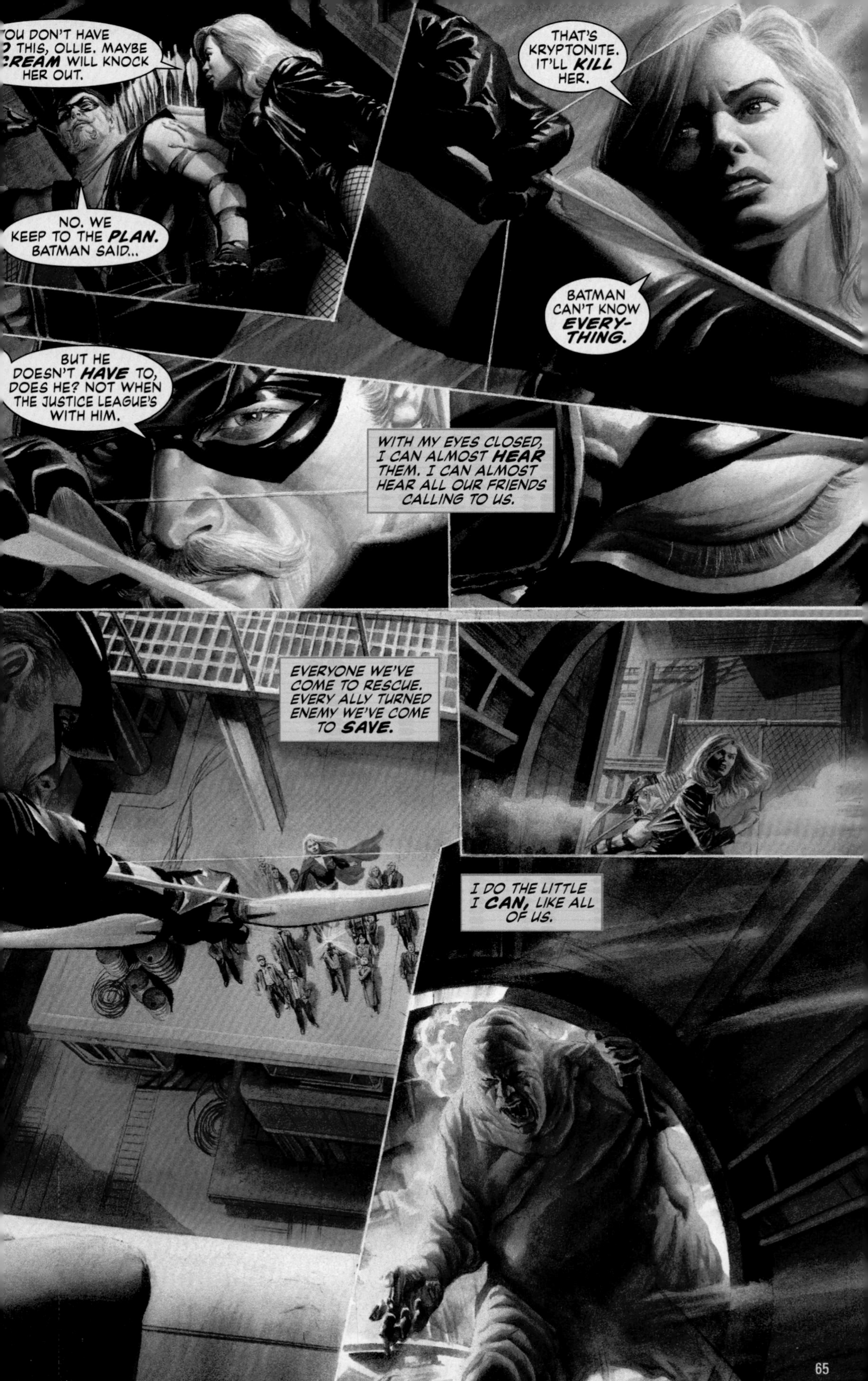
OU DON'T HAVE O THIS, OLLIE. MAYBE CREAM WILL KNOCK HER OUT.
NO. WE KEEP TO THE PLAN. BATMAN SAID...
THAT'S KRYPTONITE. IT'LL KILL HER.
BATMAN CAN'T KNOW EVERY-THING.
BUT HE DOESN'T HAVE TO, DOES HE? NOT WHEN THE JUSTICE LEAGUE'S WITH HIM.
WITH MY EYES CLOSED, I CAN ALMOST HEAR THEM. I CAN ALMOST HEAR ALL OUR FRIENDS CALLING TO US.
EVERYONE WE'VE COME TO RESCUE. EVERY ALLY TURNED ENEMY WE'VE COME TO SAVE.
I DO THE LITTLE I CAN, LIKE ALL OF US.

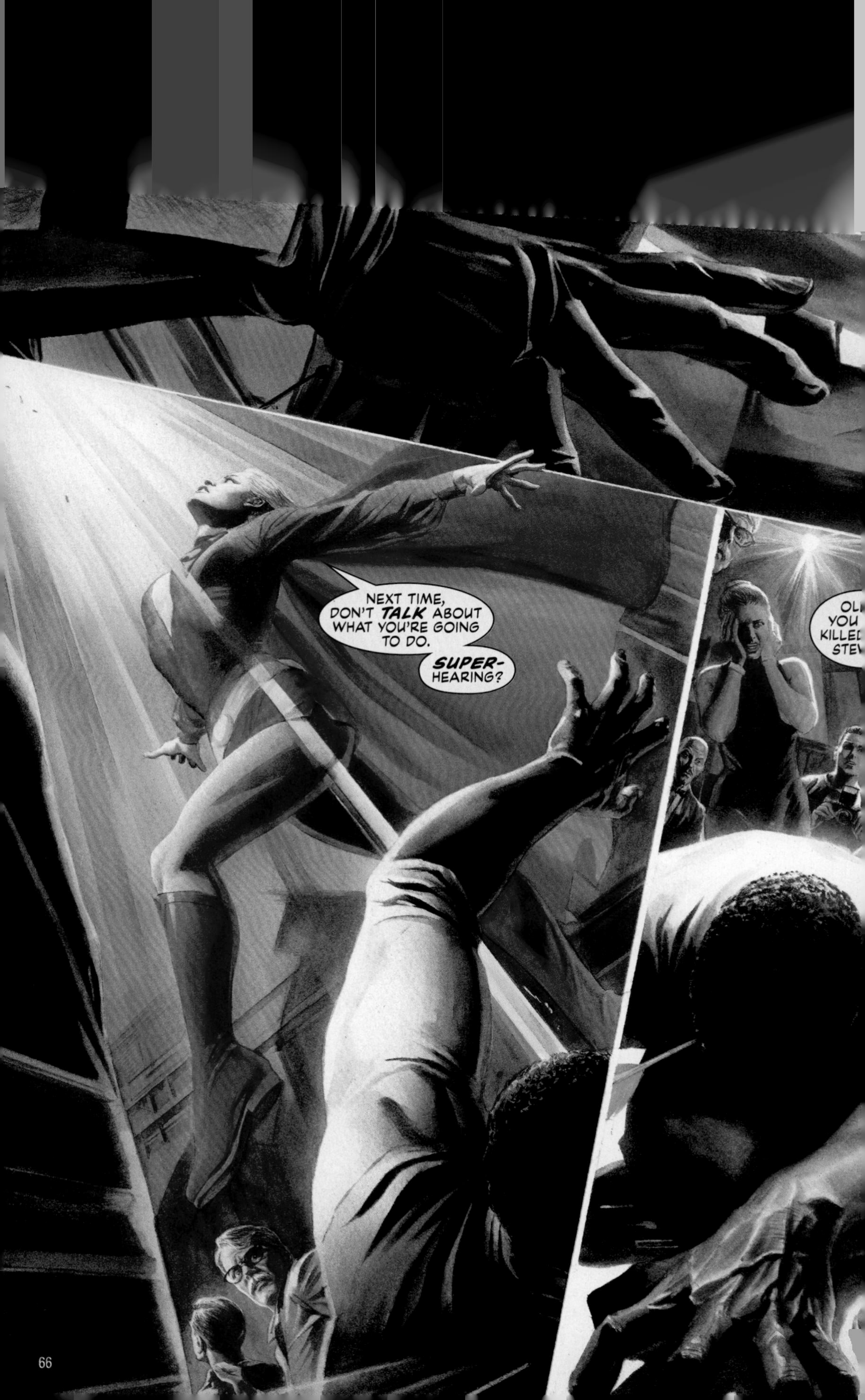
NEXT TIME, DON'T TALK ABOUT WHAT YOU'RE GOING TO DO.
SUPER-HEARING?

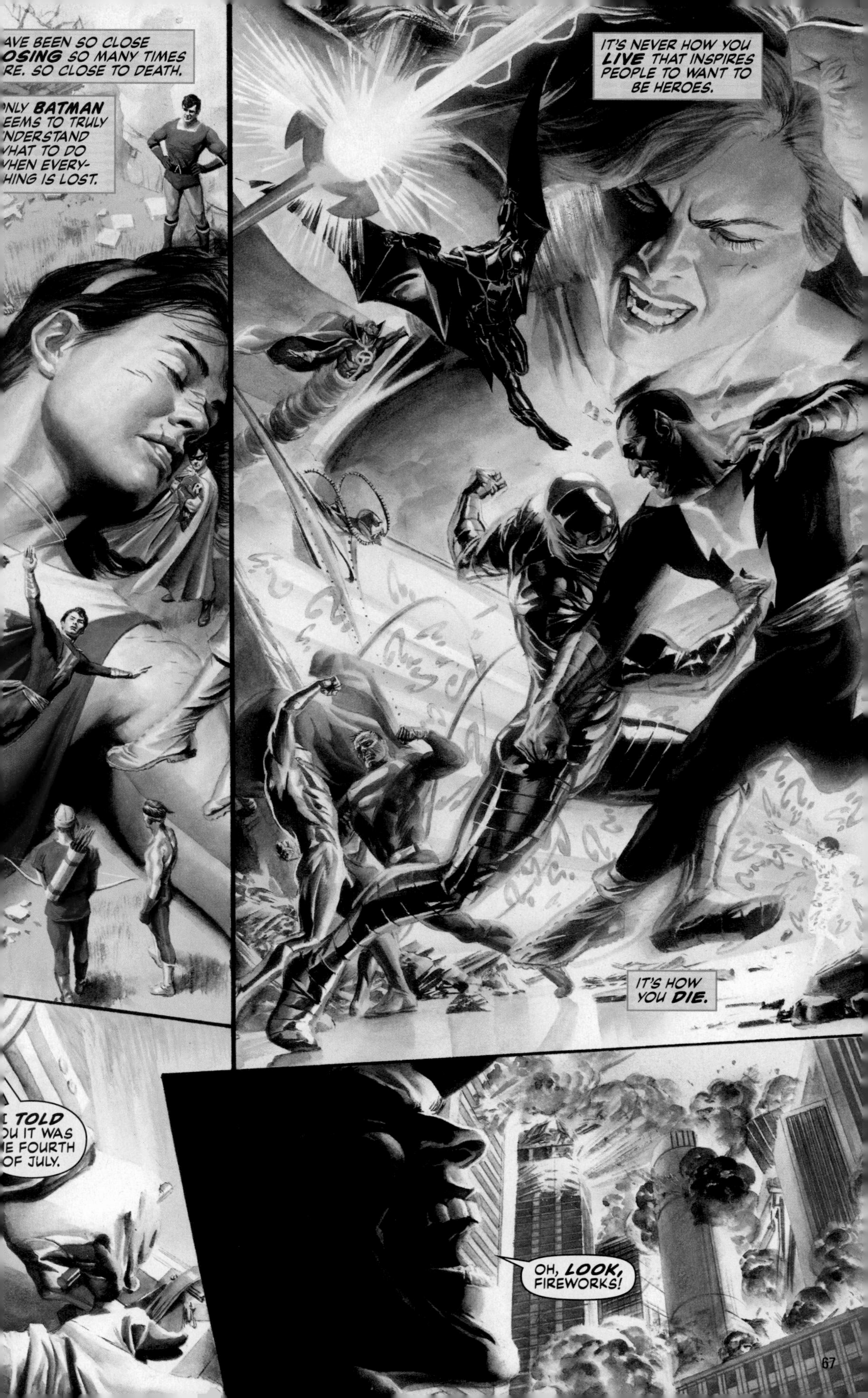
AVE BEEN SO CLOSE
OSING SO MANY TIMES
RE. SO CLOSE TO DEATH.
ONLY BATMAN
EEMS TO TRULY
NDERSTAND
WHAT TO DO
WHEN EVERY-
HING IS LOST.
IT'S NEVER HOW YOU LIVE THAT INSPIRES PEOPLE TO WANT TO BE HEROES.
IT'S HOW YOU DIE.
I TOLD
OU IT WAS
E FOURTH
OF JULY.
OH, LOOK, FIREWORKS!

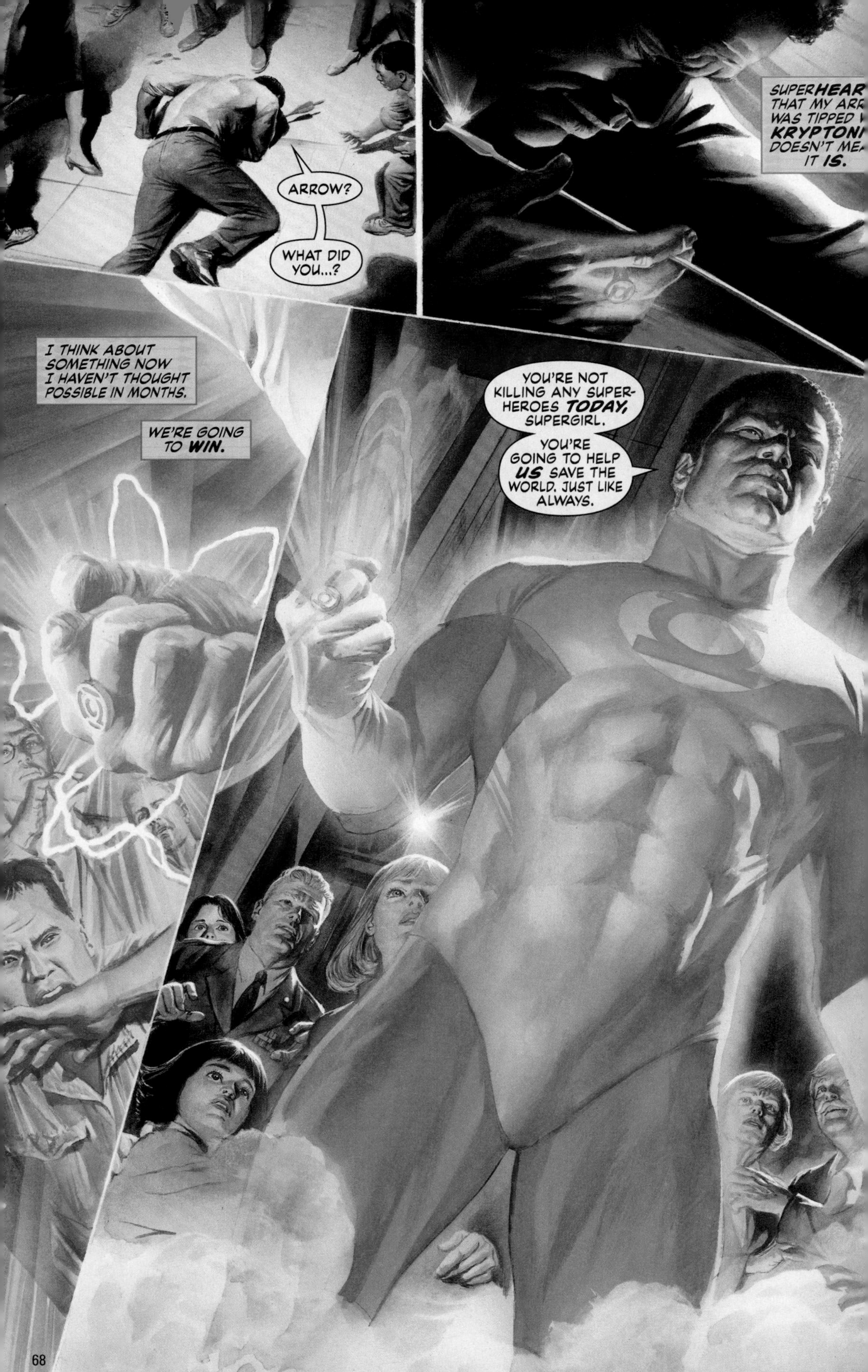
ARROW?
WHAT DID YOU...?
SUPERHEAR THAT MY ARR WAS TIPPED KRYPTON DOESN'T ME IT IS.
I THINK ABOUT SOMETHING NOW I HAVEN'T THOUGHT POSSIBLE IN MONTHS.
WE'RE GOING TO WIN.
YOU'RE NOT KILLING ANY SUPER-HEROES TODAY, SUPERGIRL.
YOU'RE GOING TO HELP US SAVE THE WORLD. JUST LIKE ALWAYS.

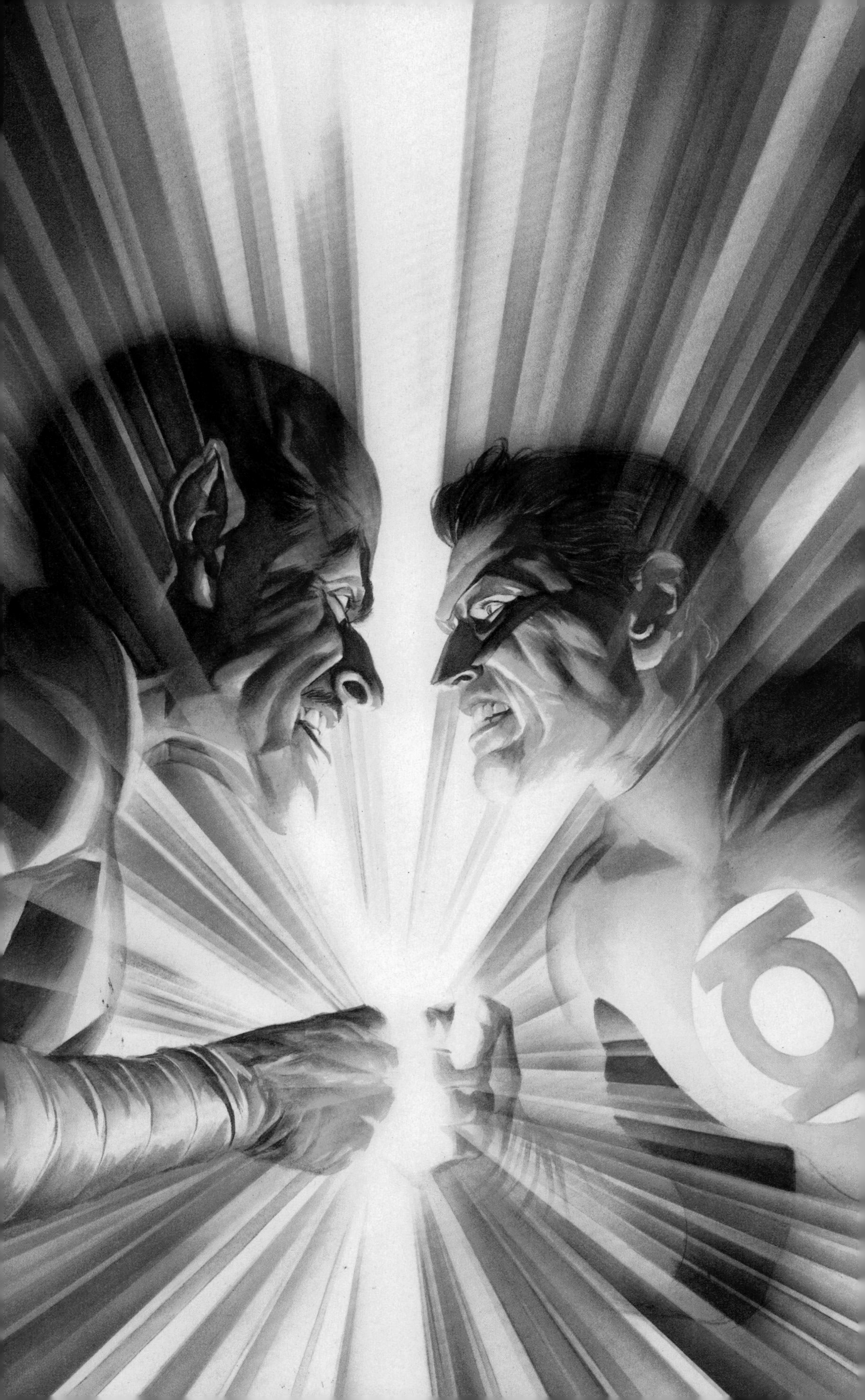

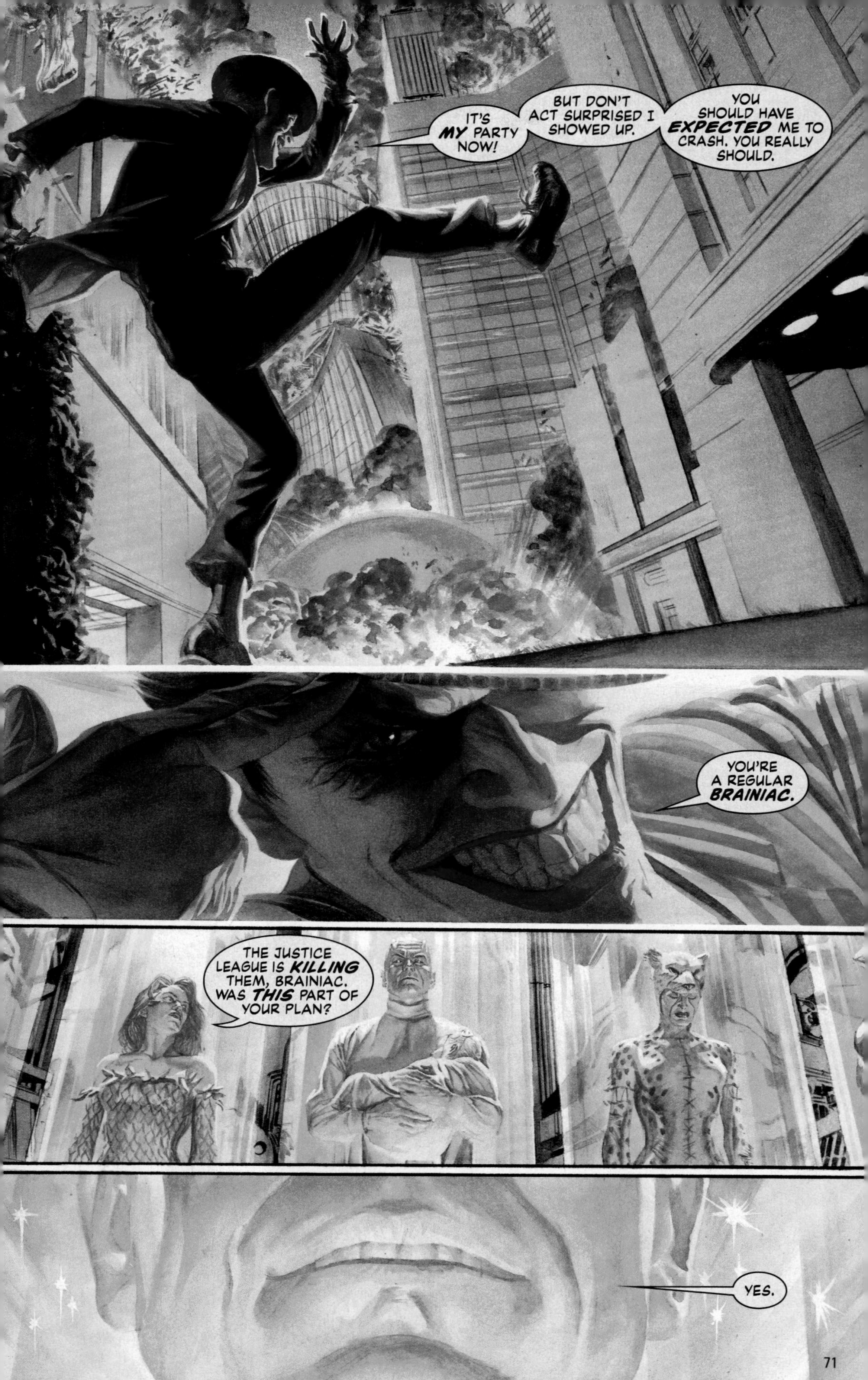
IT'S MY PARTY NOW!
BUT DON'T ACT SURPRISED I SHOWED UP.
YOU SHOULD HAVE EXPECTED ME TO CRASH. YOU REALLY SHOULD.
YOU'RE A REGULAR BRAINIAC.
THE JUSTICE LEAGUE IS KILLING THEM, BRAINIAC. WAS THIS PART OF YOUR PLAN?
YES.

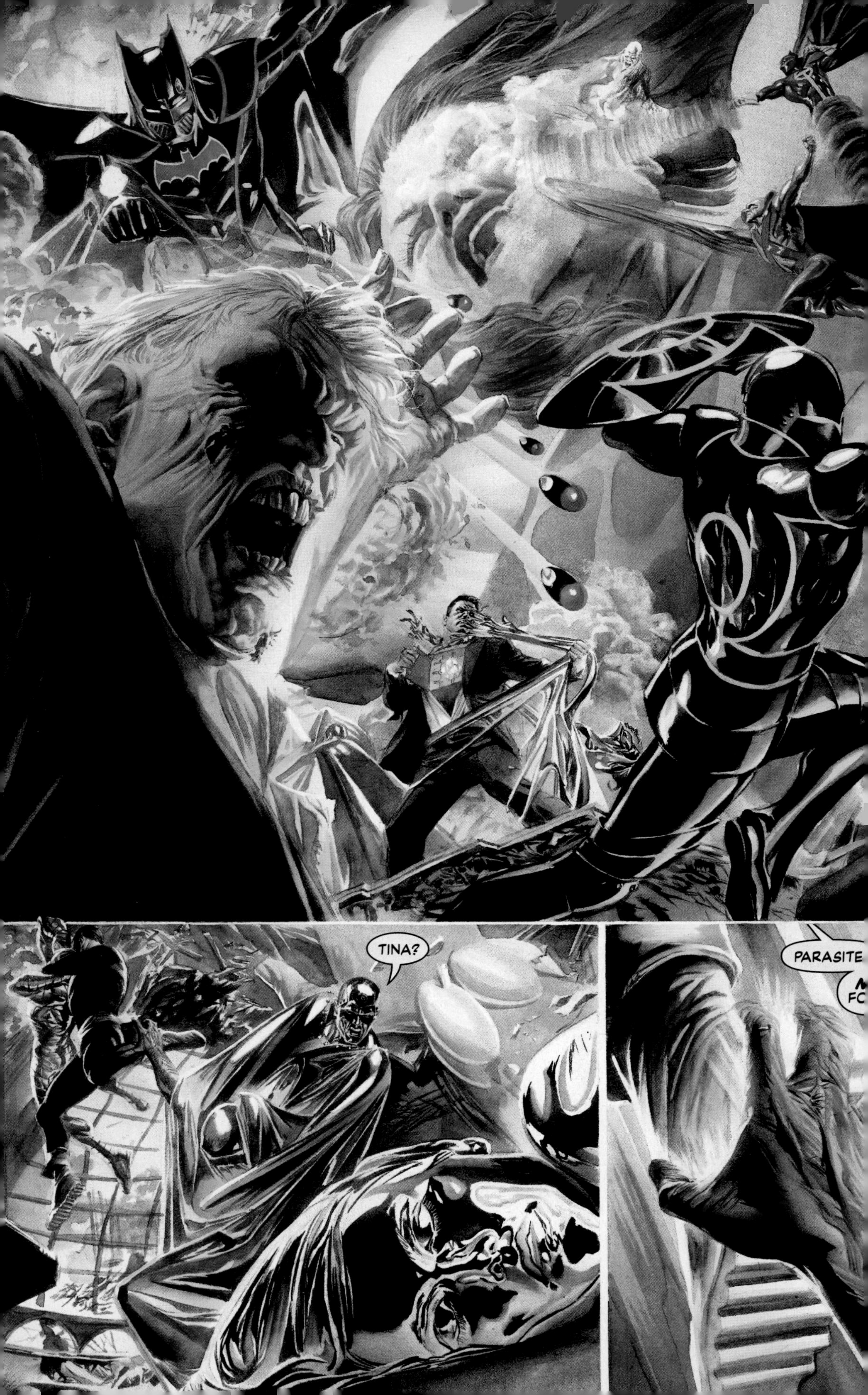
TINA?
PARASITE

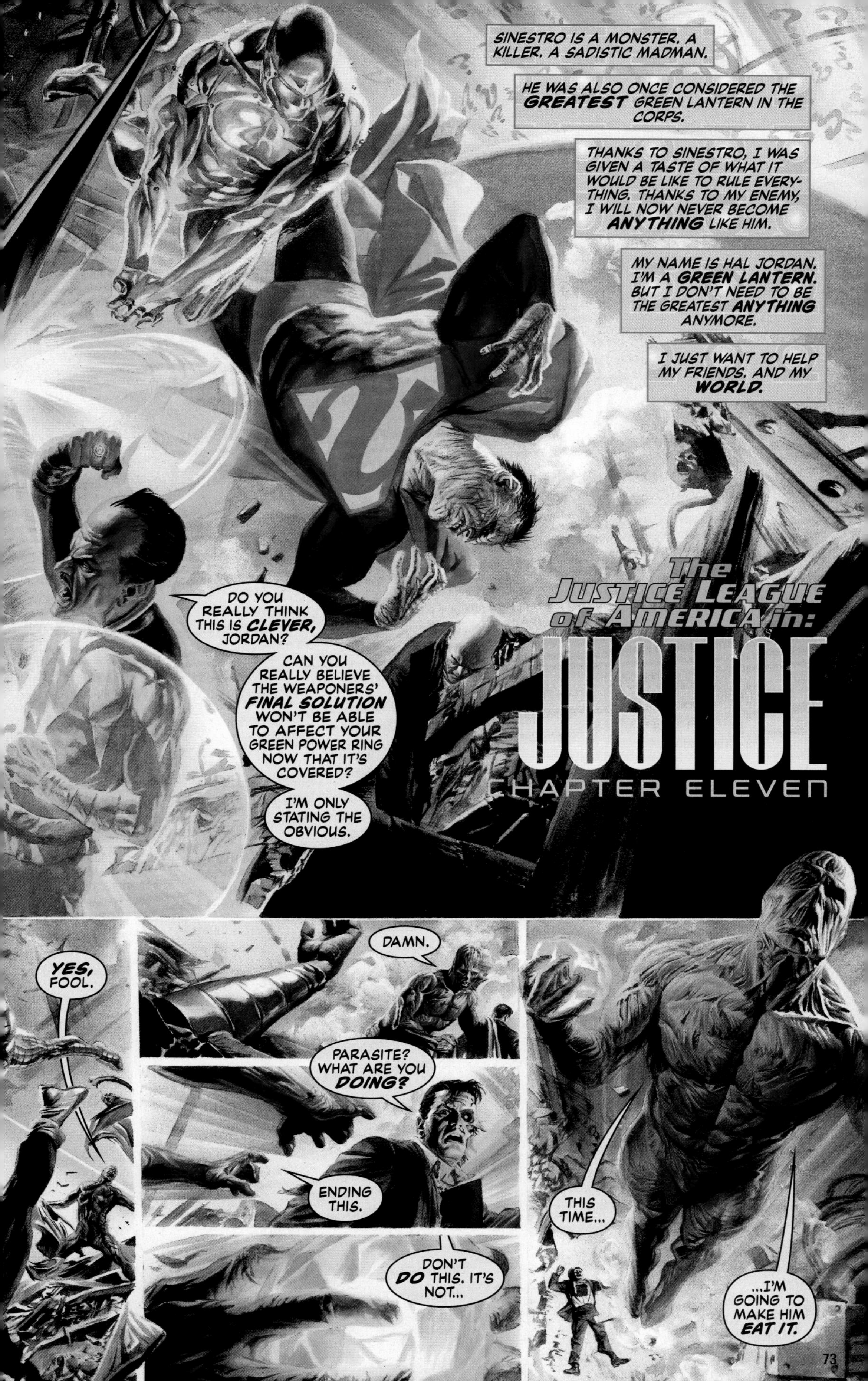
SINESTRO IS A MONSTER. A KILLER. A SADISTIC MADMAN.
HE WAS ALSO ONCE CONSIDERED THE **GREATEST** GREEN LANTERN IN THE CORPS.
THANKS TO SINESTRO, I WAS GIVEN A TASTE OF WHAT IT WOULD BE LIKE TO RULE EVERYTHING. THANKS TO MY ENEMY, I WILL NOW NEVER BECOME **ANYTHING** LIKE HIM.
MY NAME IS HAL JORDAN. I'M A **GREEN LANTERN.** BUT I DON'T NEED TO BE THE GREATEST **ANYTHING** ANYMORE.
I JUST WANT TO HELP MY FRIENDS. AND MY **WORLD.**
DO YOU REALLY THINK THIS IS **CLEVER,** JORDAN?
CAN YOU REALLY BELIEVE THE WEAPONERS' **FINAL SOLUTION** WON'T BE ABLE TO AFFECT YOUR GREEN POWER RING NOW THAT IT'S COVERED?
I'M ONLY STATING THE OBVIOUS.
The JUSTICE LEAGUE of AMERICA in:
JUSTICE
CHAPTER ELEVEN
YES, FOOL.
DAMN.
PARASITE? WHAT ARE YOU **DOING?**
ENDING THIS.
DON'T **DO** THIS. IT'S NOT...
THIS TIME...
...I'M GOING TO MAKE HIM **EAT IT.**

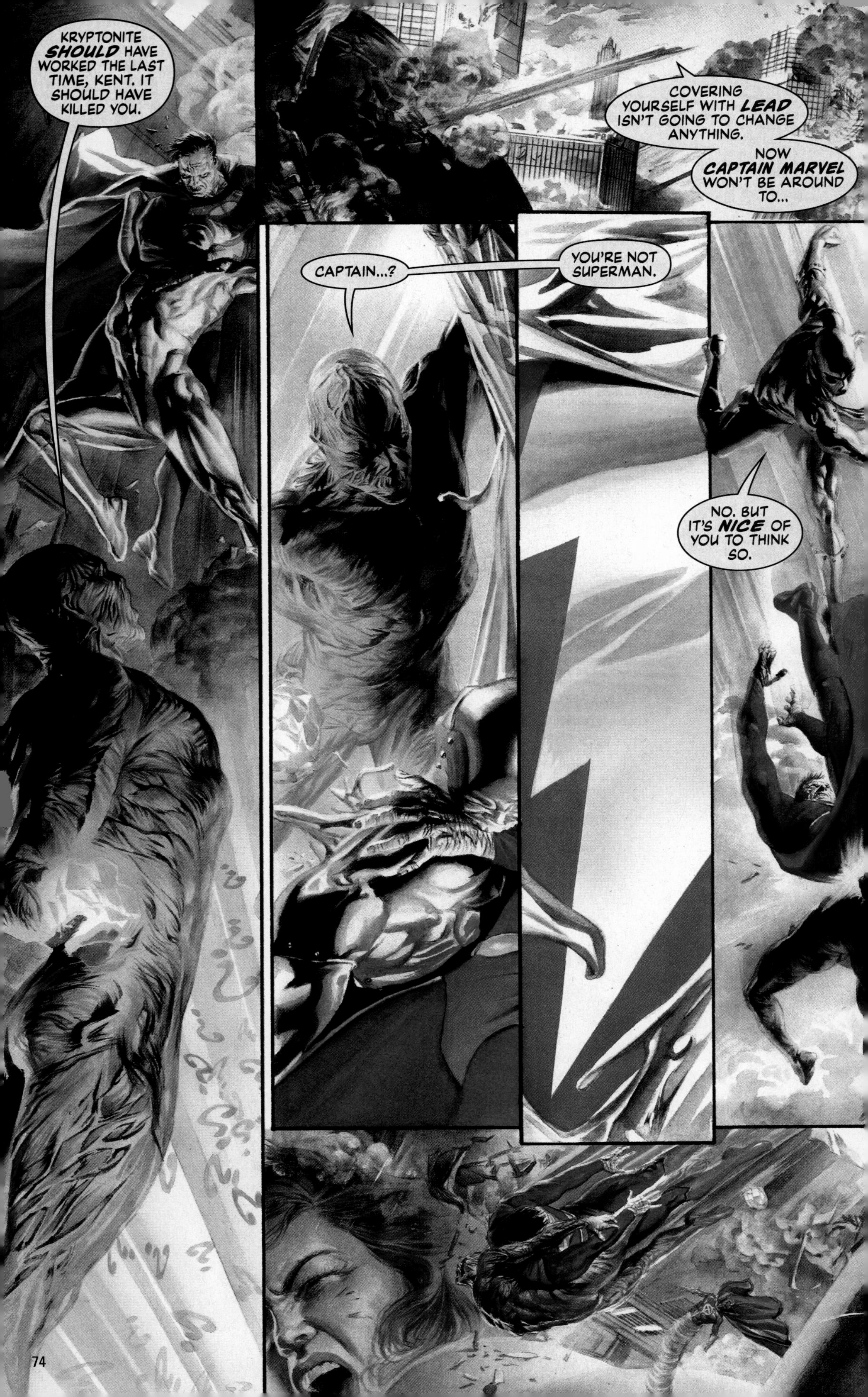
KRYPTONITE SHOULD HAVE WORKED THE LAST TIME, KENT. IT SHOULD HAVE KILLED YOU.
COVERING YOURSELF WITH LEAD ISN'T GOING TO CHANGE ANYTHING.
NOW CAPTAIN MARVEL WON'T BE AROUND TO...
CAPTAIN...?
YOU'RE NOT SUPERMAN.
NO. BUT IT'S NICE OF YOU TO THINK SO.

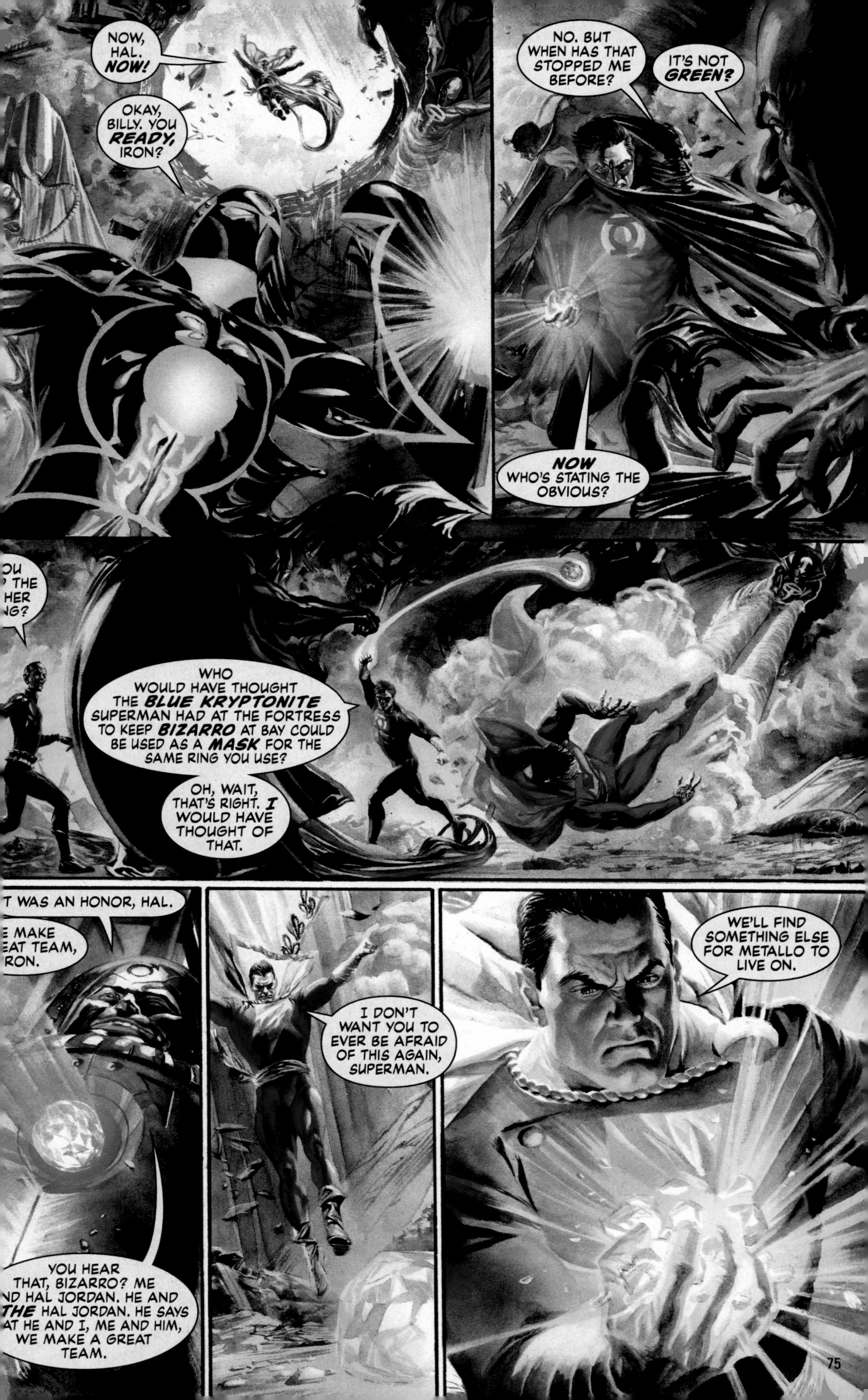
NOW, HAL. NOW!
OKAY, BILLY. YOU READY, IRON?
NO. BUT WHEN HAS THAT STOPPED ME BEFORE?
IT'S NOT GREEN?
NOW WHO'S STATING THE OBVIOUS?
OU
THE
HER
NG?
WHO WOULD HAVE THOUGHT THE BLUE KRYPTONITE SUPERMAN HAD AT THE FORTRESS TO KEEP BIZARRO AT BAY COULD BE USED AS A MASK FOR THE SAME RING YOU USE?
OH, WAIT, THAT'S RIGHT. I WOULD HAVE THOUGHT OF THAT.
T WAS AN HONOR, HAL.
E MAKE
EAT TEAM,
RON.
YOU HEAR THAT, BIZARRO? ME
ND HAL JORDAN. HE AND
THE HAL JORDAN. HE SAYS
AT HE AND I, ME AND HIM,
WE MAKE A GREAT TEAM.
I DON'T WANT YOU TO EVER BE AFRAID OF THIS AGAIN, SUPERMAN.
WE'LL FIND SOMETHING ELSE FOR METALLO TO LIVE ON.

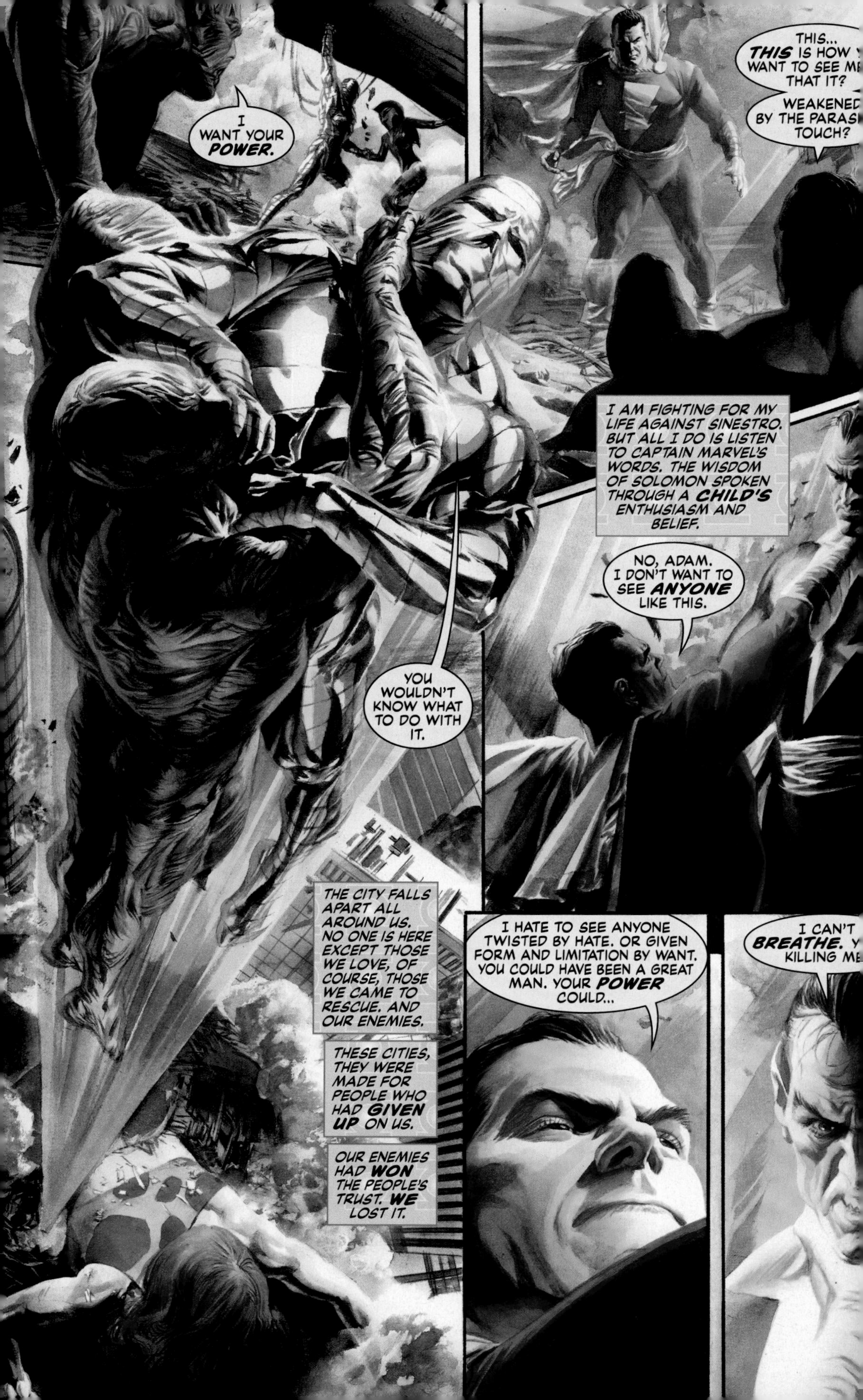
I WANT YOUR POWER.
YOU WOULDN'T KNOW WHAT TO DO WITH IT.
THE CITY FALLS APART ALL AROUND US. NO ONE IS HERE EXCEPT THOSE WE LOVE, OF COURSE, THOSE WE CAME TO RESCUE. AND OUR ENEMIES.
THESE CITIES, THEY WERE MADE FOR PEOPLE WHO HAD GIVEN UP ON US.
OUR ENEMIES HAD WON THE PEOPLE'S TRUST. WE LOST IT.
THIS... THIS IS HOW WANT TO SEE M THAT IT?
WEAKENED BY THE PARAS TOUCH?
I AM FIGHTING FOR MY LIFE AGAINST SINESTRO. BUT ALL I DO IS LISTEN TO CAPTAIN MARVEL'S WORDS. THE WISDOM OF SOLOMON SPOKEN THROUGH A CHILD'S ENTHUSIASM AND BELIEF.
NO, ADAM. I DON'T WANT TO SEE ANYONE LIKE THIS.
I HATE TO SEE ANYONE TWISTED BY HATE. OR GIVEN FORM AND LIMITATION BY WANT. YOU COULD HAVE BEEN A GREAT MAN. YOUR POWER COULD...
I CAN'T BREATHE. Y KILLING ME

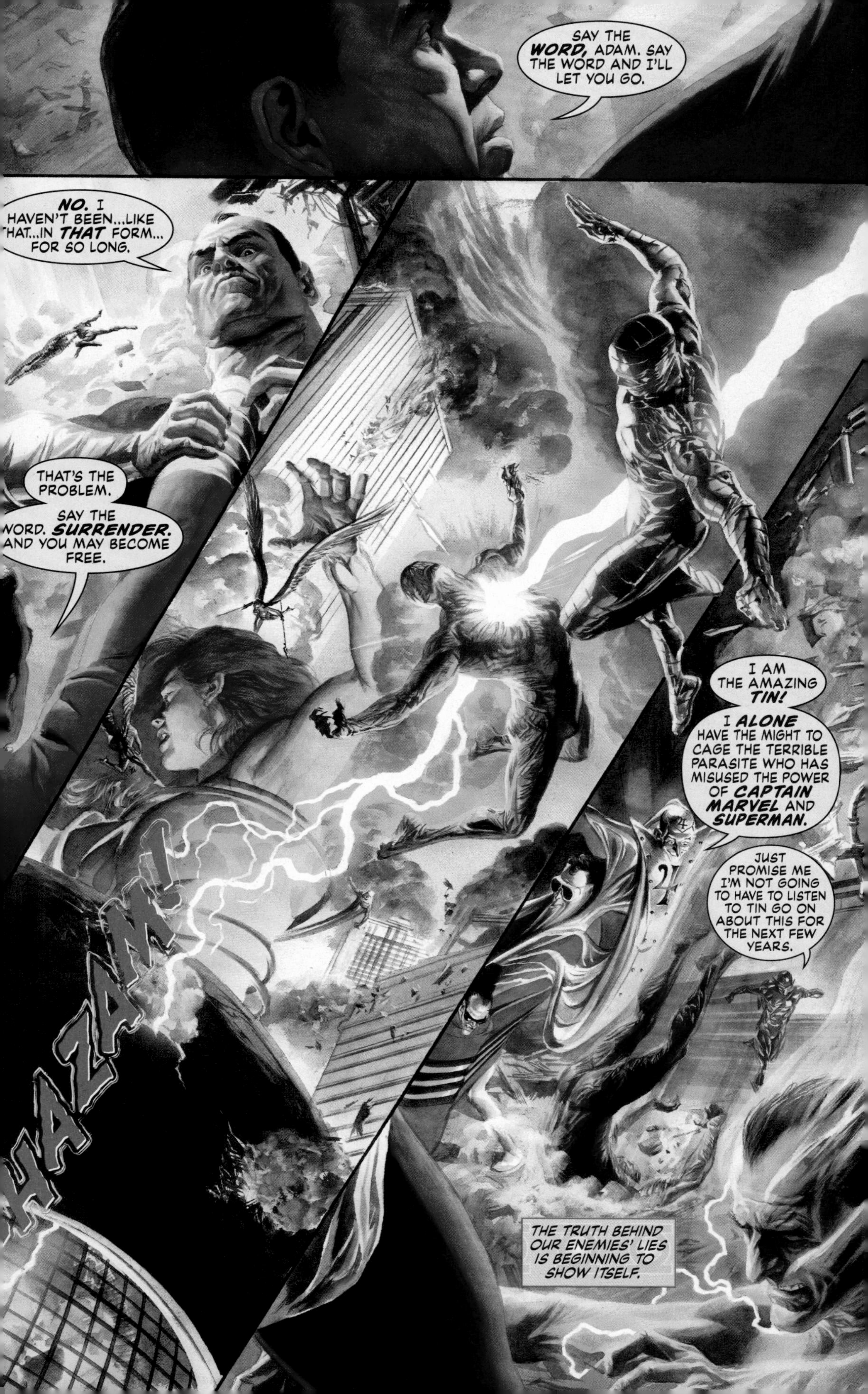
SAY THE WORD, ADAM. SAY THE WORD AND I'LL LET YOU GO.
NO. I HAVEN'T BEEN...LIKE THAT...IN THAT FORM... FOR SO LONG.
THAT'S THE PROBLEM.
SAY THE WORD. SURRENDER. AND YOU MAY BECOME FREE.
HAZAM!
I AM THE AMAZING TIN!
I ALONE HAVE THE MIGHT TO CAGE THE TERRIBLE PARASITE WHO HAS MISUSED THE POWER OF CAPTAIN MARVEL AND SUPERMAN.
JUST PROMISE ME I'M NOT GOING TO HAVE TO LISTEN TO TIN GO ON ABOUT THIS FOR THE NEXT FEW YEARS.
THE TRUTH BEHIND OUR ENEMIES' LIES IS BEGINNING TO SHOW ITSELF.

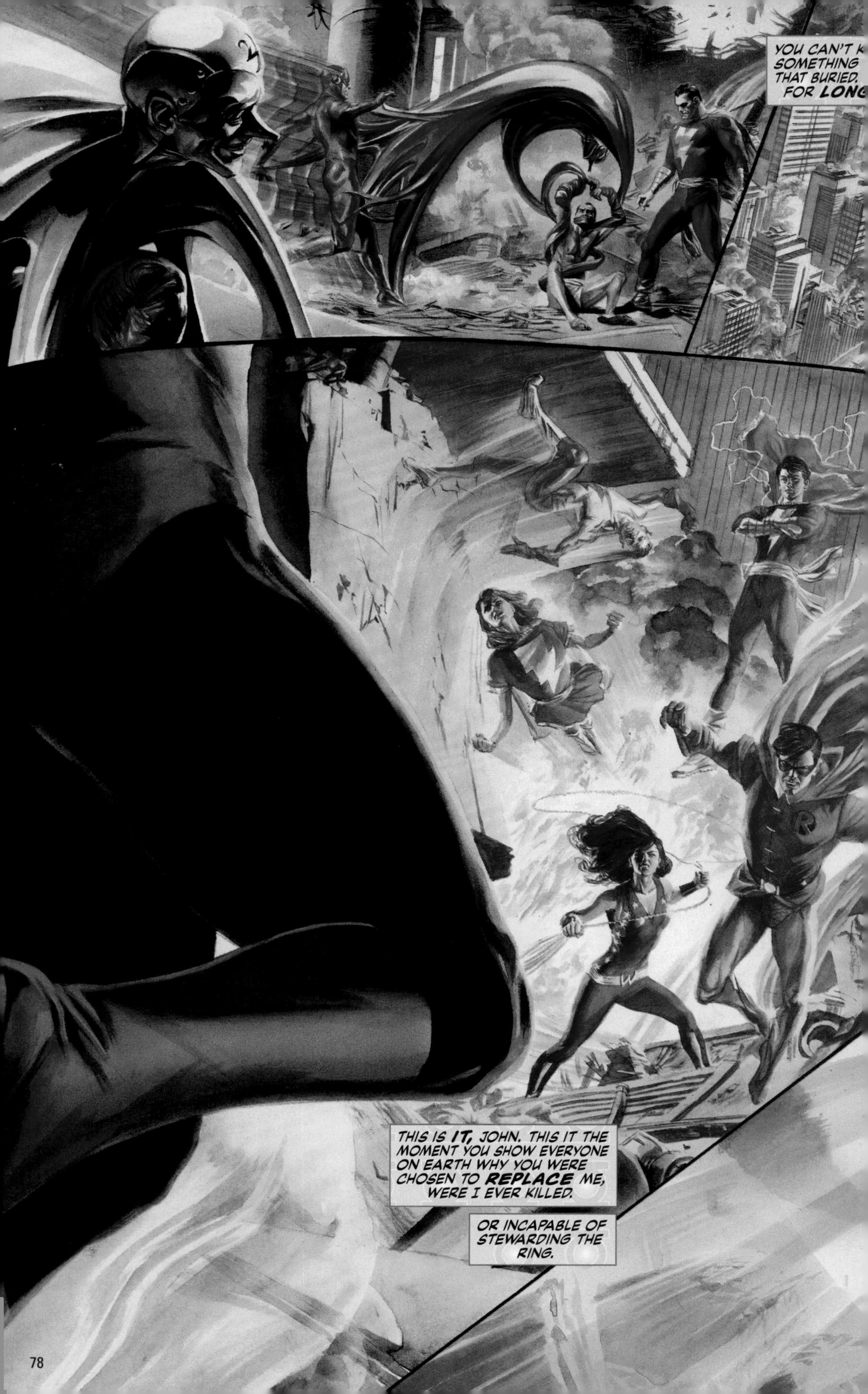
YOU CAN'T K SOMETHING THAT BURIED FOR LONG
THIS IS IT, JOHN. THIS IT THE MOMENT YOU SHOW EVERYONE ON EARTH WHY YOU WERE CHOSEN TO REPLACE ME, WERE I EVER KILLED.
OR INCAPABLE OF STEWARDING THE RING.

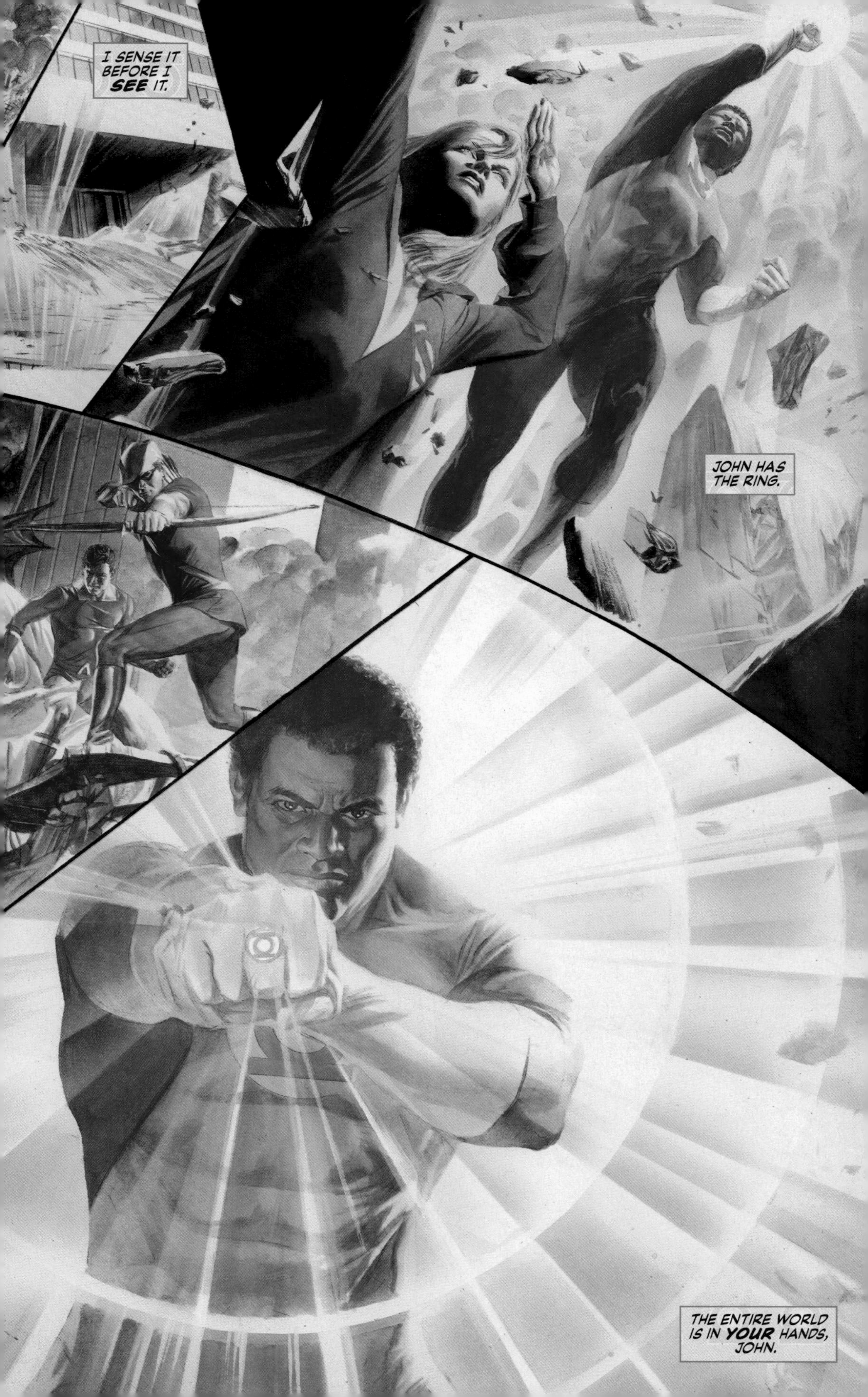
I SENSE IT BEFORE I SEE IT.
JOHN HAS THE RING.
THE ENTIRE WORLD IS IN YOUR HANDS, JOHN.

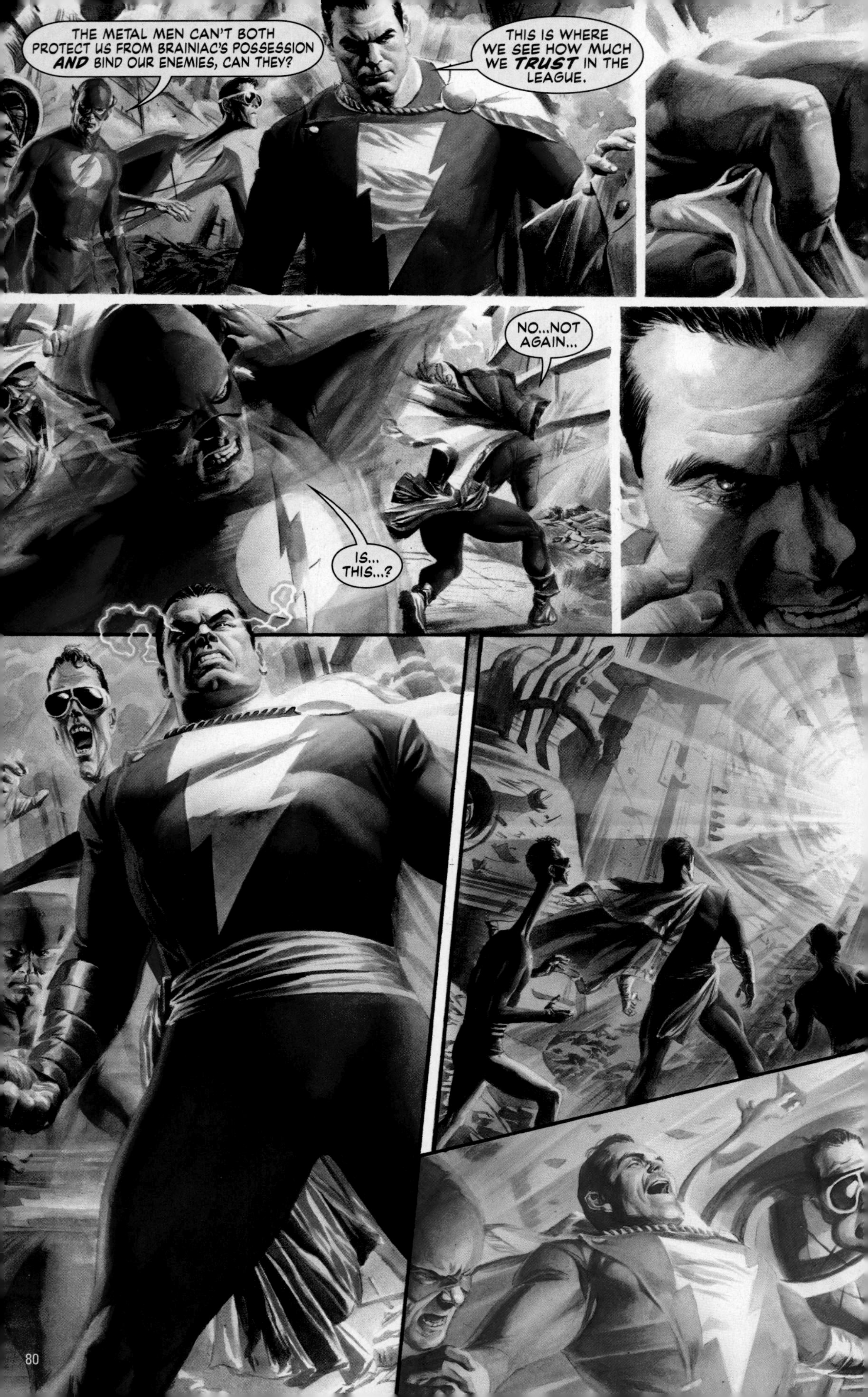
THE METAL MEN CAN'T BOTH PROTECT US FROM BRAINIAC'S POSSESSION AND BIND OUR ENEMIES, CAN THEY?
THIS IS WHERE WE SEE HOW MUCH WE TRUST IN THE LEAGUE.
NO...NOT AGAIN...
IS... THIS...?

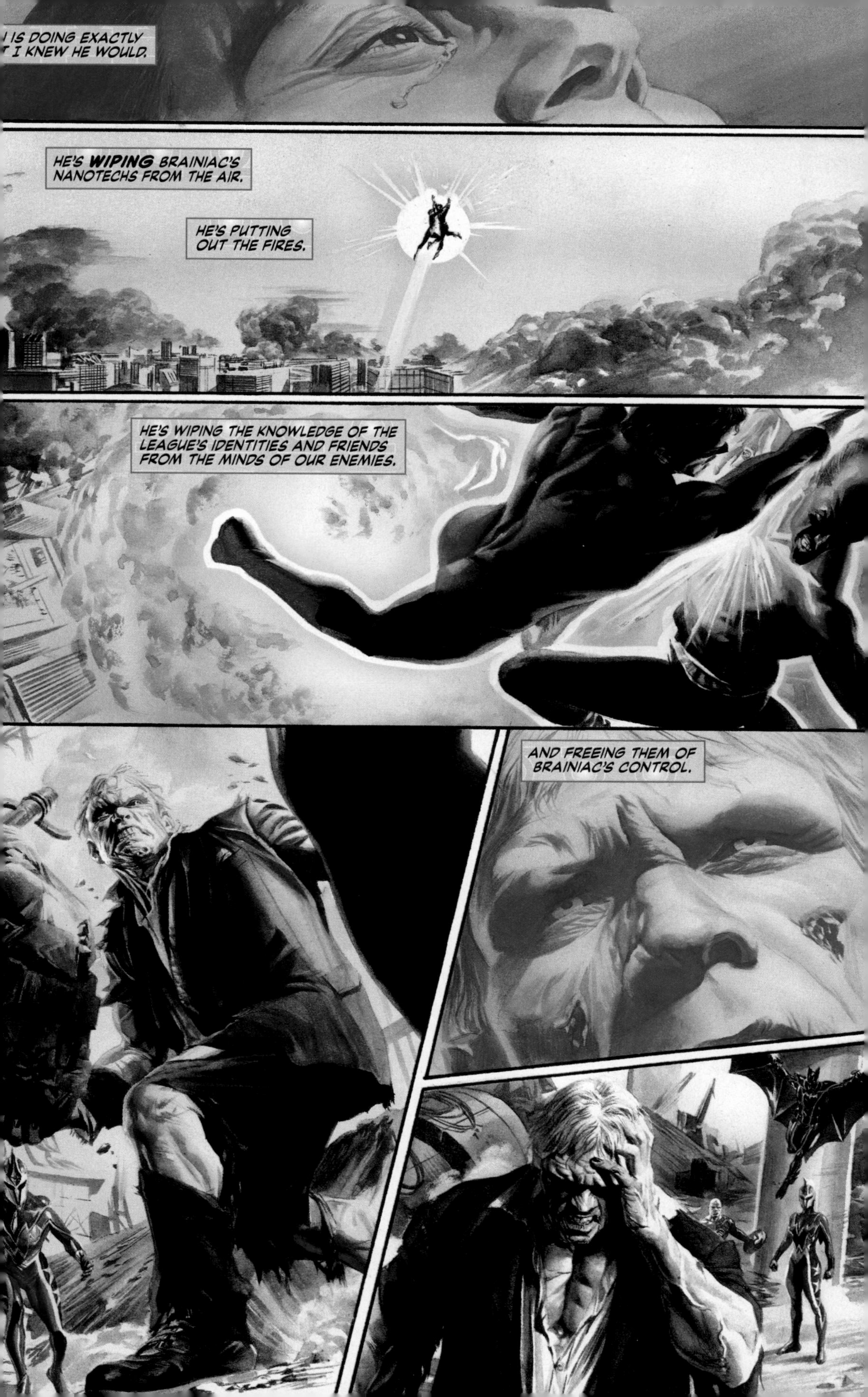

I IS DOING EXACTLY
T I KNEW HE WOULD.
HE'S WIPING BRAINIAC'S NANOTECHS FROM THE AIR.
HE'S PUTTING OUT THE FIRES.
HE'S WIPING THE KNOWLEDGE OF THE LEAGUE'S IDENTITIES AND FRIENDS FROM THE MINDS OF OUR ENEMIES.
AND FREEING THEM OF BRAINIAC'S CONTROL.

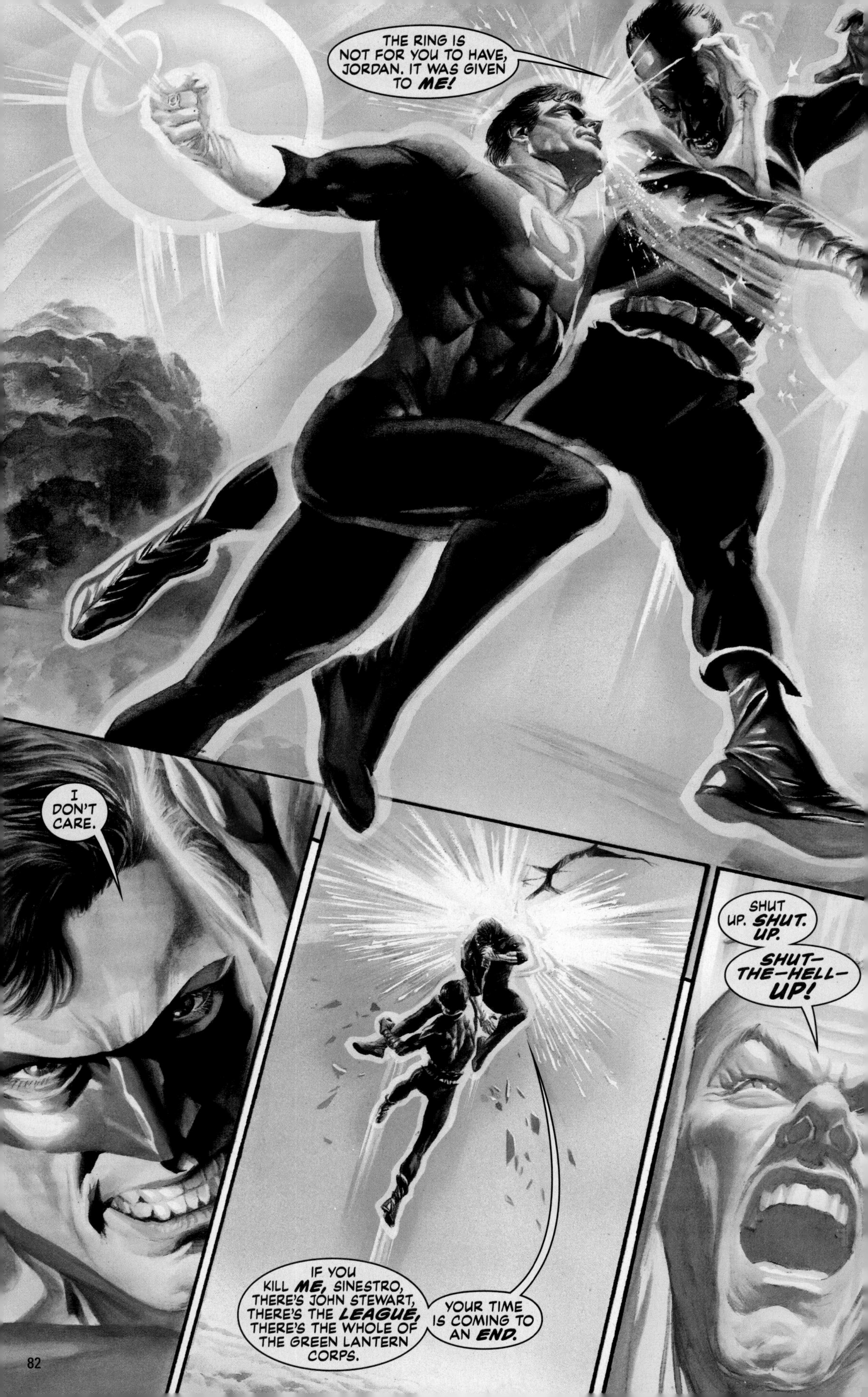
THE RING IS NOT FOR YOU TO HAVE, JORDAN. IT WAS GIVEN TO ME!
I DON'T CARE.
IF YOU KILL ME, SINESTRO, THERE'S JOHN STEWART, THERE'S THE LEAGUE, THERE'S THE WHOLE OF THE GREEN LANTERN CORPS.
YOUR TIME IS COMING TO AN END.
SHUT UP. SHUT. UP.
SHUT—THE—HELL—UP!

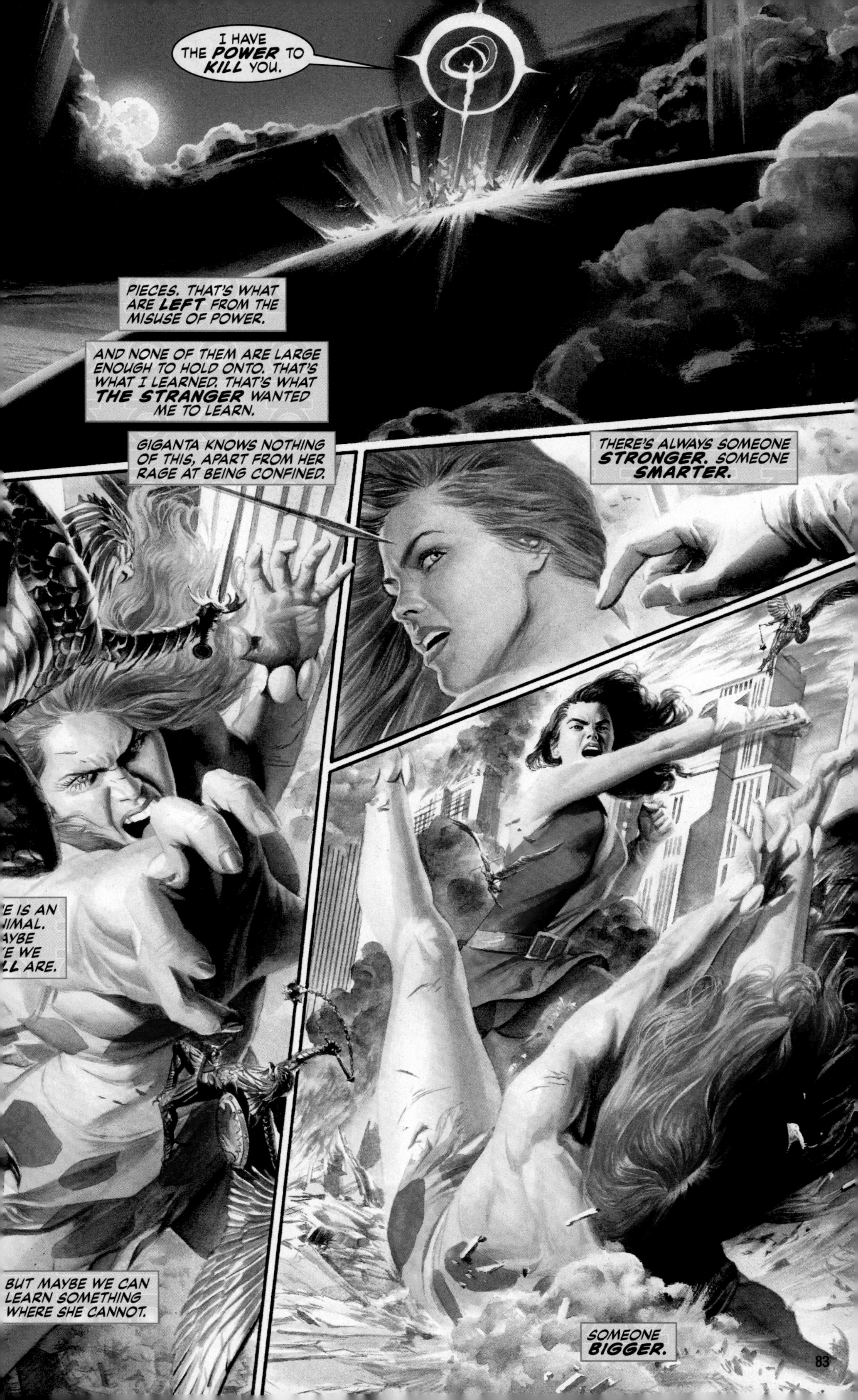
I HAVE THE POWER TO KILL YOU.
PIECES. THAT'S WHAT ARE LEFT FROM THE MISUSE OF POWER.
AND NONE OF THEM ARE LARGE ENOUGH TO HOLD ONTO. THAT'S WHAT I LEARNED. THAT'S WHAT THE STRANGER WANTED ME TO LEARN.
GIGANTA KNOWS NOTHING OF THIS, APART FROM HER RAGE AT BEING CONFINED.
THERE'S ALWAYS SOMEONE STRONGER. SOMEONE SMARTER.
E IS AN NIMAL. AYBE E WE LL ARE.
BUT MAYBE WE CAN LEARN SOMETHING WHERE SHE CANNOT.
SOMEONE BIGGER.

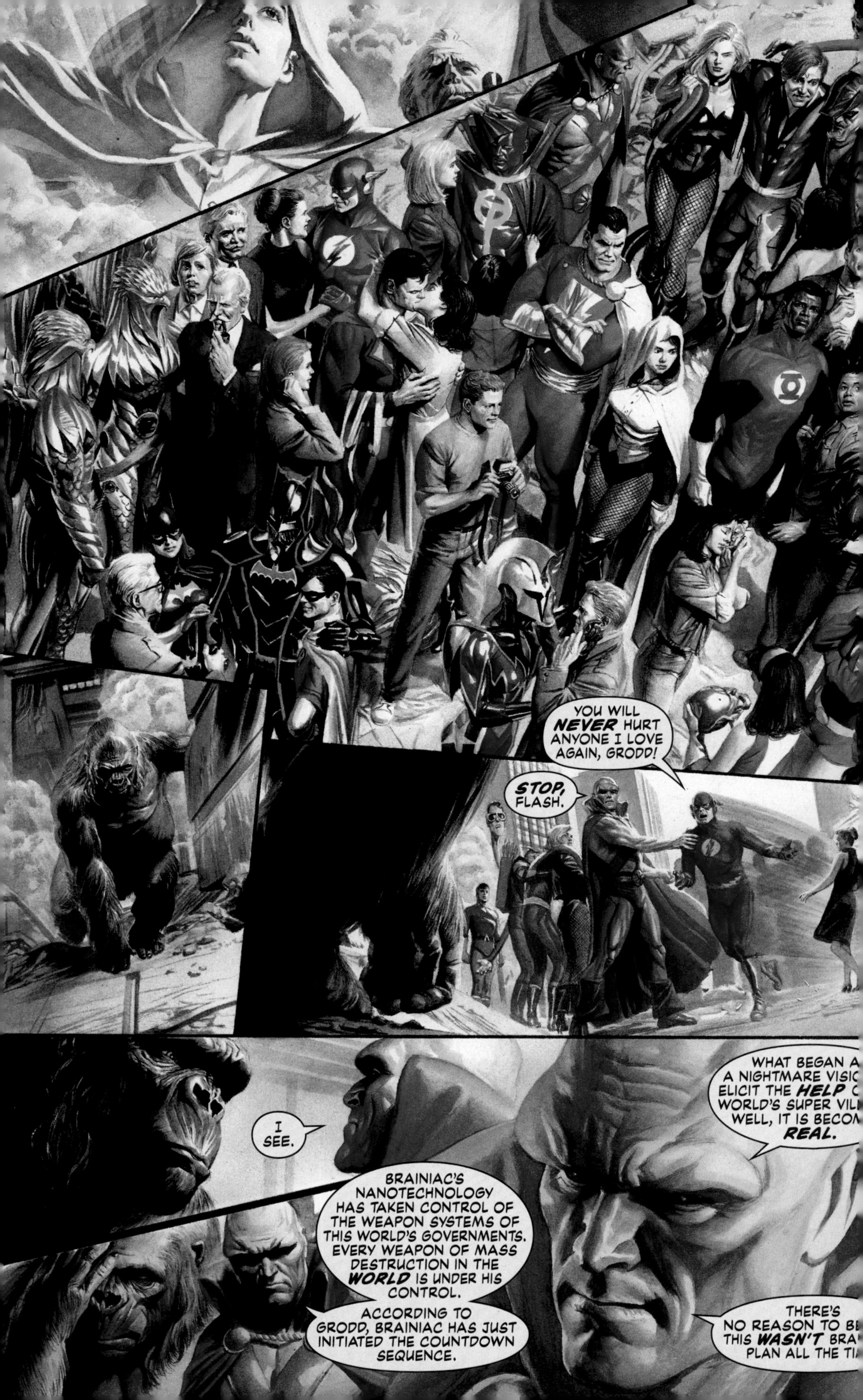

YOU WILL NEVER HURT ANYONE I LOVE AGAIN, GRODD!
STOP, FLASH.
I SEE.
WHAT BEGAN A
A NIGHTMARE VISIC
ELICIT THE HELP C
WORLD'S SUPER VIL
WELL, IT IS BECOM
REAL.
BRAINIAC'S NANOTECHNOLOGY HAS TAKEN CONTROL OF THE WEAPON SYSTEMS OF THIS WORLD'S GOVERNMENTS. EVERY WEAPON OF MASS DESTRUCTION IN THE WORLD IS UNDER HIS CONTROL.
ACCORDING TO GRODD, BRAINIAC HAS JUST INITIATED THE COUNTDOWN SEQUENCE.
THERE'S
NO REASON TO BE
THIS WASN'T BRA
PLAN ALL THE TI

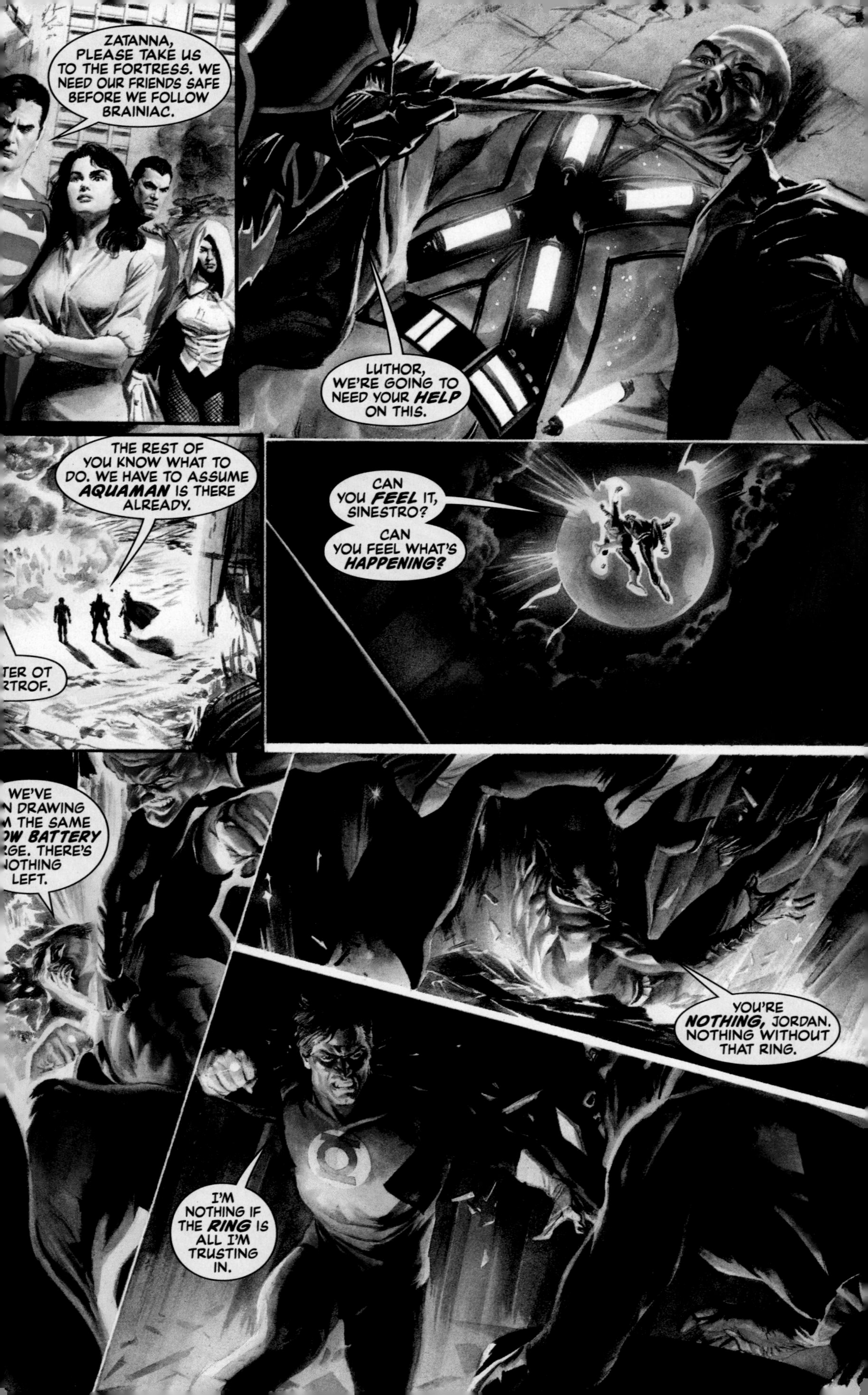
ZATANNA, PLEASE TAKE US TO THE FORTRESS. WE NEED OUR FRIENDS SAFE BEFORE WE FOLLOW BRAINIAC.
LUTHOR, WE'RE GOING TO NEED YOUR HELP ON THIS.
THE REST OF YOU KNOW WHAT TO DO. WE HAVE TO ASSUME AQUAMAN IS THERE ALREADY.
TER OT RTROF.
CAN YOU FEEL IT, SINESTRO?
CAN YOU FEEL WHAT'S HAPPENING?
WE'VE N DRAWING M THE SAME OW BATTERY RGE. THERE'S NOTHING LEFT.
YOU'RE NOTHING, JORDAN. NOTHING WITHOUT THAT RING.
I'M NOTHING IF THE RING IS ALL I'M TRUSTING IN.

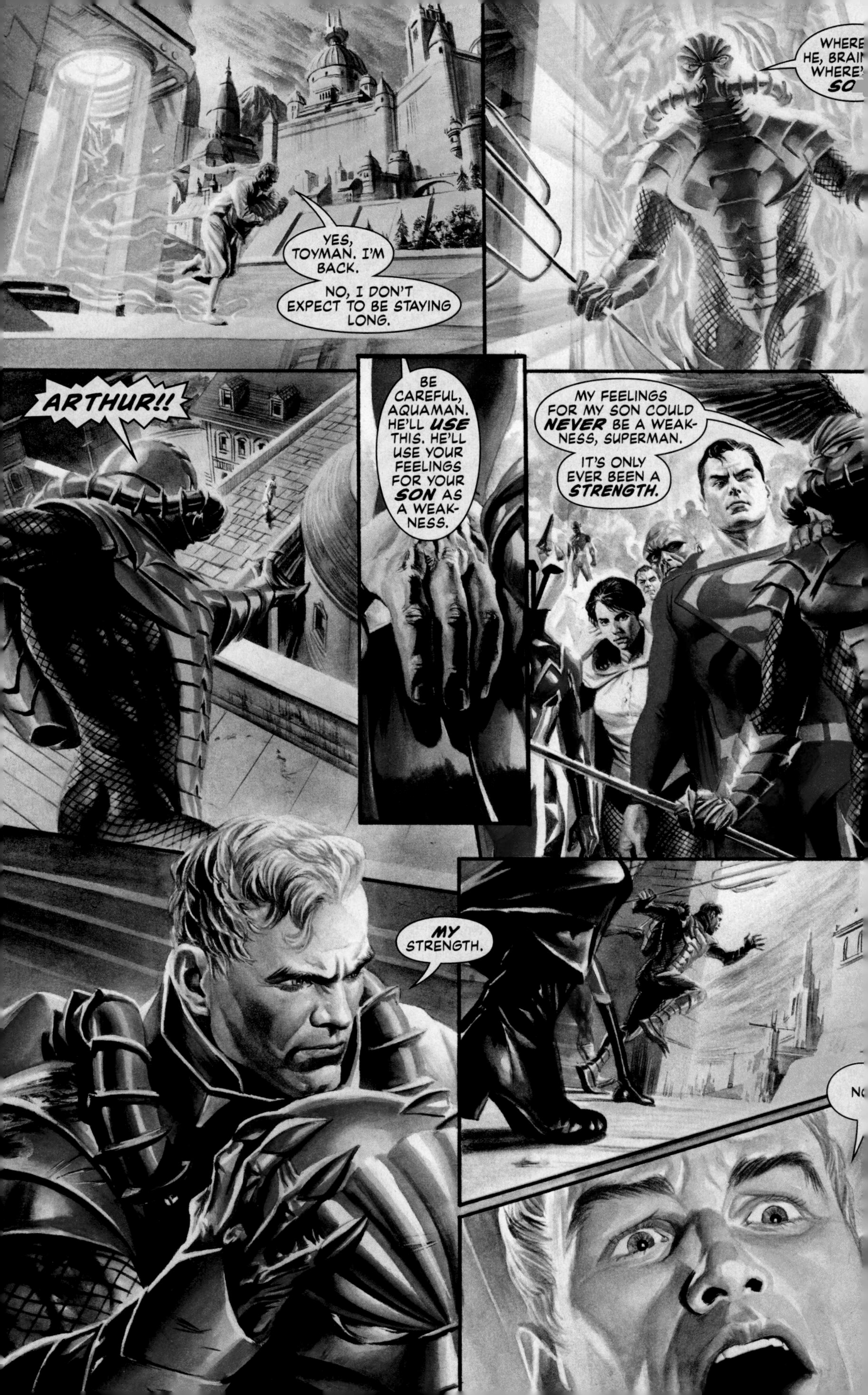

YES, TOYMAN. I'M BACK.
NO, I DON'T EXPECT TO BE STAYING LONG.
WHERE HE, BRAIN WHERE'S SO
ARTHUR!!
BE CAREFUL, AQUAMAN. HE'LL USE THIS. HE'LL USE YOUR FEELINGS FOR YOUR SON AS A WEAKNESS.
MY FEELINGS FOR MY SON COULD NEVER BE A WEAKNESS, SUPERMAN.
IT'S ONLY EVER BEEN A STRENGTH.
MY STRENGTH.
NO

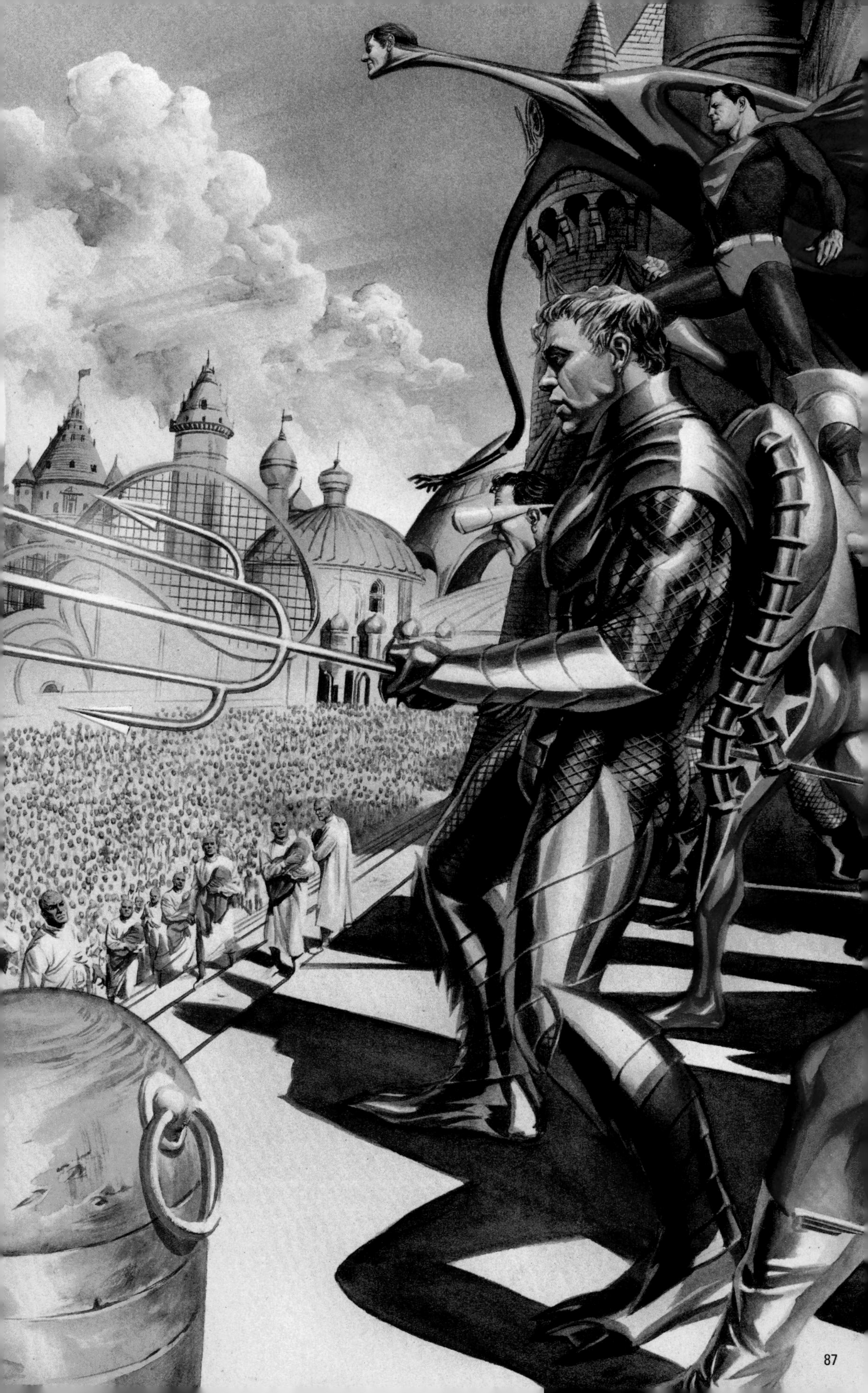

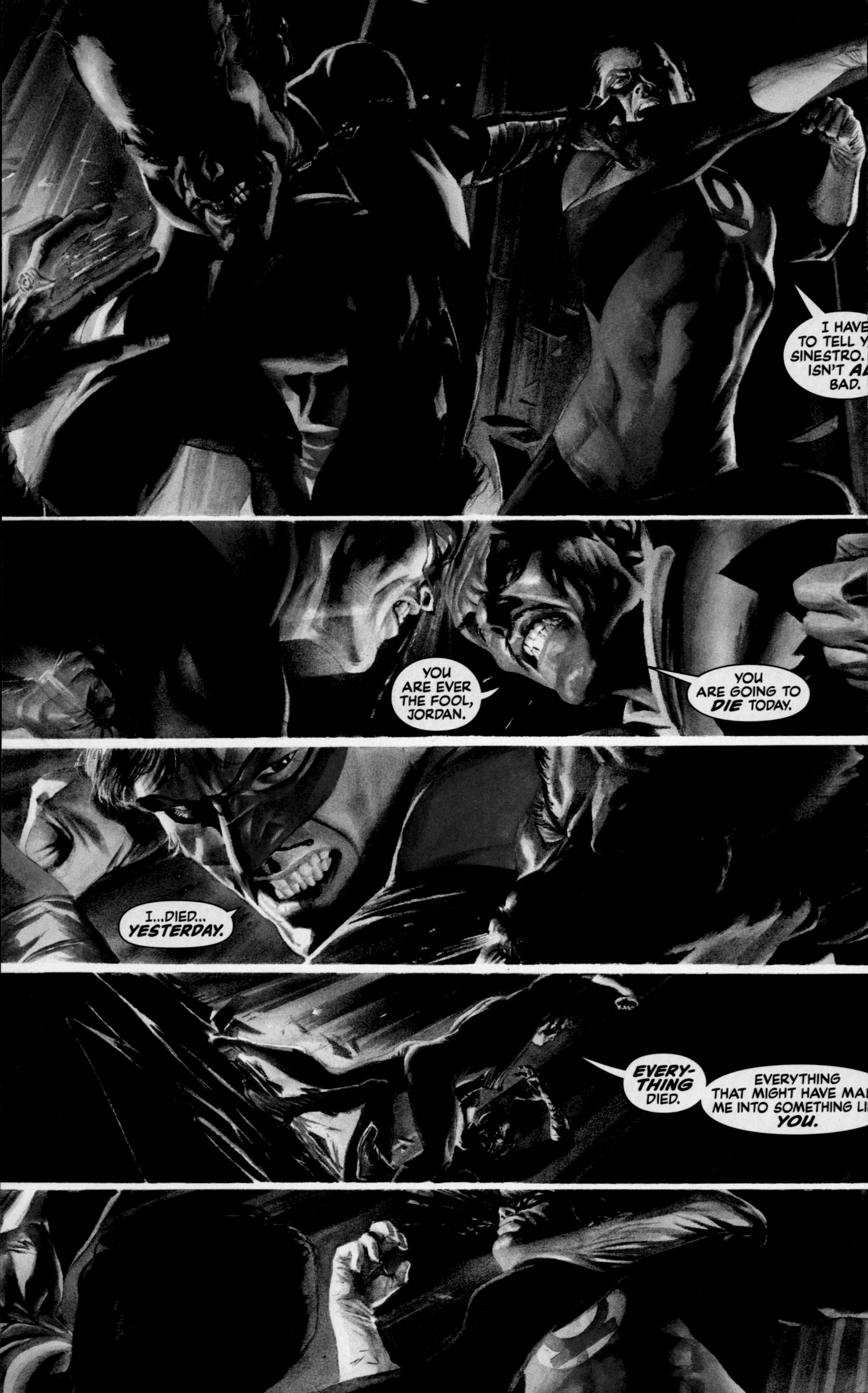
I HAVE TO TELL Y SINESTRO. ISN'T A BAD.
YOU ARE EVER THE FOOL, JORDAN.
YOU ARE GOING TO DIE TODAY.
I...DIED... YESTERDAY.
EVERY-THING DIED.
EVERYTHING THAT MIGHT HAVE MA ME INTO SOMETHING LI YOU.

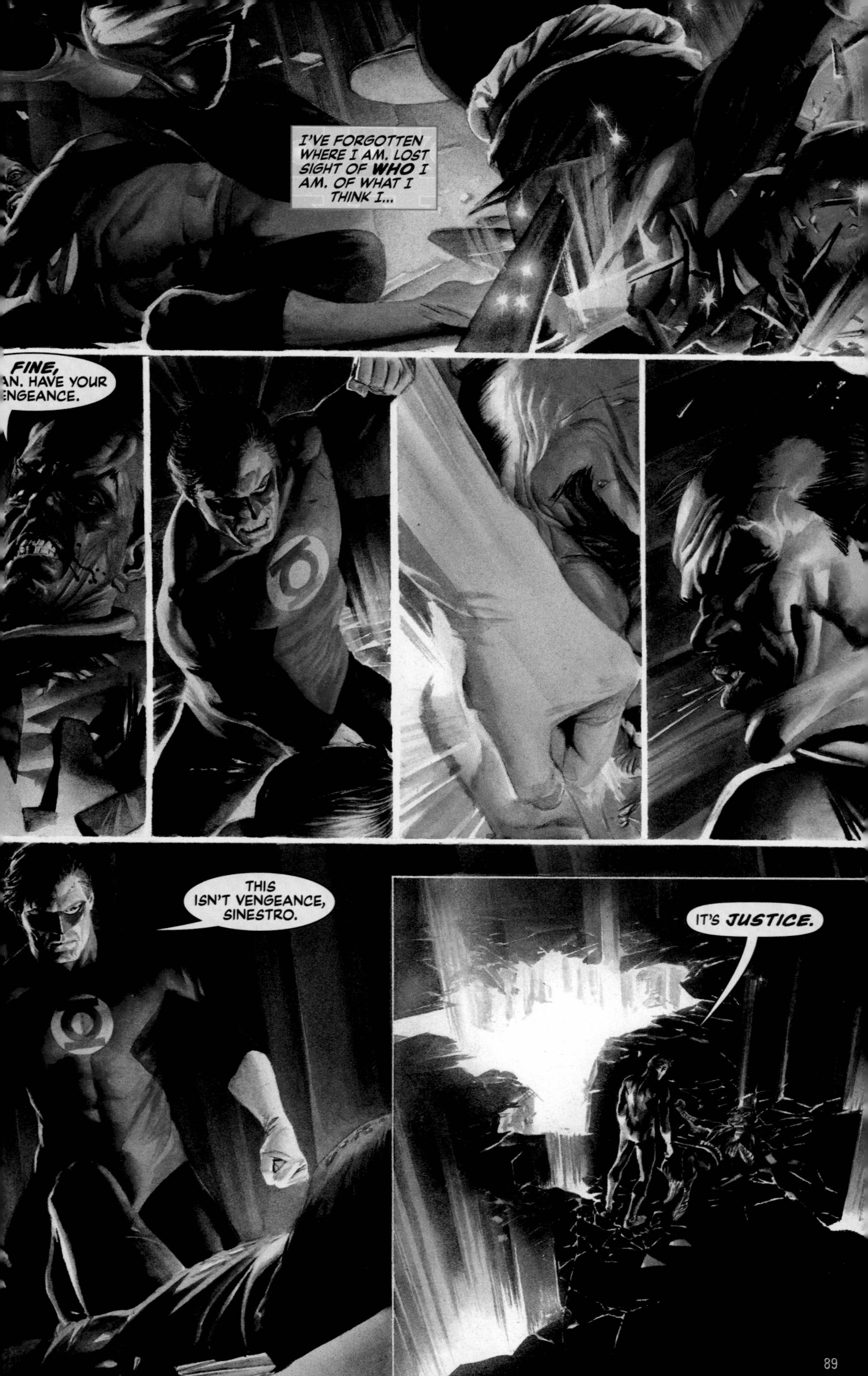
I'VE FORGOTTEN WHERE I AM. LOST SIGHT OF WHO I AM. OF WHAT I THINK I...
FINE, AN. HAVE YOUR ENGEANCE.
THIS ISN'T VENGEANCE, SINESTRO.
IT'S JUSTICE.

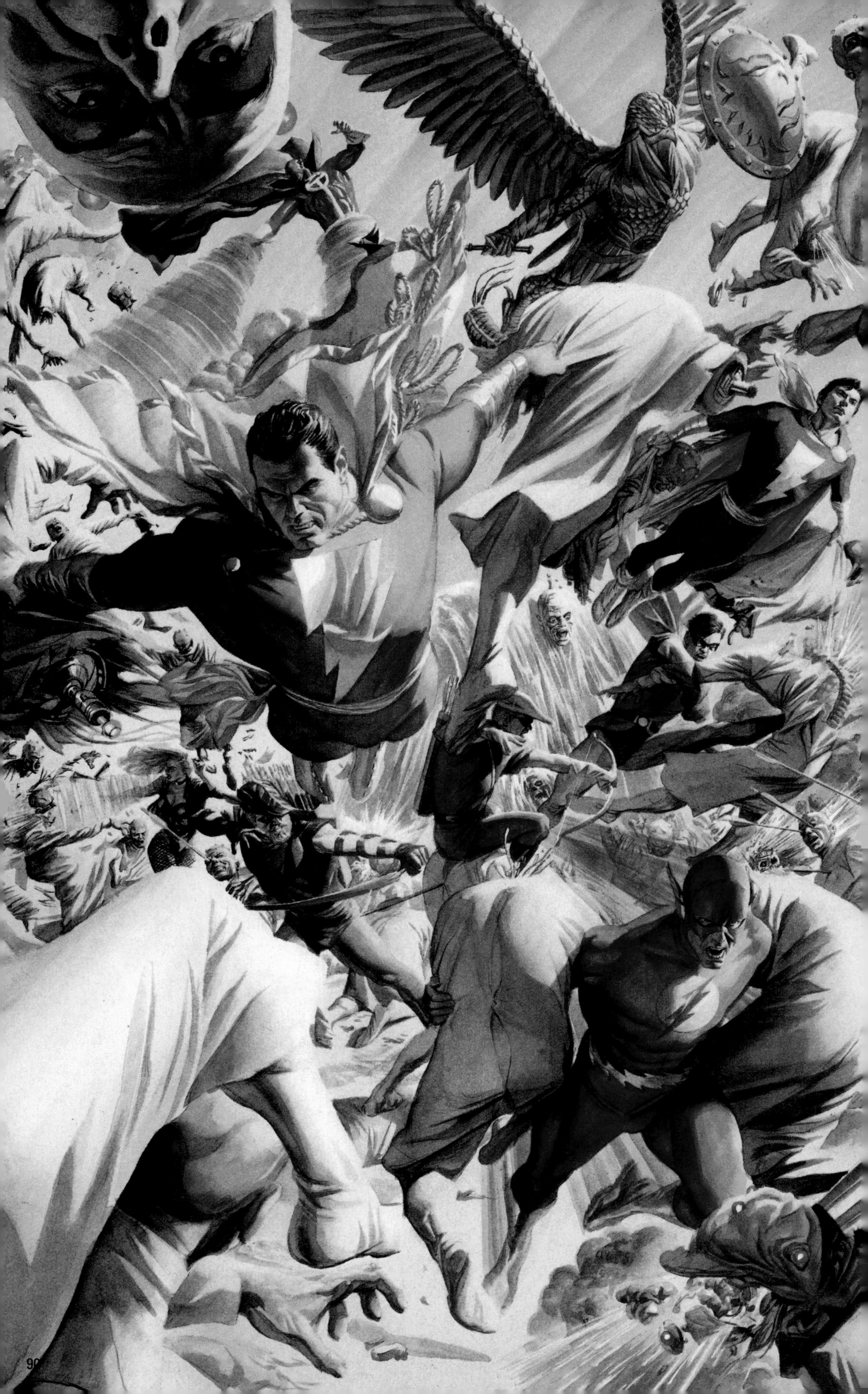

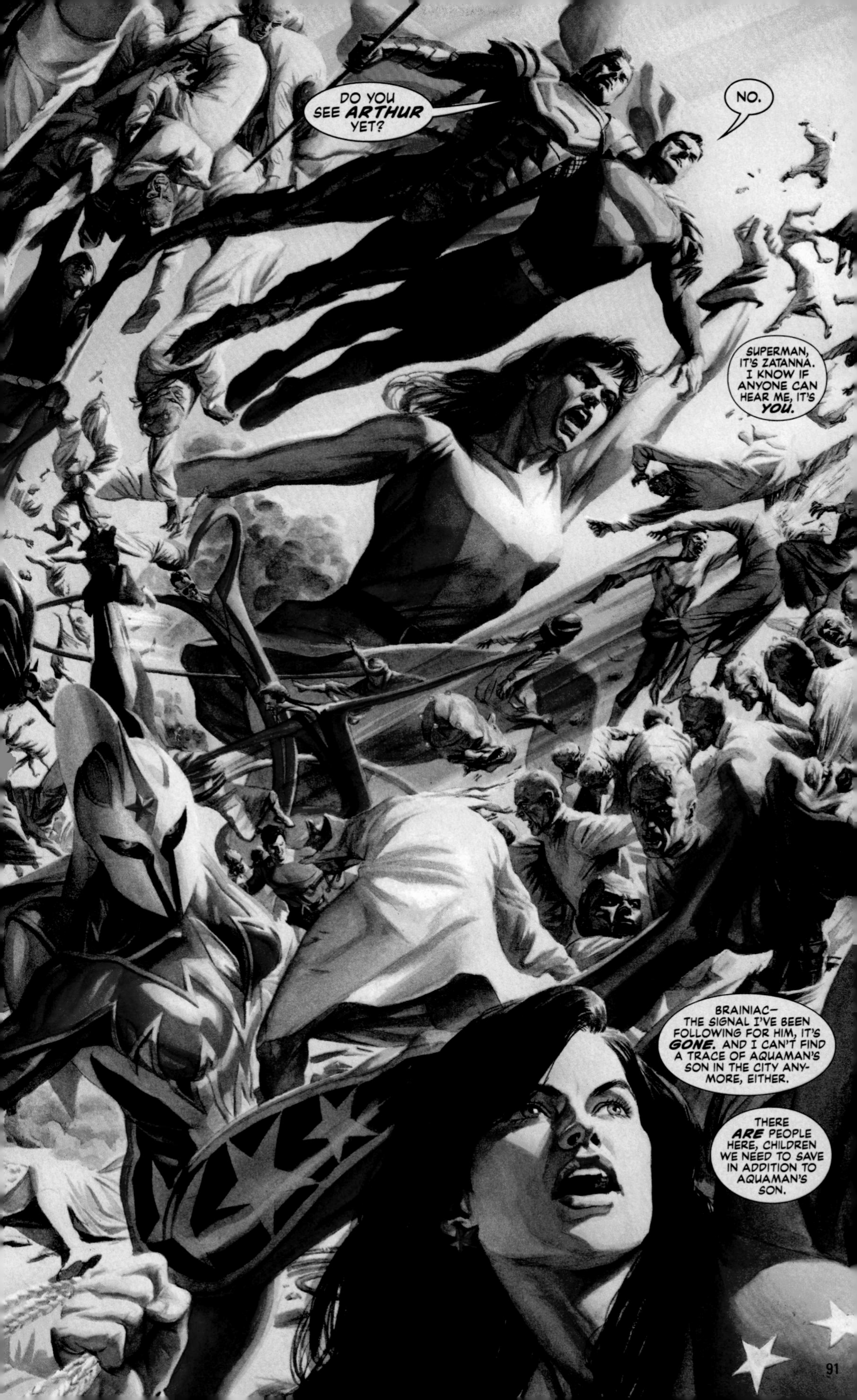
DO YOU SEE ARTHUR YET?
NO.
SUPERMAN, IT'S ZATANNA. I KNOW IF ANYONE CAN HEAR ME, IT'S YOU.
BRAINIAC— THE SIGNAL I'VE BEEN FOLLOWING FOR HIM, IT'S GONE. AND I CAN'T FIND A TRACE OF AQUAMAN'S SON IN THE CITY ANYMORE, EITHER.
THERE ARE PEOPLE HERE, CHILDREN WE NEED TO SAVE IN ADDITION TO AQUAMAN'S SON.

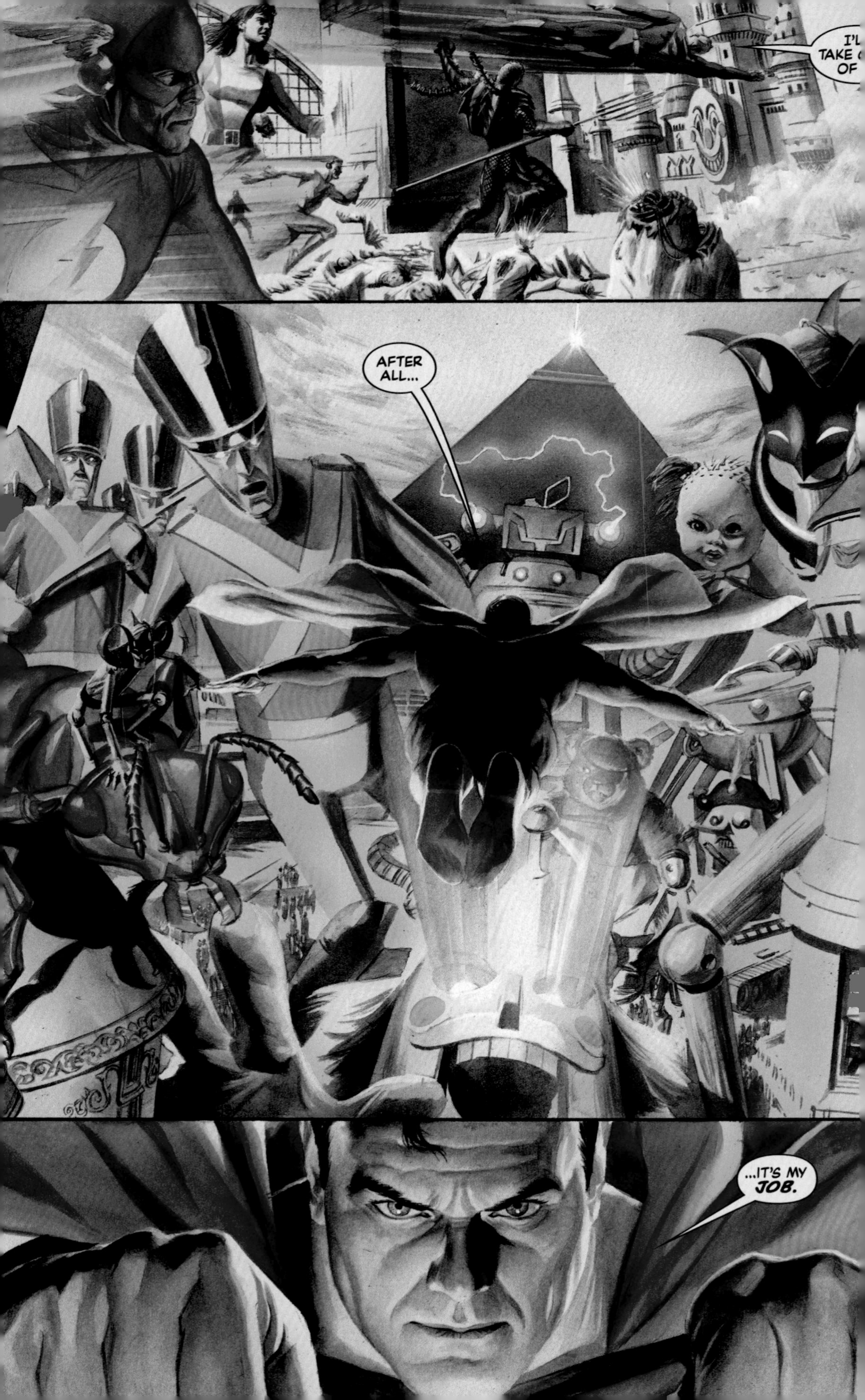
I'L TAKE OF
AFTER ALL...
...IT'S MY JOB.

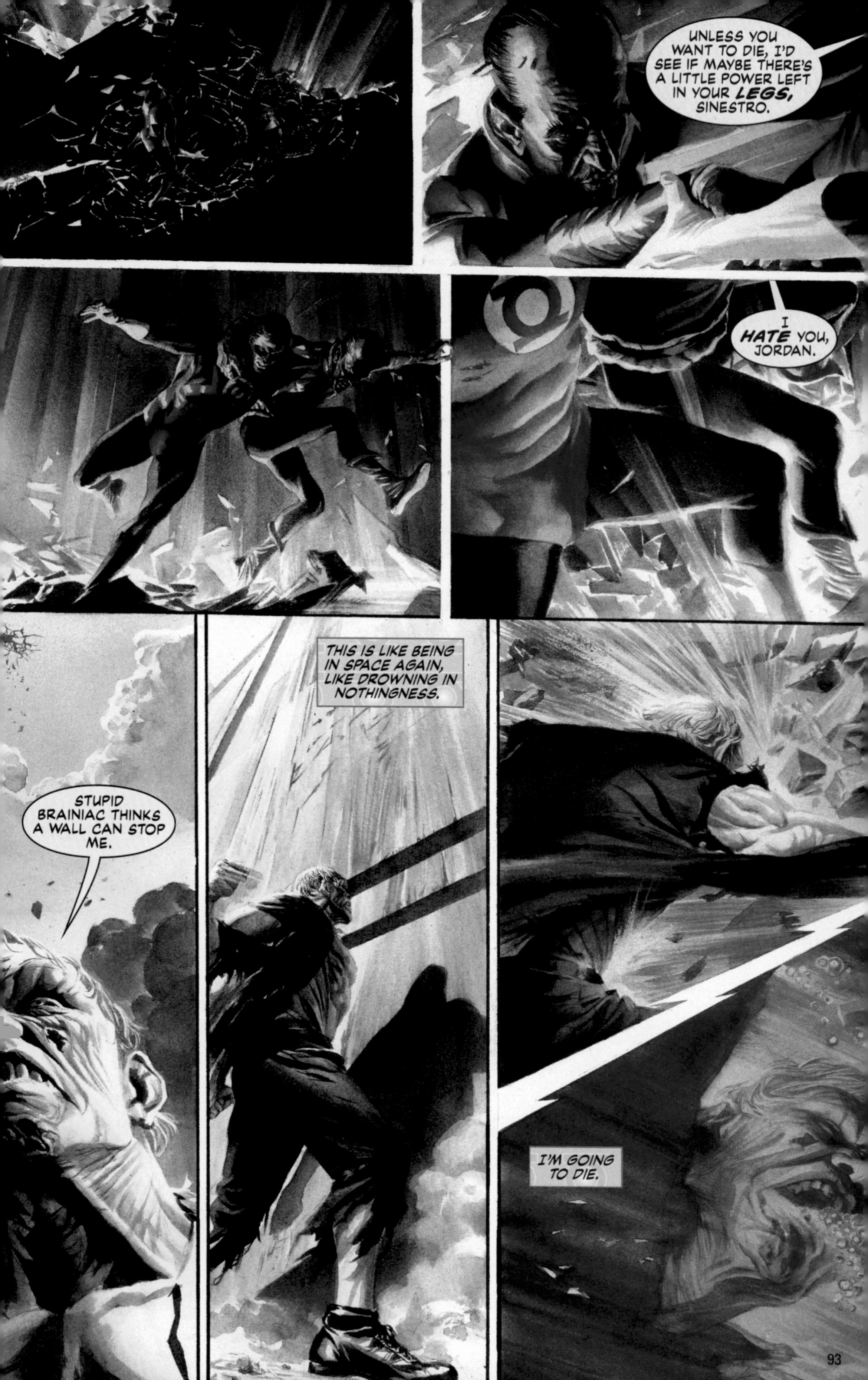

UNLESS YOU WANT TO DIE, I'D SEE IF MAYBE THERE'S A LITTLE POWER LEFT IN YOUR LEGS, SINESTRO.
I HATE YOU, JORDAN.
STUPID BRAINIAC THINKS A WALL CAN STOP ME.
THIS IS LIKE BEING IN SPACE AGAIN, LIKE DROWNING IN NOTHINGNESS.
I'M GOING TO DIE.

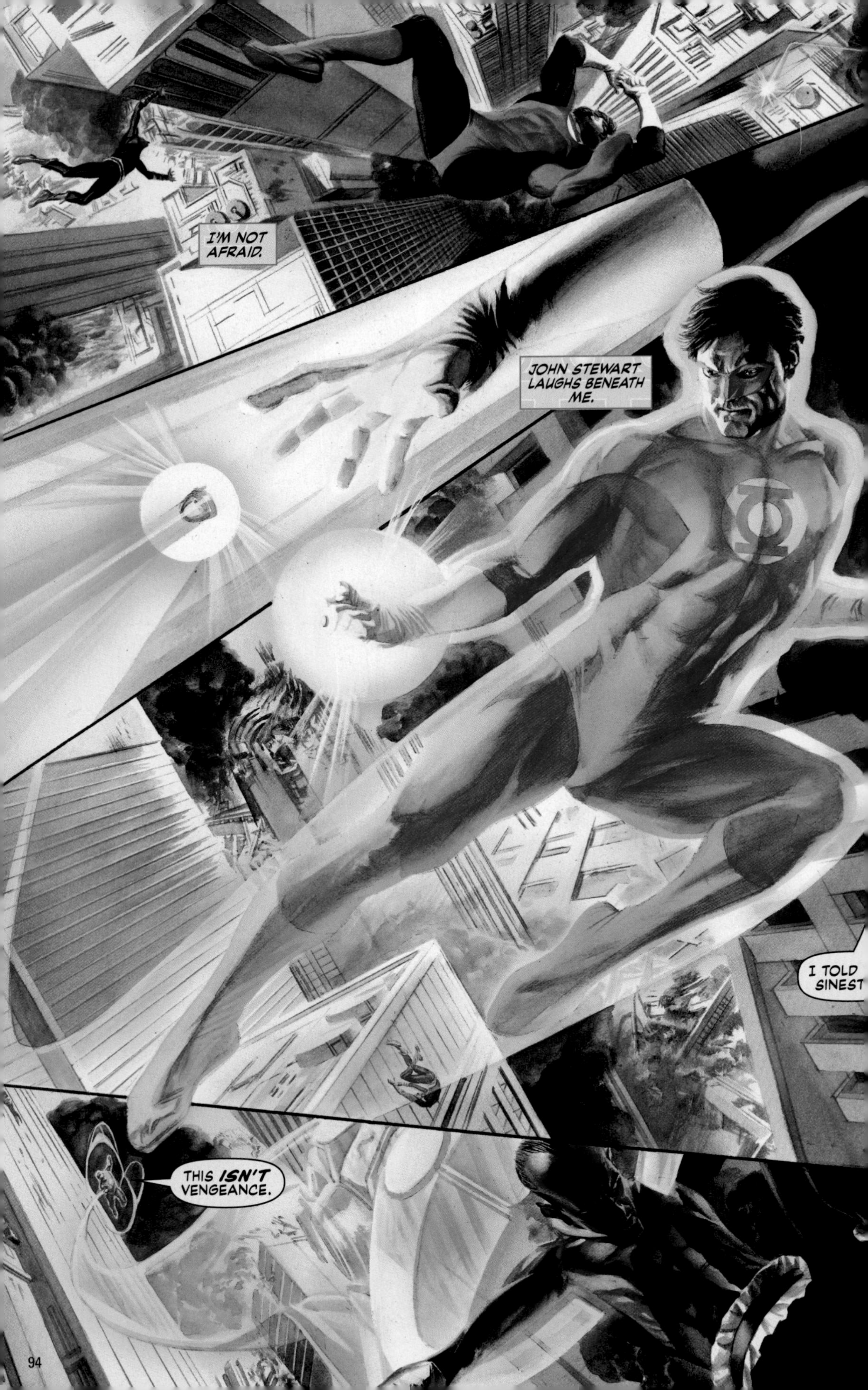
I'M NOT AFRAID.
JOHN STEWART LAUGHS BENEATH ME.
I TOLD SINEST
THIS ISN'T VENGEANCE.

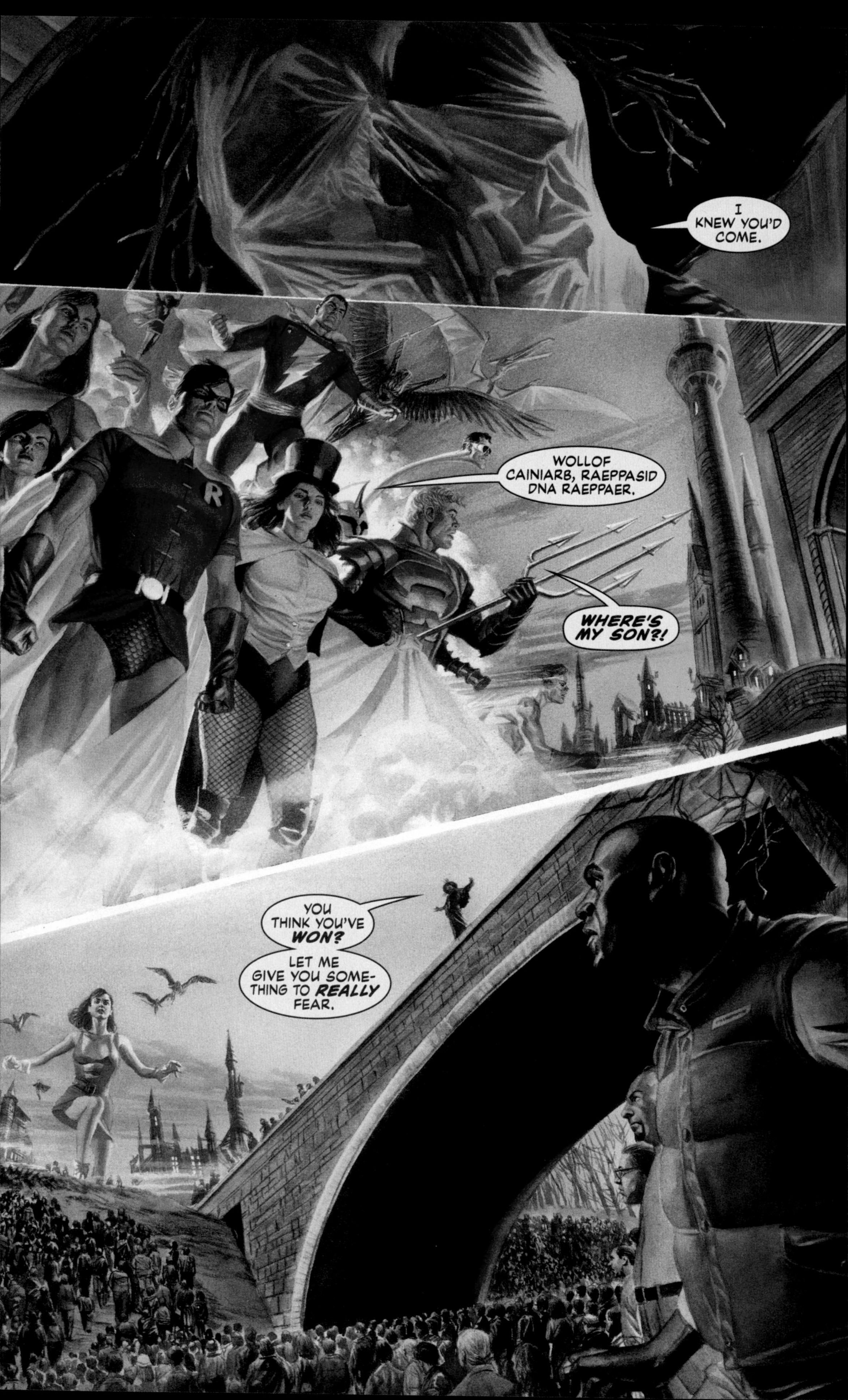
I KNEW YOU'D COME.
WOLLOF CAINIARB, RAEPPASID DNA RAEPPAER.
WHERE'S MY SON?!
YOU THINK YOU'VE WON?
LET ME GIVE YOU SOME-THING TO REALLY FEAR.

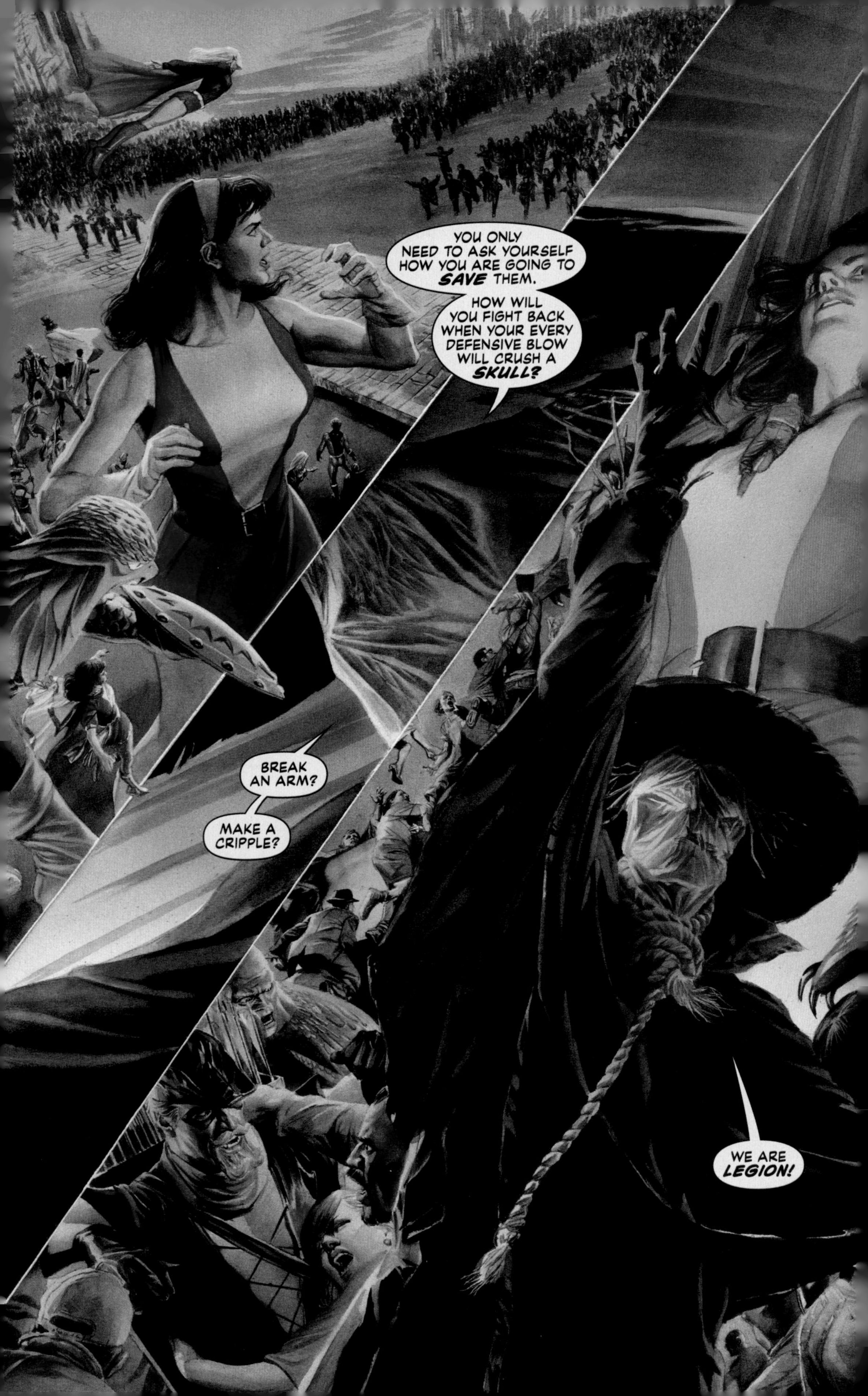
YOU ONLY NEED TO ASK YOURSELF HOW YOU ARE GOING TO SAVE THEM.
HOW WILL YOU FIGHT BACK WHEN YOUR EVERY DEFENSIVE BLOW WILL CRUSH A SKULL?
BREAK AN ARM?
MAKE A CRIPPLE?
WE ARE LEGION!

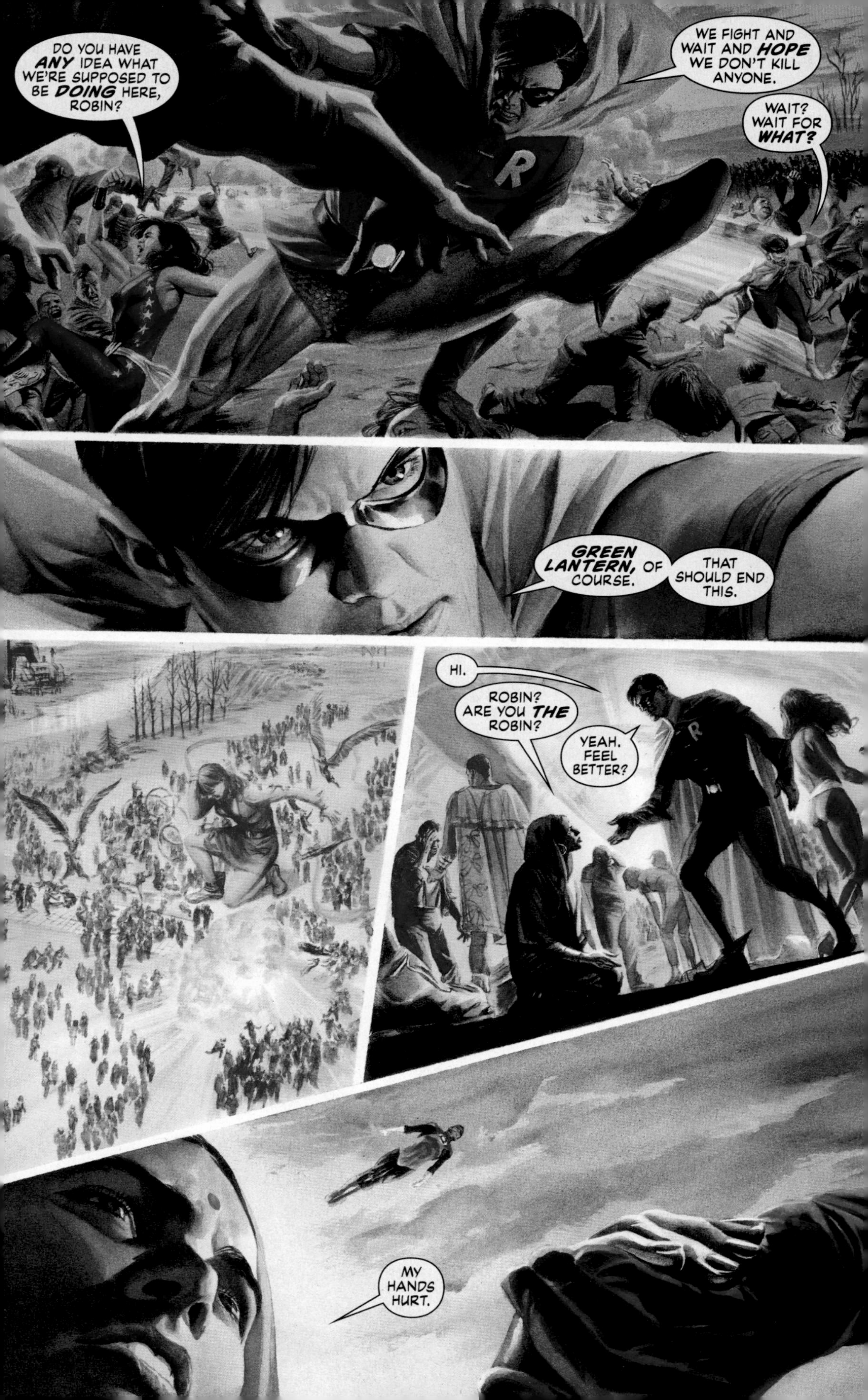
DO YOU HAVE ANY IDEA WHAT WE'RE SUPPOSED TO BE DOING HERE, ROBIN?
WE FIGHT AND WAIT AND HOPE WE DON'T KILL ANYONE.
WAIT? WAIT FOR WHAT?
GREEN LANTERN, OF COURSE.
THAT SHOULD END THIS.
HI.
ROBIN? ARE YOU THE ROBIN?
YEAH. FEEL BETTER?
MY HANDS HURT.

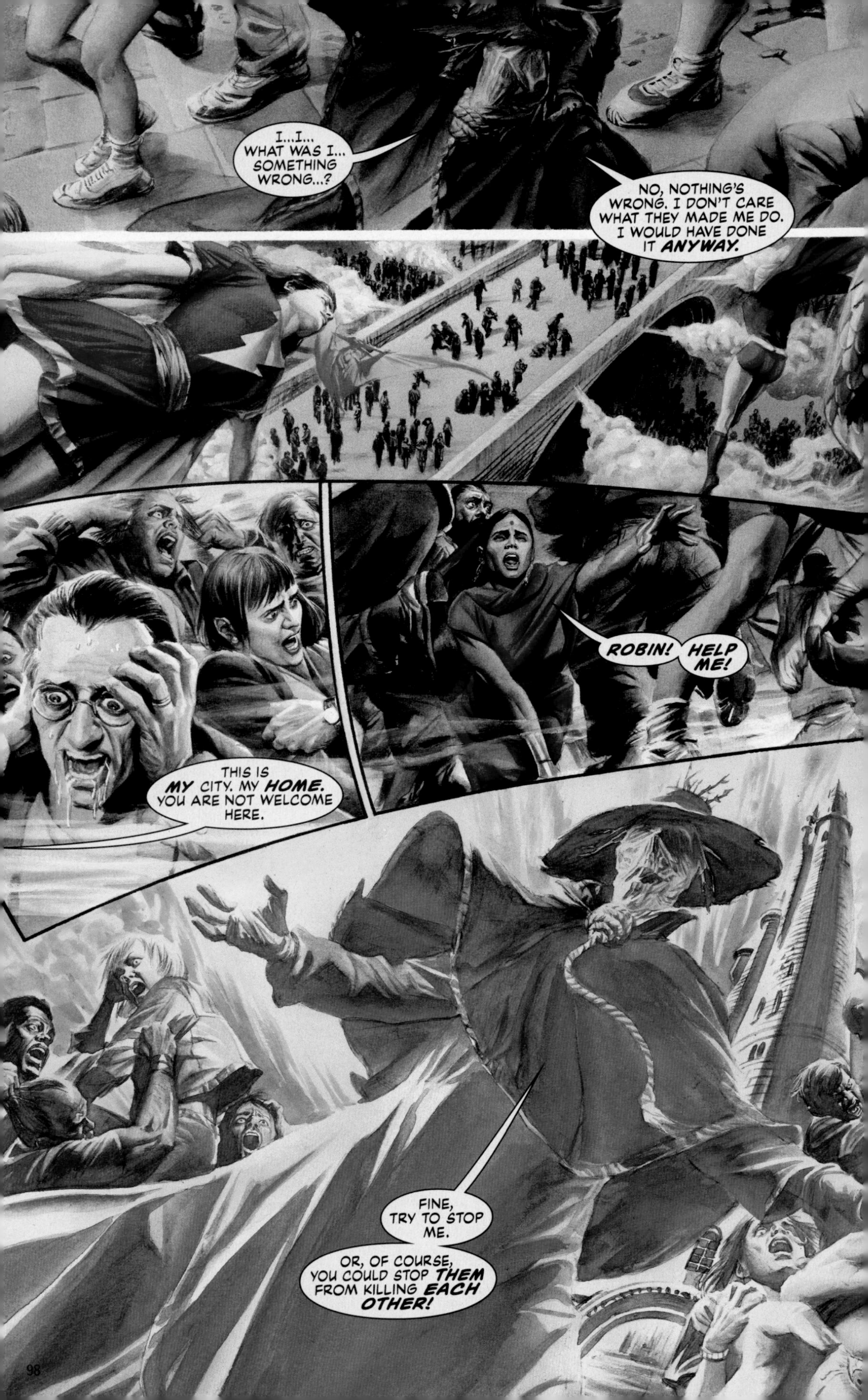
I...I...
WHAT WAS I...
SOMETHING
WRONG...?
NO, NOTHING'S
WRONG. I DON'T CARE
WHAT THEY MADE ME DO.
I WOULD HAVE DONE
IT ANYWAY.
ROBIN!
HELP
ME!
THIS IS
MY CITY. MY HOME.
YOU ARE NOT WELCOME
HERE.
FINE,
TRY TO STOP
ME.
OR, OF COURSE,
YOU COULD STOP THEM
FROM KILLING EACH
OTHER!

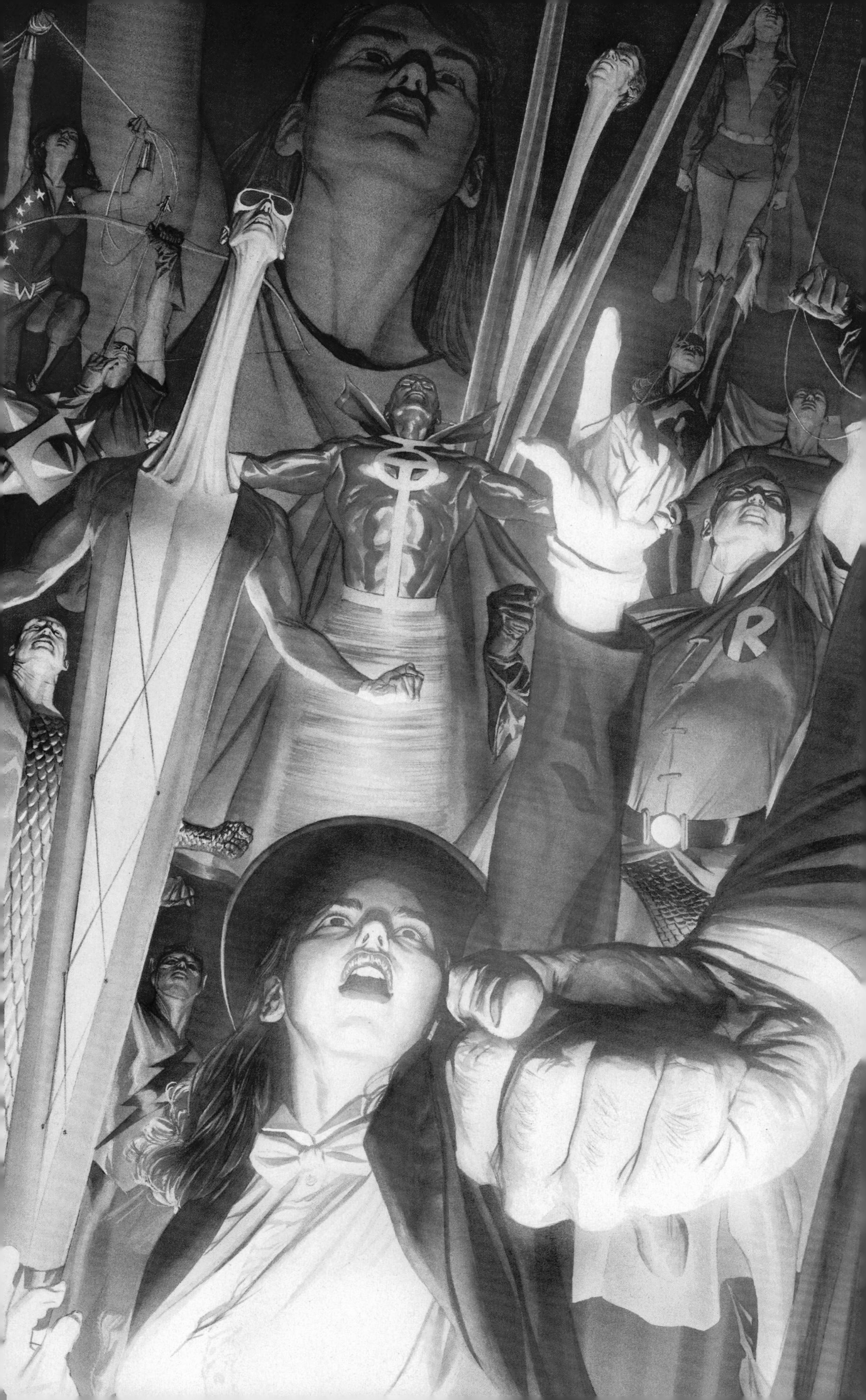

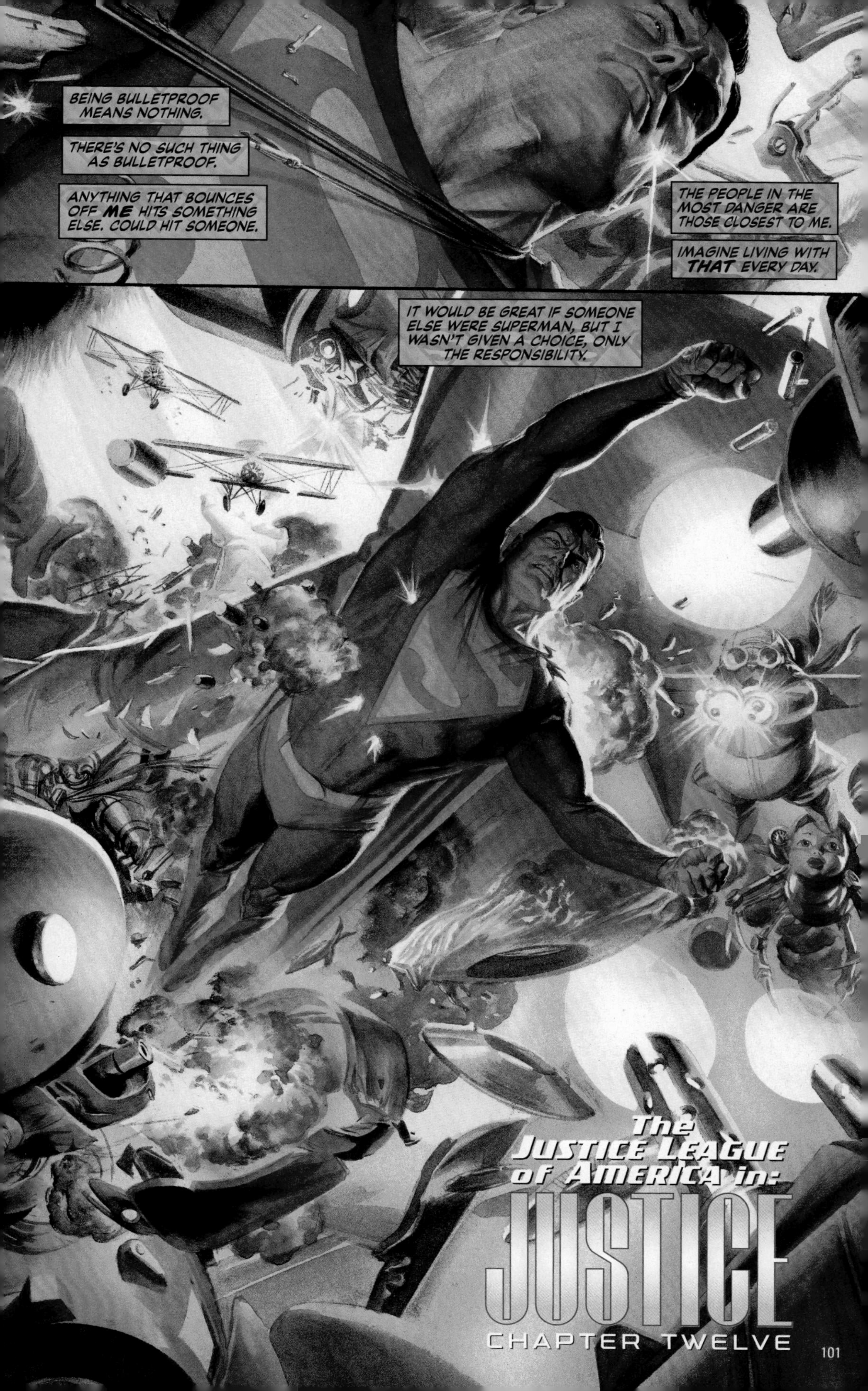
BEING BULLETPROOF MEANS NOTHING.
THERE'S NO SUCH THING AS BULLETPROOF.
ANYTHING THAT BOUNCES OFF ME HITS SOMETHING ELSE. COULD HIT SOMEONE.
THE PEOPLE IN THE MOST DANGER ARE THOSE CLOSEST TO ME.
IMAGINE LIVING WITH THAT EVERY DAY.
IT WOULD BE GREAT IF SOMEONE ELSE WERE SUPERMAN, BUT I WASN'T GIVEN A CHOICE, ONLY THE RESPONSIBILITY.
The JUSTICE LEAGUE of AMERICA in:
JUSTICE
CHAPTER TWELVE

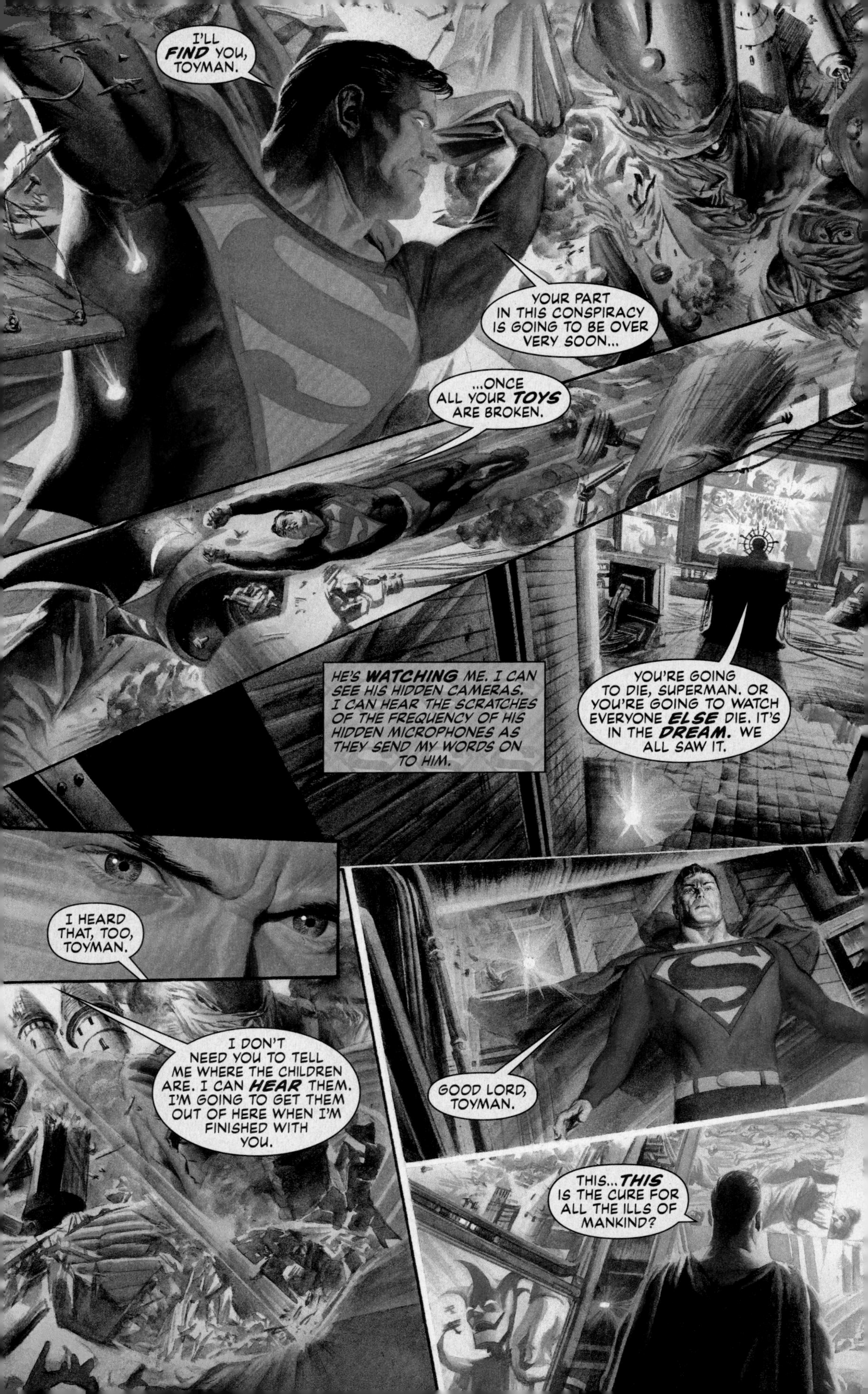
I'LL FIND YOU, TOYMAN.
YOUR PART IN THIS CONSPIRACY IS GOING TO BE OVER VERY SOON...
...ONCE ALL YOUR TOYS ARE BROKEN.
HE'S WATCHING ME. I CAN SEE HIS HIDDEN CAMERAS. I CAN HEAR THE SCRATCHES OF THE FREQUENCY OF HIS HIDDEN MICROPHONES AS THEY SEND MY WORDS ON TO HIM.
YOU'RE GOING TO DIE, SUPERMAN. OR YOU'RE GOING TO WATCH EVERYONE ELSE DIE. IT'S IN THE DREAM. WE ALL SAW IT.
I HEARD THAT, TOO, TOYMAN.
I DON'T NEED YOU TO TELL ME WHERE THE CHILDREN ARE. I CAN HEAR THEM. I'M GOING TO GET THEM OUT OF HERE WHEN I'M FINISHED WITH YOU.
GOOD LORD, TOYMAN.
THIS...THIS IS THE CURE FOR ALL THE ILLS OF MANKIND?

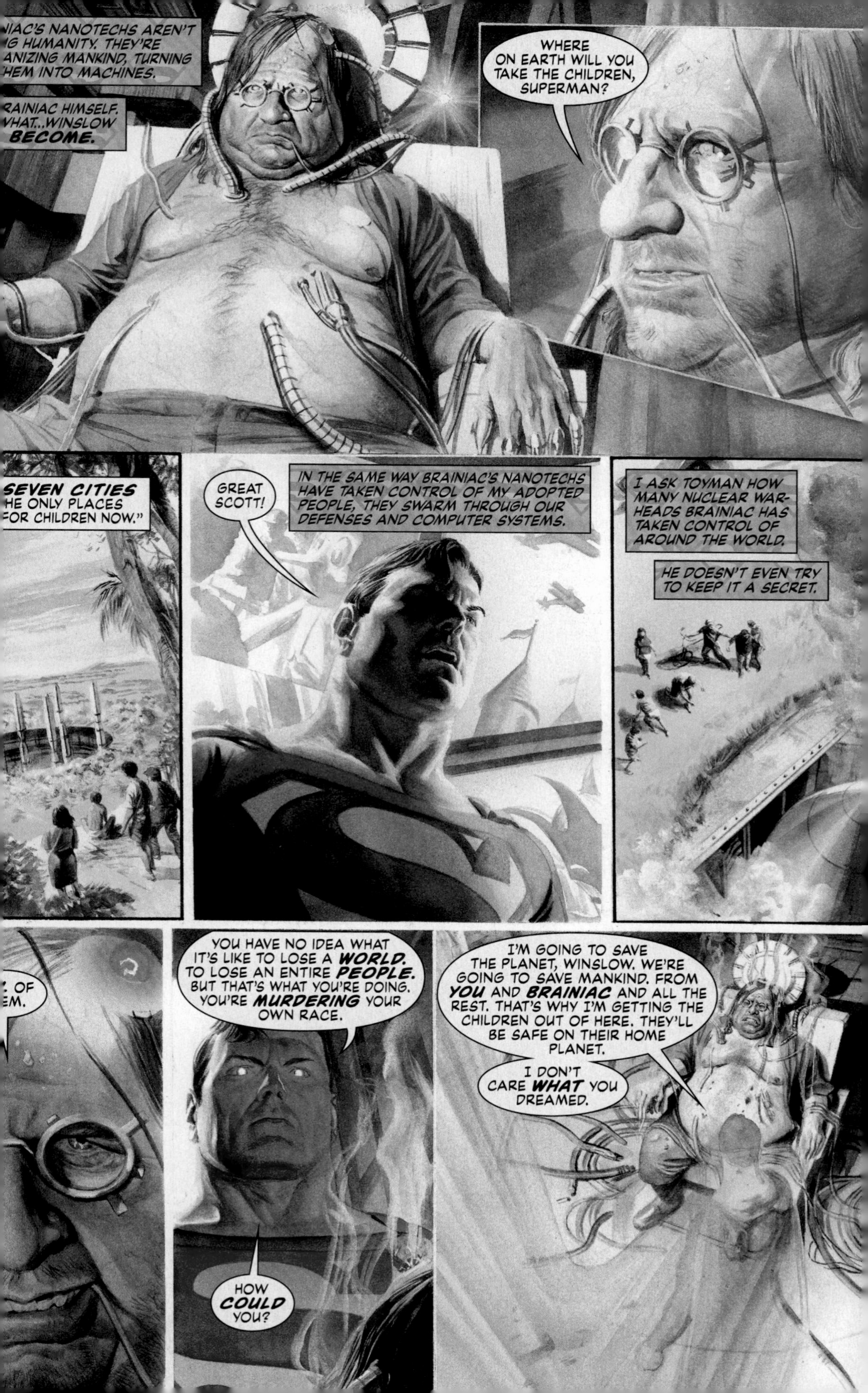

NIAC'S NANOTECHS AREN'T
G HUMANITY. THEY'RE
ANIZING MANKIND, TURNING
THEM INTO MACHINES.
RAINIAC HIMSELF.
WHAT...WINSLOW
BECOME.
WHERE ON EARTH WILL YOU TAKE THE CHILDREN, SUPERMAN?
SEVEN CITIES
HE ONLY PLACES
FOR CHILDREN NOW."
GREAT SCOTT!
IN THE SAME WAY BRAINIAC'S NANOTECHS HAVE TAKEN CONTROL OF MY ADOPTED PEOPLE, THEY SWARM THROUGH OUR DEFENSES AND COMPUTER SYSTEMS.
I ASK TOYMAN HOW MANY NUCLEAR WAR-HEADS BRAINIAC HAS TAKEN CONTROL OF AROUND THE WORLD.
HE DOESN'T EVEN TRY TO KEEP IT A SECRET.
OF
EM.
YOU HAVE NO IDEA WHAT IT'S LIKE TO LOSE A WORLD. TO LOSE AN ENTIRE PEOPLE. BUT THAT'S WHAT YOU'RE DOING. YOU'RE MURDERING YOUR OWN RACE.
HOW COULD YOU?
I'M GOING TO SAVE THE PLANET, WINSLOW. WE'RE GOING TO SAVE MANKIND. FROM YOU AND BRAINIAC AND ALL THE REST. THAT'S WHY I'M GETTING THE CHILDREN OUT OF HERE. THEY'LL BE SAFE ON THEIR HOME PLANET.
I DON'T CARE WHAT YOU DREAMED.

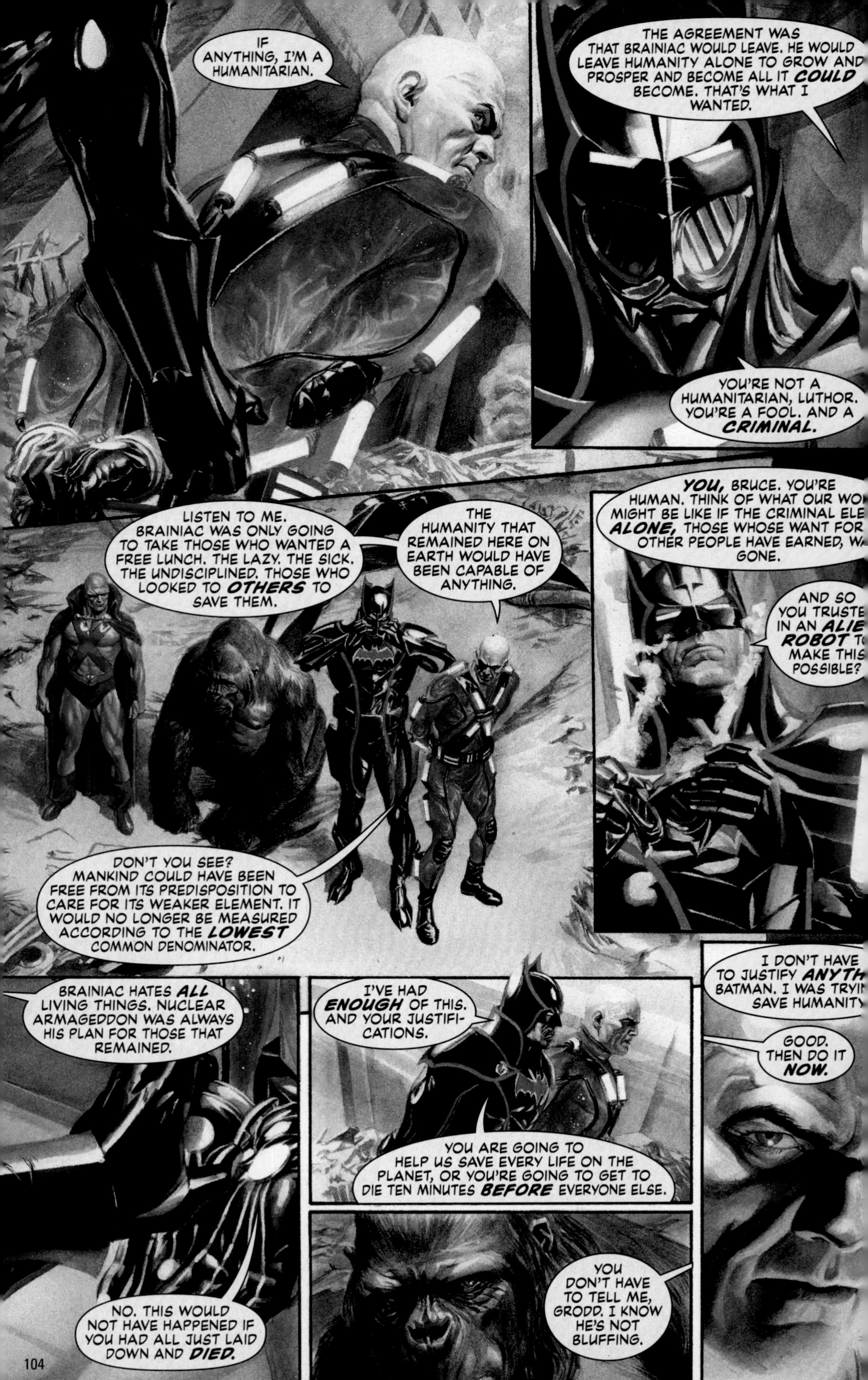

IF ANYTHING, I'M A HUMANITARIAN.
THE AGREEMENT WAS THAT BRAINIAC WOULD LEAVE. HE WOULD LEAVE HUMANITY ALONE TO GROW AND PROSPER AND BECOME ALL IT COULD BECOME. THAT'S WHAT I WANTED.
YOU'RE NOT A HUMANITARIAN, LUTHOR. YOU'RE A FOOL. AND A CRIMINAL.
LISTEN TO ME. BRAINIAC WAS ONLY GOING TO TAKE THOSE WHO WANTED A FREE LUNCH. THE LAZY. THE SICK. THE UNDISCIPLINED. THOSE WHO LOOKED TO OTHERS TO SAVE THEM.
THE HUMANITY THAT REMAINED HERE ON EARTH WOULD HAVE BEEN CAPABLE OF ANYTHING.
DON'T YOU SEE? MANKIND COULD HAVE BEEN FREE FROM ITS PREDISPOSITION TO CARE FOR ITS WEAKER ELEMENT. IT WOULD NO LONGER BE MEASURED ACCORDING TO THE LOWEST COMMON DENOMINATOR.
YOU, BRUCE. YOU'RE HUMAN. THINK OF WHAT OUR WO MIGHT BE LIKE IF THE CRIMINAL ELE ALONE, THOSE WHOSE WANT FOR OTHER PEOPLE HAVE EARNED, W GONE.
AND SO YOU TRUSTE IN AN ALIE ROBOT T MAKE THIS POSSIBLE?
BRAINIAC HATES ALL LIVING THINGS. NUCLEAR ARMAGEDDON WAS ALWAYS HIS PLAN FOR THOSE THAT REMAINED.
NO. THIS WOULD NOT HAVE HAPPENED IF YOU HAD ALL JUST LAID DOWN AND DIED.
I'VE HAD ENOUGH OF THIS. AND YOUR JUSTIFI-CATIONS.
YOU ARE GOING TO HELP US SAVE EVERY LIFE ON THE PLANET, OR YOU'RE GOING TO GET TO DIE TEN MINUTES BEFORE EVERYONE ELSE.
YOU DON'T HAVE TO TELL ME, GRODD. I KNOW HE'S NOT BLUFFING.
I DON'T HAVE TO JUSTIFY ANYTH BATMAN. I WAS TRYIN SAVE HUMANITY
GOOD. THEN DO IT NOW.

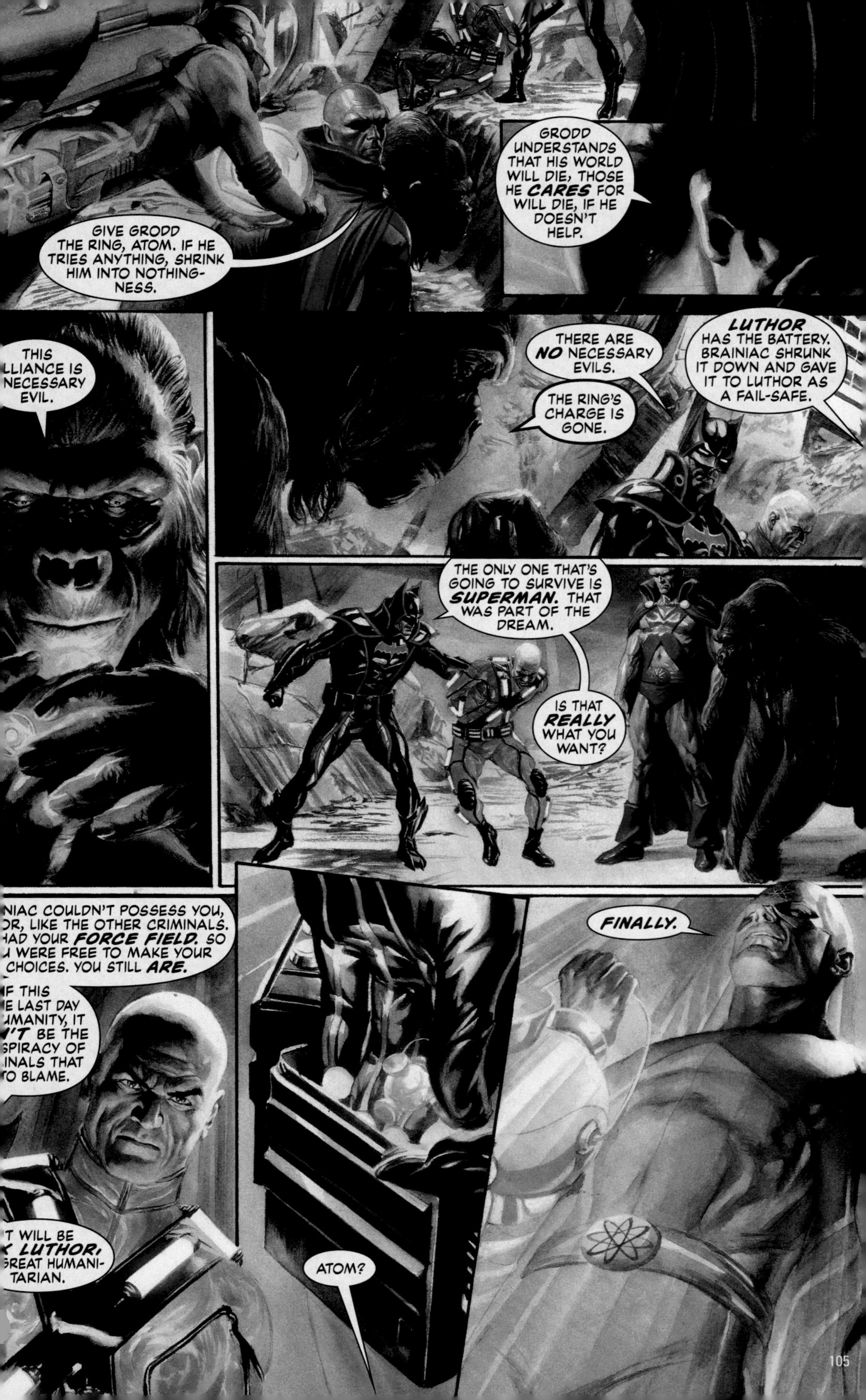

GIVE GRODD THE RING, ATOM. IF HE TRIES ANYTHING, SHRINK HIM INTO NOTHINGNESS.
GRODD UNDERSTANDS THAT HIS WORLD WILL DIE, THOSE HE CARES FOR WILL DIE, IF HE DOESN'T HELP.
LLIANCE IS NECESSARY EVIL.
THERE ARE NO NECESSARY EVILS.
THE RING'S CHARGE IS GONE.
LUTHOR HAS THE BATTERY. BRAINIAC SHRUNK IT DOWN AND GAVE IT TO LUTHOR AS A FAIL-SAFE.
THE ONLY ONE THAT'S GOING TO SURVIVE IS SUPERMAN. THAT WAS PART OF THE DREAM.
IS THAT REALLY WHAT YOU WANT?
NIAC COULDN'T POSSESS YOU, OR, LIKE THE OTHER CRIMINALS. HAD YOUR FORCE FIELD. SO U WERE FREE TO MAKE YOUR CHOICES. YOU STILL ARE.
F THIS E LAST DAY UMANITY, IT N'T BE THE SPIRACY OF INALS THAT O BLAME.
T WILL BE X LUTHOR, GREAT HUMANITARIAN.
ATOM?
FINALLY.

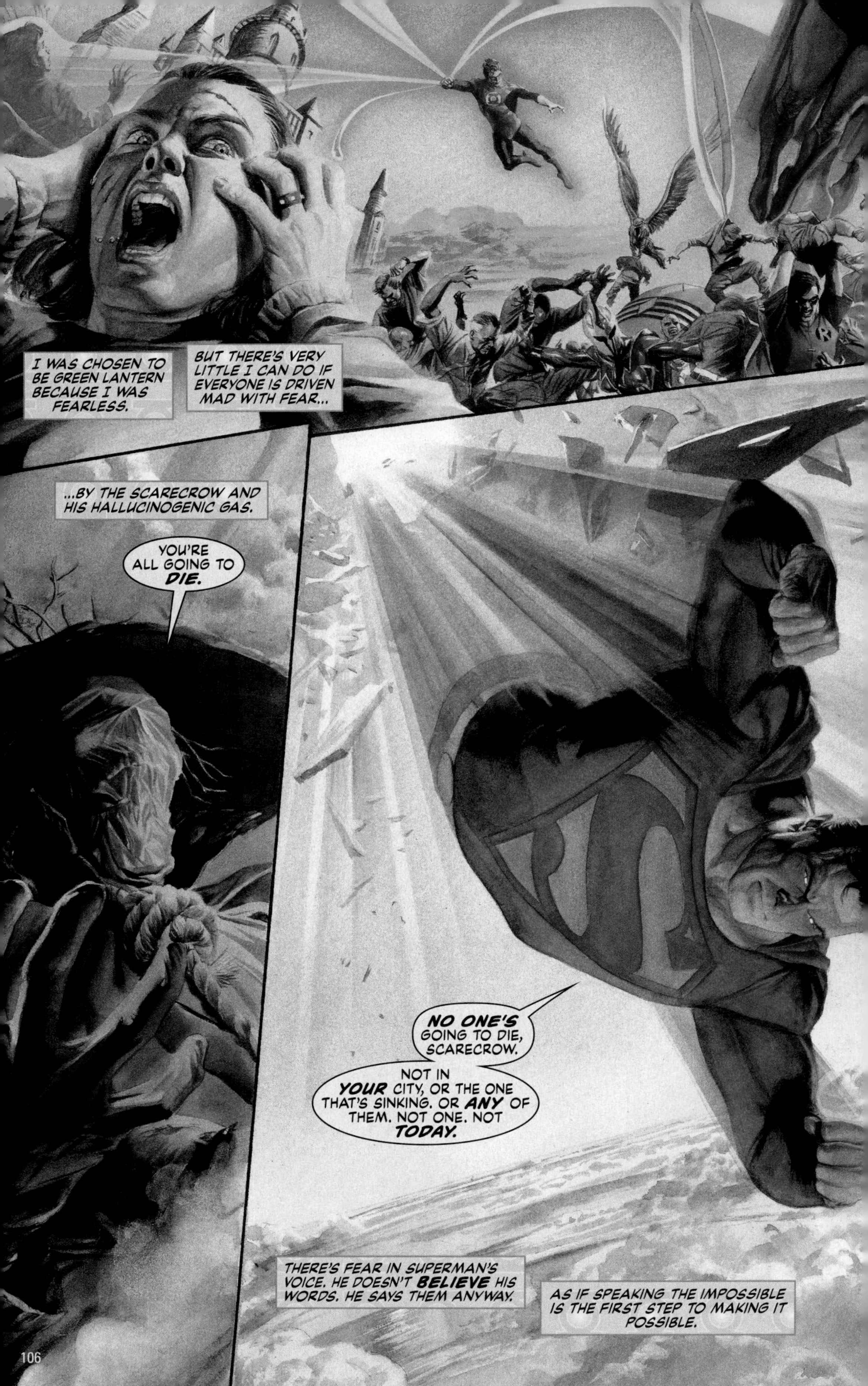
I WAS CHOSEN TO BE GREEN LANTERN BECAUSE I WAS FEARLESS.
BUT THERE'S VERY LITTLE I CAN DO IF EVERYONE IS DRIVEN MAD WITH FEAR...
...BY THE SCARECROW AND HIS HALLUCINOGENIC GAS.
YOU'RE ALL GOING TO DIE.
NO ONE'S GOING TO DIE, SCARECROW.
NOT IN YOUR CITY, OR THE ONE THAT'S SINKING. OR ANY OF THEM. NOT ONE. NOT TODAY.
THERE'S FEAR IN SUPERMAN'S VOICE. HE DOESN'T BELIEVE HIS WORDS. HE SAYS THEM ANYWAY.
AS IF SPEAKING THE IMPOSSIBLE IS THE FIRST STEP TO MAKING IT POSSIBLE.

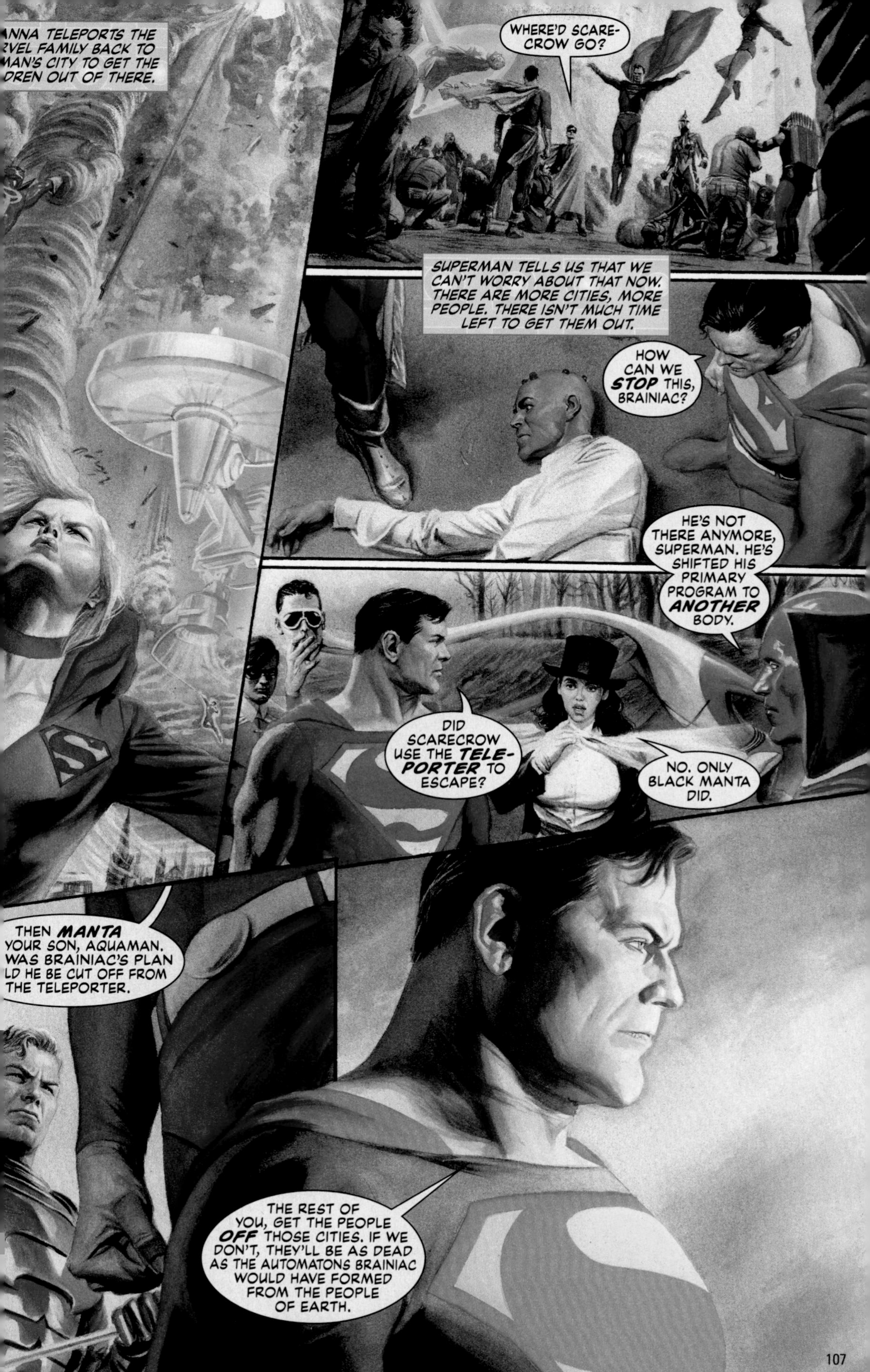

ANNA TELEPORTS THE RVEL FAMILY BACK TO MAN'S CITY TO GET THE DREN OUT OF THERE.
WHERE'D SCARE-CROW GO?
SUPERMAN TELLS US THAT WE CAN'T WORRY ABOUT THAT NOW. THERE ARE MORE CITIES, MORE PEOPLE. THERE ISN'T MUCH TIME LEFT TO GET THEM OUT.
HOW CAN WE STOP THIS, BRAINIAC?
HE'S NOT THERE ANYMORE, SUPERMAN. HE'S SHIFTED HIS PRIMARY PROGRAM TO ANOTHER BODY.
DID SCARECROW USE THE TELE-PORTER TO ESCAPE?
NO. ONLY BLACK MANTA DID.
THEN MANTA YOUR SON, AQUAMAN. WAS BRAINIAC'S PLAN LD HE BE CUT OFF FROM THE TELEPORTER.
THE REST OF YOU, GET THE PEOPLE OFF THOSE CITIES. IF WE DON'T, THEY'LL BE AS DEAD AS THE AUTOMATONS BRAINIAC WOULD HAVE FORMED FROM THE PEOPLE OF EARTH.

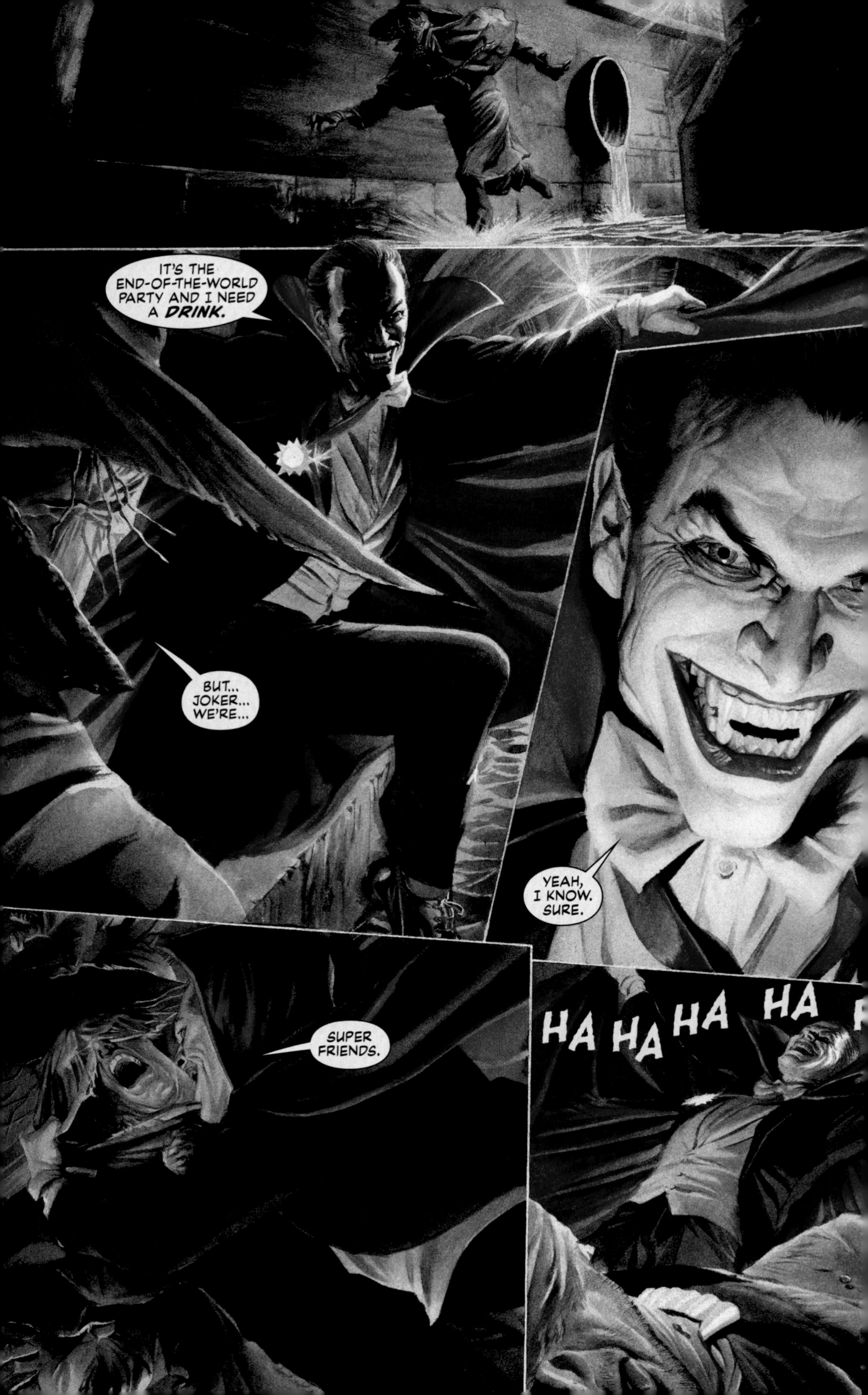
IT'S THE END-OF-THE-WORLD PARTY AND I NEED A DRINK.
BUT... JOKER... WE'RE...
YEAH, I KNOW. SURE.
SUPER FRIENDS.
HA HA HA HA

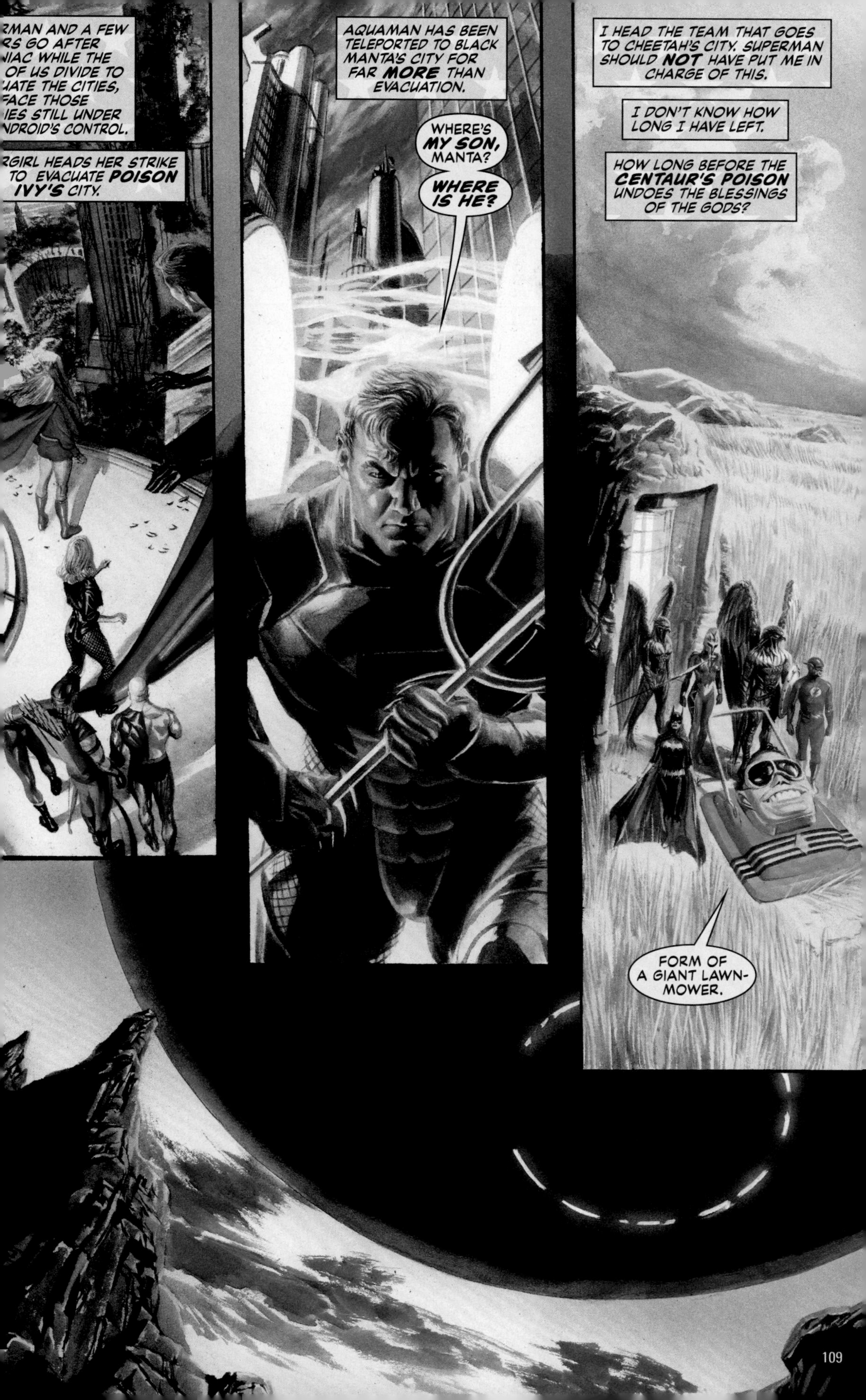
RMAN AND A FEW
RS GO AFTER
NIAC WHILE THE
OF US DIVIDE TO
UATE THE CITIES,
FACE THOSE
IES STILL UNDER
NDROID'S CONTROL.
RGIRL HEADS HER STRIKE
TO EVACUATE POISON
IVY'S CITY.
AQUAMAN HAS BEEN TELEPORTED TO BLACK MANTA'S CITY FOR FAR MORE THAN EVACUATION.
WHERE'S MY SON, MANTA?
WHERE IS HE?
I HEAD THE TEAM THAT GOES TO CHEETAH'S CITY. SUPERMAN SHOULD NOT HAVE PUT ME IN CHARGE OF THIS.
I DON'T KNOW HOW LONG I HAVE LEFT.
HOW LONG BEFORE THE CENTAUR'S POISON UNDOES THE BLESSINGS OF THE GODS?
FORM OF A GIANT LAWN-MOWER.

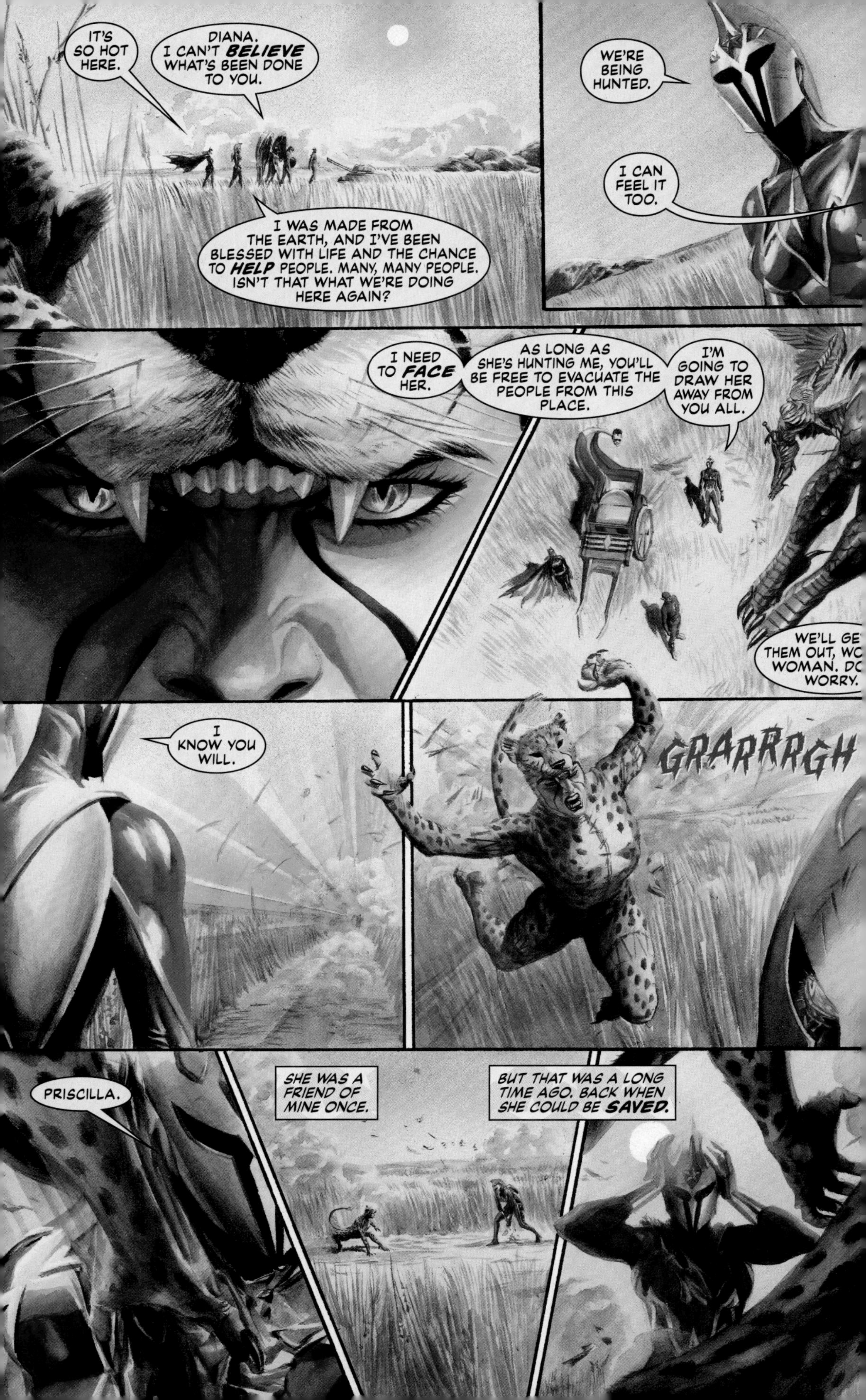
IT'S SO HOT HERE.
DIANA. I CAN'T BELIEVE WHAT'S BEEN DONE TO YOU.
I WAS MADE FROM THE EARTH, AND I'VE BEEN BLESSED WITH LIFE AND THE CHANCE TO HELP PEOPLE. MANY, MANY PEOPLE. ISN'T THAT WHAT WE'RE DOING HERE AGAIN?
WE'RE BEING HUNTED.
I CAN FEEL IT TOO.
I NEED TO FACE HER.
AS LONG AS SHE'S HUNTING ME, YOU'LL BE FREE TO EVACUATE THE PEOPLE FROM THIS PLACE.
I'M GOING TO DRAW HER AWAY FROM YOU ALL.
WE'LL GE THEM OUT, WO WOMAN. DO WORRY.
I KNOW YOU WILL.
GRARRRGH
PRISCILLA.
SHE WAS A FRIEND OF MINE ONCE.
BUT THAT WAS A LONG TIME AGO. BACK WHEN SHE COULD BE SAVED.

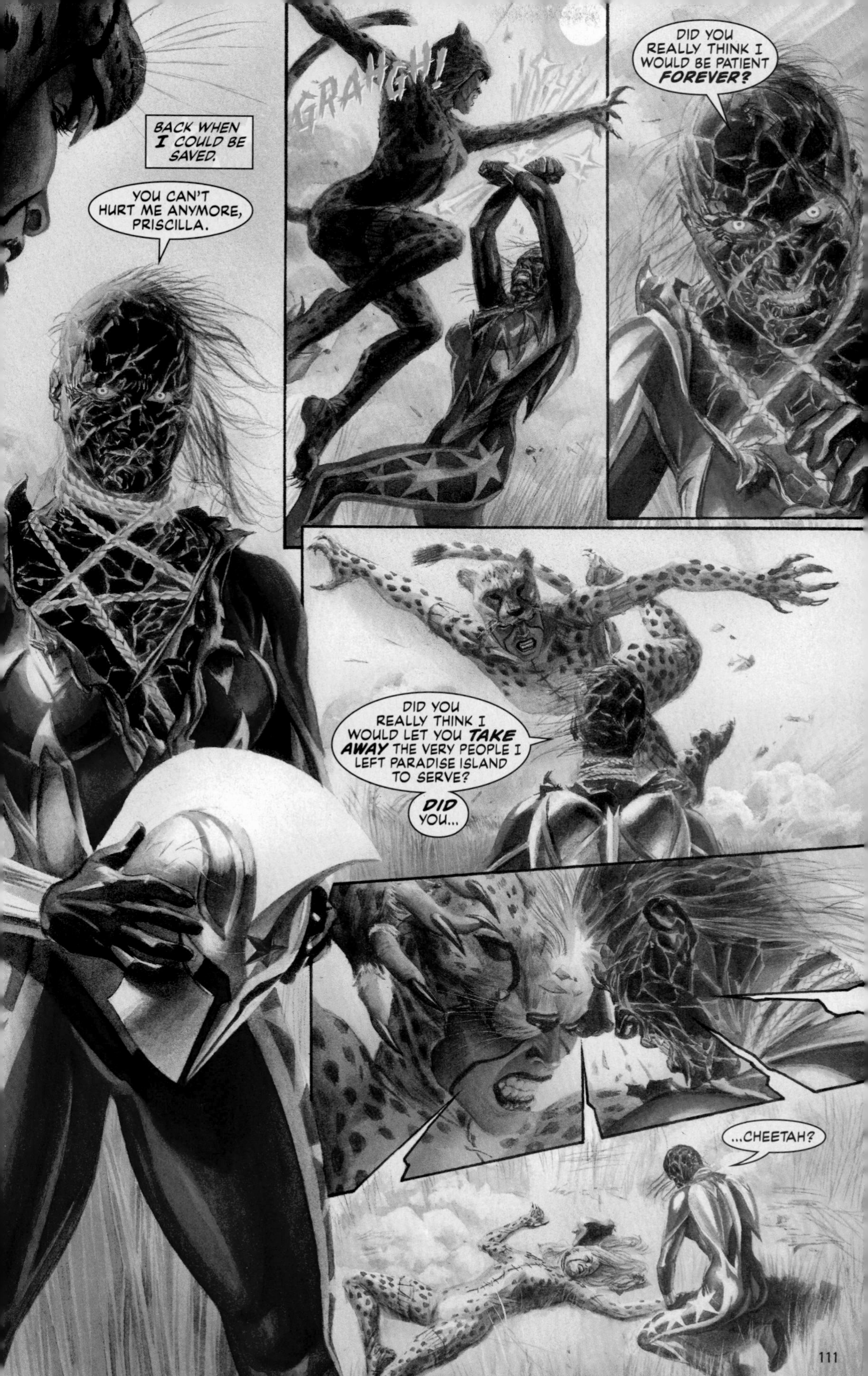
BACK WHEN I COULD BE SAVED.
YOU CAN'T HURT ME ANYMORE, PRISCILLA.
GRAAGH!
DID YOU REALLY THINK I WOULD BE PATIENT FOREVER?
DID YOU REALLY THINK I WOULD LET YOU TAKE AWAY THE VERY PEOPLE I LEFT PARADISE ISLAND TO SERVE?
DID YOU...
...CHEETAH?

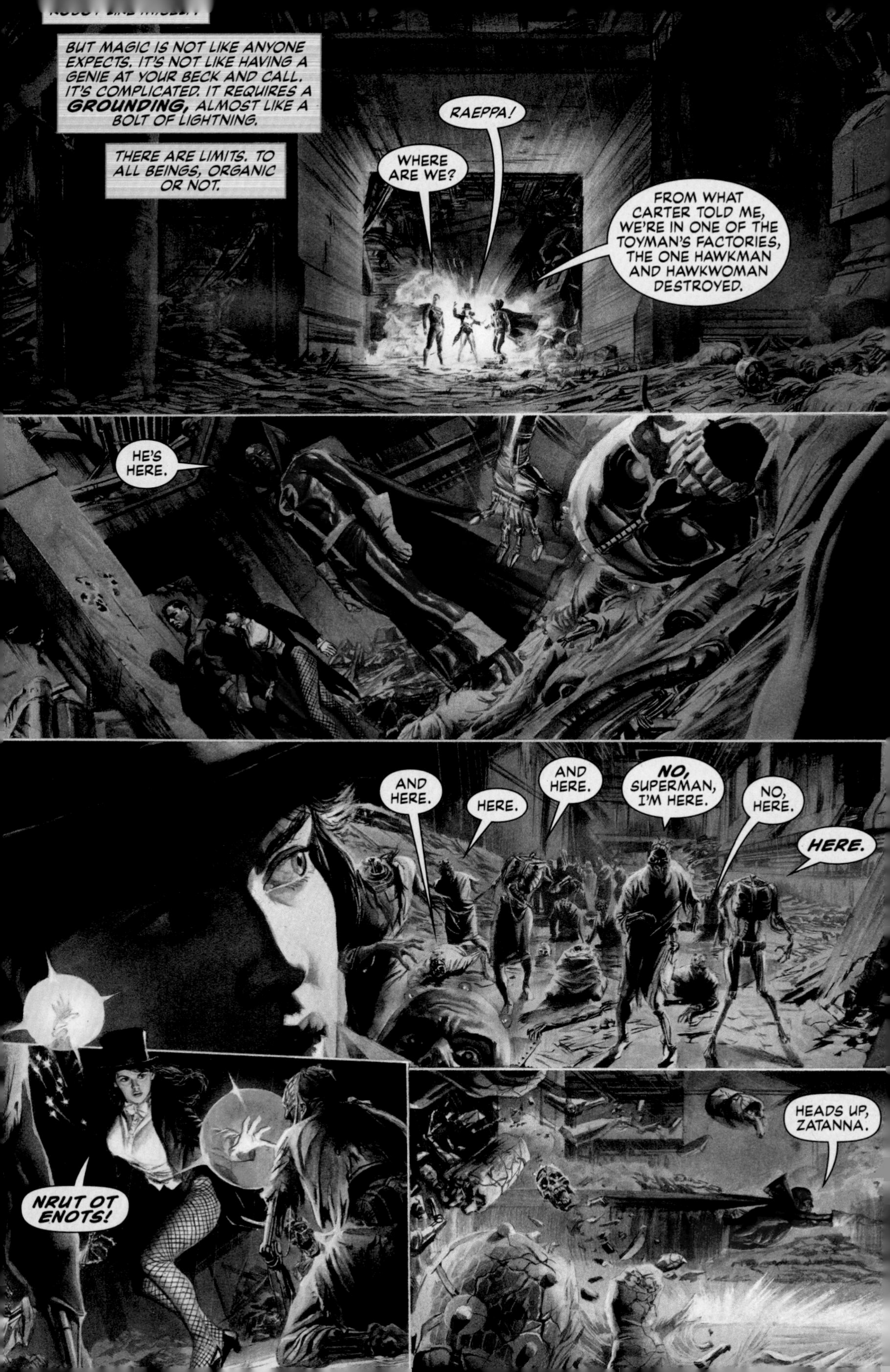
BUT MAGIC IS NOT LIKE ANYONE EXPECTS. IT'S NOT LIKE HAVING A GENIE AT YOUR BECK AND CALL. IT'S COMPLICATED. IT REQUIRES A **GROUNDING,** ALMOST LIKE A BOLT OF LIGHTNING.
THERE ARE LIMITS. TO ALL BEINGS, ORGANIC OR NOT.
RAEPPA!
WHERE ARE WE?
FROM WHAT CARTER TOLD ME, WE'RE IN ONE OF THE TOYMAN'S FACTORIES, THE ONE HAWKMAN AND HAWKWOMAN DESTROYED.
HE'S HERE.
AND HERE.
HERE.
AND HERE.
NO, SUPERMAN, I'M HERE.
NO, HERE.
HERE.
NRUT OT ENOTS!
HEADS UP, ZATANNA.

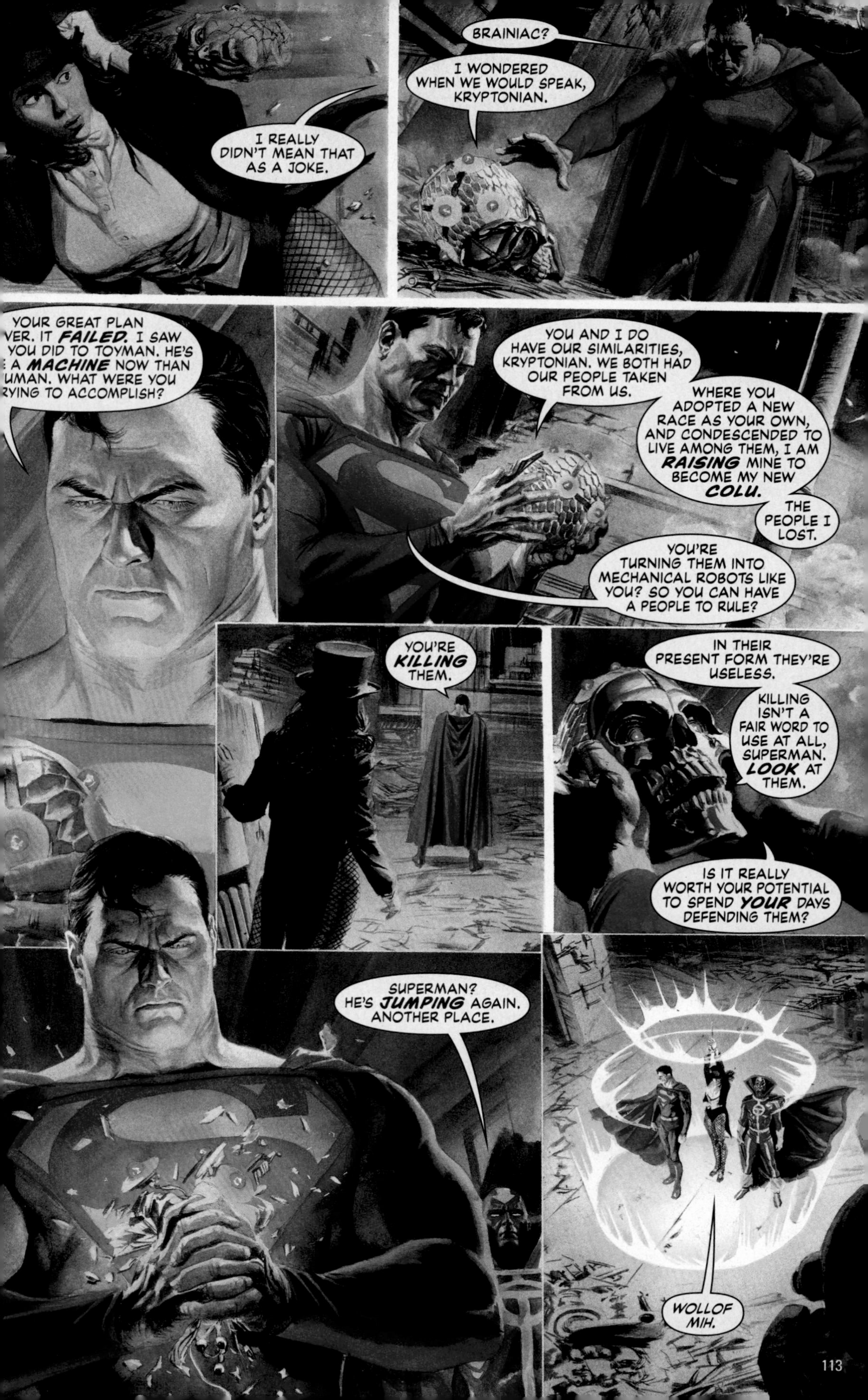
I REALLY DIDN'T MEAN THAT AS A JOKE.
BRAINIAC?
I WONDERED WHEN WE WOULD SPEAK, KRYPTONIAN.
YOUR GREAT PLAN VER. IT FAILED. I SAW YOU DID TO TOYMAN. HE'S E A MACHINE NOW THAN UMAN. WHAT WERE YOU RYING TO ACCOMPLISH?
YOU AND I DO HAVE OUR SIMILARITIES, KRYPTONIAN. WE BOTH HAD OUR PEOPLE TAKEN FROM US.
WHERE YOU ADOPTED A NEW RACE AS YOUR OWN, AND CONDESCENDED TO LIVE AMONG THEM, I AM RAISING MINE TO BECOME MY NEW COLU.
THE PEOPLE I LOST.
YOU'RE TURNING THEM INTO MECHANICAL ROBOTS LIKE YOU? SO YOU CAN HAVE A PEOPLE TO RULE?
YOU'RE KILLING THEM.
IN THEIR PRESENT FORM THEY'RE USELESS.
KILLING ISN'T A FAIR WORD TO USE AT ALL, SUPERMAN. LOOK AT THEM.
IS IT REALLY WORTH YOUR POTENTIAL TO SPEND YOUR DAYS DEFENDING THEM?
SUPERMAN? HE'S JUMPING AGAIN. ANOTHER PLACE.
WOLLOF MIH.

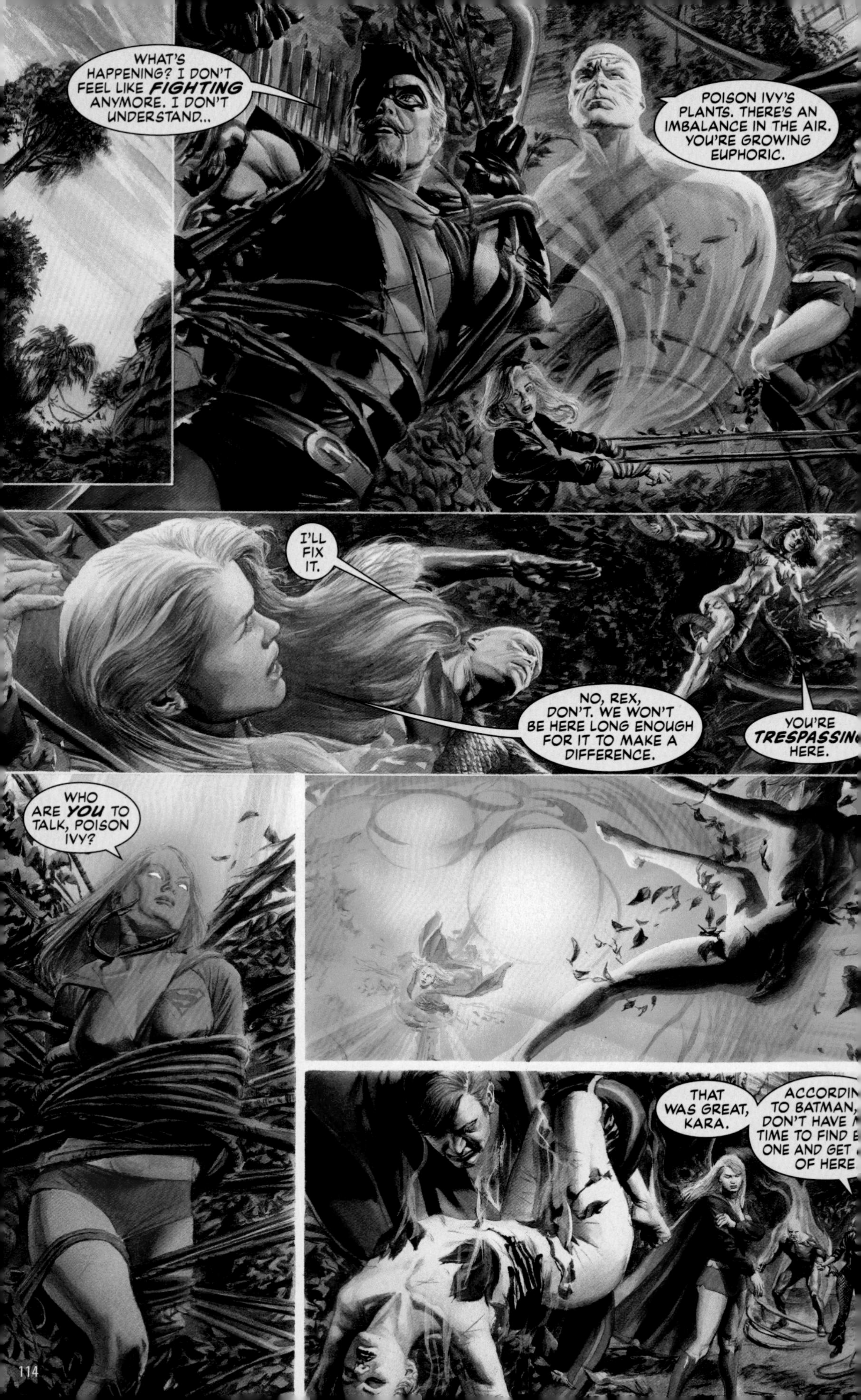
WHAT'S HAPPENING? I DON'T FEEL LIKE FIGHTING ANYMORE. I DON'T UNDERSTAND...
POISON IVY'S PLANTS. THERE'S AN IMBALANCE IN THE AIR. YOU'RE GROWING EUPHORIC.
I'LL FIX IT.
NO, REX, DON'T. WE WON'T BE HERE LONG ENOUGH FOR IT TO MAKE A DIFFERENCE.
YOU'RE HERE.
WHO ARE YOU TO TALK, POISON IVY?
THAT WAS GREAT, KARA.
TO BATMAN,
TIME TO FIND
ONE AND GET
OF HERE

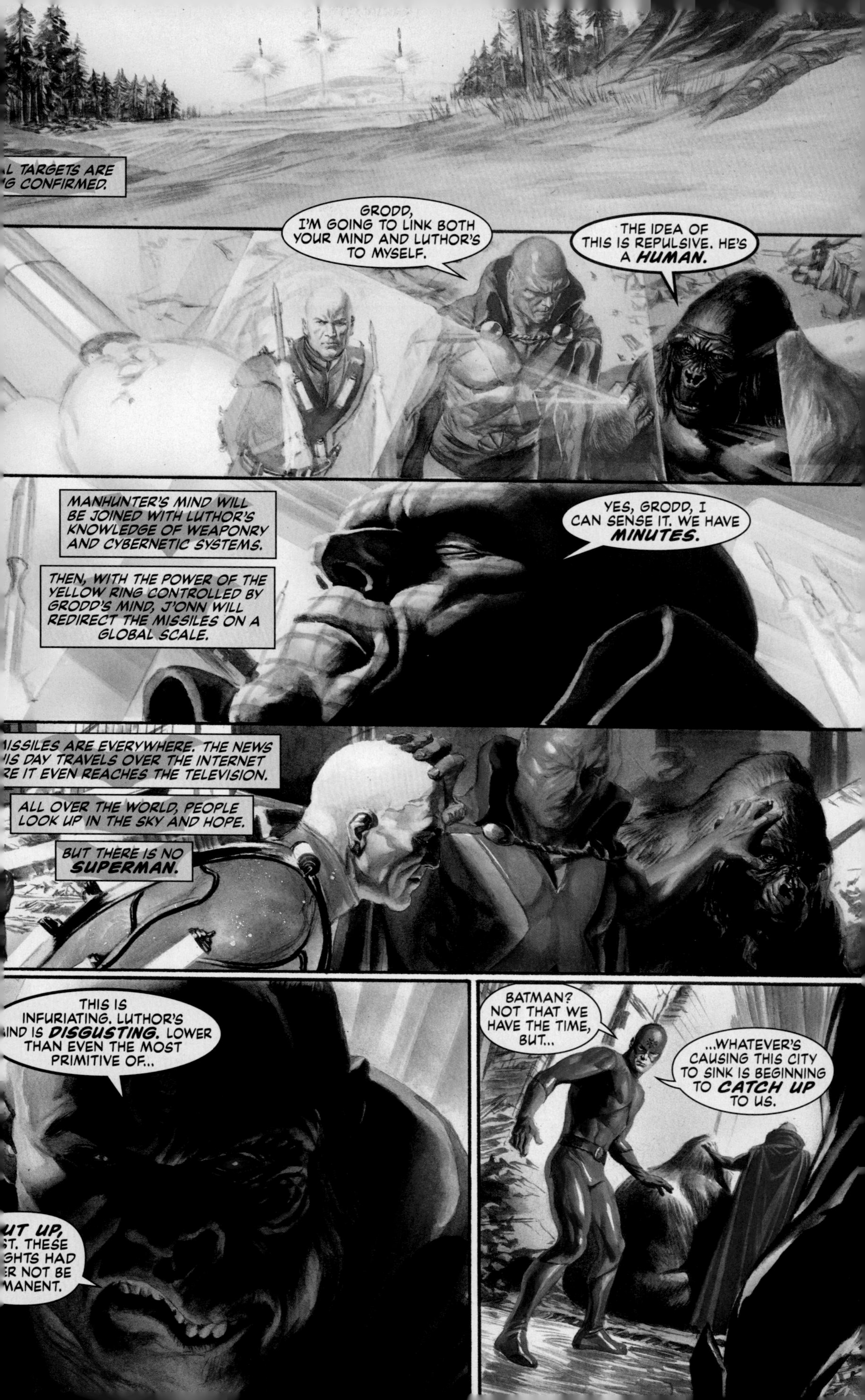
L TARGETS ARE
G CONFIRMED.
GRODD, I'M GOING TO LINK BOTH YOUR MIND AND LUTHOR'S TO MYSELF.
THE IDEA OF THIS IS REPULSIVE. HE'S A HUMAN.
MANHUNTER'S MIND WILL BE JOINED WITH LUTHOR'S KNOWLEDGE OF WEAPONRY AND CYBERNETIC SYSTEMS.
THEN, WITH THE POWER OF THE YELLOW RING CONTROLLED BY GRODD'S MIND, J'ONN WILL REDIRECT THE MISSILES ON A GLOBAL SCALE.
YES, GRODD, I CAN SENSE IT. WE HAVE MINUTES.
ISSILES ARE EVERYWHERE. THE NEWS
IS DAY TRAVELS OVER THE INTERNET
RE IT EVEN REACHES THE TELEVISION.
ALL OVER THE WORLD, PEOPLE LOOK UP IN THE SKY AND HOPE.
BUT THERE IS NO SUPERMAN.
THIS IS INFURIATING. LUTHOR'S
IND IS DISGUSTING. LOWER THAN EVEN THE MOST PRIMITIVE OF...
UT UP,
T. THESE
GHTS HAD
ER NOT BE
MANENT.
BATMAN? NOT THAT WE HAVE THE TIME, BUT...
...WHATEVER'S CAUSING THIS CITY TO SINK IS BEGINNING TO CATCH UP TO US.

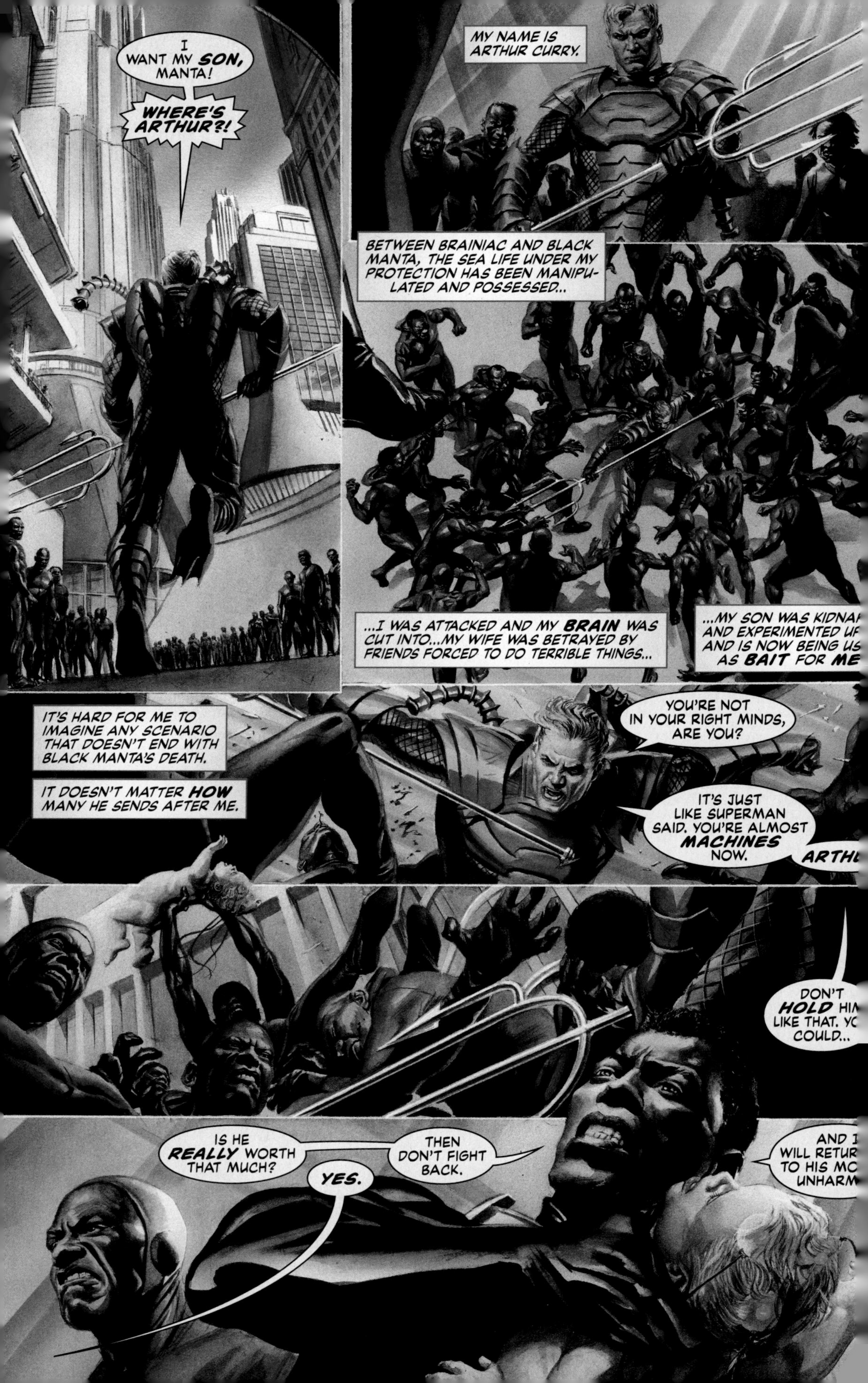
I WANT MY **SON**, MANTA!
WHERE'S ARTHUR?!
MY NAME IS ARTHUR CURRY.
BETWEEN BRAINIAC AND BLACK MANTA, THE SEA LIFE UNDER MY PROTECTION HAS BEEN MANIPULATED AND POSSESSED...
...I WAS ATTACKED AND MY **BRAIN** WAS CUT INTO...MY WIFE WAS BETRAYED BY FRIENDS FORCED TO DO TERRIBLE THINGS...
...MY SON WAS KIDNA AND EXPERIMENTED U AND IS NOW BEING U AS **BAIT** FOR **ME**
IT'S HARD FOR ME TO IMAGINE ANY SCENARIO THAT DOESN'T END WITH BLACK MANTA'S DEATH.
IT DOESN'T MATTER **HOW** MANY HE SENDS AFTER ME.
YOU'RE NOT IN YOUR RIGHT MINDS, ARE YOU?
IT'S JUST LIKE SUPERMAN SAID. YOU'RE ALMOST **MACHINES** NOW.
ARTH
DON'T **HOLD** HI LIKE THAT. Y COULD...
IS HE **REALLY** WORTH THAT MUCH?
THEN DON'T FIGHT BACK.
YES.
AND I WILL RETUR TO HIS MO UNHARM

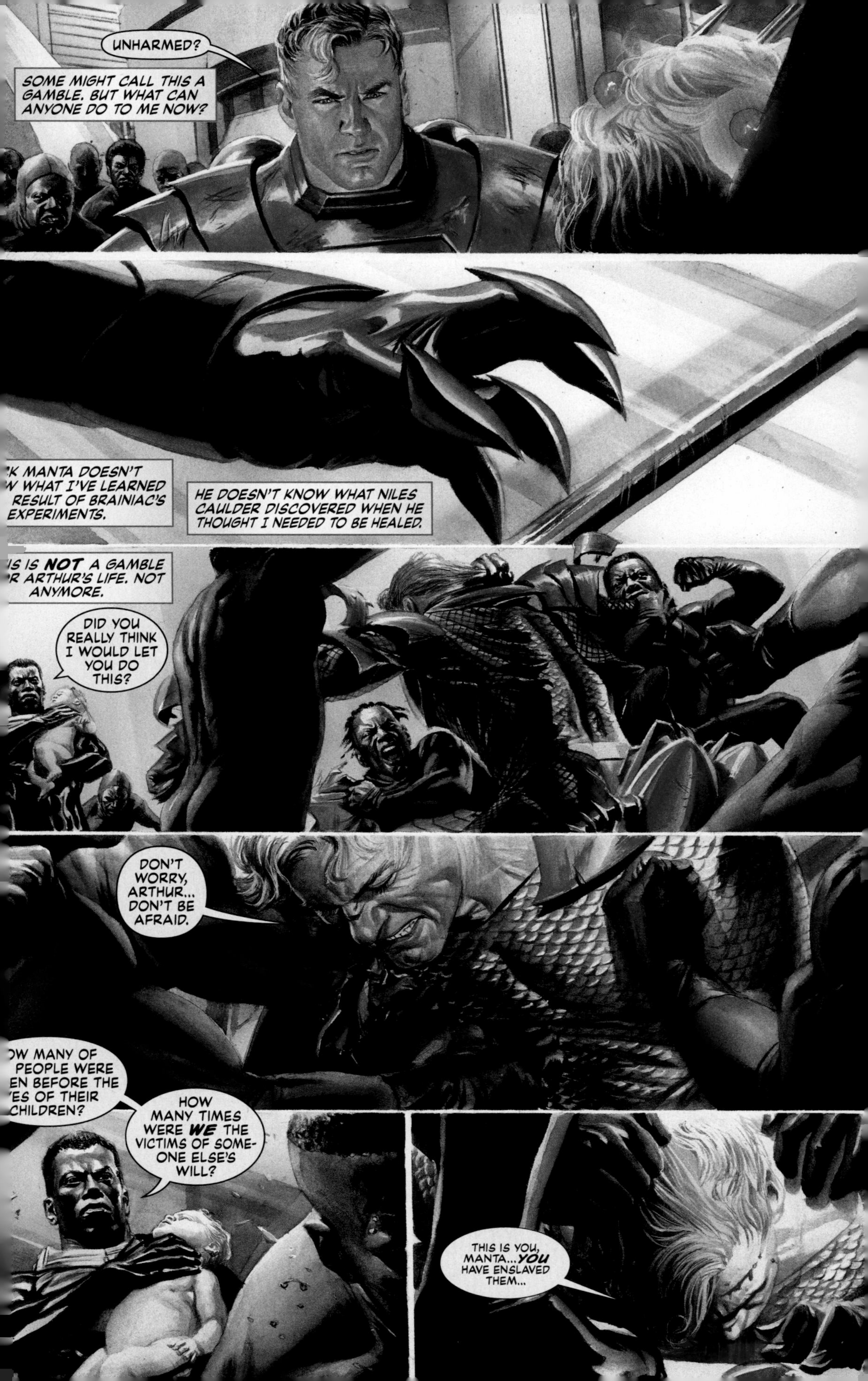
UNHARMED?
SOME MIGHT CALL THIS A GAMBLE. BUT WHAT CAN ANYONE DO TO ME NOW?
K MANTA DOESN'T W WHAT I'VE LEARNED RESULT OF BRAINIAC'S EXPERIMENTS.
HE DOESN'T KNOW WHAT NILES CAULDER DISCOVERED WHEN HE THOUGHT I NEEDED TO BE HEALED.
IS IS NOT A GAMBLE R ARTHUR'S LIFE. NOT ANYMORE.
DID YOU REALLY THINK I WOULD LET YOU DO THIS?
DON'T WORRY, ARTHUR... DON'T BE AFRAID.
OW MANY OF PEOPLE WERE EN BEFORE THE ES OF THEIR CHILDREN?
HOW MANY TIMES WERE WE THE VICTIMS OF SOME-ONE ELSE'S WILL?
THIS IS YOU, MANTA... YOU HAVE ENSLAVED THEM...

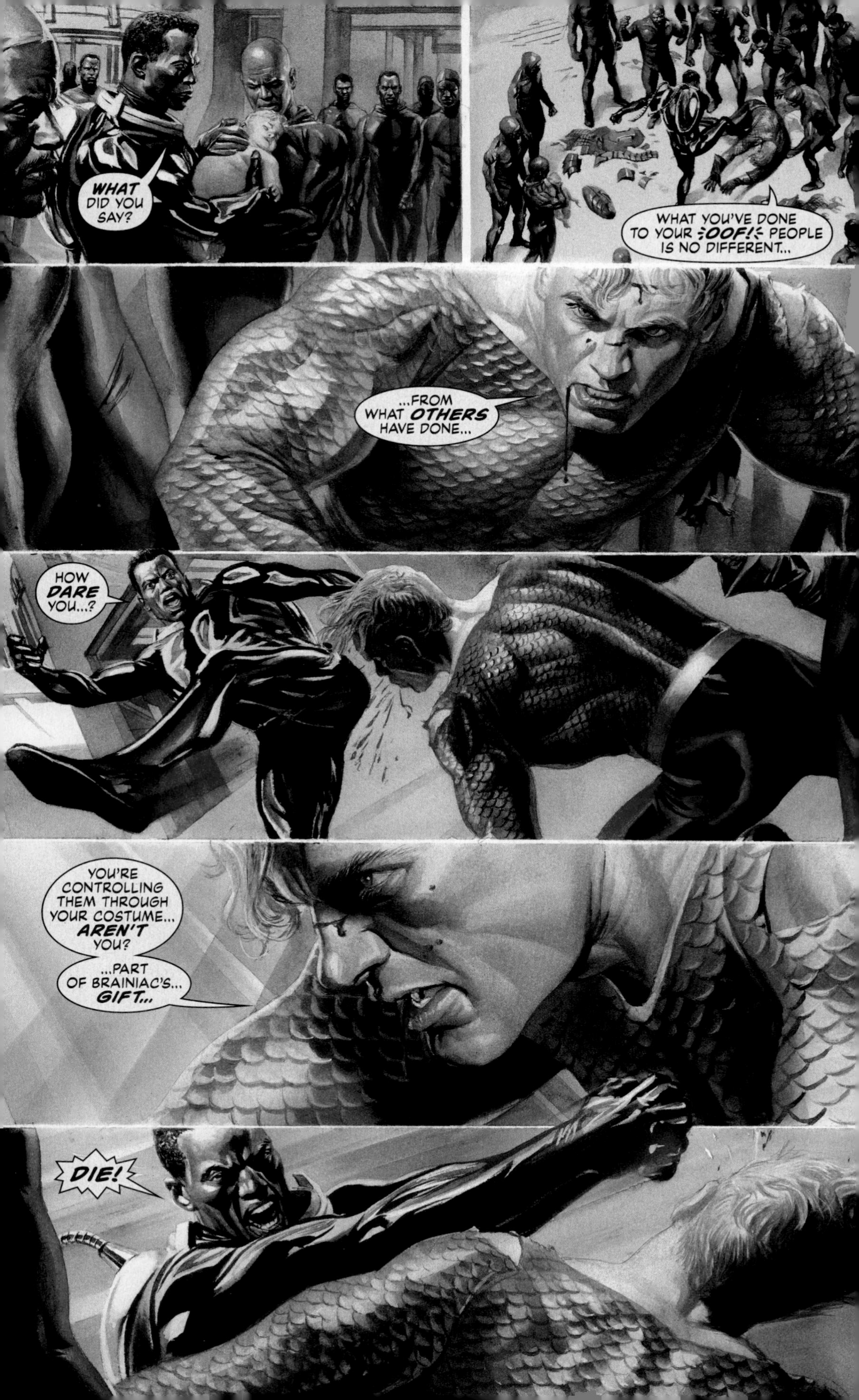
WHAT DID YOU SAY?
WHAT YOU'VE DONE TO YOUR OOF! PEOPLE IS NO DIFFERENT...
...FROM WHAT OTHERS HAVE DONE...
HOW DARE YOU...?
YOU'RE CONTROLLING THEM THROUGH YOUR COSTUME... AREN'T YOU?
...PART OF BRAINIAC'S... GIFT...
DIE!

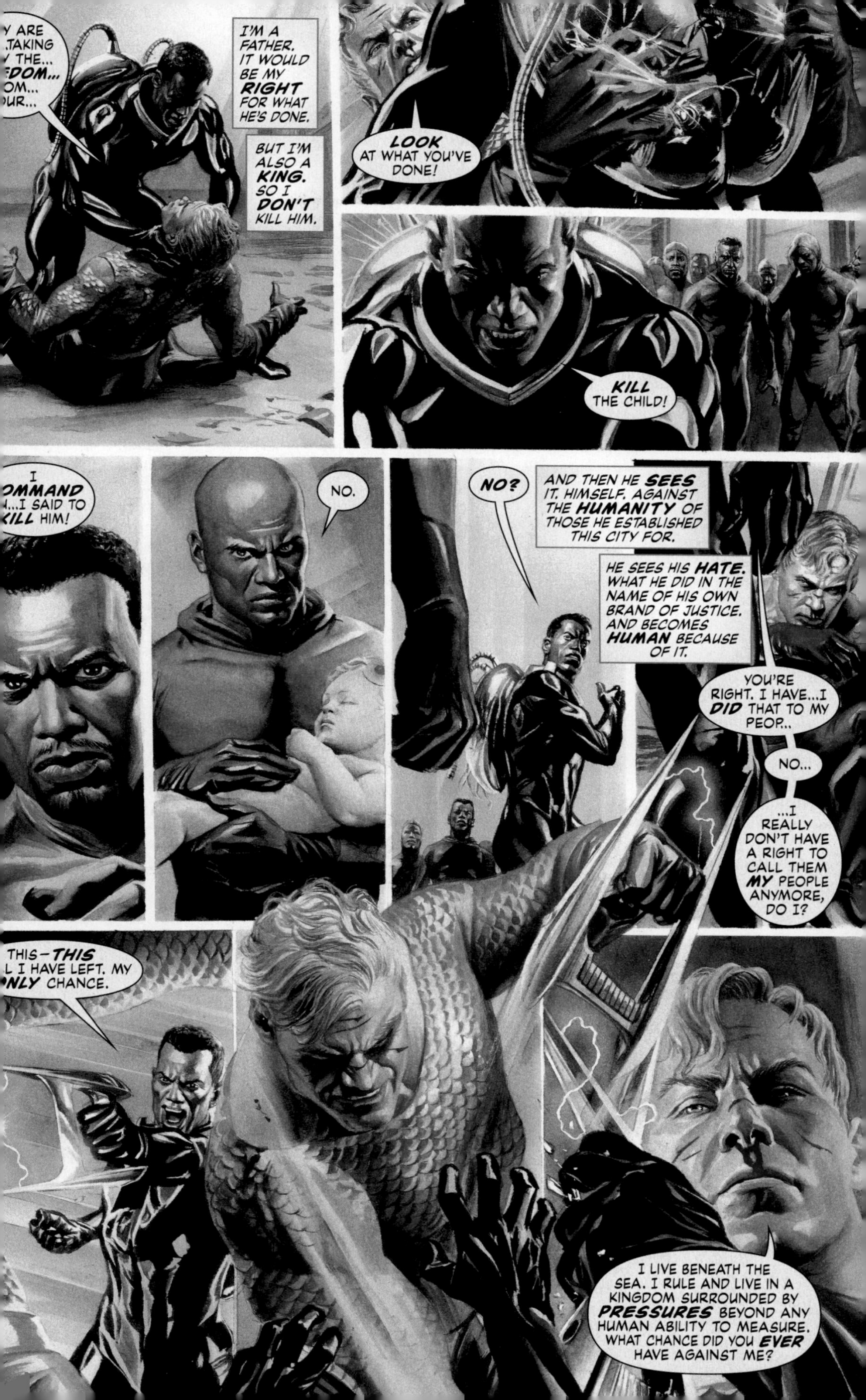
Y ARE TAKING Y THE... EDOM... OM... OUR...
I'M A FATHER. IT WOULD BE MY RIGHT FOR WHAT HE'S DONE.
BUT I'M ALSO A KING. SO I DON'T KILL HIM.
LOOK AT WHAT YOU'VE DONE!
KILL THE CHILD!
I OMMAND ...I SAID TO KILL HIM!
NO.
NO?
AND THEN HE SEES IT. HIMSELF. AGAINST THE HUMANITY OF THOSE HE ESTABLISHED THIS CITY FOR.
HE SEES HIS HATE. WHAT HE DID IN THE NAME OF HIS OWN BRAND OF JUSTICE. AND BECOMES HUMAN BECAUSE OF IT.
YOU'RE RIGHT. I HAVE...I DID THAT TO MY PEOP...
NO...
...I REALLY DON'T HAVE A RIGHT TO CALL THEM MY PEOPLE ANYMORE, DO I?
THIS—THIS L I HAVE LEFT. MY NLY CHANCE.
I LIVE BENEATH THE SEA. I RULE AND LIVE IN A KINGDOM SURROUNDED BY PRESSURES BEYOND ANY HUMAN ABILITY TO MEASURE. WHAT CHANCE DID YOU EVER HAVE AGAINST ME?

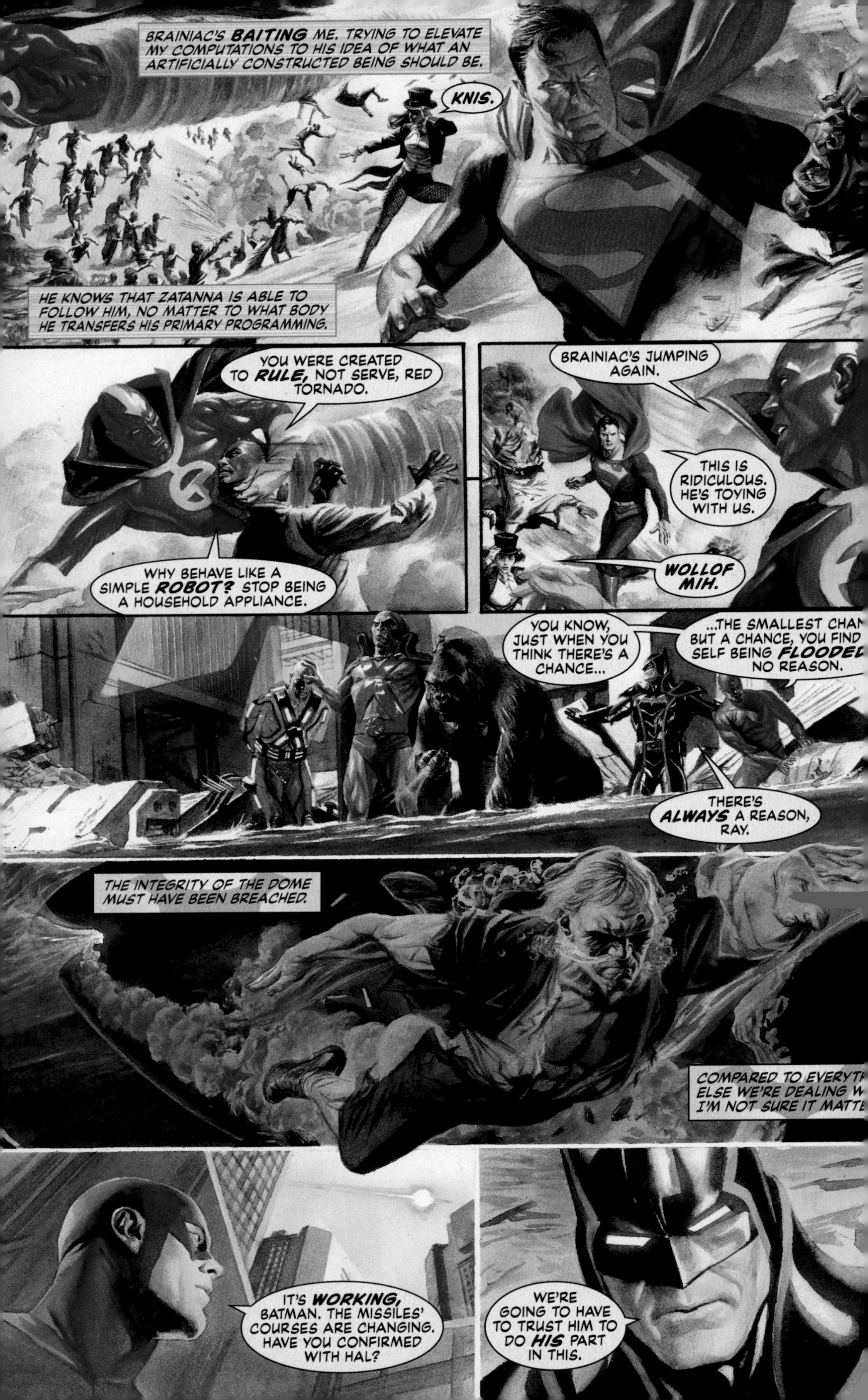
BRAINIAC'S BAITING ME. TRYING TO ELEVATE MY COMPUTATIONS TO HIS IDEA OF WHAT AN ARTIFICIALLY CONSTRUCTED BEING SHOULD BE.
KNIS.
HE KNOWS THAT ZATANNA IS ABLE TO FOLLOW HIM, NO MATTER TO WHAT BODY HE TRANSFERS HIS PRIMARY PROGRAMMING.
YOU WERE CREATED TO RULE, NOT SERVE, RED TORNADO.
WHY BEHAVE LIKE A SIMPLE ROBOT? STOP BEING A HOUSEHOLD APPLIANCE.
BRAINIAC'S JUMPING AGAIN.
THIS IS RIDICULOUS. HE'S TOYING WITH US.
WOLLOF MIH.
YOU KNOW, JUST WHEN YOU THINK THERE'S A CHANCE...
...THE SMALLEST CHAN BUT A CHANCE, YOU FIND SELF BEING FLOODED NO REASON.
THERE'S ALWAYS A REASON, RAY.
THE INTEGRITY OF THE DOME MUST HAVE BEEN BREACHED.
COMPARED TO EVERYTH ELSE WE'RE DEALING W I'M NOT SURE IT MATTE
IT'S WORKING, BATMAN. THE MISSILES' COURSES ARE CHANGING. HAVE YOU CONFIRMED WITH HAL?
WE'RE GOING TO HAVE TO TRUST HIM TO DO HIS PART IN THIS.

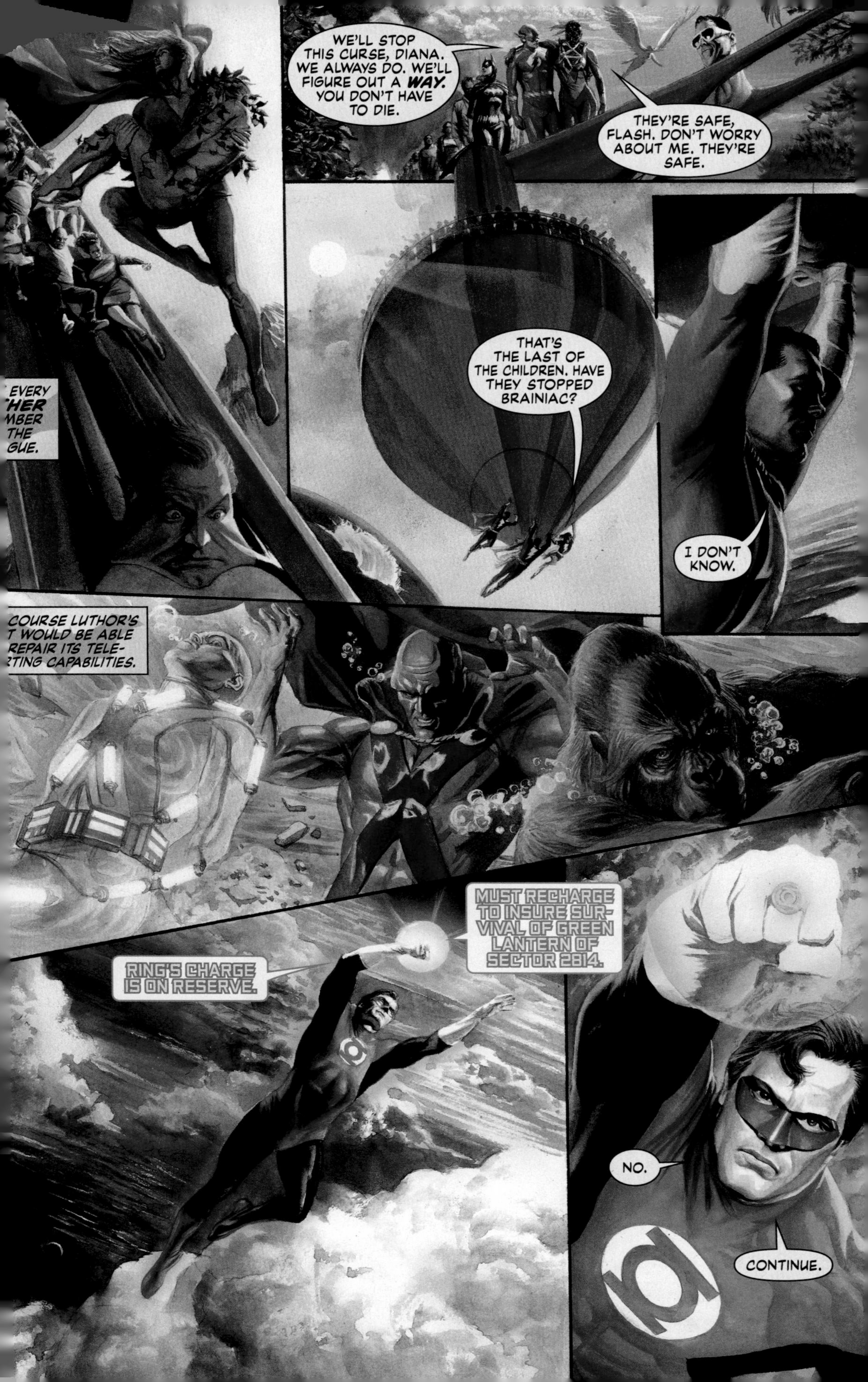
EVERY
THER
MBER
THE
GUE.
WE'LL STOP THIS CURSE, DIANA. WE ALWAYS DO. WE'LL FIGURE OUT A WAY. YOU DON'T HAVE TO DIE.
THEY'RE SAFE, FLASH. DON'T WORRY ABOUT ME. THEY'RE SAFE.
THAT'S THE LAST OF THE CHILDREN. HAVE THEY STOPPED BRAINIAC?
I DON'T KNOW.
COURSE LUTHOR'S
T WOULD BE ABLE
REPAIR ITS TELE-
RTING CAPABILITIES.
RING'S CHARGE IS ON RESERVE.
MUST RECHARGE TO INSURE SURVIVAL OF GREEN LANTERN OF SECTOR 2814.
NO.
CONTINUE.

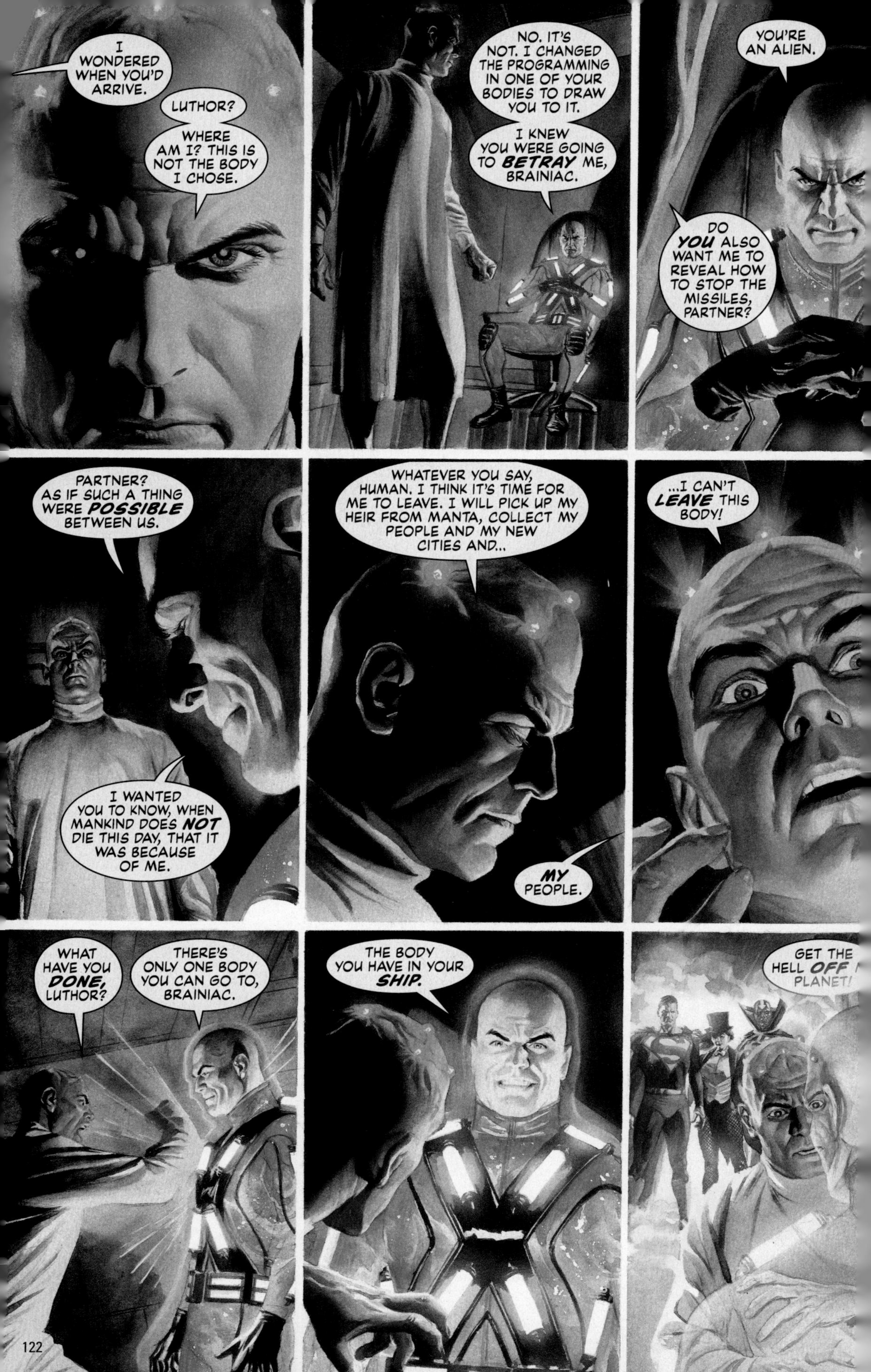
I WONDERED WHEN YOU'D ARRIVE.
LUTHOR?
WHERE AM I? THIS IS NOT THE BODY I CHOSE.
NO. IT'S NOT. I CHANGED THE PROGRAMMING IN ONE OF YOUR BODIES TO DRAW YOU TO IT.
I KNEW YOU WERE GOING TO BETRAY ME, BRAINIAC.
YOU'RE AN ALIEN.
DO YOU ALSO WANT ME TO REVEAL HOW TO STOP THE MISSILES, PARTNER?
PARTNER? AS IF SUCH A THING WERE POSSIBLE BETWEEN US.
I WANTED YOU TO KNOW, WHEN MANKIND DOES NOT DIE THIS DAY, THAT IT WAS BECAUSE OF ME.
WHATEVER YOU SAY, HUMAN. I THINK IT'S TIME FOR ME TO LEAVE. I WILL PICK UP MY HEIR FROM MANTA, COLLECT MY PEOPLE AND MY NEW CITIES AND...
MY PEOPLE.
...I CAN'T LEAVE THIS BODY!
WHAT HAVE YOU DONE, LUTHOR?
THERE'S ONLY ONE BODY YOU CAN GO TO, BRAINIAC.
THE BODY YOU HAVE IN YOUR SHIP.
GET THE HELL OFF
PLANET!

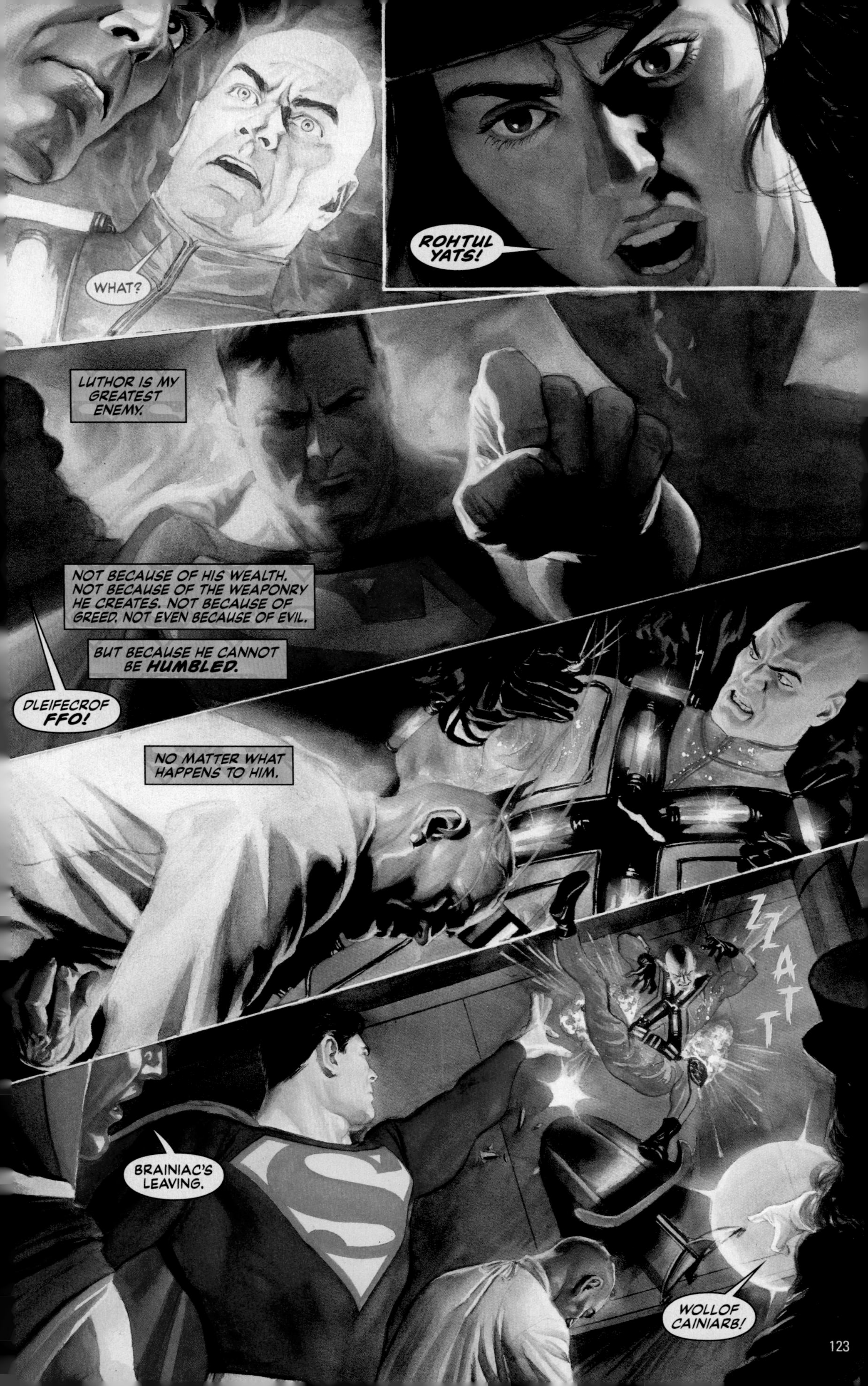
WHAT?
ROHTUL YATS!
LUTHOR IS MY GREATEST ENEMY.
NOT BECAUSE OF HIS WEALTH. NOT BECAUSE OF THE WEAPONRY HE CREATES. NOT BECAUSE OF GREED. NOT EVEN BECAUSE OF EVIL.
BUT BECAUSE HE CANNOT BE HUMBLED.
DLEIFECROF FFO!
NO MATTER WHAT HAPPENS TO HIM.
ZZZATT
BRAINIAC'S LEAVING.
WOLLOF CAINIARB!

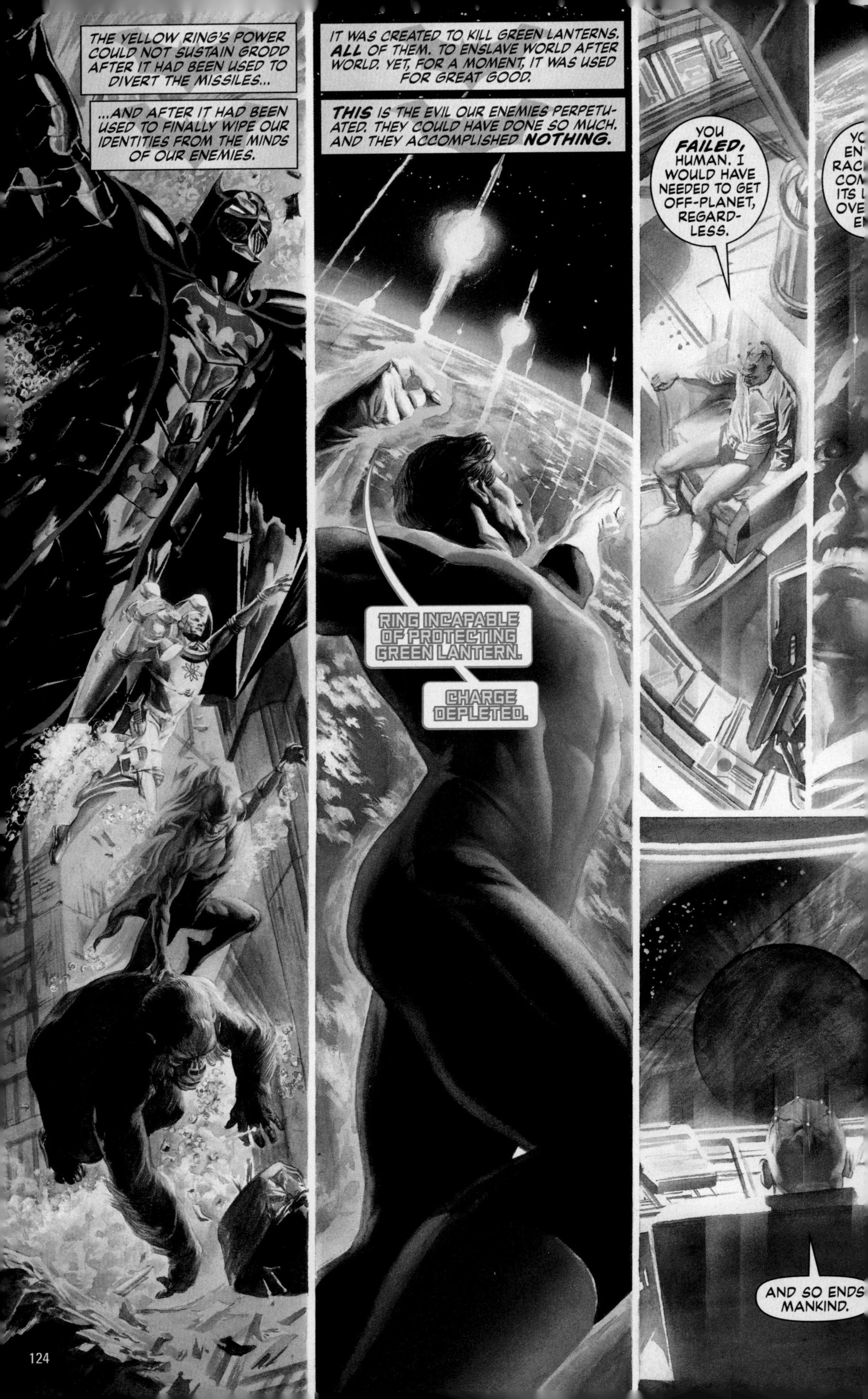
THE YELLOW RING'S POWER COULD NOT SUSTAIN GRODD AFTER IT HAD BEEN USED TO DIVERT THE MISSILES...
...AND AFTER IT HAD BEEN USED TO FINALLY WIPE OUR IDENTITIES FROM THE MINDS OF OUR ENEMIES.
IT WAS CREATED TO KILL GREEN LANTERNS. ALL OF THEM. TO ENSLAVE WORLD AFTER WORLD. YET, FOR A MOMENT, IT WAS USED FOR GREAT GOOD.
THIS IS THE EVIL OUR ENEMIES PERPETUATED. THEY COULD HAVE DONE SO MUCH. AND THEY ACCOMPLISHED NOTHING.
RING INCAPABLE OF PROTECTING GREEN LANTERN.
CHARGE DEPLETED.
YOU FAILED, HUMAN. I WOULD HAVE NEEDED TO GET OFF-PLANET, REGARDLESS.
AND SO ENDS MANKIND.

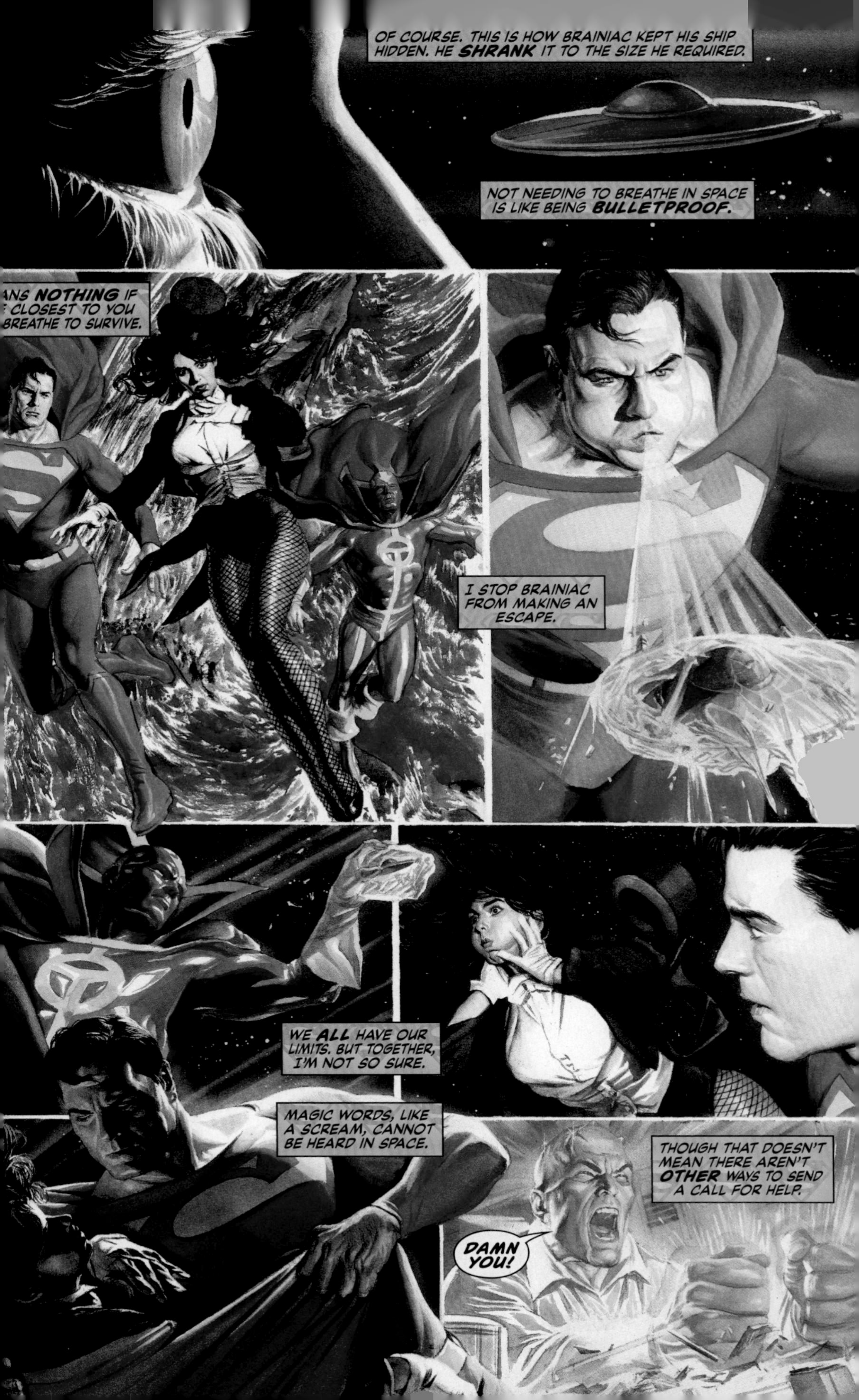
OF COURSE. THIS IS HOW BRAINIAC KEPT HIS SHIP HIDDEN. HE SHRANK IT TO THE SIZE HE REQUIRED.
NOT NEEDING TO BREATHE IN SPACE IS LIKE BEING BULLETPROOF.
ANS NOTHING IF
CLOSEST TO YOU
BREATHE TO SURVIVE.
I STOP BRAINIAC FROM MAKING AN ESCAPE.
WE ALL HAVE OUR LIMITS. BUT TOGETHER, I'M NOT SO SURE.
MAGIC WORDS, LIKE A SCREAM, CANNOT BE HEARD IN SPACE.
THOUGH THAT DOESN'T MEAN THERE AREN'T OTHER WAYS TO SEND A CALL FOR HELP.
DAMN YOU!

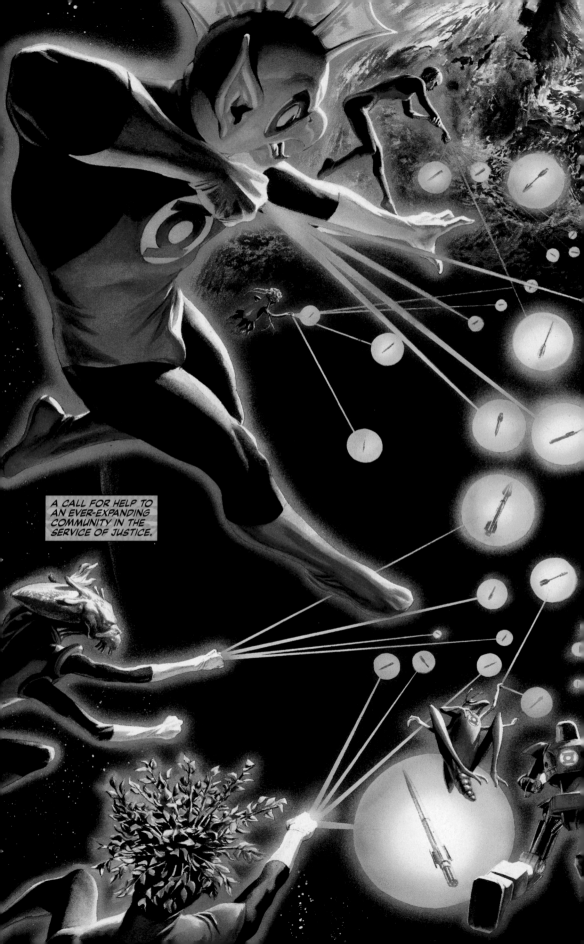

A CALL FOR HELP TO AN EVER-EXPANDING COMMUNITY IN THE SERVICE OF JUSTICE.

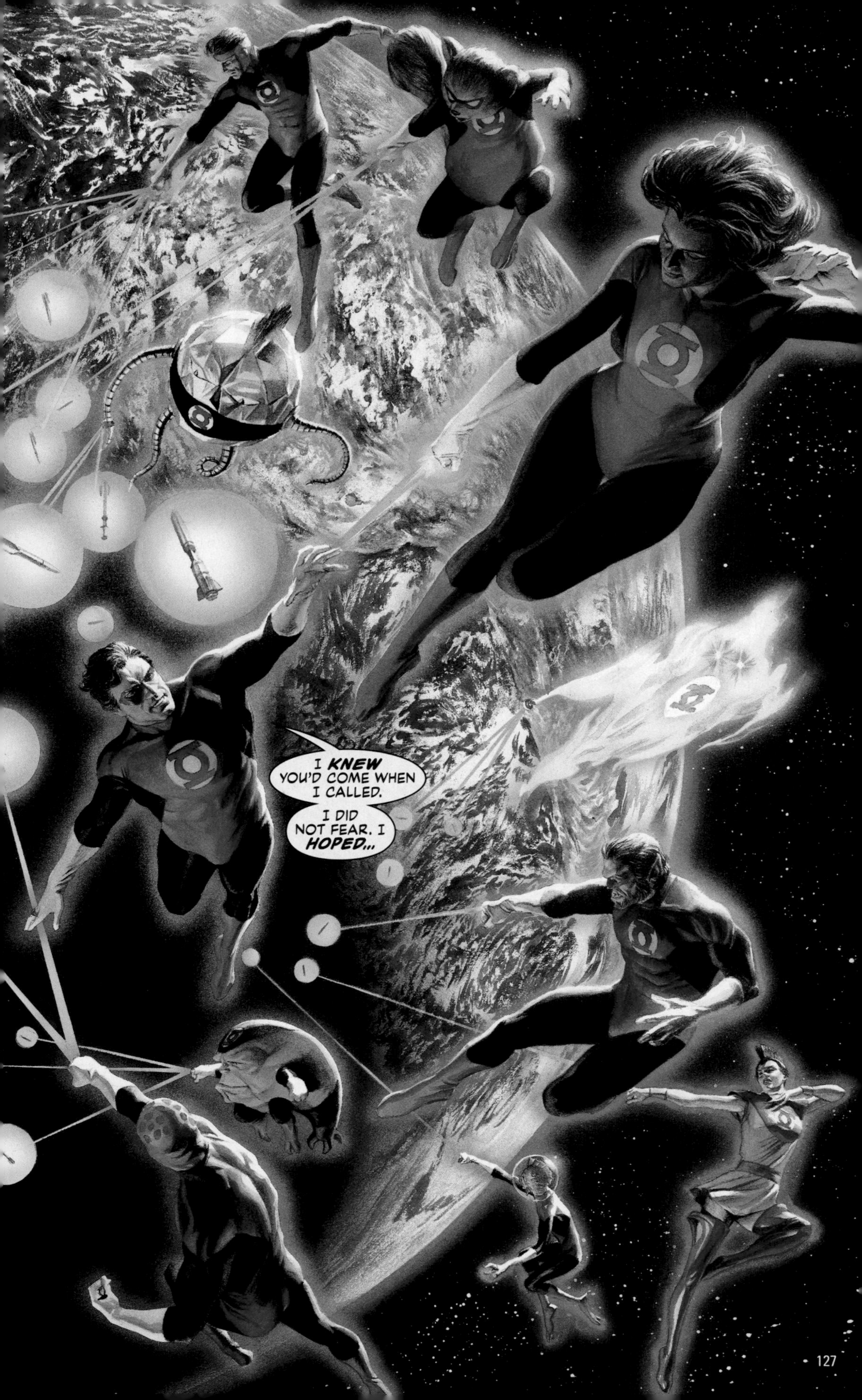
I KNEW YOU'D COME WHEN I CALLED.
I DID NOT FEAR. I HOPED...

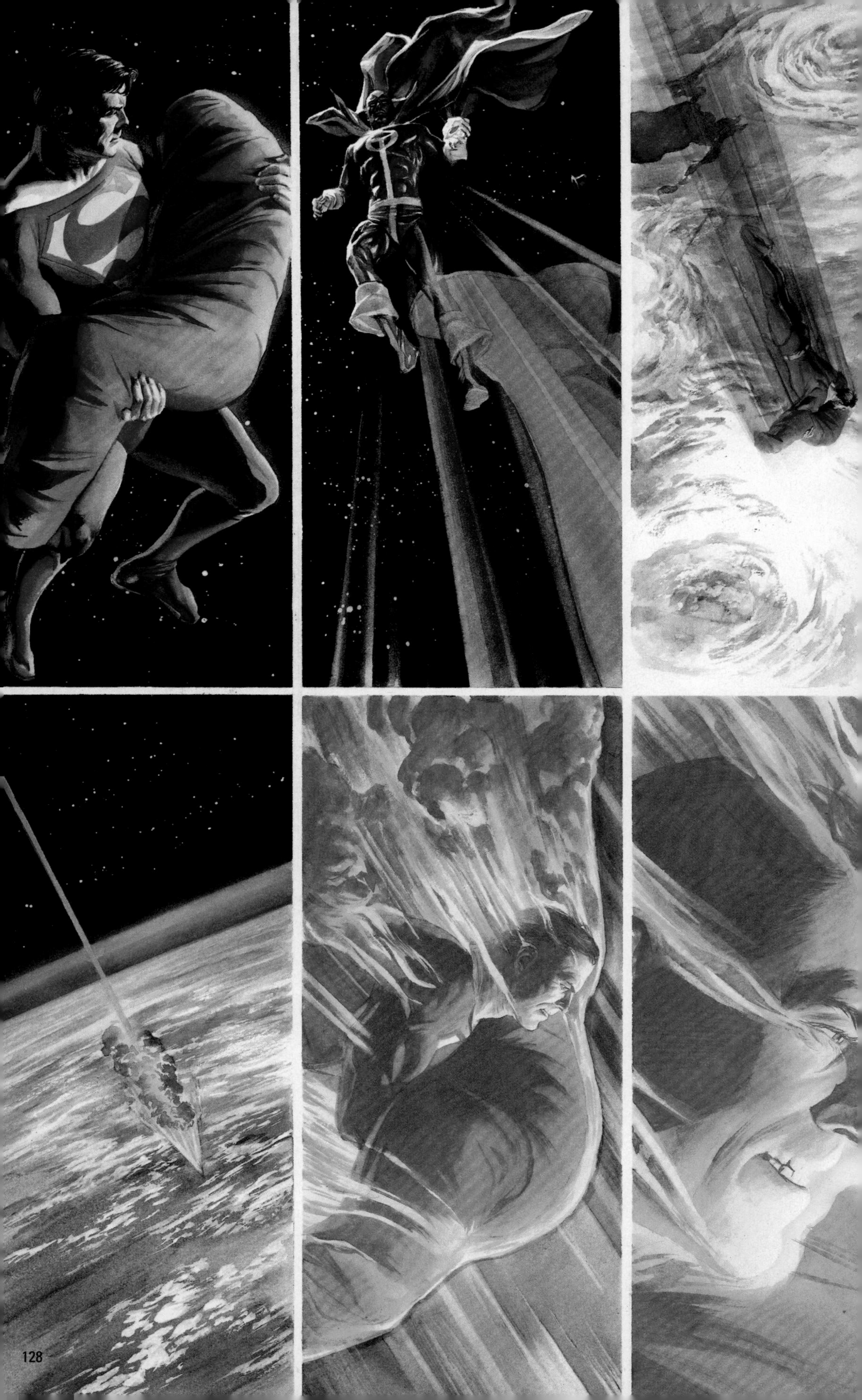

IT'S GOING TO BE OKAY, ZATANNA.
IT'S GOING...NO ONE DIES TODAY.
ZATANNA?
DO YOU HEAR ME?
GENTLY, CLARK, GENTLY.
...TWO... THREE...FOUR... FIVE...
...BREATHE, ZATANNA, BREATHE...
NOT LIKE THIS. NO ONE. NOT TODAY.
...EIGHT... NINE...TEN...
BREATHE.
...AHHHHHHH...
KOFF
KAFF
KOFF
SKNAHT...
SKNAHT?
...I MEAN... THANKS.

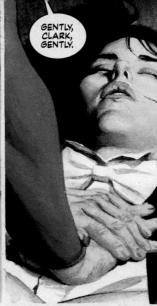

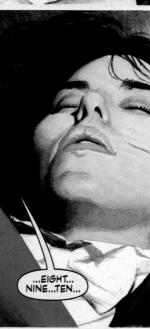

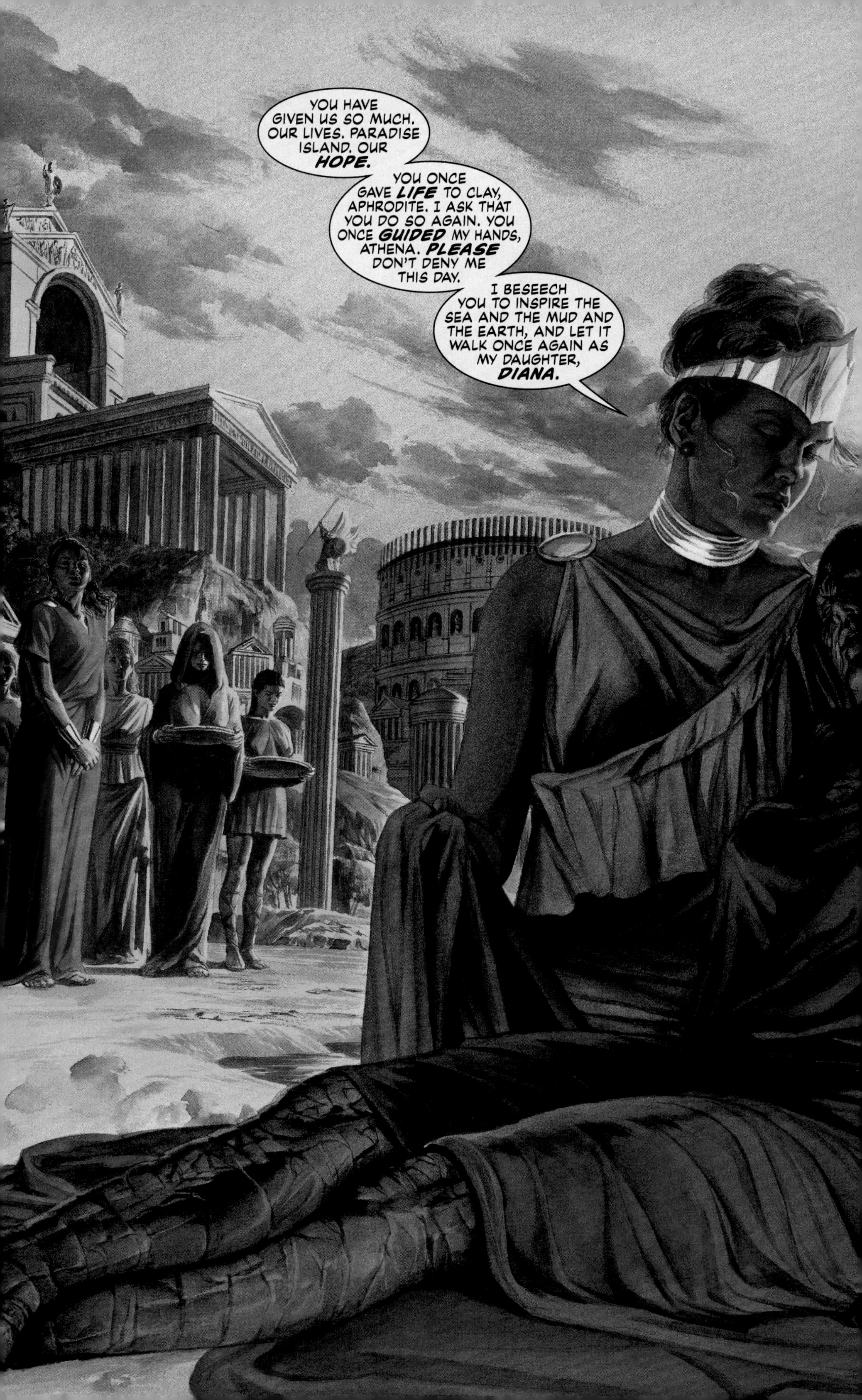
YOU HAVE GIVEN US SO MUCH. OUR LIVES. PARADISE ISLAND. OUR **HOPE.**
YOU ONCE GAVE **LIFE** TO CLAY, APHRODITE. I ASK THAT YOU DO SO AGAIN. YOU ONCE **GUIDED** MY HANDS, ATHENA. **PLEASE** DON'T DENY ME THIS DAY.
I BESEECH YOU TO INSPIRE THE SEA AND THE MUD AND THE EARTH, AND LET IT WALK ONCE AGAIN AS MY DAUGHTER, **DIANA.**

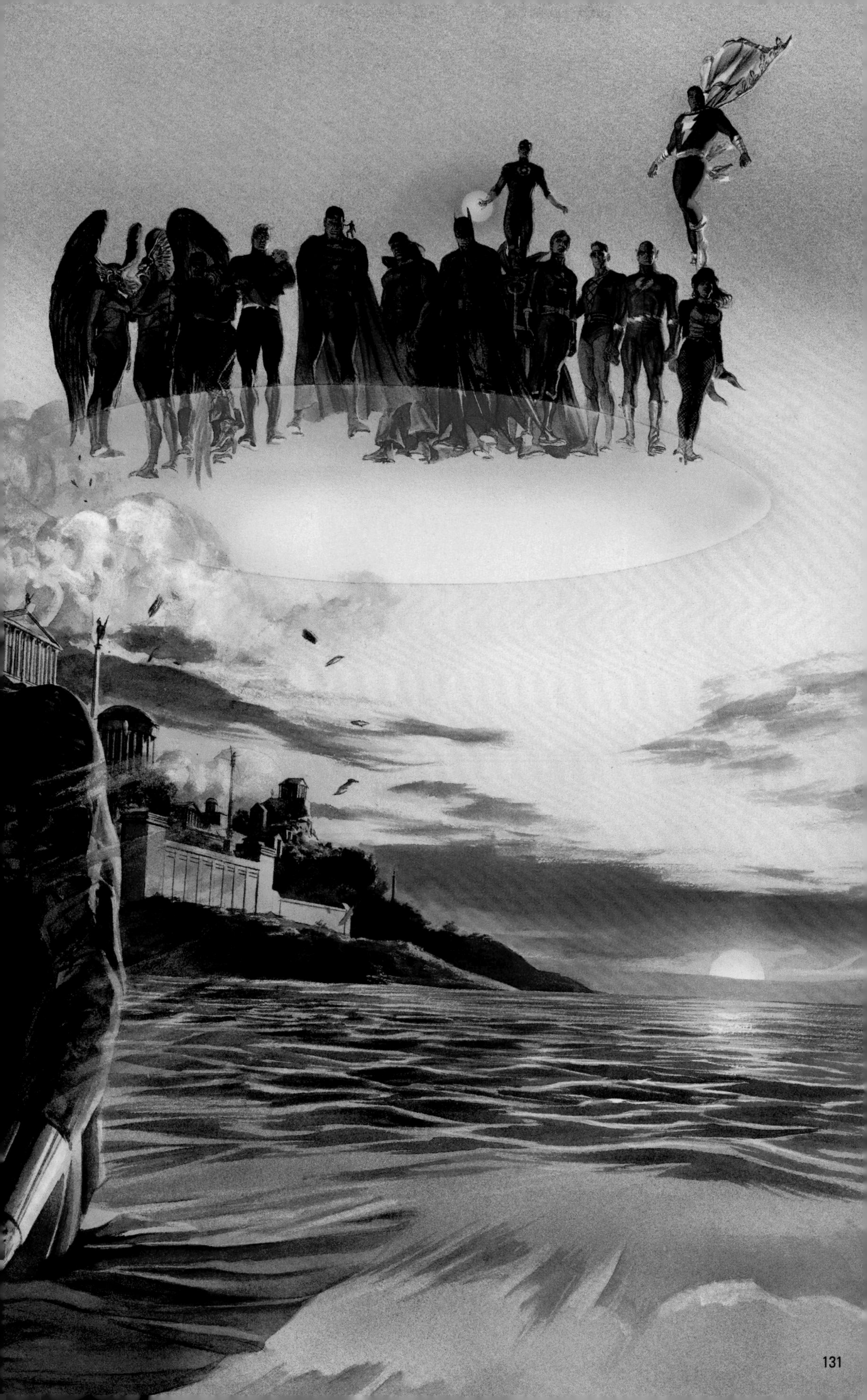

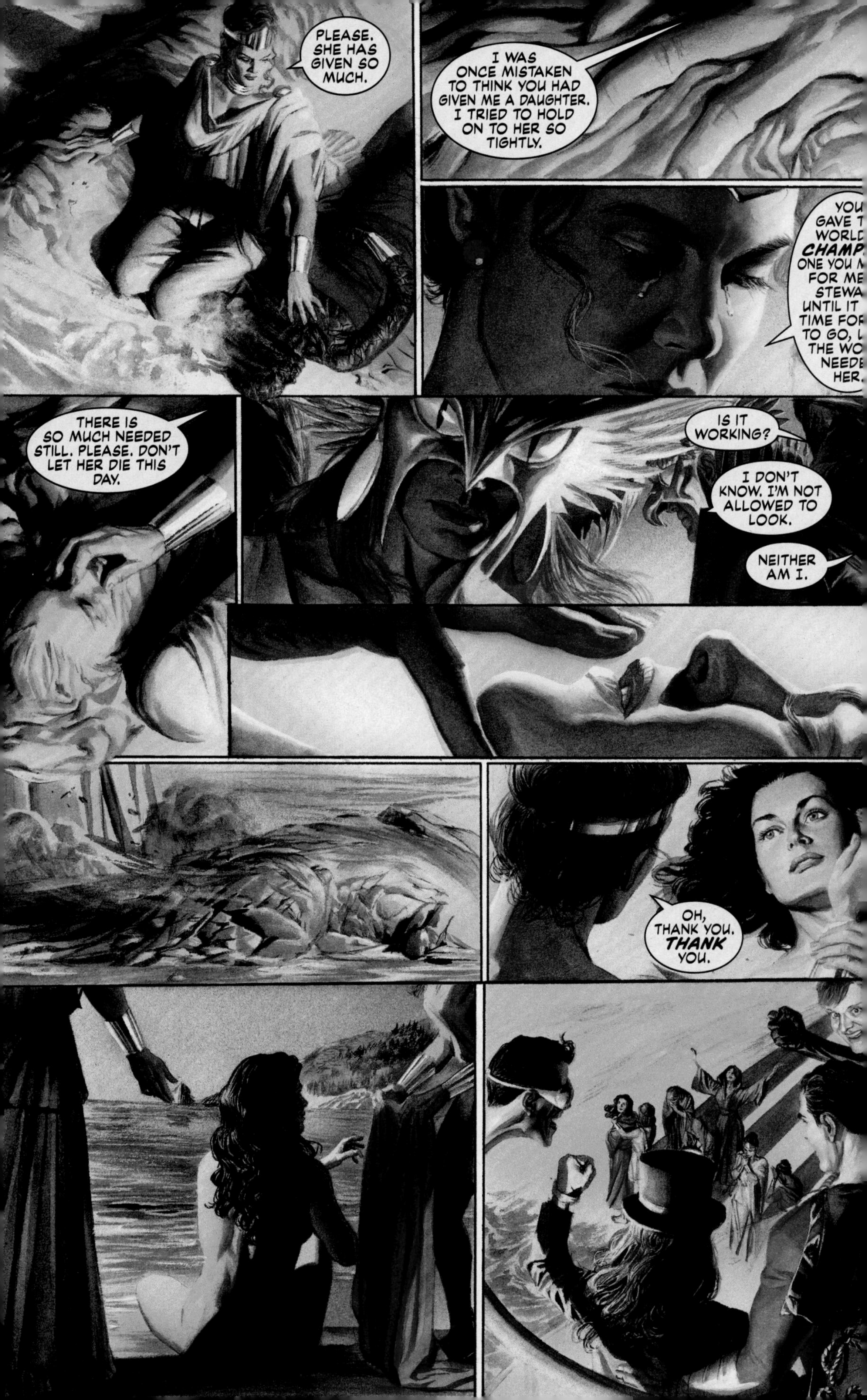
PLEASE. SHE HAS GIVEN SO MUCH.
I WAS ONCE MISTAKEN TO THINK YOU HAD GIVEN ME A DAUGHTER. I TRIED TO HOLD ON TO HER SO TIGHTLY.
YOU GAVE T WORLD CHAMP ONE YOU M FOR ME STEWA UNTIL IT TIME FOR TO GO, L THE WO NEEDE HER.
THERE IS SO MUCH NEEDED STILL. PLEASE. DON'T LET HER DIE THIS DAY.
IS IT WORKING?
I DON'T KNOW. I'M NOT ALLOWED TO LOOK.
NEITHER AM I.
OH, THANK YOU. THANK YOU.

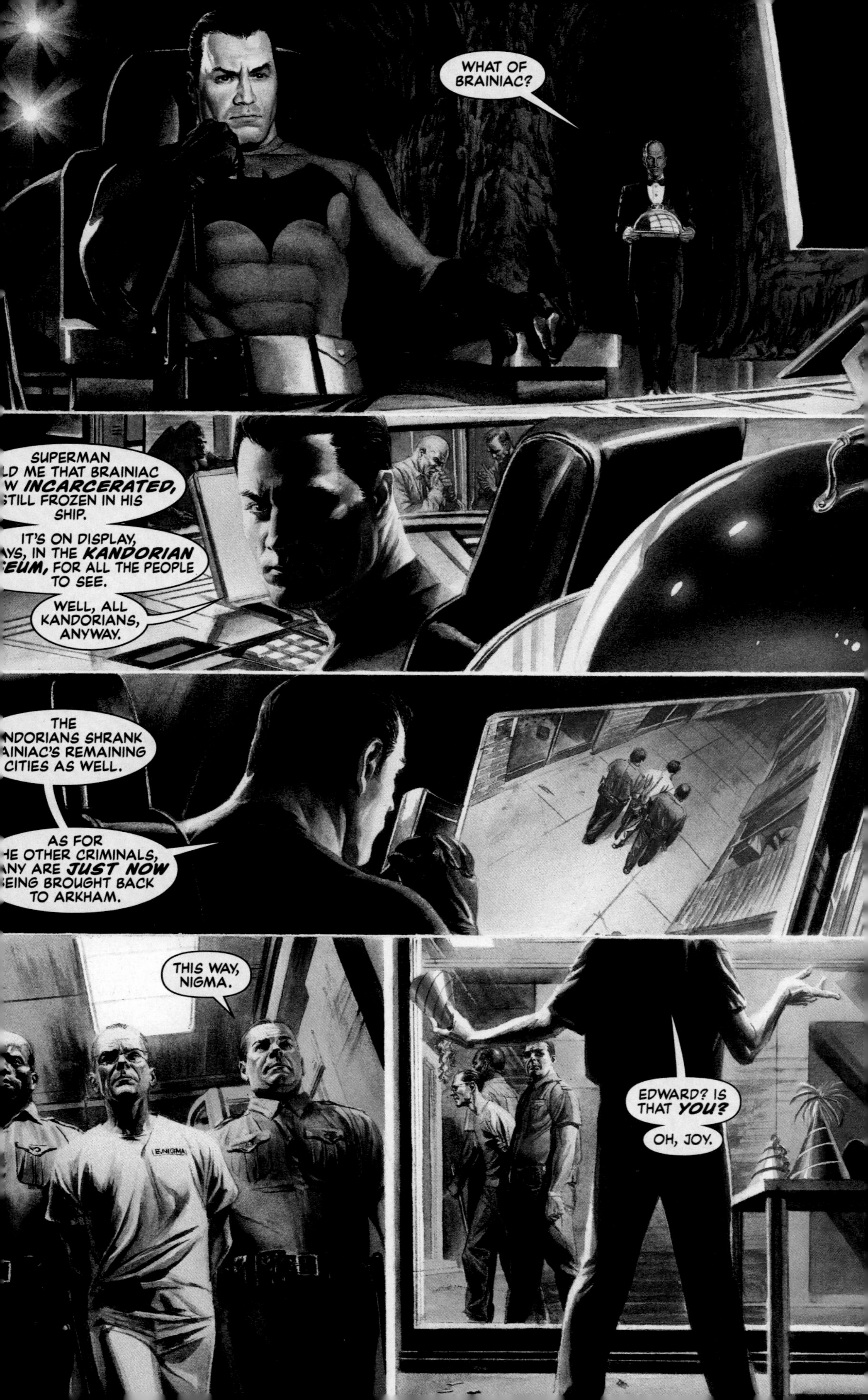
WHAT OF BRAINIAC?
SUPERMAN LD ME THAT BRAINIAC W INCARCERATED, STILL FROZEN IN HIS SHIP.
IT'S ON DISPLAY, AYS, IN THE KANDORIAN SEUM, FOR ALL THE PEOPLE TO SEE.
WELL, ALL KANDORIANS, ANYWAY.
THE NDORIANS SHRANK AINIAC'S REMAINING CITIES AS WELL.
AS FOR HE OTHER CRIMINALS, ANY ARE JUST NOW BEING BROUGHT BACK TO ARKHAM.
THIS WAY, NIGMA.
E.NIGMA
EDWARD? IS THAT YOU?
OH, JOY.

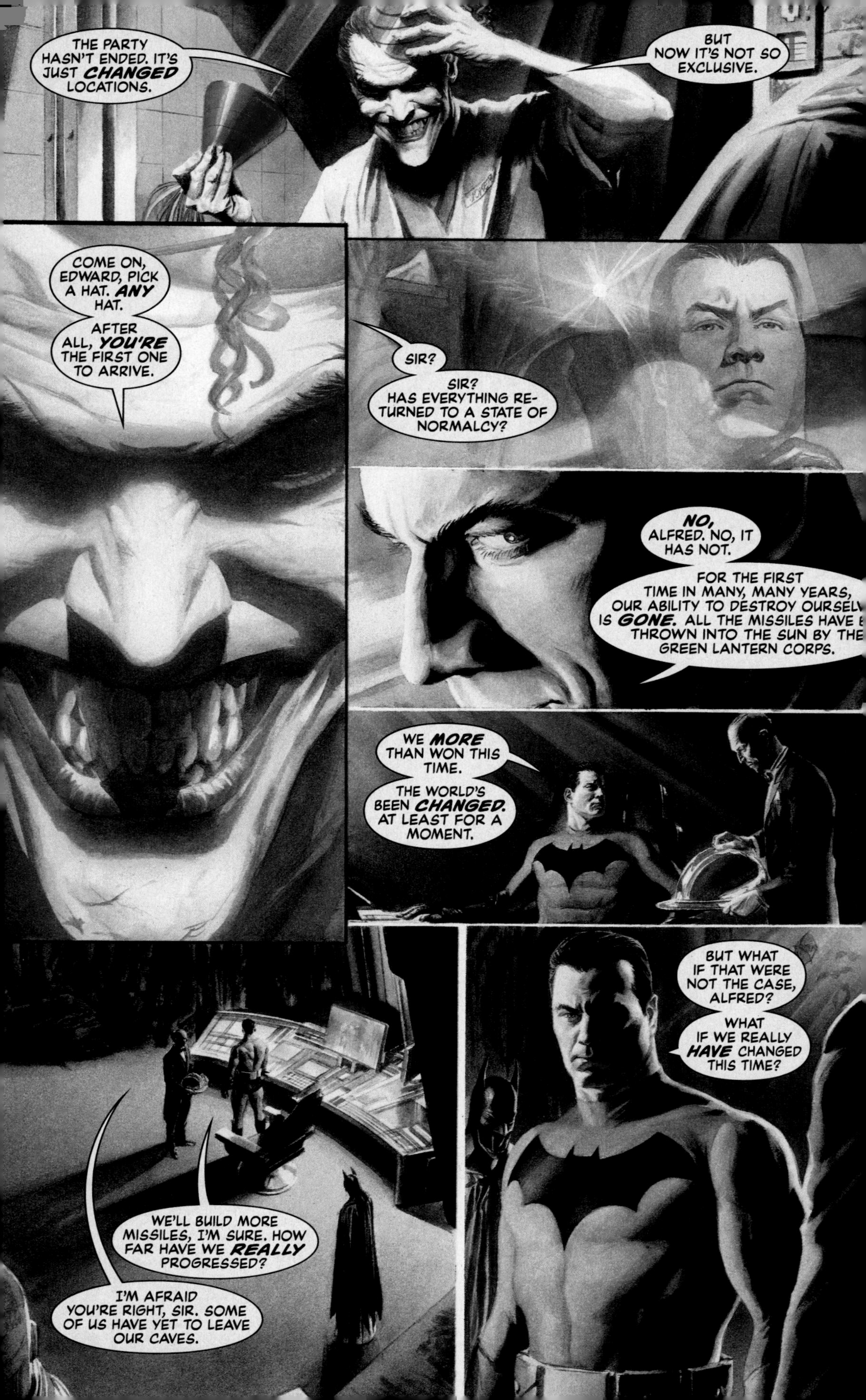
THE PARTY HASN'T ENDED. IT'S JUST CHANGED LOCATIONS.
BUT NOW IT'S NOT SO EXCLUSIVE.
COME ON, EDWARD, PICK A HAT. ANY HAT.
AFTER ALL, YOU'RE THE FIRST ONE TO ARRIVE.
SIR?
SIR? HAS EVERYTHING RE-TURNED TO A STATE OF NORMALCY?
NO, ALFRED. NO, IT HAS NOT.
FOR THE FIRST TIME IN MANY, MANY YEARS, OUR ABILITY TO DESTROY OURSELV IS GONE. ALL THE MISSILES HAVE THROWN INTO THE SUN BY THE GREEN LANTERN CORPS.
WE MORE THAN WON THIS TIME.
THE WORLD'S BEEN CHANGED. AT LEAST FOR A MOMENT.
WE'LL BUILD MORE MISSILES, I'M SURE. HOW FAR HAVE WE REALLY PROGRESSED?
I'M AFRAID YOU'RE RIGHT, SIR. SOME OF US HAVE YET TO LEAVE OUR CAVES.
BUT WHAT IF THAT WERE NOT THE CASE, ALFRED?
WHAT IF WE REALLY HAVE CHANGED THIS TIME?

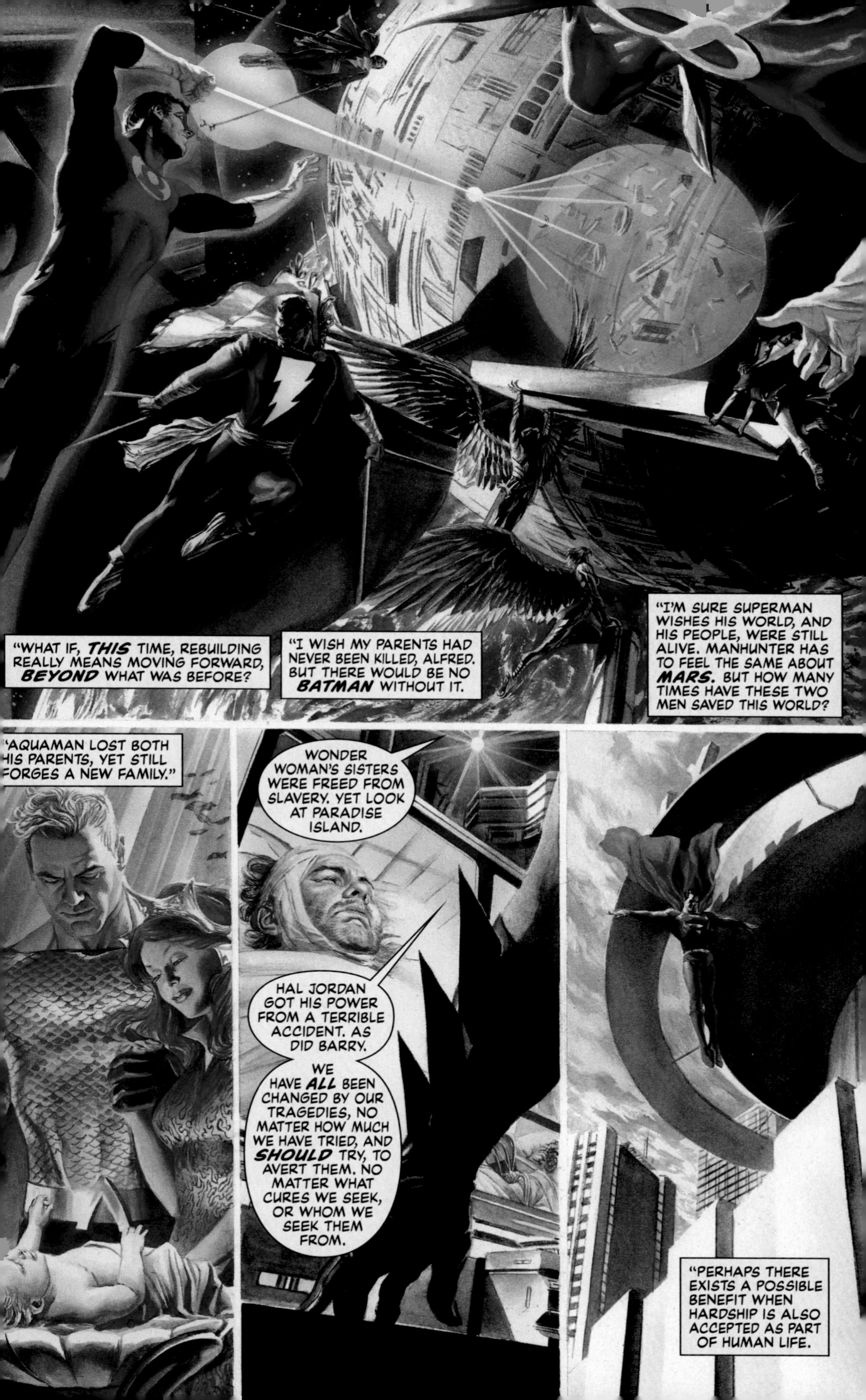
"WHAT IF, THIS TIME, REBUILDING REALLY MEANS MOVING FORWARD, BEYOND WHAT WAS BEFORE?
"I WISH MY PARENTS HAD NEVER BEEN KILLED, ALFRED. BUT THERE WOULD BE NO BATMAN WITHOUT IT.
"I'M SURE SUPERMAN WISHES HIS WORLD, AND HIS PEOPLE, WERE STILL ALIVE. MANHUNTER HAS TO FEEL THE SAME ABOUT MARS. BUT HOW MANY TIMES HAVE THESE TWO MEN SAVED THIS WORLD?
"AQUAMAN LOST BOTH HIS PARENTS, YET STILL FORGES A NEW FAMILY."
WONDER WOMAN'S SISTERS WERE FREED FROM SLAVERY. YET LOOK AT PARADISE ISLAND.
HAL JORDAN GOT HIS POWER FROM A TERRIBLE ACCIDENT. AS DID BARRY.
WE HAVE ALL BEEN CHANGED BY OUR TRAGEDIES, NO MATTER HOW MUCH WE HAVE TRIED, AND SHOULD TRY, TO AVERT THEM. NO MATTER WHAT CURES WE SEEK, OR WHOM WE SEEK THEM FROM.
"PERHAPS THERE EXISTS A POSSIBLE BENEFIT WHEN HARDSHIP IS ALSO ACCEPTED AS PART OF HUMAN LIFE.

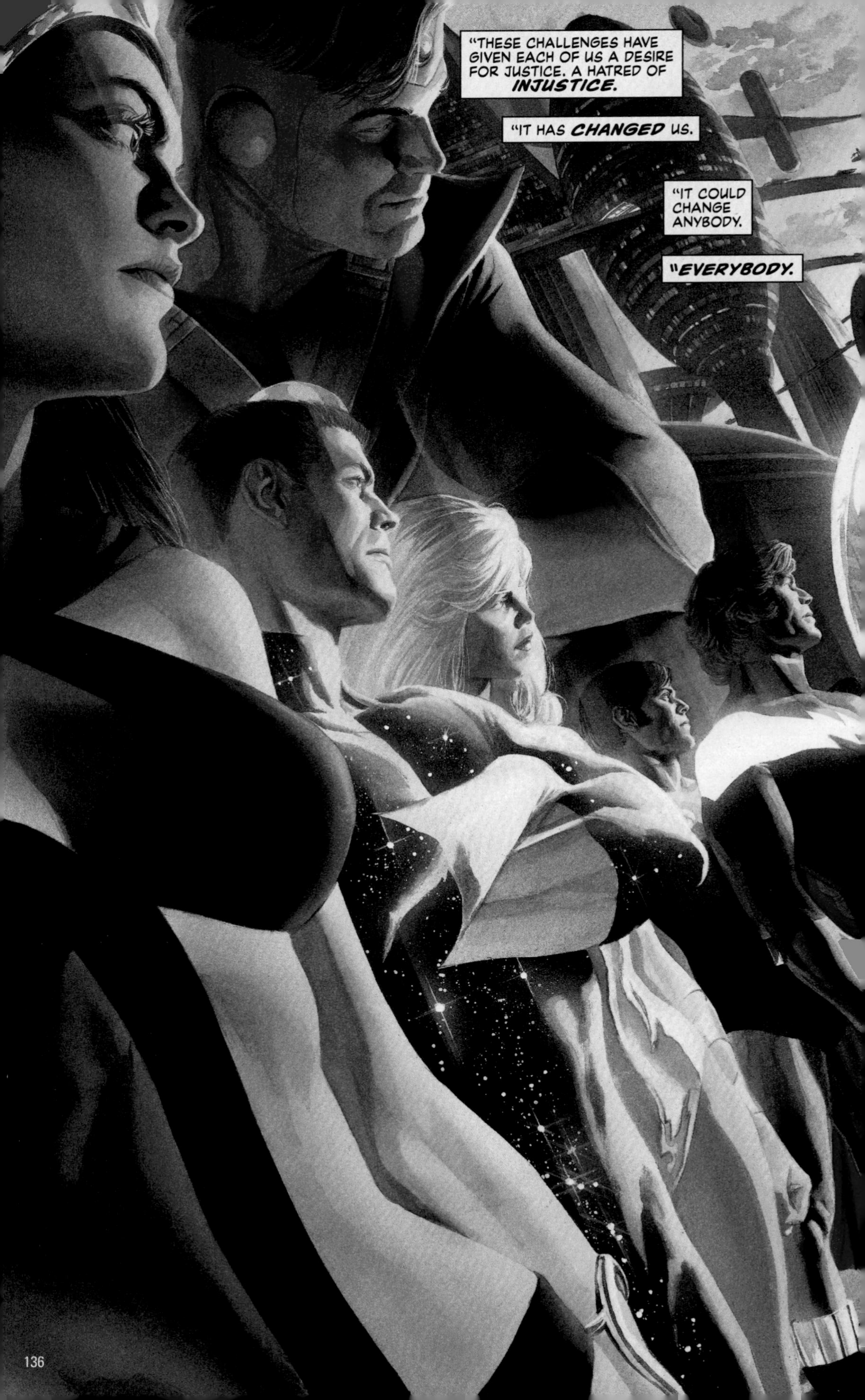
"THESE CHALLENGES HAVE GIVEN EACH OF US A DESIRE FOR JUSTICE. A HATRED OF ***INJUSTICE.***
"IT HAS ***CHANGED*** US.
"IT COULD CHANGE ANYBODY.
"***EVERYBODY.***

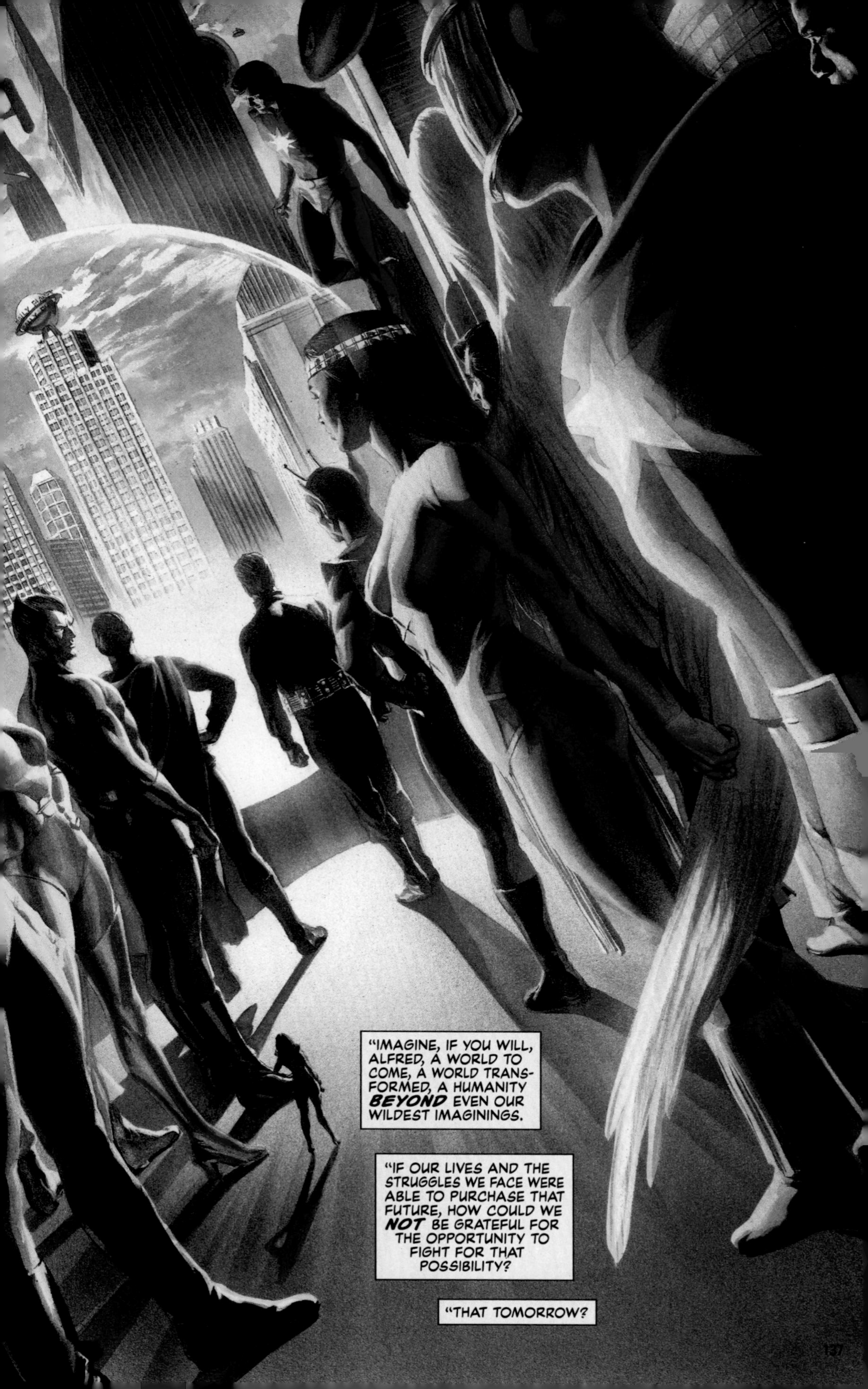
"IMAGINE, IF YOU WILL, ALFRED, A WORLD TO COME, A WORLD TRANS-FORMED, A HUMANITY *BEYOND* EVEN OUR WILDEST IMAGININGS.
"IF OUR LIVES AND THE STRUGGLES WE FACE WERE ABLE TO PURCHASE THAT FUTURE, HOW COULD WE *NOT* BE GRATEFUL FOR THE OPPORTUNITY TO FIGHT FOR THAT POSSIBILITY?
"THAT TOMORROW?

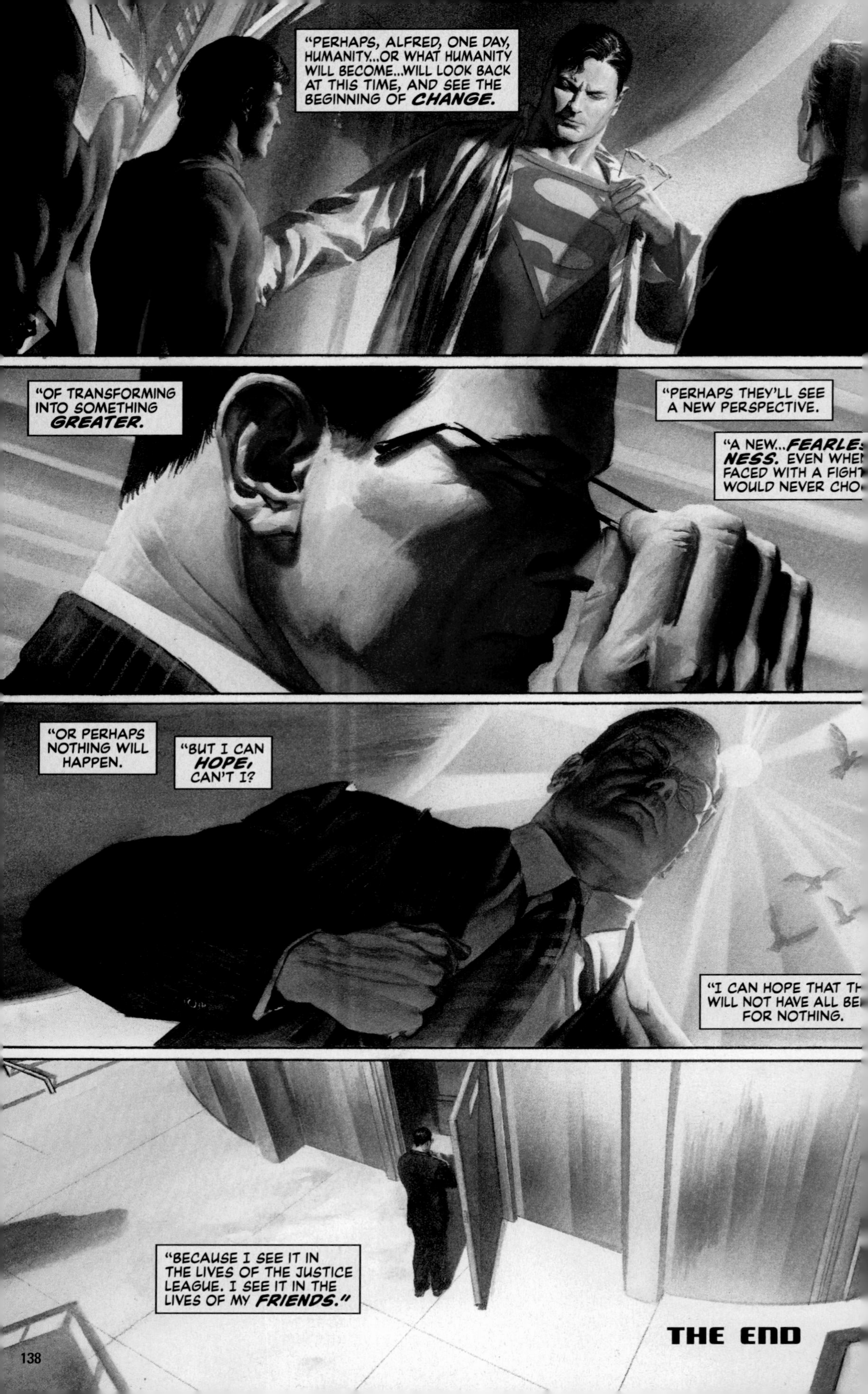
"PERHAPS, ALFRED, ONE DAY, HUMANITY...OR WHAT HUMANITY WILL BECOME...WILL LOOK BACK AT THIS TIME, AND SEE THE BEGINNING OF CHANGE.
"OF TRANSFORMING INTO SOMETHING GREATER.
"PERHAPS THEY'LL SEE A NEW PERSPECTIVE.
"A NEW...FEARLE NESS. EVEN WHE FACED WITH A FIGHT WOULD NEVER CHO
"OR PERHAPS NOTHING WILL HAPPEN.
"BUT I CAN HOPE, CAN'T I?
"I CAN HOPE THAT TH WILL NOT HAVE ALL BE FOR NOTHING.
"BECAUSE I SEE IT IN THE LIVES OF THE JUSTICE LEAGUE. I SEE IT IN THE LIVES OF MY FRIENDS."
THE END

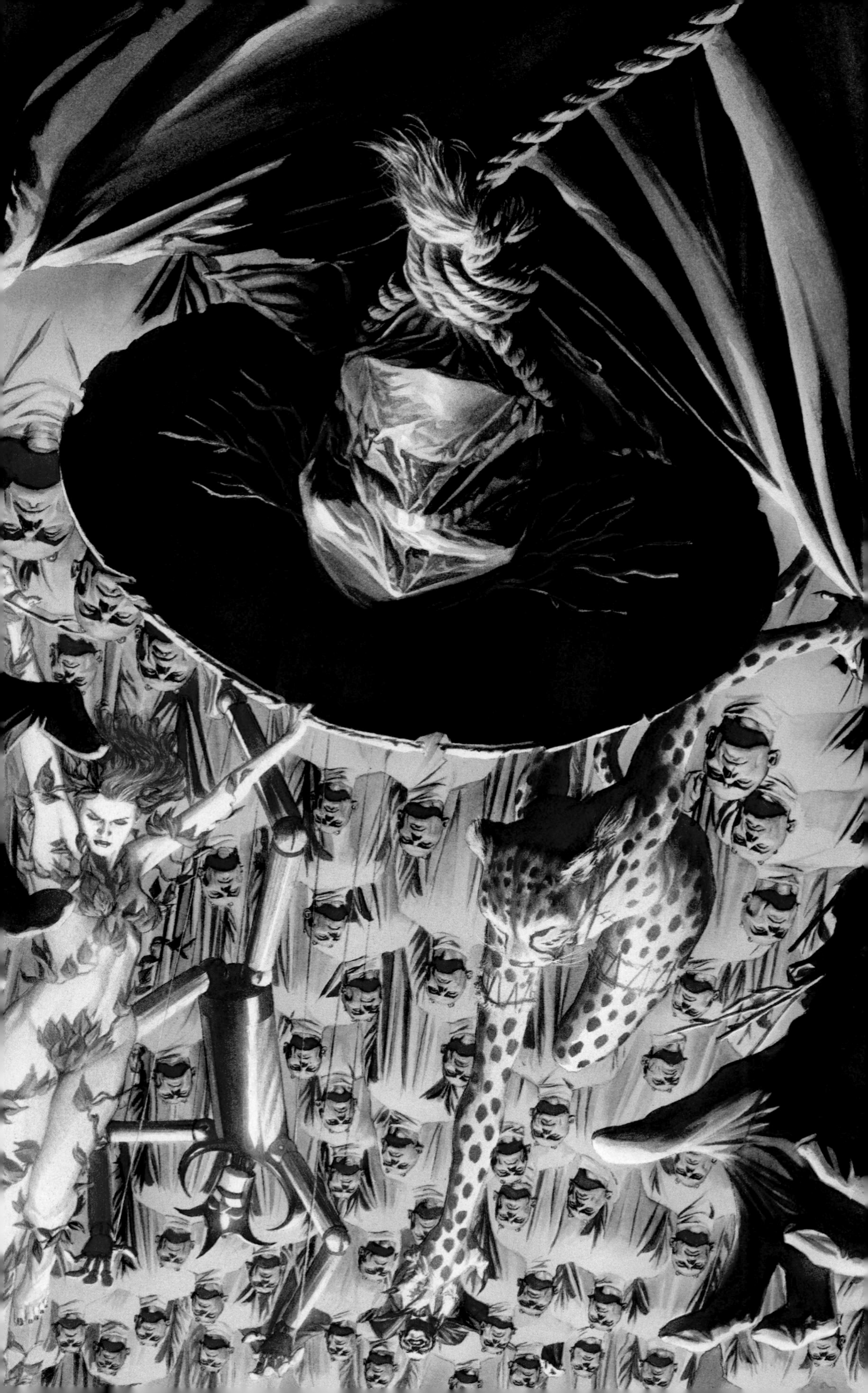

FROM BRUCE WAYNE'S PRIVATE FILES IN THE BATCOMPUTER

CAPTAIN MARVEL

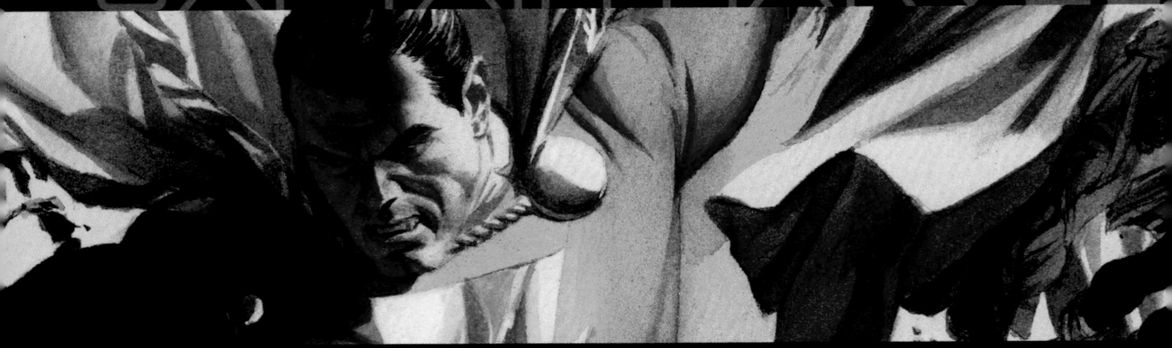

He was a child on the streets, visited by a mysterious stranger, taken to a secret place...

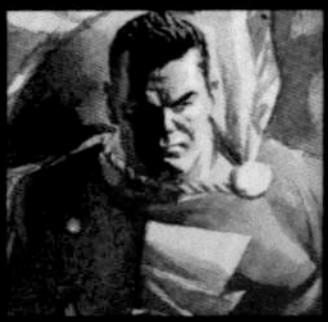

It's not that Billy Batson *is* **CAPTAIN MARVEL**. It's more like he *becomes* Captain Marvel. Like Clark, like me, Batson is an orphan. But unlike Clark and myself, Billy is still a child. Perhaps that is why his story is more like a fairy tale. He did not have a home; that was taken from him. He was a child on the streets, visited by a mysterious stranger, taken to a secret place, shown the seven primary weaknesses of man, and introduced to a wizard. The Wizard gave Batson magical powers capable of fighting mankind's weaknesses, powers derived from the Wizard's name – SHAZAM.

When Batson speaks the magic word, the Wizard's name, he transforms into an adult with the mythic wisdom of Solomon, the strength of Hercules, the stamina of Atlas, the power of Zeus, the courage of Achilles, and the speed of Mercury.

Captain Marvel can fly. While his form is similar to that of Superman, Batson is also much like Clark Kent. Batson learns of the needs of the world around him by working as the youngest newscaster at a local radio station. His sister Mary has also been given powers. And there are others still in the mythos established by the magician. There is a sort of Marvel family, as if it is the battle that forges community.

Sometimes I wonder what would have happened if Billy had had a parent present. Would he have become the world's mightiest mortal? Or would he have been told that he was not allowed to grow up to be a hero? I wonder if the same could be said of me.

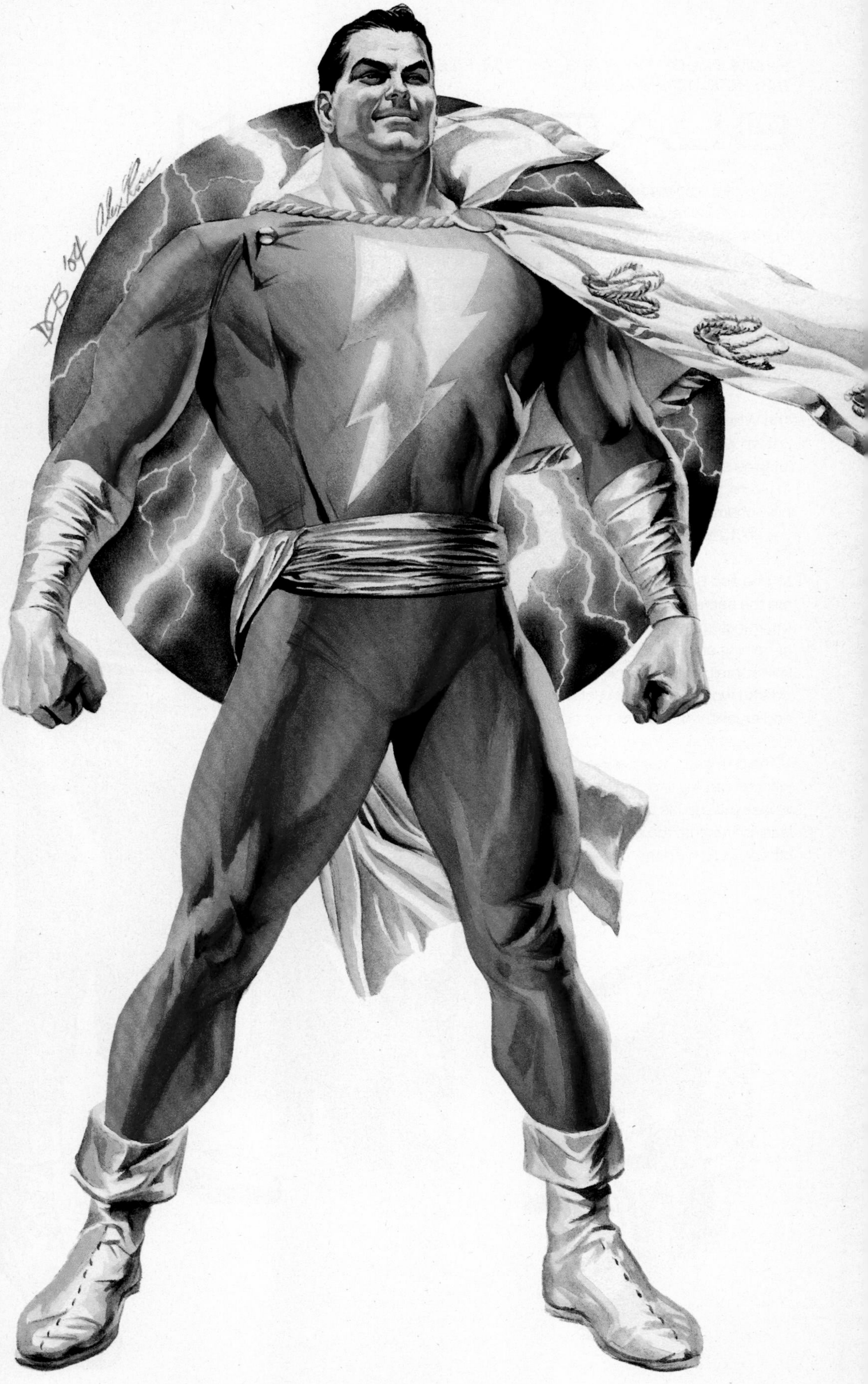

FROM BRUCE WAYNE'S PRIVATE FILES
IN THE BATCOMPUTER

BLACK ADAM

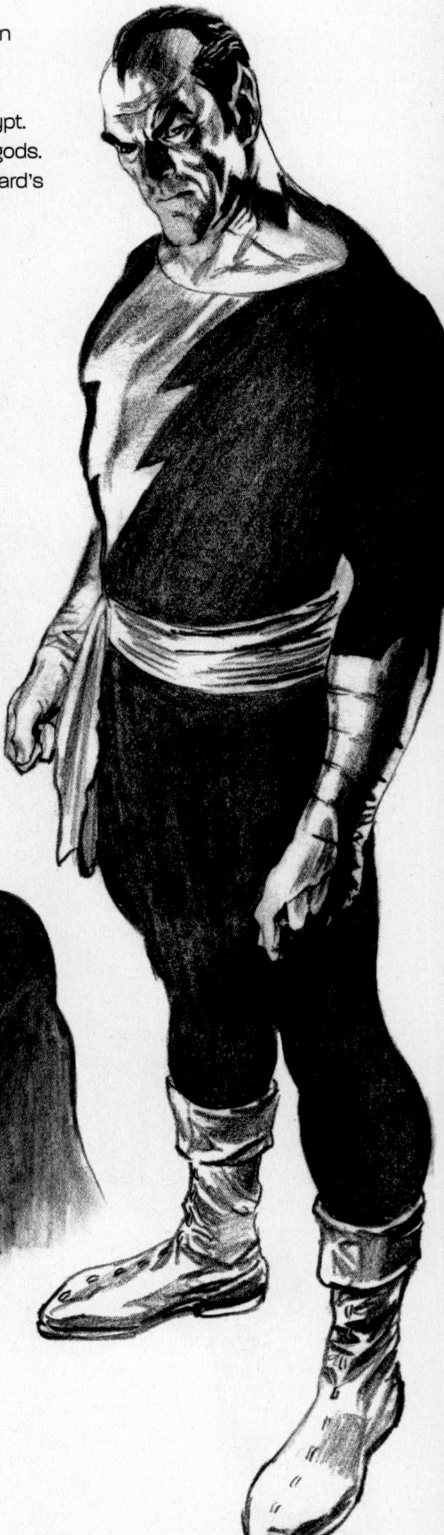

The wizard who made it possible for Billy Batson to become Captain Marvel is also responsible for empowering the monster known as **BLACK ADAM**. From what I have pieced together, this enemy of Captain Marvel was born sometime during the 19th dynasty of Egypt. Like Captain Marvel, his power is an amalgamation of six different gods. But unlike him, the power corrupted the man chosen to be the Wizard's champion. Perhaps that is why the Wizard chose a boy when he came to Batson. Children are easier to mold, quicker to learn, easier to put on a path from which they won't deviate.

The Wizard banished Black Adam, casting him beyond all known worlds and solar systems. It seems difficult even to imagine such a possibility, but it took Adam thousands of years to return. His return was marked by the Wizard's choosing of a new champion — Captain Marvel. He has speed, strength, and the ability to match all of Captain Marvel's powers.

My life and Batson's are so similar. Our losses are the same. Yet, there is a difference. My transformation came through years of training and discipline. His came immediately. When I think of Black Adam, I wonder, between Batson and myself, which of us might be more susceptible to corruption — the one given magical wisdom without earning it, or the one whose pride in his training and learning resents the other's otherworldly wisdom.

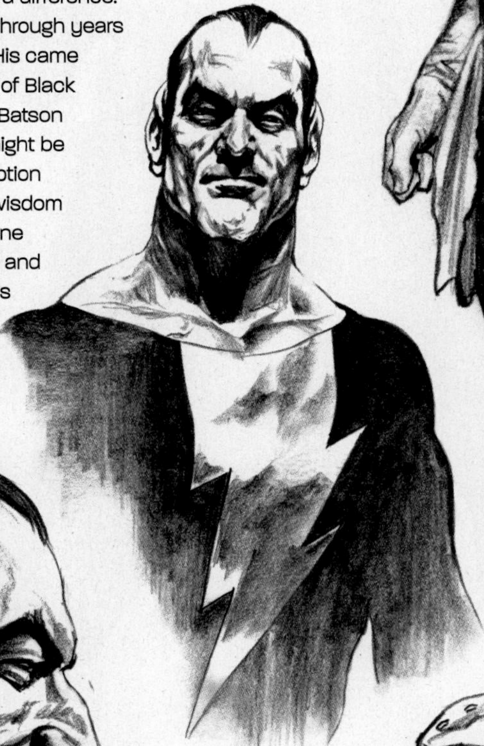

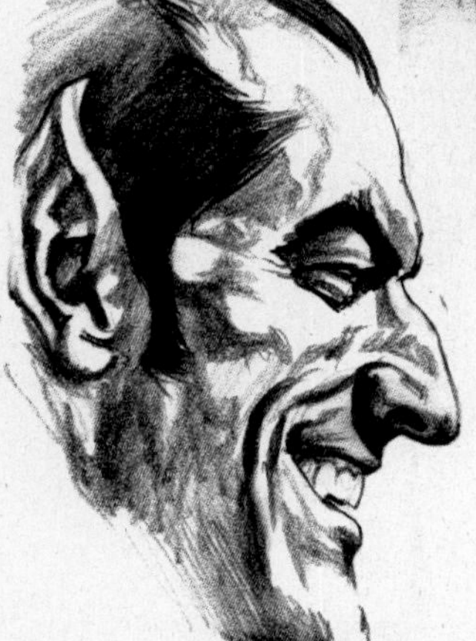

FROM BRUCE WAYNE'S PRIVATE FILES IN THE BATCOMPUTER

SIVANA

HADDEUS B. SIVANA has fought Captain Marvel more often than any of the World's Mightiest Mortal's enemies. ust as the Joker, who mocks death and revels in the suffering and losses of others, is my antithesis, Sivana is the pposite of Captain Marvel. While Captain Marvel is a being of magic, Sivana knows only the secrets of science, nly what the intelligence of man can discover. He has been widowed twice, and the pain of those losses led to is becoming twisted and embittered against the very humanity he once invented and created for.

is knowledge is more than Earth-based, though. He spent years in self-imposed exile on another planet, studying race of creatures there, becoming adept in the secrets of that world. Perhaps his time there further twisted him nto what he is. He has no physical power or strength, but he has developed a means to walk through walls by peaking a scientific formula of sorts.

ore magic words, even if they are clothed in science. wonder if Sivana is even aware how affected he is by rces beyond his control.

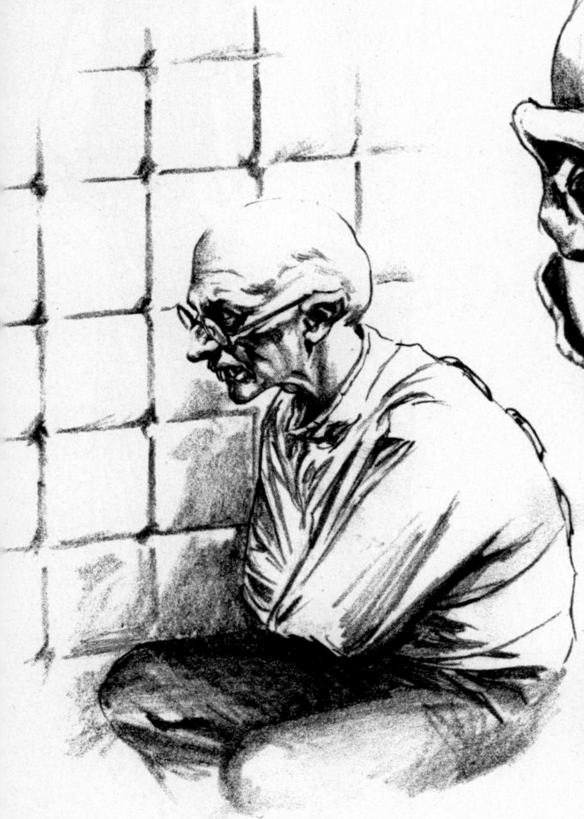

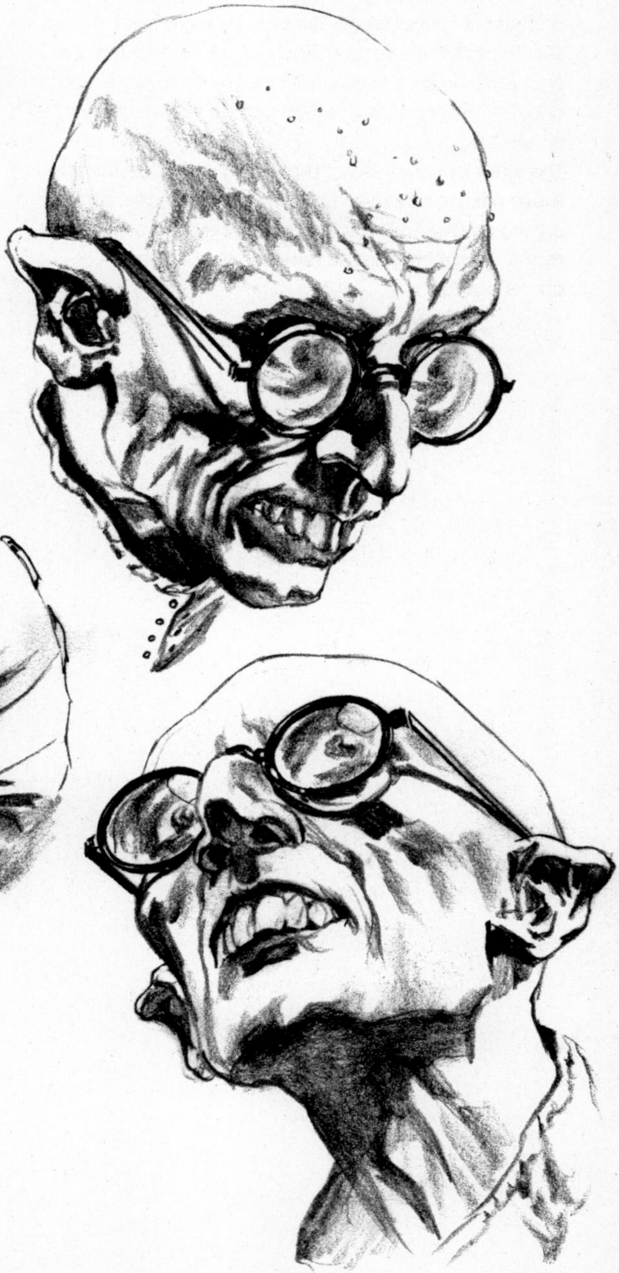

FROM BRUCE WAYNE'S PRIVATE FILES
IN THE BATCOMPUTER

SCARECROW

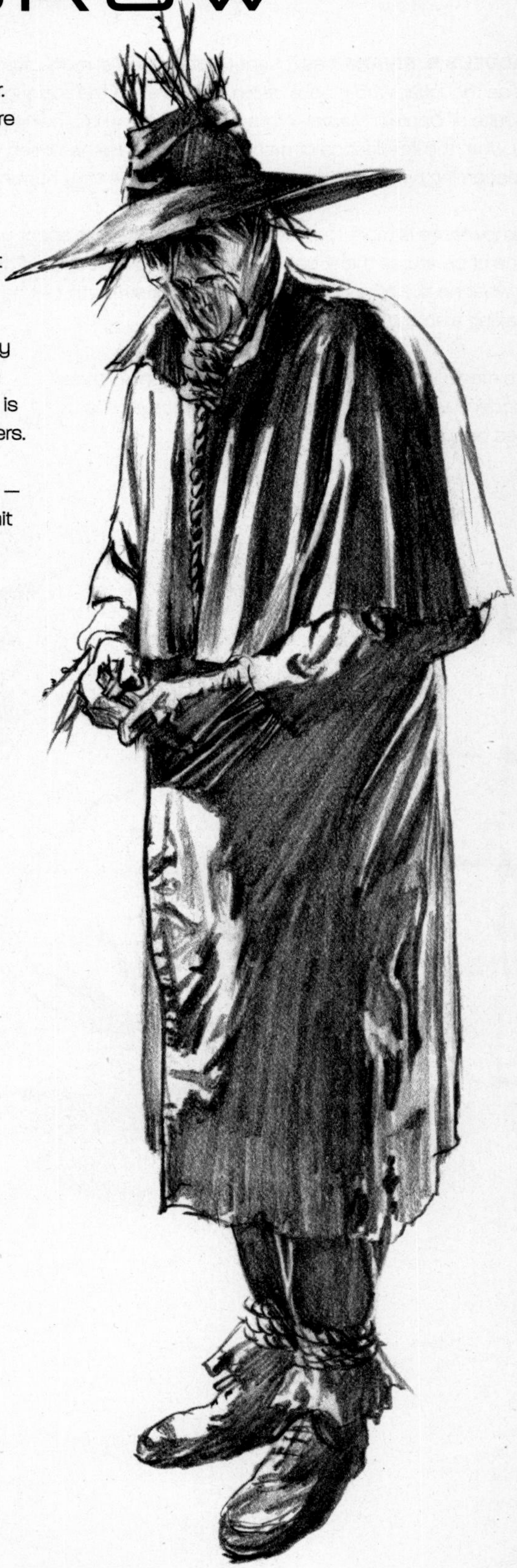

I became a bat so that the criminal element would fear me. But I must never forget that they, too, use fear. **JONATHAN CRANE** was called a scarecrow long before he turned to crime, wore a costume, and created fear-based hallucination-inducing gases to render his victims powerless before him.

There are some, in academic circles, who suggest that Crane turned to crime and his masquerade because of the jeers and taunts of peers back when he was a professor of psychology. But crime is more than merely the result of the effects of such oppression. Crime is a choice. The desire to take advantage of someone else is one that overwhelms the desire to live rightly with others.

The want for power over others, the need to be feared — these are common elements among those who commit crime and those who fight it. It may be this truth that Crane fears most: that he had a choice, and he chose poorly.

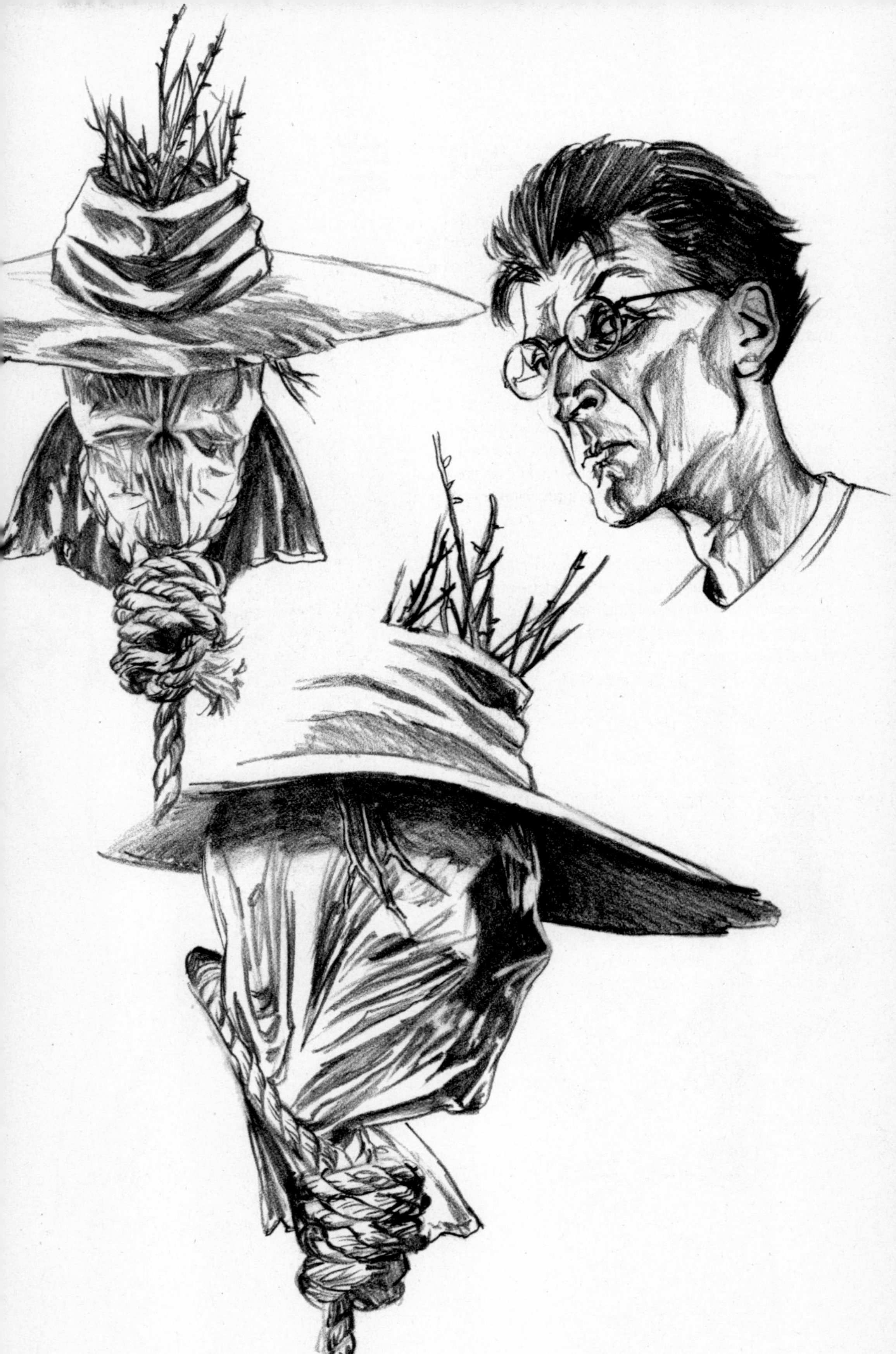

FROM BRUCE WAYNE'S PRIVATE FILES IN THE BATCOMPUTER

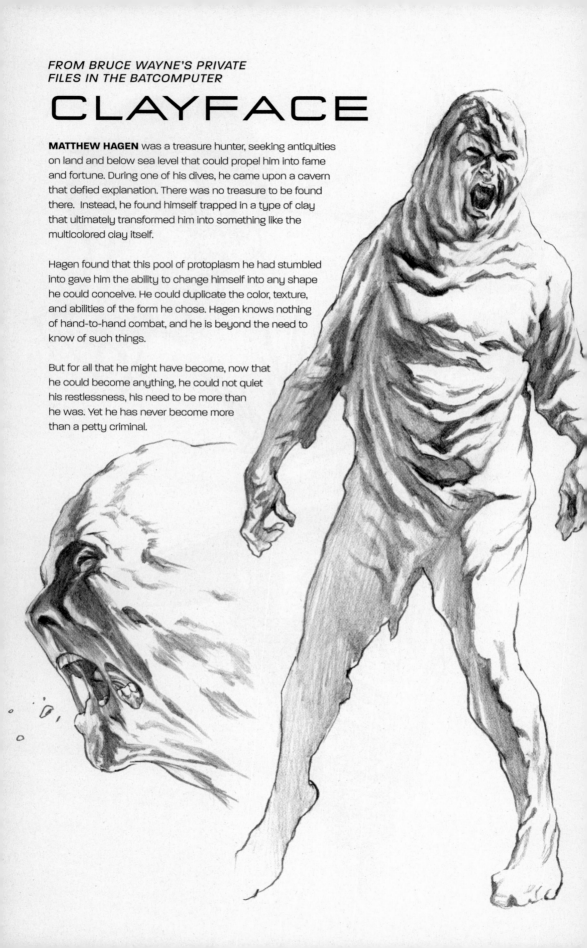

CLAYFACE

MATTHEW HAGEN was a treasure hunter, seeking antiquities on land and below sea level that could propel him into fame and fortune. During one of his dives, he came upon a cavern that defied explanation. There was no treasure to be found there. Instead, he found himself trapped in a type of clay that ultimately transformed him into something like the multicolored clay itself.

Hagen found that this pool of protoplasm he had stumbled into gave him the ability to change himself into any shape he could conceive. He could duplicate the color, texture, and abilities of the form he chose. Hagen knows nothing of hand-to-hand combat, and he is beyond the need to know of such things.

But for all that he might have become, now that he could become anything, he could not quiet his restlessness, his need to be more than he was. Yet he has never become more than a petty criminal.

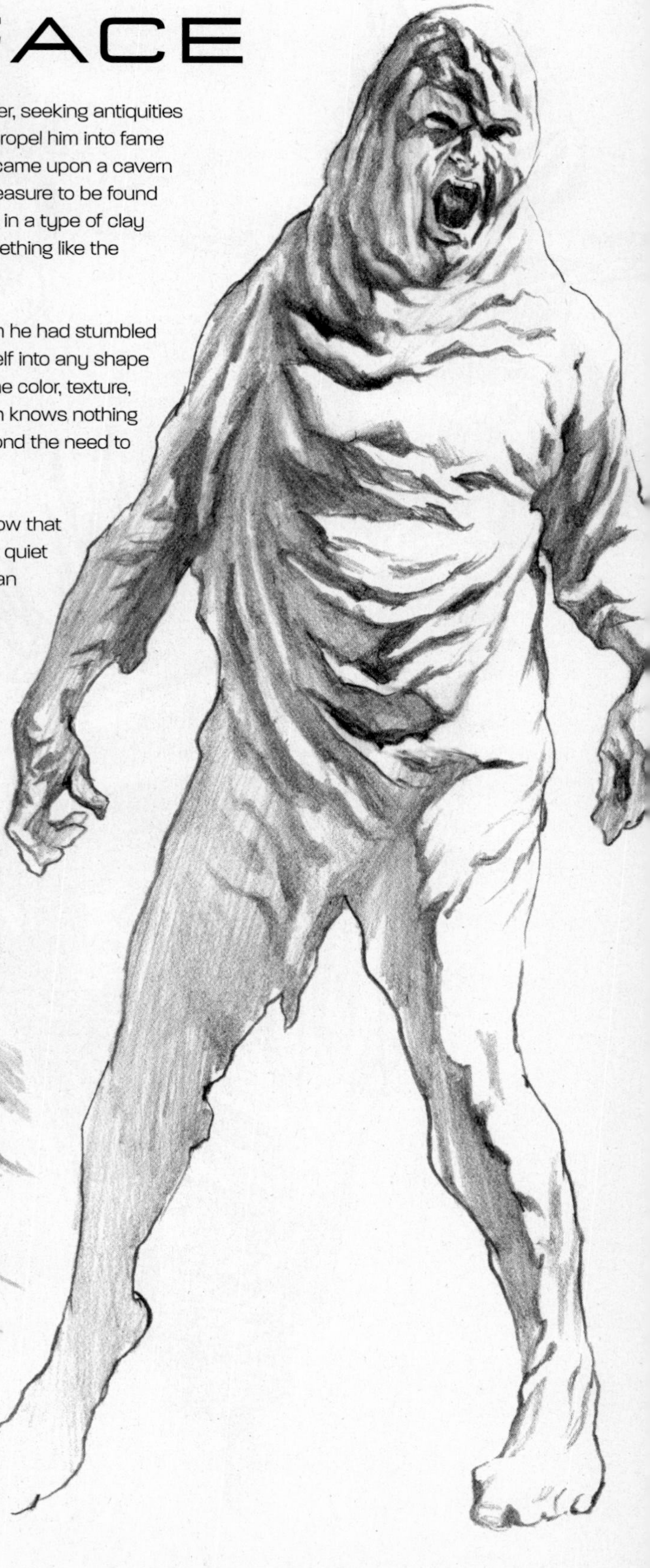

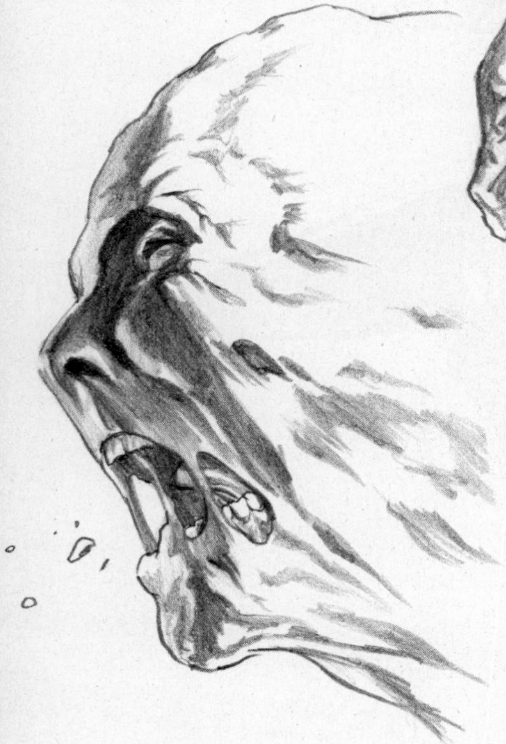

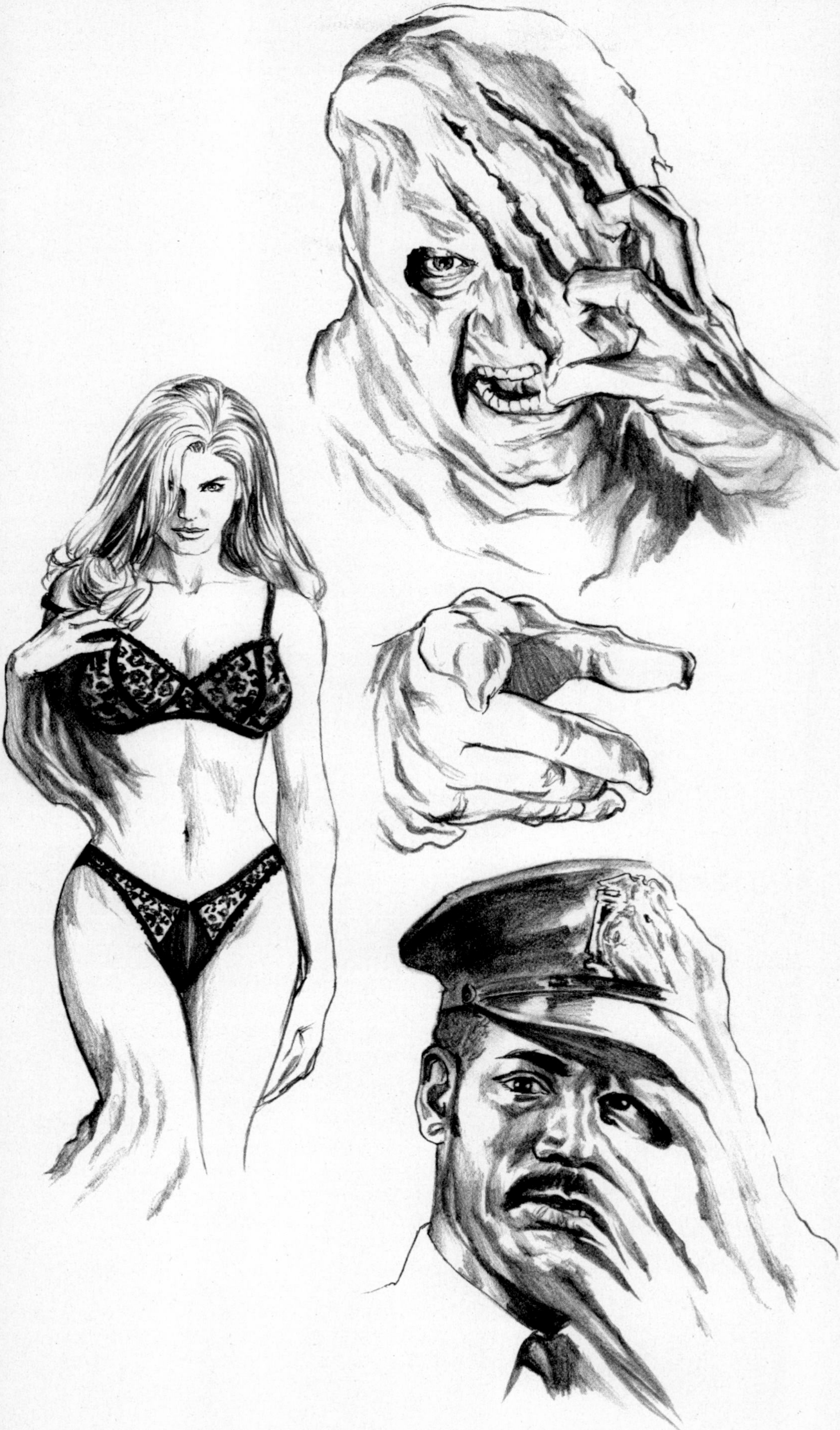

FROM BRUCE WAYNE'S PRIVATE FILES IN THE BATCOMPUTER

GREEN ARROW/ BLACK CANARY

...ironically, a band of criminals who nearly put an end to him might instead have been his salvation.

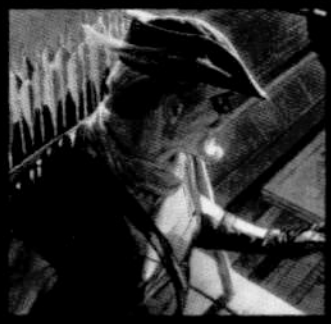

I knew of **OLIVER QUEEN** long before I chose to become Batman. That was long before Oliver faced a challenge that would make him the Justice Leaguer known as Green Arrow.

Queen was born to wealth, like me. His family was not taken from him as mine was, so he grew accustomed to comfort and a quality of life that can detach some from their humanity. That could have been his fate. But ironically, a band of criminals who nearly put an end to him might instead have been his salvation.

His boat was overtaken by modern-day pirates. Queen was knocked overboard. He survived but was lost on an uncharted island. This forced the rich man to live in the most primitive way imaginable. If he did not work to build a shelter, he spent his nights in the rain. If he did not hunt, he did not eat. So, after assembling a makeshift bow and carving arrows, he learned to hunt. He became proficient at it and created a life for himself, until the pirates who stole his boat and former life visited his island.

With his new weapons, he defeated the thieves and rescued their newest victims. When he could return to his riches, they no longer matched his tastes. Still, the money proved useful for the purpose that now consumed him, confronting urban crime. To this end, he created a series of trick arrows, capable of launching nets, exploding upon impact, and even "punching out" assailants.

Queen's story is different from mine, yet in many ways we reached the same place. He has no enhanced abilities or magical weapons save what has been possible through the application of design and skill. The Green Arrow is a valuable ally. His longtime alliance with the Black Canary has become a source of strength and focus

---

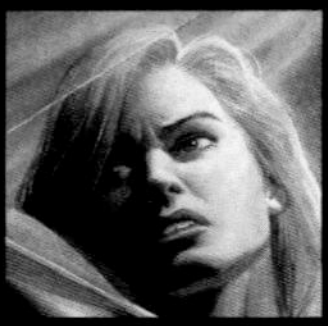

Dinah Lance is the **BLACK CANARY**, but this is her second life. She was a costumed adventurer with her detective husband until the day she was widowed, when her world changed forever. She joined the Justice League of America, searching for something that passed for stability and community. It was in their midst, during a battle with one of the League's enemies, that she received the power of a voice that can shatter wood and stone.

...she began fighting crime out of human empathy, but became something more than human while fighting alongside the League.

In many ways, she began fighting crime out of human empathy, but became something more than human while fighting alongside the League. Her relationship with Green Arrow has been vital to both of them. Both lost their worlds. While I normally consider relationships a disadvantage to our mission, this relationship gives her strength. Together, Green Arrow and Black Canary have fought against local crime as well as the interplanetary variety we often face in the Justice League.

Dinah also runs a local business, as manager and owner of a flower shop. Her relationship with those whose lives she has saved over and over again is therefore closer than perhaps anyone else in the League. She doesn't merely save the city; she lives within it and with its people.

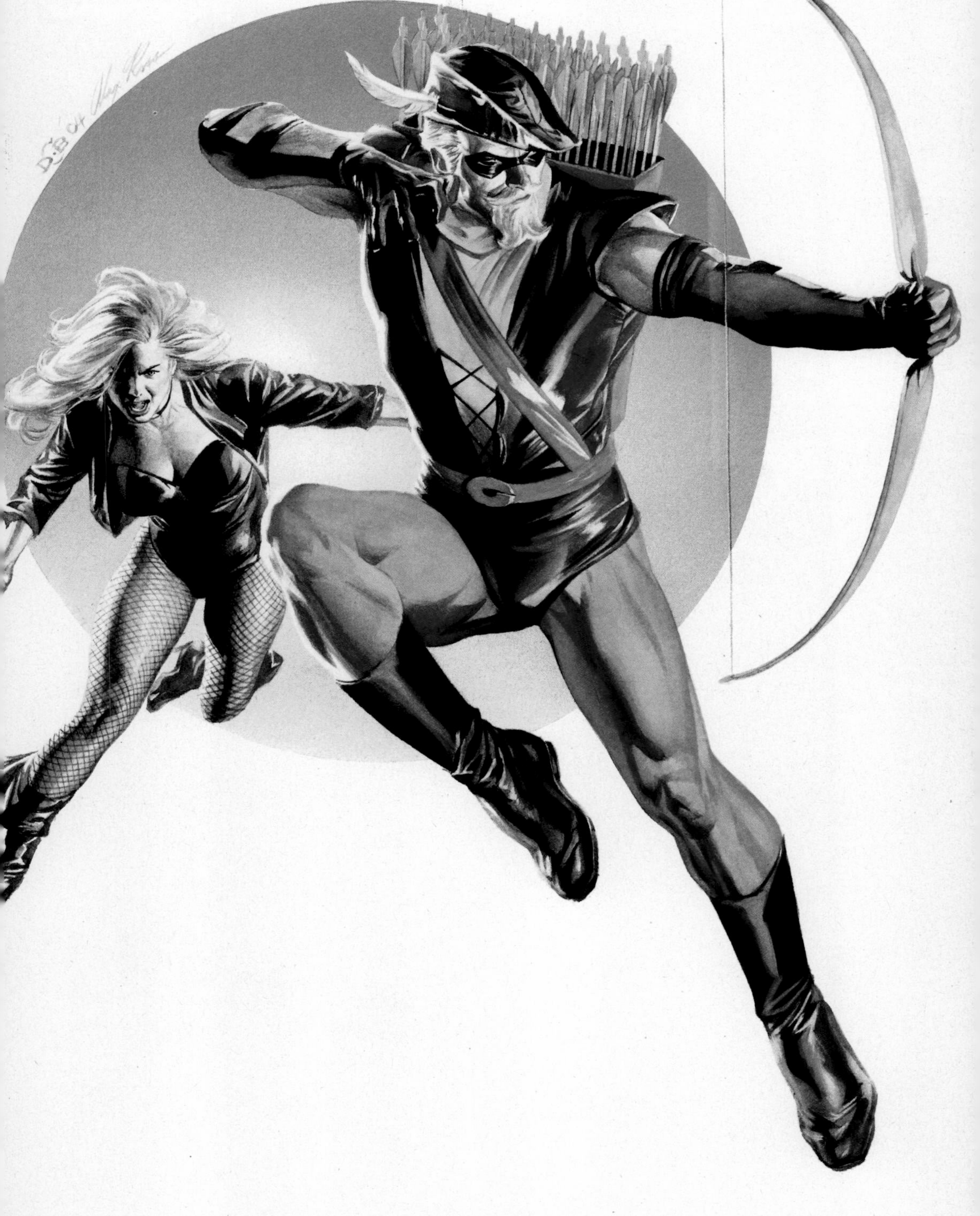

FROM BRUCE WAYNE'S PRIVATE FILES
IN THE BATCOMPUTER

GREEN LANTERN

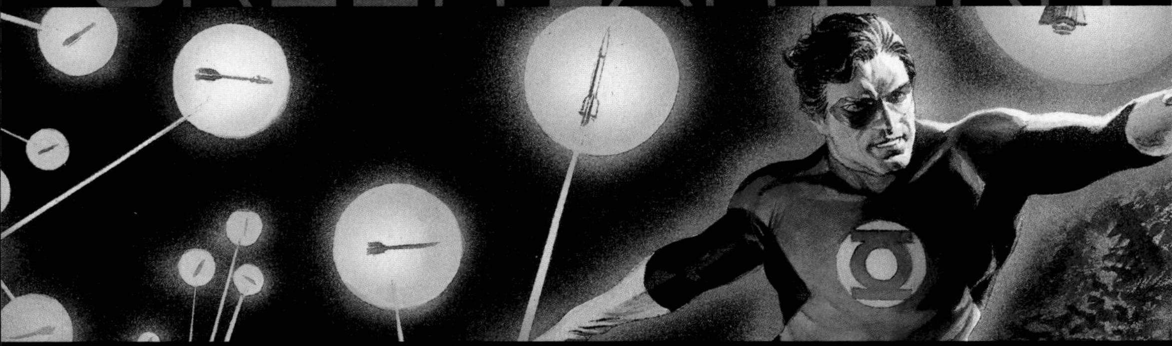

HAL JORDAN is a test pilot for Ferris Aircraft who has gone faster, farther and higher than anything he could ever hope or dream. Of all the members of the Justice League, of all of those who wield strange powers and abilities, he concerns me the most.

Years ago, he was given a ring by a dying alien. The ring was powered by another world's energy source. It allows Jordan to create, through imagination alone, whatever he desires. With it, he can fly, form giant objects to be used as weapons or tools, or survive the rigors of space. His is not the only ring. He is a member of the Green Lantern Corps. This alien league polices the universe, and they are led by a race known as the Guardians.

The ring's charge lasts only about twenty-four hours. This, Jordan admits, is his only weakness. But he forgets that Jordan himself is a weakness. Superman tells me that Jordan is a hero who has saved this world many times. But his willpower to form things according to his whim is not the result of discipline. It is not the result of testing or wisdom. When the alien gave him the ring, it chose Jordan because he was fearless.

It has been my experience that fear is a necessary trait in those who would do what we do. Fear of loss. Fear of corruption. Fear of what the world will become if we don't succeed.

Superman tells me that Jordan is a hero who has saved this world many times...

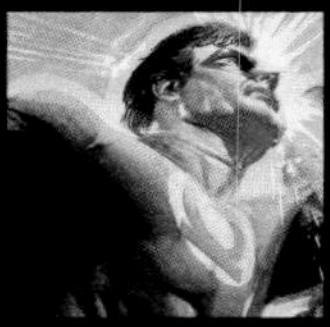

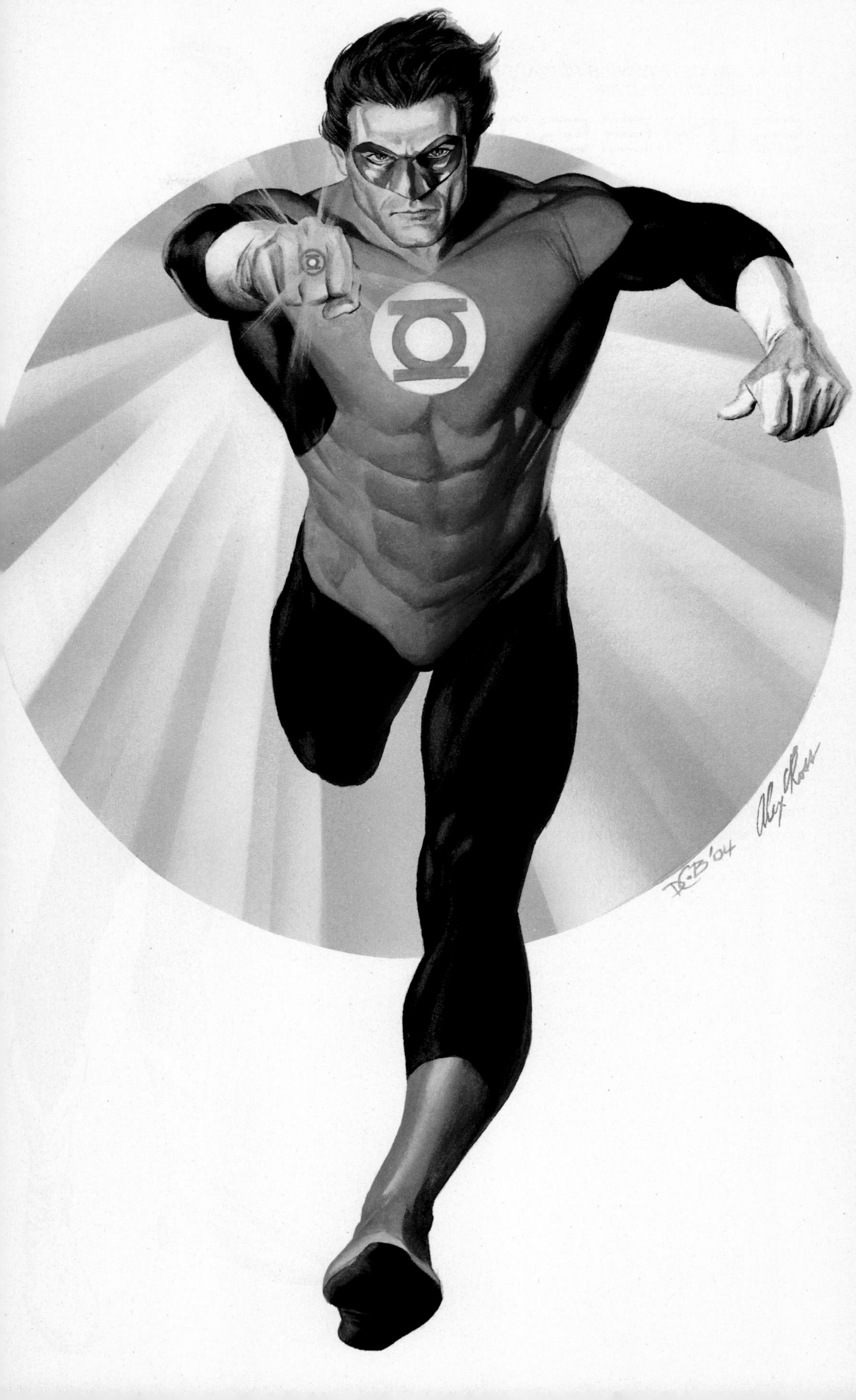
DCB'04
Alex Ross

FROM BRUCE WAYNE'S PRIVATE FILES IN THE BATCOMPUTER

SINESTRO

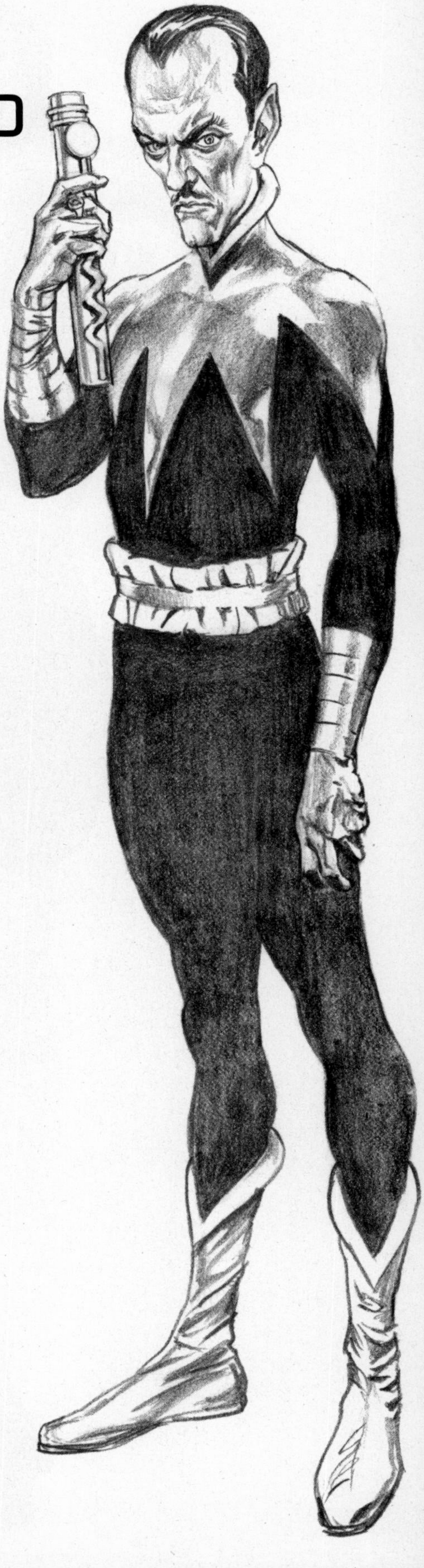

SINESTRO is what will happen to Hal Jordan if he is not kept in check. Power corrupts. And these Green Lantern rings seem to be the closest any of us could have to absolute power. Sinestro was chosen by the Green Lantern Corps to police the specified region of his home planet. He was judged to be fearless.

But over time, the power of the ring changed him. Sinestro began to rule and abuse the worlds he was charged to protect. The Guardians stopped him. They took away his ring. In their desire to teach him a lesson, they banished him to a world of terrible cruelty and despotism. But for someone like Sinestro, it was like coming home. The race that lived in that place hated the Guardians and their intergalactic police force. They created a weapon for Sinestro, one not without its own brand of irony. They gave him a ring that operated exactly like those of the Green Lantern Corps — except that his ring did not rely upon power from the central Green Lantern Corps battery. And it was capable of breaking through any form generated by a Green Lantern ring.

It is more than a desire for revenge against the Green Lantern Corps that has caused Sinestro to especially hate and strike at Hal Jordan. It is far more personal. Jordan was not corrupted by the ring as Sinestro was. Jordan was hailed as the greatest Green Lantern of them all. So, despite having a superior power ring, a weakness is revealed: Sinestro's pride.

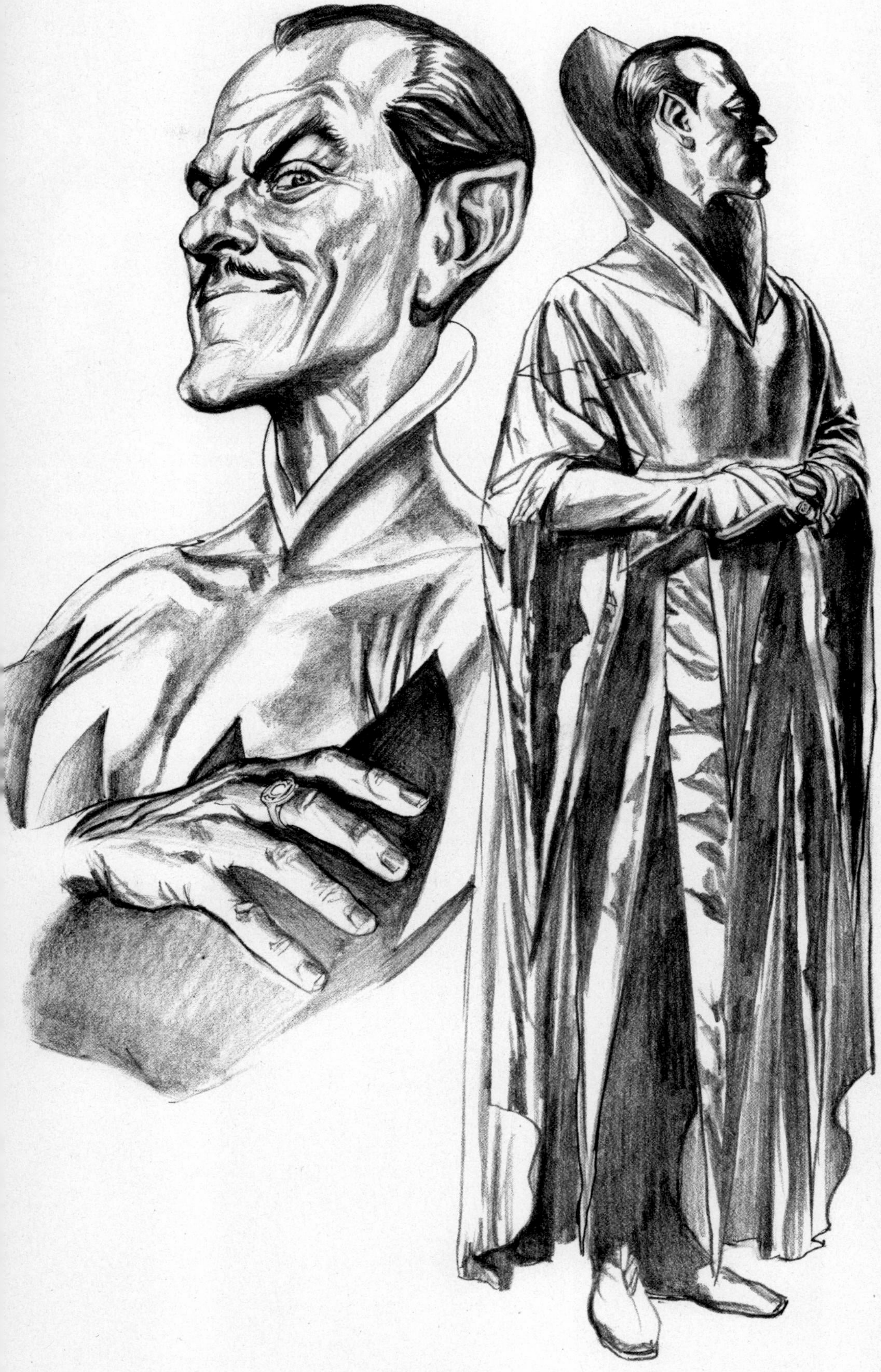

FROM BRUCE WAYNE'S PRIVATE FILES IN THE BATCOMPUTER

ZATANNA

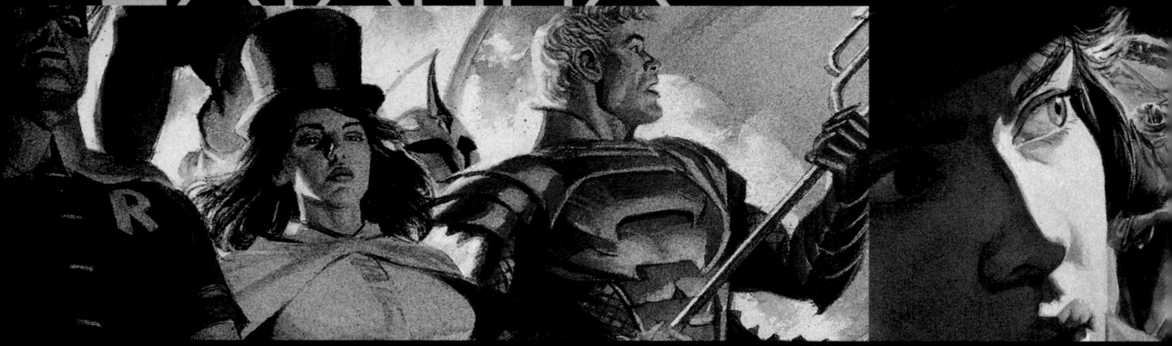

ZATANNA ZATARA is the daughter of the master magician Zatara, one-time member of the All-Star Squadron. Zatanna's mother was believed to have died shortly after Zatanna's birth, forcing John Zatara to raise his daughter alone. Because of her lineage, she had some of her father's magical gifts. But her father's prominence made her the target of dark forces. A curse was placed on Zatara by one of his enemies so that Zatanna would die if he ever saw her again. And so her father left her. With him gone, she struggled though her childhood like so many of us did, only to find a family of sorts in the Justice League of America.

Because of her lineage, she had some of her father's magical gifts.

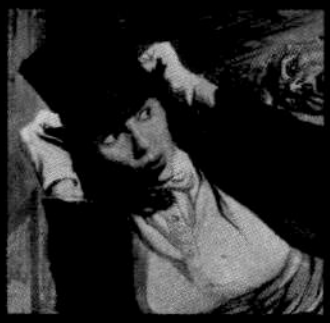

Zatanna's magical powers are limited. She generally needs a conduit to ground her magic. This is necessary for her ability to teleport as well. She has, at best, a fair amount of hand-to-hand combat knowledge. It's her talent for manipulating the odds in the Justice League's favor that makes her invaluable.

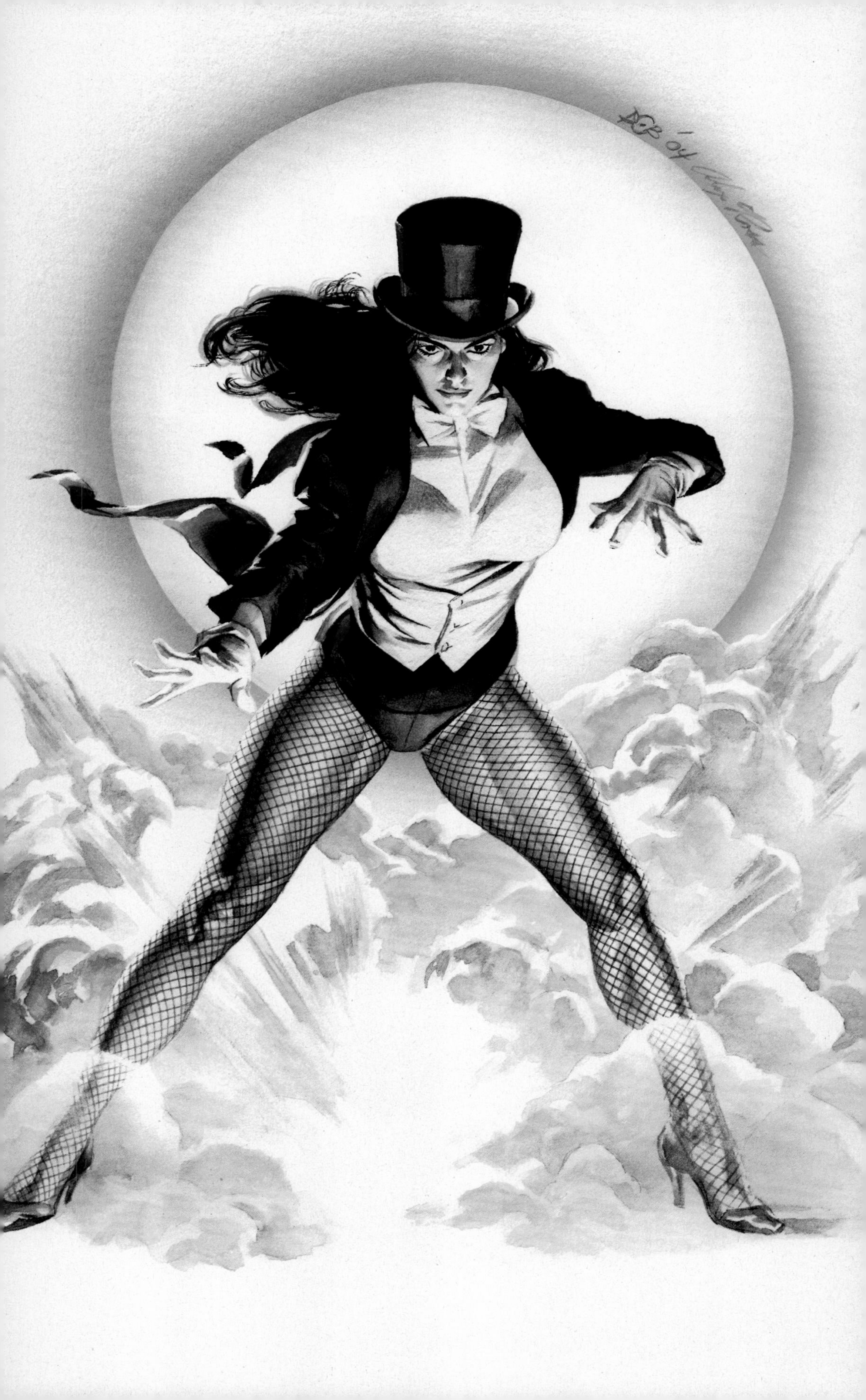

FROM BRUCE WAYNE'S PRIVATE FILES IN THE BATCOMPUTER

PLASTIC MAN

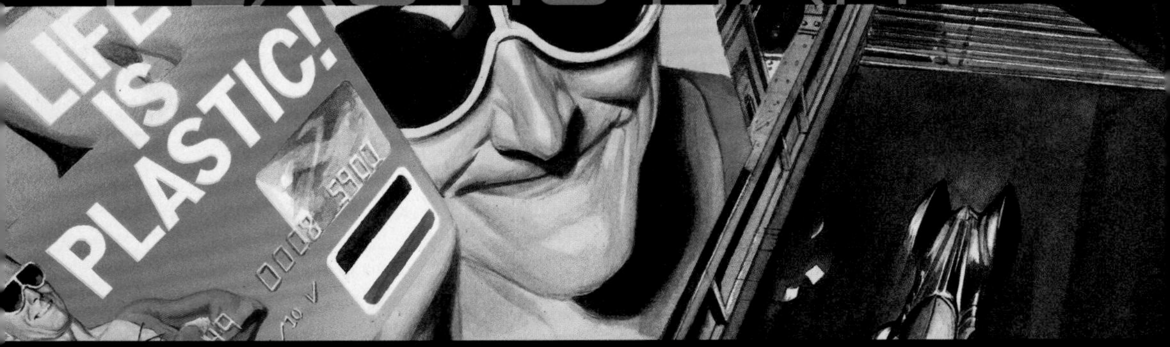
IS
PLASTIC!

Can a criminal change? Can those with a hunger for evil be transformed into more than just a citizen, but an ally in my war on crime?

...kindness and concern for a petty criminal like him shamed and cured his inclination towards selfishness...

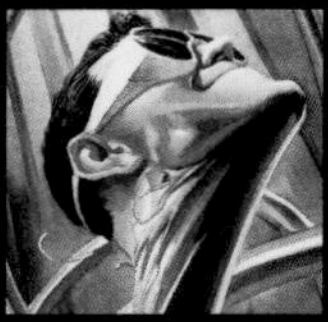

Plastic Man was once the enemy. A mediocre thief known as **PATRICK "EEL" O'BRIAN.** When he and a few other thieves attempted a burglary of a local chemical plant, he was shot by a security guard and struck by a falling drum filled with arcane substances. The chemicals, which were similar to acid, mixed with his blood, affecting him in ways science and logic cannot decipher.

He was abandoned by his fellow burglars. He escaped anyhow, wounded and dying, only to be nursed back to health by a mysterious order of monks. Their kindness and concern for a petty criminal like him shamed and cured his inclination towards selfishness as he discovered a new way to live.

The mysterious acid bath gave him the ability to stretch his body into any shape. He wears dark glasses and a red-and-yellow costume as flexible as his body. His choice in costume is garish, and he uses his form-changing abilities to fight crime in the most ridiculous of ways.

I do not appreciate his compulsion for the absurd, but am grateful he is a friend of the League, and not still a criminal.

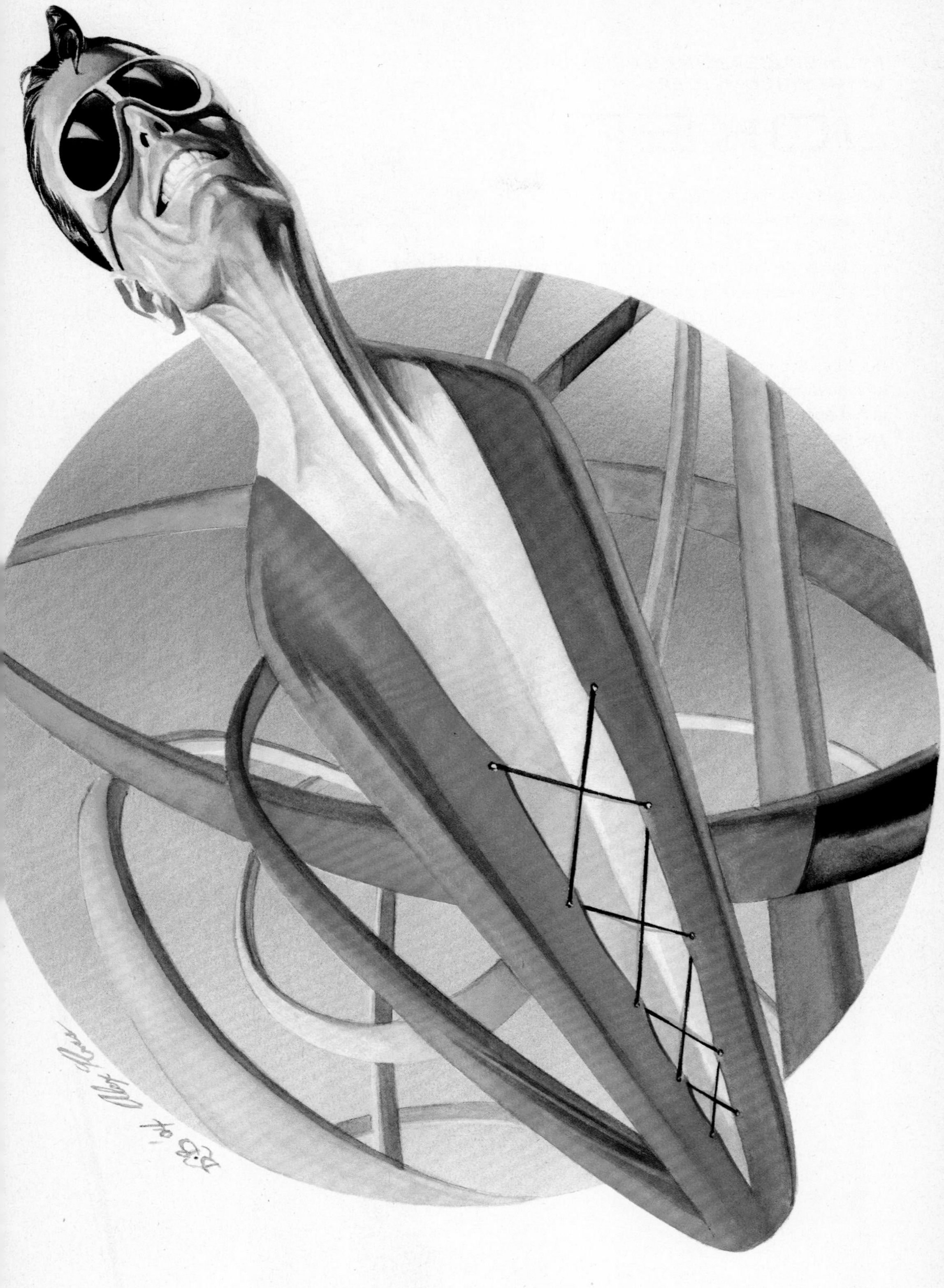

FROM BRUCE WAYNE'S PRIVATE FILES IN THE BATCOMPUTER

JOKER

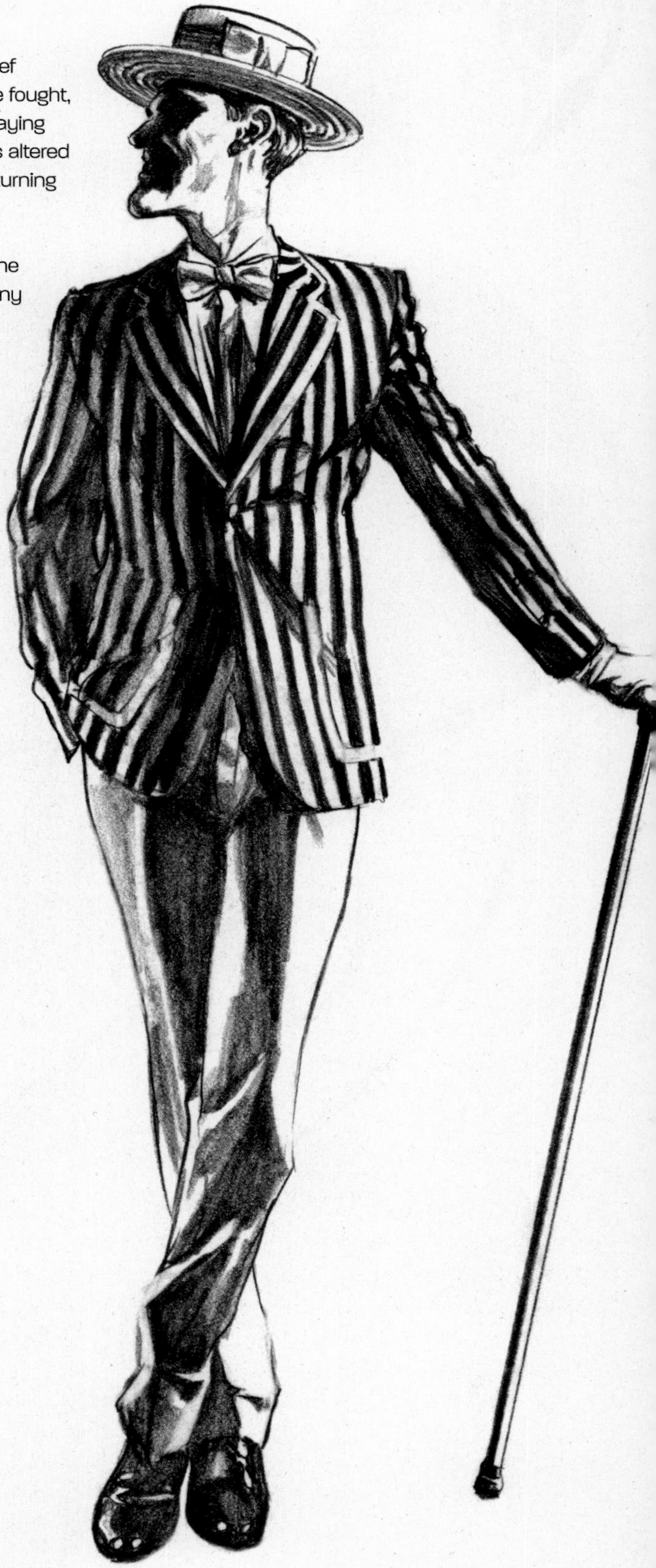

My greatest enemy began as the petty thief known as the **RED HOOD**. The first time we fought, he fell into a vat of waste chemicals in a playing card factory in Gotham City. The chemicals altered the thief's features, exaggerating his face, turning his skin white, his lips red, his hair green.

Believing that this accident was an omen, he embraced his new appearance and the irony of its happening in a playing card factory. The Red Hood became the Joker.

He has adopted a number of "jokes" as lethal weapons — including hand-buzzers that electrocute, lapel flowers that squirt acid, and far more.

I'm convinced that, while everything about the Joker — his murderous instincts, his maniacal laughter, his maddening behavior — points to his being insane, he is the farthest thing from it. The Joker's greatest prank has been to pull the wool over society's eyes all these years, masquerading as a madman so as to be thrown into an asylum and treated with kid gloves when apprehended, to be "rehabilitated" rather than punished in a penitentiary. It's a strategy worthy of a high-stakes player, so it's apt that he'd be named for a playing card.

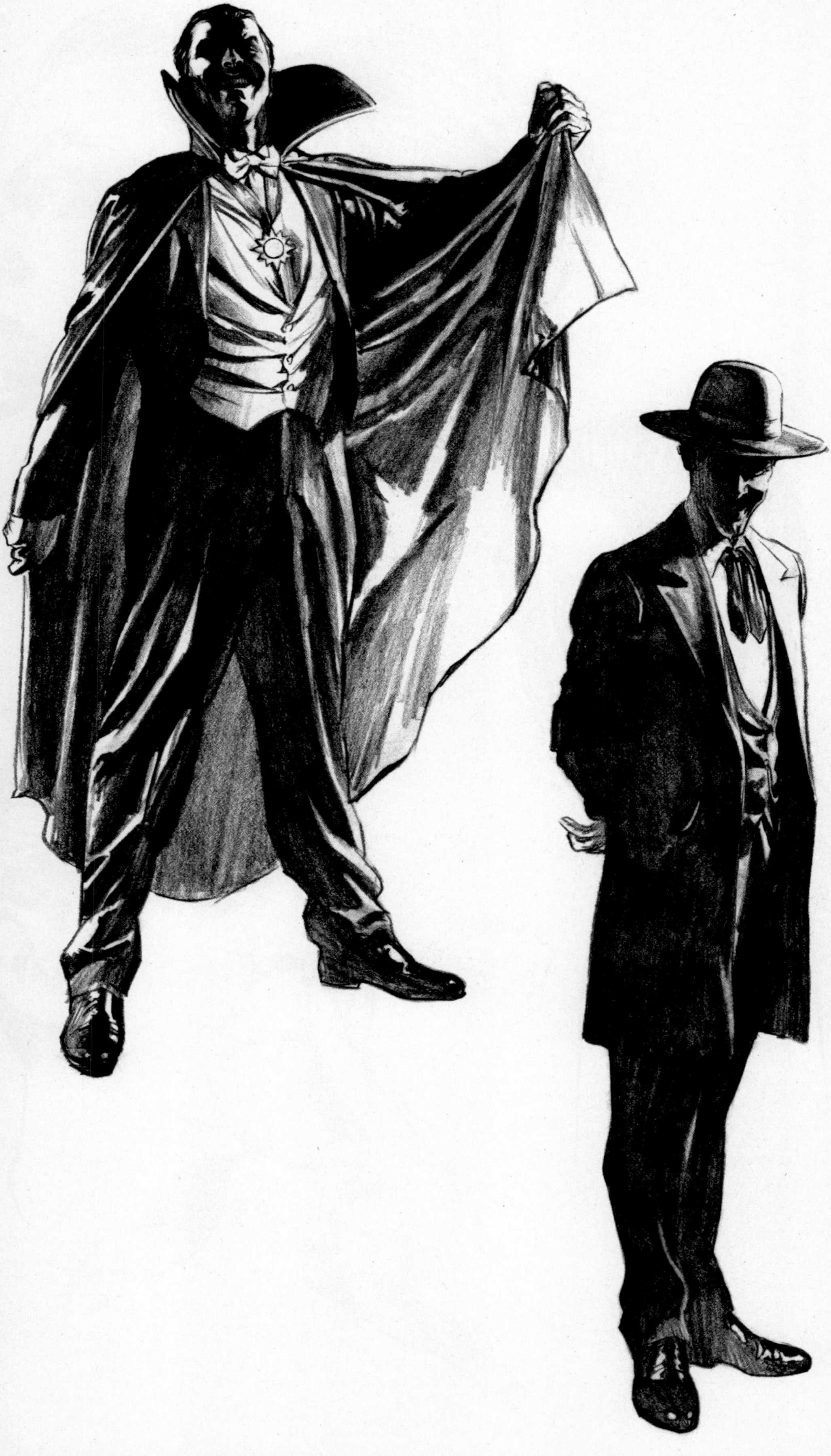

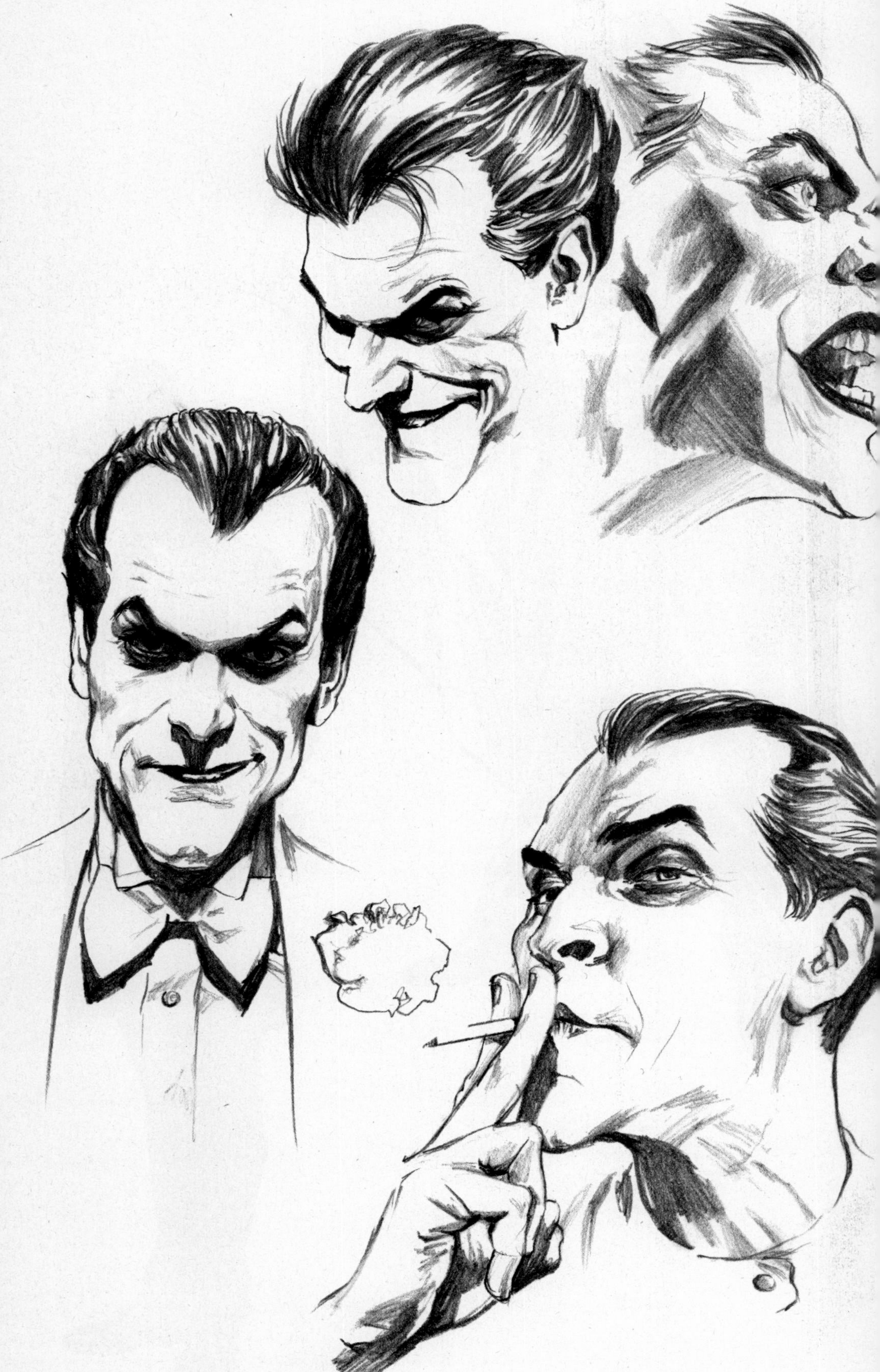